Value and Valuation

Value and Valuation

AXIOLOGICAL STUDIES

IN HONOR OF

ROBERT S. HARTMAN

edited by John William Davis

The University of Tennessee Press
Knoxville

Library of Congress Catalog Card Number 72–146661
International Standard Book Number 0–87049–130–X

Copyright © 1972 by The University of Tennessee Press.
Manufactured in the United States of America.
All Rights Reserved. First Edition.

Preface

ROBERT S. HARTMAN's international reputation and the esteem in which he is held by scholars throughout the world are reflected in this book. Distinguished scholars from eight different countries have contributed to the volume. The authors do not, of course, all share Robert Hartman's views concerning the nature of either philosophy or value, but they do share his concern for problems in the general area of value theory and its application, to which their present essays are devoted.

Much of what Robert Hartman has written during the last thirty years is related to his attempt to develop a science of values. His most recent explanation of this science is *The Structure of Value: Foundations of Scientific Axiology*, which Henry N. Wieman comments upon in the Foreword. Professor Wieman's discussions should help the reader to understand the organization of the present volume, for the book's structure reflects Robert Hartman's theory of value. While the contributors were asked to write on topics within the general area of value, they were also asked to write about their own specialties. Their essays appeared to the editor to fit into specific groups.

One group was clearly concerned with the nature and logic of value, topics which have long been the concern of Robert Hartman. Hence Part 1 begins with Thomas E. Hill's argument that the concept of good is not to be identified with any other concept or conjunction of concepts; it is, for Hill, a distinctive concept and perhaps a distinctive kind of concept as well. Hector-Neri Castañeda, on the other hand, suggests that the goodness of particulars is definable and analyzable in terms of the goodness and badness of states of affairs, which are the ultimate subjects of value predication. He also draws some interesting conclusions concerning the measurement of value. Gerhard Frey's essay leads us into the logic of value by discussing the deontic in a language of ethical systems and relating deontic logic to axiology. He concludes that deontic logical systems need not be axiological, but that it is possible to posit axiologically relevant frame norms depending on the kind of formalism used. Robert S. Brumbaugh's discussion is also concerned with the logic of value. Using Robert Hartman's categories of value, Brumbaugh derives three rules which offer axioms for an ethical calculus for guiding choice where changes in time involve changes in order of value. In contrast to these essays, William H. Werkmeister

offers an empirical approach to a definition of value. He is not interested, he says, in an analysis of value language per se or in the use and
classification of value words. He is concerned, rather, with the value
experience, which for him is constituted by feelings and attitudes
together.

The group of essays constituting Part 2 is mainly directed to problems of methodology. Manfred Moritz distinguishes between theories
about value sentences and value ontologies and relates these theories
to four types of the naturalistic ("axiological") fallacy. Oliver L. Reiser,
in contrast, applies his own philosophy of "cosmic humanism" to the
naturalistic fallacy and to the problem of the relation between facts
and values and shows, to his satisfaction, that it is not a fallacy to pass
from "facts" to "values." Wayne A. R. Leys, using a legal approach
to throw light on problems of value terminology, questions the assumption (held by some of our other authors) that correct value judgments
can always be attained by the individual's effort to correct errors in
definition. He points out that "indefinite terms" are often useful in
valuational situations; precise definition, in fact, may be a handicap.
Paul Weiss, in examining the method of phenomenology, asks whether
value or anything can be the object of a pure phenomenological study.
He concludes that we can know what things are like, apart from our
involvement with them, but only within limits. Finally, Gottfried
Martin concludes our methodological studies with the Socratic warn-
ing that our inquiry should not end with skepticism, but rather that
it should continue with the realization that we have not discovered
what value is and must, with true Socratic understanding, determine
that "tomorrow we shall search again."

The essays in Part 3 deal with the types of value in Hartman's system
of formal axiology—intrinsic, extrinsic, and systemic—and are grouped
accordingly. Seven essays deal with intrinsic value applied to various
fields. The essays of Albert Ellis, Charlotte Buhler, and Fritz-Joachim
von Rintelen may be regarded primarily as the application of the
category of intrinsic value to persons. From the point of view of the
psychotherapist, Ellis argues for the intrinsic value of the individual
and offers many reasons why individuals should not systemically or extrinsically evaluate either themselves or others (while still evaluating
their traits and performances). Buhler, writing from the perspective of
humanistic psychology, speaks of the individual as "an intentionality
directed toward fulfillment," and discusses several approaches to an
understanding of persons. Von Rintelen, who calls his theory "a logic
of value," defines intrinsic value (*Eigenwert*) as fullness of meaning
(which corresponds to Hartman's density of intension), and relates

such value to the spiritual situation of today. Paul Arthur Schilpp's essay on Kant and the problem of world peace may, I think, be viewed as an examination of the problem of applying the category of intrinsic value to groups of persons. Bertram Morris, on the other hand, offers a different approach to the intrinsic value of man, which he identifies with happiness. Happiness, he says, is the good *of* man, the intrinsic value of which all its components (activities, virtues, and pleasures) are extrinsic. David Pole and I also are concerned with intrinsic value, but as it is applied to things. Our essays are in the field of aesthetics. I give an essentially Hartmanian interpretation of aesthetic valuation in terms of the prizing of a thing's uniqueness. In contrast, Pole is concerned with a form of aesthetic excellence which he refers to as the "expressiveness," the tertiary qualities (aesthetic aspects) of artworks.

Three essays, those of Nicholas Rescher, Franz Loeser, and Elfriede Tielsch, are primarily concerned with extrinsic value. Rescher gives us a detailed examination of the foundation of the good life (welfare) and emphasizes that such a life must also include the attainment of a wide spectrum of trans-welfare goals. Loeser, starting from the point of view of Marxist ethics, offers a mathematical formula for measuring the social value of moral processes. Tielsch, too, would like a scientific ethics (based on a scientific teleology), but her argument is that the future comes about through prophets that foresee it, predict it, and formulate what the time needs or means in futuristic terms. All three essays are concerned with what Bertram Morris refers to as the extrinsic components of happiness.

Our last three essays deal with the dimension of systemic value (although the authors may not accept this classification). Luigi Bagolini, Adam Schaff, and Daniel B. Christoff discuss systems, or elements within systems, or constructions of the human mind. Bagolini gives us an analysis of time and "ought" from the perspective of the legal system. Schaff discusses stereotypes, ideology, and the influence of language on behavior. He offers semantics as social therapy, or in Hartman's terms, an extrinsic valuation of systemic value. (In Schaff's essay stereotypes are systemic valuations of intrinsic values.) Christoff's essay on the sign is, I think, the clearest example of a treatment of systemic value, although here, too, an extrinsic valuation of a systemic thing is evident.

Those scholars who should like to have honored Robert S. Hartman by writing for this volume but who, for one reason or another, could not are: Virgil C. Aldrich, Chris Argyris, Abraham Edel, Hugo Fischer, William K. Frankena, Risieri Frondizi, Charles Hartshorne, Johannes Erich Heyde, Susanne K. Langer, Morris Lazerowitz, Dorothy Lee, Ruth Barcan Marcus, Juri K. Melvil, George K. Plochmann, Charles L.

Stevenson, and Georg Henrik von Wright, who join the authors of the essays in their appreciation for Robert S. Hartman.

Professor Abraham Maslow's untimely death prevented completion of his contribution to this volume. Maslow used Hartman's categories in his work regarding human peak-experiences as kinds of intrinsic valuation.

I have known Robert Hartman for more than twenty years, first as my teacher, now as a colleague in the department which I head, always as a friend. I have never known a more brilliant, comprehensive, creative mind; or a more enthusiastic, eloquent teacher; I am grateful, therefore, for the privilege of editing his *Festschrift*. Rita D. S. Hartman, the wife of our honoree, deserves special thanks for the many translations which she prepared for this volume and for compiling the Bibliography. Without her help it is doubtful that this *Festschrift* could have been completed.

I wish also gratefully to acknowledge the contribution of Merritt H. Moore, who translated Christoff's essay, and to thank Paul Weiss for reminding me of the date of Robert Hartman's sixtieth birthday (January 21, 1970) and for urging me to undertake the editing of this *Festschrift*. I am also grateful for the help of my secretaries, Miss Deborah Ann Hoogesteger, and especially Mrs. Dolores Scates, who had the thankless task of typing the entire manuscript.

JOHN WILLIAM DAVIS

The University of Tennessee
Knoxville, Tennessee

Foreword: The Axiology of Robert S. Hartman

HENRY NELSON WIEMAN

IN THE FORM OF NATURAL SCIENCE we have an ever increasing power to transform existence in any way desired. But we have no proportionate and parallel increase in range, fullness, and coherent system of values to direct the use of this power. Robert S. Hartman, in his book *The Structure of Value: Foundations of Scientific Axiology* and in other works, seeks to correct this dangerous, one-sided development by creating a science of values to cooperate with natural science.

This scientific axiology will provide that access to values which the human mind must have to direct the use of the power of natural science to the end of increasing indefinitely the range and fullness of values to be had in human existence. A science of values cooperating with natural science will also protect us from misusing the power of natural science in such a way as to result in the self-destruction of human existence.

In order to develop a science of values, Hartman recognizes that two preliminary tasks must be accomplished. These he accomplishes with skill and insight. One of these is to demonstrate that science is of such a nature that it can be applied to values. To this end, Hartman examines science to show that it has an essential nature that can be applied to values, even as natural science is applied to the processes of nature. The two kinds of science will have different subject matter for inquiry but will be the same in that distinctive feature which makes them both instances of science. What is this essential nature of science? Hartman's answer to that question will be given a little later.

But there is a second preliminary task required for this undertaking: The nature of value must be so interpreted as to make it accessible to science. Since science deals with "facts," the relation of value to fact must be interpreted in a way to meet the demands of scientific inquiry. Hartman approaches this problem of the relation between fact and value by examining G. E. Moore's struggle with this problem.

Moore recognized that a described object can be identified with the described qualities found in it. But he insisted also that these same qualities can be viewed as values independent of the natural object to which they pertain. This seemed a contradiction which Moore never could surmount. How can qualities be identical with the object they describe and yet be values not identified with any natural object?

Hartman resolves this difficulty in Moore's thinking by saying that values are found in the concept of the object but not in the object itself *when we consider the intension of the concept and not its extension.* The *extension* of a concept is that class of objects to which it applies by indicating features these objects have in common. The *intension* of the concept is that set of qualities which the concept prescribes for any object fit to belong to the class covered by the concept. For example, that class of objects called chairs must have seat, back, and legs fit to support the human organism in a sitting position. A chair is a good chair or not a good chair, depending on the degree to which it meets these prescriptions found in the intension of the concept. The back may be broken, the legs shaky, the seat split, etc. So it is with every concept. Its intension is prescriptive for the objects to which it applies. Thus, the intension of the concept determines whether an object is good or bad, better or worse, so far as concerns its fitness to belong to the class to which the concept applies.

This explanation shows the difference between fact and value and their intimate relation to one another. When qualities serve merely to identify an object as a member of a class, they are fact. But when they are the intensions of a concept, prescribing what an object ought to be to fulfill the requirements of membership in a class, these qualities are value. This system enables us to apply concepts to values with all the logical structure which concepts must have. It opens the way for developing a science of values.

Of course this is only the beginning. Scientific axiology arises from the unfolding of the following axiom: *Value is the degree in which a thing possesses the set of qualities corresponding to the set of attributes in the intension of its concept.* Since there are three kinds of sets of attributes, there are three kinds of concepts, and their fulfillment gives rise to three kinds of value: systemic value, the fulfillment of a *synthetic* concept whose intension is a finite set of attributes; extrinsic value, the fulfillment of an *analytic* concept whose intension is a denumerably infinite set of attributes; and intrinsic value, the fulfillment of a *singular* concept whose intension is a nondenumerable infinite set of attributes. Let us take a brief look at these categories of value.

First, *systemic* value is the value of that structure of concepts by which all concepts, including those of value, are brought into a system. It is the value of the logical thing, a construction of the human mind, as are geometrical circles. Such things have the value of perfection; they must have all the properties of their concepts, a finite and definite number of properties, for they come into being by definition. Second, *extrinsic* value is the value objects, empirical things, have to the measure that they meet the demands of belonging to a class as determined by the intension of an analytic concept. The intension of an analytic concept arises from the abstraction of the common qualities of a group of things. Such an intension consists of a denumerably infinite—and indefinite—number of attributes, for such abstractions, theoretically, can be continued *ad infinitum*. Unlike systemic things, an empirical thing does not have to have all the attributes of its concept to be a member of the class designated by that concept. A chair, for example, can be a chair and not have all the properties of the concept "chair." Finally, *intrinsic* value is the value to be found in any uniquely individual object not subject to the limitations of those values shared in common with some class of other individuals. It is the value of a thing that fulfills a singular concept. Hartman refers to such concepts, or proper names, as "unicepts," for instead of being an entity that grasps together the common features of several things, it is the experiencing of a thing in its concreteness. In such an experience the "concept," thing, and values, become one, thus forming a continuum with a nondenumerable infinity of properties, and the extent to which they become one is the extent to which the thing fulfills its concept.

Summarizing the distinction between fact and value, we can put it this way. Within the *extension* of a concept, qualities are facts identifying any object as a member of a class. Within the *intension* of a concept, qualities are values prescribing the qualities an object ought to have to meet fully the requirements of membership in a class or to be unique. With the *extension* of a concept we freeze qualities into fixed forms called facts, using these fixed forms to seek values that have not been frozen in this way. But to gain full access to values we must have a science that does not freeze values into facts. We achieve this goal by giving primacy to the intension of concepts.

When qualities are liberated from the fixed form of fact, they can be combined in all manner of different ways to form sets designed to quicken the valuing consciousness. This opens the way to an infinity of values otherwise hidden from the valuing consciousness. This infinity cannot reach awareness until it is given rational order by a science of values.

We do not first have facts and then have values derived from these facts. We first have values in confusion. The infant seeking the mother's breast is not concerned with facts but only with values. Facts are devices by which we bring some order into the chaos of values. But the transformation of values into facts blinds us to many values and confines our quest for values.

Basic reality is value and not fact. Facts are devices for putting values into a manageable order preliminary to the time when we can have a scientific axiology fit to give conceptual structure to the fullness of values without confining them to the artificial structure of fact. Such a rational order applicable to values is what Hartman has long sought to develop.

Natural science has created the illusion that objective reality is the universe of facts, making it appear that values are subjective. If Hartman is correct, the reverse of this theory is the truth of the matter. Facts are values caught into a pattern designed to identify objects for the purpose of scientific inquiry and technological control. Thus, facts are artificial constructions and in that sense "subjective," whereas the reality out of which they are constructed is the infinity of values.

So far we have been explaining only one of the two preliminary tasks Hartman must perform to develop his science of value, otherwise called scientific axiology. The preliminary task we have been considering is to show how facts and values are related to one another. The other task is to show the essential nature of science whereby it can be applied to values as well as to facts. To show this essential nature of science, Hartman distinguishes what he calls analytic inquiry from synthetic. Synthetic inquiry is what distinguishes science while analytic inquiry is practiced by common sense and philosophy.

The analytic inquiry of common sense and philosophy seeks to find in the thronging fullness of immediate, concrete experience those abstractions (generalizations) which can be distinguished more or less continuously or repeatedly throughout the changing fullness of immediate experience. In this way we identify objects and situations as having in common some of these generalizations. In this way we are able to recognize trees, houses, persons, friends, enemies, sky, earth, and whatever the focus of attention can mark out from the all-encompassing fullness of sense and feeling. But this knowledge is vague and unreliable. Furthermore, the farther we extend any generalization to include a wider range of objects, the more meager is the information it provides about any one of them.

Over against this analytic knowledge of common sense and philosophy is the synthetic knowledge of science. Science reverses the procedure of common sense and philosophy. Instead of first seeking in the world what the inquiring mind can discover, it first creates a rational structure of concepts which the human mind can know with precision and can expand to infinity without loss of accuracy and complex fullness. The chief examples of this are pure logic and mathematics developed by the rational powers of the mind without application to the world. But after this structure of concepts has been developed within the mind in the form of mathematics, it can be applied to the world.

By intricate procedures this rational structure of concepts is applied to the world of experience to select from it those elements that can be fitted into this structure and, reciprocally, to develop those structures of concepts that can fit these chosen elements. In analytic inquiry we try to fit the powers of the knowing mind to what is experienced in the world; in synthetic inquiry we fit what is experienced in the world to meet the demands of the rational powers of the human mind. Thus, the essential nature of science is to transform the world of experience into a rational structure rather than trying to find a rational structure ready-made in the world of experience.

With this understanding of science, we can have a science of values. Instead of trying to find a rational order in the thronging, chaotic experience of what we like and dislike and otherwise experience as better and worse, right and wrong, what ought to be and ought not to be, we develop a structure of rational concepts and identify value with the intension of these concepts. Thus, as natural science transforms the world of sense experience into a rational structure of applied concepts, the science of axiology can transform the chaotic world of values into a rational structure of applied concepts.

On this basis, Hartman develops a vast complexity of logical forms and distinctions of values, meaning by *value* what ought to be and what actually is so far as it approximates the *ought*. The *ought* is determined by the intension of concepts.

Running through the infinite realm of values thus exposed are the three basic kinds of values mentioned, systemic, extrinsic, and intrinsic. Any set of qualities found in the intension of concepts can be combined in every imaginable way within the limits of logical structure. In this way we find ourselves living in an infinity of infinities of values to be brought to consciousness by the proper use and application of concepts.

Hartman suggests how this rational structure of concepts with their intensions can be applied to ethics, psychology, physiology, jurisprudence, political science, social ethics, sociology, law of persons and institutions, aesthetics, economics, technology, science of civilization, ecology, industrial technology, civil engineering, games, law of property, ritual, metaphysics, epistemology, logic, poetry, literary criticism, rhetoric, semantics, linguistic analysis, grammar, and theory of communication.

He ends *The Structure of Value* with this sentence: "As the achievements of the natural scientists analyzing natural situations in terms of mathematics have led to the building of factories turning out new and undreamed-of things, so the achievements of the moral scientists of the future, analyzing moral situations in terms of formal axiology, will lead to the building of a new society with new people, living on higher levels of awareness and possessing undreamed-of insights into the subtleties and depths of moral reality."

I am inclined to agree with this statement. If we can develop an axiological system with the power and scope comparable to the power and scope of natural science, the human race may rise to a higher level of existence for which all the past might be viewed as preparation. Natural science is a necessary first step in this direction. But the human personality and society cannot be organized, and institutions cannot be shaped to maximize the experience of value until a science of values is developed. Human existence cannot become the medium by which the universe is transformed into an infinite system of consciously experienced values until such a science is created.

Hartman does not claim to have done more than establish the foundations of such a science. Much more work must be done before we have such an axiology. I feel that Hartman's efforts have been somewhat misdirected by using G. E. Moore's work as a starting point. Instead of starting with sets of qualities it might have been more profitable to start with sets of goal-seeking activities. Goal-seeking activities can carry with them the experience of qualities but can be better treated by a science. Goal-seeking activity does not mean that the value is in the goal any more than in the activity. Furthermore, all thinking and all feeling are goal-seeking, as well as physiological behavior. Also, the goal of any activity is never an ending so long as life lasts, but is some further activity.

Whether or not my suggestion is valid, I believe that this work by Hartman is one of the most constructive and revolutionary undertakings suggested in modern times. The confusion and frustration of our time might be the turmoil driving us to choose between a science of values on the one hand and self-destruction of the human race on the other.

Contents

1. The Nature and Logic of Value

The Distinctiveness of the Concept of Good

THOMAS E. HILL

For a long time now the character of the concept of good has been a subject of controversy between naturalists, who claim that this concept can be reduced to ordinary descriptive concepts; non-naturalists, who reject this claim; and emotivists and prescriptivists, who claim that the significant feature of the use of the term *good* is not its cognitive import but its expressive and dynamic force. In recent years the second of these positions, the non-naturalistic one, has been widely held to be untenable, and for good reasons. The concept of good is neither simple nor, for the most part, intuitively applicable; and naturalistic attempts to formulate it in terms of descriptive concepts need not commit any such "naturalistic fallacy" as non-naturalists suppose. Besides, some non-naturalists, by insisting that good is a simple property and thereby cutting off analysis at the start, tend to preclude such insights as may be obtained by careful inquiry into the role of the concept of good in our conceptual schemes and in our way of life. Nevertheless, implicit in what the non-naturalists are saying is at least one important claim that seems to merit serious consideration in the contemporary philosophical setting; namely, that the concept of good retains, whatever may be its relations to other concepts, a significant distinctiveness.

The notion of the distinctiveness of good that I shall try to defend requires some preliminary explanation. By a concept I mean a pattern of possible experience dispositionally linked with a word or some other symbol in such fashion as to be available for use in thought, communication, and action. Under the concept of good I include all of the concepts constituting the principal meanings of the word *good* and all those aspects of the meanings of other words that could be represented by the word *good* in any of its characteristic senses. The words in English with which the concept of good is most directly linked are, of course, the word *good* itself and its cognates in other parts of speech. Fairly closely, but by no means precisely, parallel are the word *valuable* and its cognates. Virtually all languages seem to include words having meanings similar to that of *good*. In addition to the words most closely linked with the concept of good, the English language, and most other languages, include multitudes of other words whose meanings involve, in conjunction with the concept of good, a variety of other factors. For example, the meanings of such English words as *brave*, *kind*, *wise*, *strong, resolute, substantial, beautiful, faithful, harmonious,* and *splendid* include, along with concepts that could well be represented by the word *good,* other concepts indicating special features of the things and events to which they apply. The same thing is true, in many contexts, even of such words as *colorful, careful, solid, steady,* and *vivid.* Nearly all words the meanings of which include the concept of good have a variety of senses. A thing or event may be good in any of many different ways, for any of many different reasons, and for any of many different purposes. Indeed, so varied are the senses and uses of the word *good* that one could well speak of concepts of good rather than of the concept of good. The mere occurrence of a word usually associated with the concept of good is, however, no assurance that any concept of good is being ascribed; for even the words most characteristically associated with the concept of good have "degenerate" uses (sometimes indicated by inverted commas) that ascribe, not a concept of good, but a concept of being commonly and perhaps incorrectly taken to be good. However, except for the exclusion of "degenerate" uses of the term *good* and related words, neither the variety of the senses and uses of *good* and related words nor the fact that one may well speak of many concepts of good need, for present purposes, be of any special concern; for the sort of distinctiveness to be discussed here is applicable to virtually all senses and uses of *good,* except the "degenerate" ones, and no confusion need result from continuing to speak of the concept of good provided the diversity indicated is kept in mind.

Although concepts are of many and deeply different kinds that may be ordered in a variety of ways, one useful way of classifying them is as descriptive, existential, semantic, and normative. A *descriptive* concept is, for present purposes, taken to be one in which the correctness of an ascription of it can be in some degree confirmed either directly or indirectly by sensory experiences or introspection or a combination of the two. An *existential* concept is one that affirms or denies that something is, or exists. The concepts that I am grouping loosely under a broad sense of the term *semantic* are concepts having to do both with the application of verbal expressions to the world and with the logical relations between verbal expressions. Included are such concepts as those of truth, consistency, entailment, and coherence. *Normative* concepts are taken here to be concepts by the use of which one undertakes to set or apply standards for the guidance of practical activity.

By distinctiveness of a concept I mean in general that the concept is not to be identified with any other concept or conjunction of concepts. In the course of the discussion more specific and more interesting features of a distinctiveness of good may, of course, emerge. What I shall attempt to do is not to prove that good is distinctive in the sense indicated or any other, for that is scarcely possible, but to consider the notion of a distinctiveness of good in several kinds of contexts that seem likely to disclose the character of this concept. The kinds of contexts that would appear most suitable to this end include the contexts of ascription or predication of good,[1] those of justification of such ascription, those of the teaching of the concept, and those of the origin of the concept.

Perhaps the most direct way in which the character of the concept of good may be disclosed is to place in juxtaposition a statement in which an ordinary descriptive concept is ascribed to or predicated of something and a statement in which the concept of good is ascribed to the state of affairs described by the first statement. Examples of such related sets of statements are:

(1) A bright little boy named John comes running up to his mother: "Mom, Jim [his older brother] caught a fish and the fish was wiggling fiercely." And then a little later: "Mom, it was good that Jim caught a fish, wasn't it?" (2) A few years later, John comes into the house carrying a newspaper and saying: "Mom! Jim shot down an enemy flier." And then, reflectively: "Mom, it was good that Jim shot down an enemy flier, wasn't it?" (3) Sydney Carton, dissolute character in Dickens' *A Tale of Two Cities,* takes the place of a condemned prisoner and goes voluntarily to the guillotine. Of this act he says: "It is a far, far better thing that I do, than I have ever done . . . ." (4) An engineering student reports to his class on an assigned observation of the procedures used by the builders of a nearby bridge: "They used one cubic yard of cement for four cubic yards of sand and gravel." He continues: "According to my calculations, this was a good mixture." (5) An art student, reporting on his observation of the procedure of an artist of undetermined ability, says: "The painter placed the scarlet robe of the central figure against the background of a dark-brown wall." He continues: "As I see it, that was a quite acceptable use of color." (6) A banker reports to his economist friend: "There is a substantial decline in interest rates." "Splendid!" replies the economist.

If the first statement in each set is construed as either descriptive or existential, the two statements of each set are, prima facie at any rate, strikingly different from one another. In each instance the first statement tells how things are; the second, how they should be. One may in some degree confirm the first by observation, introspection, and inductive inference alone; not so the second. The first lies wholly within the province of the science, but not the second. One may be quite sure of the first and remain in doubt concerning the second. The first is, in an important sense, complete in itself and needs no reference to the second; the second embraces the first and remains indeterminately apart from the state of affairs described by the first. The first implies nothing about conformity to or non-conformity to any standard; the second does. The first implies nothing about what one ought to do; the second one does. The first does not indicate that anything has any worth; to say that something is in some degree worthwhile is the major point of the second. The first implies nothing about the value of the events that bring about the situation to which it refers; the second implies that such events have value.

But may the differences in question not be more apparent than real for the reason that the concept of good is in fact identical with some such psychological concept as that of being desired, liked, or pleasing, which—far from being remote from descriptive concepts—is in fact a descriptive concept? Apparently not; for, apart from other well-known difficulties in such identifications, the same sorts of differences are to be found between statements ascribing being desired, liked, or pleasing to something and statements ascribing the concept of good to something as desired, liked, or pleasing, as are found between statements ascribing other descriptive properties to something and statements ascribing the concept of good to something as characterized by these properties. Thus, for example, statements to the effect that catching a fish, giving one's life for another, achieving a certain mix of concrete, or finding a declining interest rate are desired, liked, or pleasing are statements of what is the case, could be confirmed (or disconfirmed) by observation, introspection, and inductive inference alone, and imply nothing concerning conformity to standards, obligations, or worth; but statements that these things as desired or liked or good are statements of what should be the case, presumably cannot be determined by observation, introspection, and induction alone, and do imply standards, obligations, and worth.

Another possible reason for rejecting the apparently significant difference between ascriptions of descriptive concepts and ascriptions of concepts of good is that many ordinary concepts considered primarily descriptive include implicit concepts of good. Man develops his concepts for practical as well as theoretical purposes, and initially he has no occasion to distinguish sharply between descriptive and valuational concepts. Thus, even such nominally descriptive terms as *man, flower, tree, cave, horse, eat,* and *caress* carry, in many contexts, considerable value import. However, under the pressure of scientific interest, on the one hand, and aesthetic and moral interest, on the other, an intelligible distinction between descriptive concepts and concepts of good does emerge; and any primarily descriptive concept can, by abstraction at any rate, be so construed as to render it relatively pure description. When the distinction between descriptive concepts and concepts of good has emerged, the problem of the depth of the difference between these two must be confronted seriously; and for this purpose the crucial instances are those in which descriptive concepts are relatively pure rather than mixed with concepts of good. Accordingly, if such ordinary descriptive concepts as those ascribed to things and events in the examples given above were, despite their containing some value feature, strikingly different from ascriptions of concepts of good as such, the differences become far deeper and more significant when the descriptive concepts in question come to be construed, as they can be, as purely descriptive. Thus, far from explaining away the prima facie difference between descriptive concepts and concepts of good, discernment of the valuational element in ordinary descriptive concepts tends to confirm the depth and significance of the differences between these two kinds of concepts.

Contexts concerning the concept of good that are likely to be more revealing than those of ascription itself are the ones that justify ascription of that concept; for whereas one may correctly apply a concept without much insight into its character, he must possess considerable understanding of the concept to be able to justify its application. The justification that I have in mind is not confined to that practical justification ordinarily in demand which makes many unacknowledged assumptions and attempts only to answer difficulties. Instead it is the justification that consists of ordered reference to the major factors that render the ascription of a concept reasonable; for nothing less is likely to yield a balanced understanding of the concept in question.

Obviously, ascriptions of ordinary descriptive, existential, and semantic concepts often play substantial roles in the justification of ascriptions of the concept of good. We frequently employ logical principles to show that because something is properly described as an instance of that which is already known to be good, it is good; or that because something which would be good if it existed does exist, it is good. Not only so, but the very kind of thing to which the concept of good is characteristically ascribed is something having descriptive and existential characteristics by virtue of which it is good and apart from which it would not be. If the application of the concept of good could properly vary without some corresponding change in the descriptive, existential, or semantic properties or relations of that to which it applied, the concept would be of little use, if, indeed, it would then be a concept at all. Thus, John is ready to give as reasons for Jim's catching a fish's being good that Jim enjoys catching a fish and that Jim will have fish to eat. Carton is ready to give as a reason for his act's being good that it gives him peace and affords his beloved an opportunity for happiness. And the engineering student is ready to offer in support of the goodness of the concrete mix employed that it will make the bridge strong and durable. In like manner, in support of the notion that it would be good to undertake certain sanitary measures, one might call attention to the existence of a mild epidemic; and in support of the value of anything one might remind his hearers of the consistency and truth of the grounds already offered in support of the claims that that thing is good.

What is in question concerning the justification of ascriptions of the concept of good is not, then, whether or not ascriptions of descriptive, existential, or semantic concepts are involved. It is agreed on every hand that they are. What is in question is, instead, whether ascriptions of such concepts are sufficient by themselves to justify ascriptions of the concept of good. What I want to suggest in this connection is that ascriptions of these other concepts alone never seem to provide ample justifications for ascriptions of the concept of good, but rather that every ascription of the concept of good must either be inferred from a set of judgments including a basic ascription of the concept of good (a synthetic value judgment) that is significantly distinct from ascriptions of descriptive, existential, or semantic concepts and requires no further justification, or else must be justified directly by just such an ascription, rooted in ascertained facts and inferences, but not itself an ascription of any descriptive, existential, or semantic concept.

If this claim is correct, its applicability must manifest itself in the principal kinds of instances of ascription of the concept of good. Such instances fall roughly into two classes. In the first class, which may be referred to as the *predicative* one, the concept of good is ascribed to a thing or event generally, rather than with special reference to the kind of thing or event it is. In the second class, which may be referred to as the *attributive* one, the concept of good is ascribed to a thing or event as the kind of thing or event it is.

With regard to the first class the need for a basic judgment ascribing the concept of good somewhere within any adequate set of justifying reasons becomes readily apparent upon examination of instances. If we ask an old fisherman why catching a fish is good, he may reply that it contributes to his livelihood; and in answer to our question why contributing to his livelihood is good, he may well say that it enables him to eat and drink and to do the things he wants to do. As to why these are good, he may just say that, of course, anyone will find them so. Or he may take another tack and say that fishing provides food for people. "And why is that good?" "Well, anyone can see that that is good." Again, on the basis of many experiences and the telescoping of many facts, he may say that, in his judgment, catching fish simply is good, and that's all there is to it. In any case, however many descriptive or existential statements he offers us, he always comes back as a fundamental part of his reason to a basic judgment, not merely that something is of such and such descriptive character or exists, but that something is good. If we ask an electrician why the use of armored cable in interior wiring is good, he may well present us with a complex set of propositions regarding the behavior of electrical currents under overload conditions. In answer to our queries about why these facts justify his claim that the use of the cable is good, he may point to the prevention of fire, and thence to the preservation of life or something else that he may find good without the need for further reasons; but he has to come at least that far before his justification can begin to be complete. If a philosopher claims that his meticulous and apparently remote-from-life analysis is nevertheless a good thing, he may cite as reasons the light that it throws on the character of the human mind, the functioning of language, or the nature of the universe. In support of the relevance of these considerations he may, in turn, cite all manner of descriptive facts and invoke a wide variety of semantic and logical principles. But, in the end, if he is to explain adequately to us why what he does is a good thing, he must either make the dubious claim which one may judge directly, in the light of what his activity is—that it is a good thing—or else he must undertake to link the grounds which he offers with something that can be found good without further need of justification.

With respect to the justification of instances of what I have called attributive ascriptions of the concept of good, dependence upon judgments directly ascribing this concept is less readily apparent than with respect to instances of predicative ascriptions. The reason is that ample justificatory grounds seem to be suggested by the character and purposes of the *kinds* of things in question. Nevertheless, reference to what is found good without need of further justification continues to be required. When I say that here is a good book or pen or saw or even a good pistol or a good poison, the descriptive properties that lead us to say that the book, pen, saw, pistol, or poison is good are surely relevant to the thing's being of the kind that it is and, hence, to its being good of its kind. However, one is still entitled to inquire why having these properties makes the thing in question good of its kind; and the answer must, in the end, always include a reference to some self-justifying good, such as the satisfaction of smooth writing or pleasant reading. In like manner one's saying that a book or pen or pistol quickly and easily achieves the ends of the kind of thing it is must surely be relevant to its being good of its kind; but the notion of accomplishing an end quickly and easily already includes a concept of good, and one can explain why accomplishing just these ends is good only by reference to some self-justifying good, such as being a pleasant or satisfying experience.

If the suggestion now being made that in every adequate justification of an ascription of the concept of good a basic ascription of this concept must itself somewhere appear is to be rejected, such rejection must take the form either of a claim that ascriptions of the concept of good can be inferred solely from ascriptions of other kinds of concepts or else of a claim that ascriptions of some other kind of concept are equivalent to ascriptions of the concept of good.

If ascriptions of the concept of good are to be inferred from ascriptions of some other kind of concept, the inferences must be either entailments or inductions or related kinds of inferences. Inferences of the first kind, entailments of ascriptions of the concept of good by ascriptions of other kinds of concepts, are generally rejected on the ground that conclusions of entailments should not contain factors of kinds not included in the premises. Inferences of the second kind, inferences of ascriptions of the concept of good from ascriptions of other kinds of concepts by inductive or other related arguments, are more persistent and less obviously invalid.

Actually, the claim that some ascriptions of other kinds of concepts imply ascriptions of the concept of good makes a sound and important point; namely, that from a very great many kinds of ordinary statements commonly taken to be ascriptions of descriptive and existential concepts, ascriptions of the concepts of good can be correctly inferred. Thus, in many contexts, from the statement that John struck his brother without reason, one may correctly infer that John's conduct was rude and, therefore, not good. From the statement that Carton gave his life for his friend, one may perhaps correctly infer that Carton's conduct was good or even saintly; and from the statement that a painting is colorful and symmetrical, one may sometimes infer that the painting may well be beautiful and, therefore, good.

Nevertheless, the claim involved in such instances—that ascriptions of the concept of good can be inferred from ascriptions of other concepts—rests upon a confusion, the confusion of supposing that ordinary ascriptions of descriptive and existential concepts are just that and

nothing more and, accordingly, that in inferring ascriptions of the
concept of good from them, one is inferring ascriptions of good from
ascriptions of other concepts. If, as has been previously noted, a great
many expressions employed in what appear to be wholly descriptive
or existential statements involve, as aspects of their meanings alongside
explicit descriptive and existential concepts, implicit concepts of good,
then statements ascribing the concept of good may indeed follow from
them; but the inferences by which these statements follow are not, as
they seem, inferences from ascriptions of other concepts alone but
inferences from ascriptions of other concepts together with concepts
of good. Thus, when one infers from a statement that someone has
freely given his life for another, fed the hungry, cared for the aged,
loved his neighbor, increased production, or been creative, that what
he has done is good, one is not, as might appear, inferring ascriptions
of concepts of good from ascriptions of other concepts, but rather inferring ascriptions of the concepts of good from ascriptions of concepts already implicitly containing such concepts. When one is tempted
to suppose that in inferring from such statements as "the child kept
chattering cheerfully," "the boy covered the whole assignment," "the
old man smiled with delight," or "wages are rising without a corresponding rise in prices" he is inferring ascriptions of concepts of
good from ascriptions of other kinds of concepts, he should try abstracting from these initial statements every element of the concept
of good or, even better, placing each episode in contexts of culture
in which no notion of good is built into the conception initially ascribed. If he succeeds in doing so, the inferences to ascriptions of the
concept of good almost inevitably disintegrate, and the illusion of
having inferred ascriptions of concepts of good from ascriptions of
other concepts loses its grip.

I turn now from the supposition that ascriptions of the concept of
good can be inferred from ascriptions of other concepts to the other
way of attempting to justify ascriptions of the concept of good without
referring to any basic ascription of a significantly distinctive concept
of good; namely, that of identifying the concept of good with some
other concept, such as being desired, liked, or pleasing. Upon such a
view, to justify an ascription of the concept of good might indeed require, as has been claimed here, a reference to a basic ascription of the
concept of good or to an inference from such an ascription; but this
requirement could be fulfilled by an ascription of a concept of good
which was identical with another descriptive concept such as being
desired, liked, or pleasing. However, quite apart from other well-
known objections to the sorts of identifications indicated, this account

of the justification of ascriptions of the concept is confronted, once the proposed definitions are substituted for the concept of good, with the very same kind of demand for justification concerning the ascription of the concept of good to a thing or event as characterized by the defining property as was initially present concerning the ascription of the concept of good to the thing or event itself; and there seems to be no way of eventually satisfying this demand save by reference to basic ascriptions of concepts of good that are not identifiable with being desired, liked, pleasing, or anything else of the sort. Thus, for example, one may undertake to justify the claim that the latest sculpture by Pablo Picasso is good by asserting that it is pleasing to cultured people, and that this condition is what being good is. But then one can scarcely avoid asking why the sculpture's being pleasing is good, and the answer that the sculpture's being pleasing is pleasing is scarcely an adequate answer.

Whereas one may often correctly apply and even give adequate justifications for applications of a concept on the basis of apprehension of only a very limited part of the range of the concept, one can scarcely teach another person to understand and to use a concept without some grasp of the full range of the concept. Accordingly, inquiry concerning what one must teach if his pupil is to have an adequate apprehension of the concept of good may be even more revealing with reference to the character of that concept than inquiry concerning the manner of ascriptions or justifications of ascriptions of the concept.

Although there is no one right way in which the concept of good, or any other concept, must be taught, a successful teacher is very likely to begin with the cruder, more obvious aspects of a concept and gradually work out into the refinements. Thus, in teaching a child to understand and to use the concept of good, a wise parent may well begin by explaining that for something to be good is for it to be something we like, desire, or are pleased with—as, for example, we like, desire, and are pleased with ice-cream cones, cherry pies, smiling faces, clean hands, polite manners, pretty girls, and kind friends.

This first lesson must, however, soon be modified. Who are included in the *we?* and for what purposes is a thing or event liked, desired, or pleasing? Is the *we* the parent and the child? or both parents and the child? or the whole family and the community? or everybody? or who? Sooner or later the child must learn that the answers vary in quite flexible and complex ways with the context of the use of the word *good*, and that no fully general answers can be given. He must also learn that the purposes for which a thing is taken to be good are widely varied and are likely to be implicit in the verbal, physical, and social setting; and that just what these purposes are makes a considerable difference concerning whether the thing said to be good really is good. He must come to see, for example, that a house jack is properly said to be a good thing when one is speaking of leveling a sagging floor, but not when one is decorating a living room; and that a pipe wrench can properly be called good with reference to tightening pipe joints, but not with reference to adjusting wrist watches. The child must also be taught that although what is called good is roughly what we like, desire, and are pleased with, it is not just that and can more accurately be said to be what we like, desire, and are pleased with when we are thoughtful and when we are well aware of what the thing or event we are calling good will lead to. He must be led to see that to call eating a fourth ice-cream cone a good thing when in fact that would make him ill for two days is not to make a correct statement. Another related lesson that the child must learn is that a thing or event is not properly said to be good unless its effect upon everyone embraced within the reference group and included in the purpose for which the thing is being said to be good is duly and impartially considered. Thus, though the child's having fresh peaches every day during the year is something that he desires, likes, and is pleased with even when he knows its effects, it may nevertheless not be a good thing with respect to the economy of the family.

Another refinement that the child must be taught to cope with concerns the problem of just where to place the notion of good with respect to the differences between liking, desiring, being pleased, and other favorable attitudes. These attitudes are different from one another, and that difference makes a difference regarding the concept of good. For example, one often desires something very strongly but is not pleased with it when he gets it, and he should then be hesitant to call it good. Or, not having desired a thing or an event at all or even having had an aversion to it, one may like it very much when it occurs; and in the process one may have shifted his judgment concerning its goodness from a negative to a strong positive.

When our child has learned to qualify the initially conveyed account of the concept of good in the foregoing ways, he may still remain a long way from having learned the concept of good until he has learned that, for the various purposes for which a thing is said to be good, there are standards that are to be met by what is properly said to be good. Apples are good only if they are sweet and juicy; corn, if it is full and tender; knives, if they are easy to handle and hold their cutting edges; actions, if they are fair and considerate; and people, if they are just and kind. Such standards, our child must sooner or later learn, can be quite detailed, and they vary with cultures and subcultures. Although they can become so rigid that the term *good* comes, in a "degenerate" sense, to be used as almost equivalent to them, they are never fully independent of other more basic factors in the concept of good, and they are subject to correction when they cease to conform to these factors; e. g., to what people would reflectively and impartially desire. Thus, our teacher may well explain to his pupil that although the segregation of races is, in his area, commonly considered good, it is not what he or anyone else would want if he knew the consequences and had to exchange places with those persons adversely affected.

Even when a child has learned that things and events are good when they are in accord with standards conformable to what one in full knowledge of relevant facts would impartially like, desire, or be pleased with, he would, presumably, still be commonly acknowledged not yet to have fully grasped the concept of good. Presumably for something to be good is not just for it to be what one would, under specifiable conditions, desire, like, or be pleased with but what one should (in some sense of *should*) desire, like, or be pleased with. Even when what one should desire or like is just what he does reflectively and impartially desire or like, its being good is as much a function of the fact that it should be desired or liked as of the fact that it is reflectively and impartially desired or liked. Moreover, if one's capacity for reflective impartial valuation happens to be limited or distorted, what one does desire or like impartially and reflectively will not be what he should desire or like.

There is still at least one more lesson that our child in quest of the concept of good must learn; namely, how to distinguish the concept of good from other normative concepts, for the concept of good is only one of a number of normative concepts and is distinguished by a positive quality lacking in most of the others. However, this aspect of two concepts can best be discussed in connection with the topic of the following paragraphs.

The final kind of context in which the distinctiveness of the concept of good is to be considered consists of those contexts in which this concept originates and renews itself,[2] and attention to those contexts should be revealing not only with respect to the whole range of the concept of good but also with respect to the place of this concept in our conceptual schemes and in our way of life. It should, accordingly, throw light, not only upon what this concept is, but also upon what the character of any concept must be if it is even roughly to fulfill the need that this one does. To be sure, the details of the historical origin of the concept of good, or of a term playing the role that *good* does in modern English, are lost in antiquity. However, we have some knowledge of the manner in which, in general, concepts arise and of the character of the needs out of which this concept in particular arises; and this knowledge should be helpful for present purposes.

Concepts never emerge in a vacuum. Always they appear within complex settings involving already operative conceptual systems and in response to experiences and needs. Sometimes the experiences and needs from which new concepts spring can be related to other experiences in a fairly clear-cut manner; and sometimes, usually in formal systems, emerging concepts stand in quite clearly defined relations to existing systems of concepts. More characteristically, however, the experiences out of which new concepts emerge are new experiences standing in no neat set of relations with prior experiences, and the concepts they produce are not initially part of, and are not readily relatable to, previously existing systems of concepts.

Perhaps the general character of the situations out of which the concept of good arose and from which it repeatedly renews itself may be briefly characterized somewhat as follows. When living, conscious organisms, capable of vast ranges of sensible, conceptual, and volitional experiences, come to be able to anticipate, and in some degree to regulate, the future and, hence, to develop desires, likings, and satisfactions, they stand in need of a general concept that may be used to guide their free choices by designating those things and events that they find worth desiring, liking, being satisfied with, and seeking to attain.

If this be so, it is plain, to begin with, why both existing concepts of good and any concept of good that is to serve even roughly the same purpose must make reference to man's desires, likings, and satisfactions; for nothing could suitably guide the practical activity of a being in whom these factors play so vital a role as they do in man without taking these factors into account. Indeed, apart from these factors, the notion of one thing's being better than another scarcely seems to make sense at all. It is also plain that what is suited to guide the free activity of a creature such as man must be in accord, not merely with his desires, likings, and satisfactions as they are at any given moment, but more especially with man's desires, likings, and satisfactions as are likely to emerge in his attempt to regulate his life in the light of his character and that of the world in which he lives. Again, any concept that is to meet the demands of the situation sketched must be such as to take full account of the many purposes for which a thing is taken to be good and to preserve a substantial degree of impartiality with reference to persons affected by what is regarded as good. Accounts of the conditions under which desires, likings, and satisfactions may properly be said to define the concept of good may be in fact progressively refined along the lines indicated; and in this way the concept of good may be characterized with increasing precision. Proceeding in this fashion, one may well be able to construct a complex of descriptive, existential, and semantic concepts answering to salient features of the concept of good and quite sufficient to distinguish the concept of good from any other existing concept. The possibility of achieving such a complex excludes not only the possibility of equating the concept of good with any other existing concept but also the possibility, implicit in the claims of some non-naturalists, that the concept of good is simple. It likewise excludes the possibility, implicit in the claims of most naturalists, that the concept of good is a relatively simple complex; for naturalists, like non-naturalists, err in making the concept of good too simple rather than in making it too complex.

Nevertheless, however closely the projected account of the concept of good as a complex of descriptive, existential, and semantic concepts may approximate the concept of good and however fully it may distinguish the concept of good from other concepts, it apparently cannot, for want of features that do justice to the distinctively nominative and evaluative aspects of the existing concept of good that were noted previously, be equated with the existing concept of good or constitute an adequate account of that concept. Moreover, because the situation in which the concept of good arises is one requiring a concept that not only indicates conditions under which things and events might be desired or liked and how free choices are, or could be, guided, but also discloses conditions under which things and events should be chosen and can be used to designate what is worth desiring, liking, and seeking, no complex of descriptive, existential, and semantic properties can do justice to the character of any concept that is to meet the requirements of the situation out of which the concept of good arises. Accordingly, although the complex set of features thus far indicated does distinguish the concept of good from all other concepts, it does not exhaust the distinctiveness of the concept of good.

Another feature of the existing concept of good, also required in any concept that is to meet the needs of a sensible being with capacity to anticipate and affect the future for a general concept to be used to guide his free choices and indicate what is worth desiring and seeking, is, as has been suggested previously, the normative character of the concept; that is, its signifying what should be and not merely what is.

The specific force conceptualized in this *should* is difficult to locate, but this much seems clear: it is not physical force, or logical necessity, or even social pressure as such, but rather a kind of rational constraint recognizable, and capable of being self-imposed, by those who employ concepts in which it is implicit. Among the normative concepts by way of which this rational constraint is operative are such concepts as those of morality, right, obligation, and duty. The normative character of the concept of good has already been encountered in general in earlier inquiries concerning ascriptions of value and justifications of such ascriptions and, more specifically, in the discussion of the teaching of the concept of value. It is encountered still more pointedly when one inquires into the situations out of which the concept of good arises, for here man's need for effective guidance concerning both the ends to be pursued and the means of pursuing them comes into focus. Being a normative concept in the manner indicated is quite enough by itself to distinguish the concept of good from all descriptive, existential, and semantic concepts as such; for however much such concepts may be made to coincide with normative concepts in extension, they never become equivalent to normative concepts in intension. Nevertheless, being a normative concept does not distinguish the concept of good from all other concepts; for normative concepts also include concepts of right, duty, obligation, and many other concepts that cannot be construed as belonging directly to the concept of good or as containing that concept. Further analysis is, accordingly, required.

Among normative concepts it is possible to distinguish at least roughly between those in which the rational constraint involved can be construed as largely rational restraint and those in which this rational constraint is better construed as rational attraction. To the former group belong such concepts as those of right, duty, and obligation. To the latter belong those of good, value, merit, desert, effectiveness, and many more specific ones. Of all these latter concepts the most general and indeed the all-embracing one is the concept of good. Accordingly, the mark, implicit in the demand of the situation out of which the concept of good emerges for a general concept by which to designate what is worth desiring and seeking, that best distinguishes the concept of good from other normative concepts would seem to be that of being the most comprehensive of what might be called the "attractive" group of the normative concepts; and since being a normative concept already distinguishes the concept of good from all descriptive, existential, and semantic concepts, this mark would seem to distinguish the concept of good from all other concepts whatever.

Is this complex concept of the most general of the "attractive" group of normative concepts equivalent to the concept of good, and has an adequate account of the distinctiveness of the concept of good at last been achieved in it? Perhaps, at any rate, a second way of distinguishing the concept of good from all other concepts—over and above the way of referring to what would be desired, liked, or pleasing under specifiable conditions—has been pointed out. But the complex concept in question is not equivalent to the concept of good, and the distinctiveness of the concept of good has not been exhausted in it. Something is missing from both of the foregoing accounts of the distinctiveness of the concept of good. Something has been said about what would be desired, liked, or pleasing under specified conditions and about the "attractive" set of normative concepts; but nothing has been said about anything's being specifically worth being desired, liked, or pleasing, or "attractively normative"; and apart from some such notion of worthwhileness there is no notion of good.

At this point some non-naturalists would be ready to say that indeed the notion of such worthwhileness—or, if one pleases, of just goodness or value—is the whole of the concept of good and that all such characters as those of being desired or liked under specifiable conditions as "attractively normative" are no more than "good-making" characters that constitute no part of the concept of good as such. However, it would be a mistake to say that any notion of worthwhileness or even goodness that failed to include the notions of being desired under certain conditions and being "attractively normative" could constitute the whole of the concept of good; for no concept can be suitably characterized apart from reference to the conditions of its application, and these latter notions are conditions of the application of the concept of good. Indeed, it would be a mistake to treat the notion of worthwhileness that seems to be essential to the concept of good as a notion separate from and to be placed alongside those of being desired under certain conditions and being "attractively normative" at all. The search for any such separate notion as that of worthwhileness as isolated from the notion of being desired or liked and being "attractively normative" is at best likely to prove a vain one; and even if any such notion could be clarified, the notion of a compound in which being desired plus being "attractively normative," plus being worthwhile would be an artificial and redundant one bearing all too little resemblance to the existing concept of good or any that could serve the same purpose.

The notion of worthwhileness that is indispensable to the concept of good is virtually the concept of good all over again, but now seen to be a product of conditions requiring a general concept to guide free choices and, hence, embracing both the notion of possessing characteristics that, under certain conditions, are desired or liked and the notion of being "attractively normative," but not exhausted by either notion or by both. To discover what other factors it may include is a subject for a continuing inquiry; but in the light of the conditions of the origin of the concept of good these factors can scarcely be expected to fit quite neatly into any ready-made conceptual scheme. The concept of good seems then to be no more a concept isolated from other concepts than one equivalent to other concepts. Like most other concepts save purely formal ones, it seems rather to be a conceptual way of meeting needs implicit in a special kind of experiential situation that is not quite like any other concept and, thus, is never quite equivalent to any other concept or set of concepts although it is intimately related to other concepts and is increasingly approximated by reference to combinations of them.

There may, however, be something more to the distinctiveness of good than this. Not only does the concept of good seem to be different in growing out of different needs, but it also seems to grow out of a different *kind* of need and is, thus, perhaps a different *kind* of concept from other kinds of concepts. Because he must anticipate the character of sensible experiences that are significant with reference to the future and those that are not, man needs existential concepts. Because man can respond more intelligently and satisfactorily to his environment when he can reflect upon his own discourse than when he cannot, man also needs semantic concepts. Because he must guide his practical life, man needs normative concepts. But since he also needs to have the guidance of his practical life formed by goals worth seeking, man also requires a concept of good. To the extent that this last need is not only a different need from the others but a different kind of need, the concept of good may be not only a distinctive concept but a distinctive kind of concept.

In presenting the distinctiveness of the concept of good in the foregoing manner, I have, of course, renounced all naturalistic attempts to equate fully the concept of good with any other concept and all emotivist-prescriptivist attempts to substitute for a concept of good—a linguistic function without a concept. However, in doing so, I have not reverted to the non-naturalistic notion of a simple property that stops the analytic process before it gets started. Instead if, as I have contended, the concept of good is, from one point of view, a complex character of being ready to be desired or liked in specifiable ways and, from another point of view, an "attractive normative" character, though not entirely either or both but a distinctive character rooted in a special kind of experiential situation and involving both, then the concept of good, rather than stopping analysis at the start, stands as a continuing challenge to analytic inquiry.

NOTES

1. That the needs of originating situations are of special importance for the understanding of many concepts that are both broad and distinctive—and of the concept of good in particular—was suggested by the reading of the first two chapters of Julius Kovesi's *Moral Notions* (New York and London: Routeledge and Kegan Paul and The Humanities Press, 1967).

2. *Ibid.*

On the Ultimate Subjects of Value Predication

HECTOR-NERI CASTAÑEDA

> When we assert that a thing is good, what we mean is that its existence or reality is good.
>
> ... Whatever definition be offered, it may be always asked, with significance, of the complex so defined [i.e., the defining complex property] whether it is itself good.
>
> ... We should know what good means before we can go on to consider what is good—what things or qualities are good.
>
> —G. E. Moore, *Principia Ethica*, § 70, 13, 86

To the unsophisticated consciousness a given property, quality, or condition is predicated of things, persons, acts, properties, or conditions when it is said that certain items are good or bad. Judging from the epigraph quoted above, G. E. Moore has assumed very much the same attitude. If so, Moore's famous open-question technique has a powerful prong that, to my knowledge, has never been appreciated by his critics. Although that prong would still be incapable of yielding proof of the unanalyzability of goodness, it would show that only properties which apply to different categories can be genuine candidates for a definiens position in a definition of goodness. Clearly, if goodness is not self-predicative, the predicability of goodness to a proposed definiens makes that definiens not identical with goodness.

In this essay I again want to consider the questions raised almost solely by Everett Hall:[1]

   1. Is primary goodness a second-order property?
   2. Is primary goodness a property of states of affairs?

I also want to take up the question:

   3. Is primary goodness one and the same property that crosses over logical ranks, or are there several different properties?

The exploration of these questions suggests that perhaps:

   1. the goodness of properties is derivative;
   2. the goodness of particulars is definable and analyzable in terms of the goodnesses and badnesses of states of affairs; so that
   3. the primary goodness is that of states of affairs that are, therefore, the ultimate subjects of value predication.

In any case, the investigation uncovers two important assumptions that underlie value measurement; namely, V.E and M.3, M.3a, or M.4, as we shall see below.

In this investigation I will use the term *state of affairs* as the most neutral way to refer to the same thing which *proposition* and *statement* refer to. *Proposition* emphasizes contents of mental acts or attributes, while *statement* emphasizes language.

I. THE VERTICAL APPROACH

The adjective *good* is used in several different ways, among which the ones illustrated by the following examples are of great importance:

A.1 This is good.
A.2 This is a good steak.
B.1 The good thing to do is . . . .
C.1 Jones is a good student.
C.2 Jones is a good man.
C.3 It was good of Jones to come (talk with Smith).
D.1 This wine is not good, but it has some good features (qualities).
E.1 It is good that you came.
E.2 It is good for Smith that Jones came.

A.1 and A.2 attribute goodness to objects; B.1 attributes goodness to an action; C.1, C.2, and C.3 attribute goodness to persons; D.1 attributes goodness to properties, or qualities; E.1 attributes goodness to states of affairs, and E.2 attributes a relation to Smith and a state of affairs. Now the question is: Do all uses of the adjective *good* predicate one and the same property? I really do not know how to support an affirmative, or for that matter, a negative answer to this question. Some philosophers would simply regard the fact that several different categories of entities are said to be good as a conclusive proof that we are dealing with different properties. For some philosophers all entities are tidily classified into separate pidgeonholes, so that no entity can belong to two or more of them. However, on reflection we can see that there are entities that cross categories. Numbers, or numerical properties, for instance, jump from category to category. Not only do physical objects exemplify numbers, but properties of physical objects and properties of properties of physical objects also exemplify numbers. Psychological relations, of course, seem to relate minds or mental acts to all categories of entities, including psychological relations.

We should also note that simply because each of the examples given above has entailments different from the others, it does not follow that the adjective *good* has a different meaning in each one. Clearly, the difference in entailments is fully accounted for by the different elements, other than goodness, in each of the statements. Indeed, even if one and the same sentence expresses two different statements so that we are justified in claiming that the sentence has an ambiguity, we have not in that fact alone a conclusive reason for claiming that some word, or term, in the sentence is ambiguous. For example, the sentence

S Jones ought not to see Mary.

can be used to make two different statements, which can be expressed more perspicuously as follows:

1. Jones ought to not-see Mary.
2. It is not the case that Jones ought to see Mary.

Thus, the ambiguity of S does not consist of S's having an ambiguous term, but of S's having two different scopes for the negative term *not*.

How can we show then that the uses of *good* cited above are, or are not, different in that they predicate different properties? One way of showing that we have different properties referred to by several uses of *good* in the forementioned examples consists of analyzing each of the uses differently. This approach I will call the *parallel approach*, because, if successful, it will provide us with parallel definitions for the goodness of objects, the goodness of persons, the goodness of states of affairs, etc. If successful, it shows at once that each property called *goodness* is analyzable. And if the analyses are entirely different it also shows that any two properties called *goodness* are different. Now, of course, it is not necessary that we find a complete analysis for each sense of *good*. It suffices that we produce partially adequate analyses that show that two properties, each called *goodness*, are different. For instance, when we claim that the word *table* is ambiguous we often offer only partial analysis: *table₁* means a diagram or a list of items; *table₂* means a piece of furniture on which to eat or around which to place seats.

The parallel approach is in fact being tried out whenever a philosopher proposes an analysis of the meaning of the adjective *good* used attributively (as the grammarians say); that is, an analysis of its use as it appears in contexts of the form *good*   , where the blank is occupied by a noun. Each such proposal is one member of the sets of parallel definitions we should have in order to analyze all the uses of *good*.

There is, however, what I call the *vertical approach*. This approach consists in attempting to analyze the goodness of one category of entities in terms of the goodness of other categories. For instance, we may try to analyze the goodness of particulars (objects or persons) in terms of the goodness of states of affairs. Let me say at once that both approaches should be tried out. While the broad application of the parallel approach hinges on the working hypothesis that each of the properties called *good* is analyzable, the vertical approach hinges on the hypothesis that only some are. But the truth of the matter is that one can experiment with both approaches, with no preconceived assumption. In this spirit I want to proceed to an experiment employing the vertical approach.

II. The Goodness of Properties

We can readily agree that the goodness of properties is analyzable in terms of the goodness of objects, persons, or actions, or the goodness of states of affairs. The fundamental insight is this: *the realm of values is the contingent,* the World of Becoming; statements attributing goodness to a contingent entity A are statements to the effect that a universe containing A is good. Properties are abstract and necessarily existing or subsisting entities, whose primary ontological status is not affected by the contents or the changes in the world. Thus, there are three points to be made:

1. The values we are interested in when we are making decisions for immediate action or long-range plans are the values of contingent things and events and states of affairs. Since properties and necessary truths are necessarily existing entities, any values which they had would be values which would belong to any possible world and would remain fixed. They can, therefore, be added or ignored, without in the least affecting our practical task of ascertaining the values characteristic of our circumstances in our actual universe, the values that are to determine which courses of action or which things we ought to choose.

2. In the first place, properties in themselves are not good. Wines are said to be good when they have good features, or properties, such as when they are dry, not sour, of a clear color, etc. But none of these properties is really good in itself. Otherwise dryness would be a good property, regardless of which things have it, or even if nothing at all has it. The fact is that dryness is not a good feature, as, for example, in a slice of bread. When we say that a certain wine is good because it has the good properties, $P_1, \ldots, P_n$, we are simply ascribing to these properties goodness only in the sense of good-making properties. That is, $P_1, \ldots, P_n$ are good because wines having $P_1, \ldots, P_n$ are good wines. This analysis of the goodness of properties, in terms of the goodness of objects, persons, or actions, seems to hold for those cases in which the good

properties in question form a sufficient set of conditions for the goodness of things of a certain kind ϕ to be good ϕ-ers.

3. When the good properties are only necessary conditions for the goodness of a ϕ, then the above analysis fails. But in such a case the good properties in question are not in themselves good; they are *good for things to have*, or not to have, as the case may be. It is the possession of properties, rather than the properties themselves, which is good or bad. Thus, when we say that an object has certain good features, or qualities, we are really ascribing goodness to unspecified states of affairs consisting of the object in question having those unspecified features, or qualities. For example, when a steak is not good, although it has some good qualities, what happens is that the steak has some qualities, say ϕ_1-ness, ϕ_2-ness, . . . , and ϕ_n-ness so that it is good that steaks be ϕ_1, be ϕ_2, . . . , and be ϕ_n.

It must be emphasized, however, that none of the three points made above, nor all of them together, constitutes *proof* that properties in themselves have no values. They only establish that such necessary values of abstract entities are irrelevant to our practical problems. If a philosopher wants a rich axiology, he is certainly free to have it. Indeed, he may retort to my third point that it only shows that simple properties do not have value, but that a very complex property, like red wine, with such and such a degree of sourness and such and such aroma and . . . is good, and that nothing having that goodness can be bad. Nevertheless, that philosopher must understand that he is adding a rather empty wrapping to his axiology. For he needs a principle connecting the goodness of properties with the goodness of particulars, such as:

P For every property ϕ-ness which is good whatever is ϕ is good.

It does not matter whether the word *good* predicates in sentence P one or two different properties. The point is that it makes no difference for action or practice whether we use P and the relevant principles for determining which properties are good, or whether we never attribute intrinsic goodness to properties and use, instead, principles of the form

S Whatever is ϕ is good,

together with the criteria for the good-making properties. In other words, it is axiologically immaterial whether in addition to being good-making, either by P or by S and some criteria, a property is intrinsically good or not. What matters is that properties be good- or bad-making.

I am opting here for a poorer ontological axiology that takes all properties to be in themselves value-indifferent, but partitions the set of all properties into good-making, bad-making, and neither.

III. THE GOODNESS OF OBJECTS

Thus, the main issue is whether intrinsic goodness is all at once a first-order property of objects and persons, a property of actions, and a property of states of affairs. Let us see whether we can analyze the goodness of objects or persons in terms of the goodness of states of affairs. To begin with, consider A.1. According to Moore (*Principia Ethica*, § 70), we have two alternative ways of putting the same statement A.1:

A.1.a1 The existence of this is good.
A.1.a2 This ought to exist.

Presumably, we can put both A.1.a1 and A.1.a2 more perspicuously as:

A.1.a1′ It is (would be) good that this exist (s) .
A.1.a2′ It ought to be that this exists.

There is a certain oddness about the claim that A.1.a1′ and A.1.a2′ are the same statement. But even if we have here two different statements, at first sight it would seem that A.1.a′ is the same statement as A.1. But before we rush to conclude that the goodness of objects is analyzable in terms of the goodness of states of affairs, let us consider A.2. Following the model of A.1.a1′ we have:

A.2.a1 This steak's existence is good.
A.2.a1′ It is good that this steak exists.

But now there is a difficulty. It is possible that the mere existence of the steak in question fails to be good. If the steak in question is being praised at dinner, very likely the steak managed to keep its goodness, thanks to, or in spite of, the manipulations of it by the cook. Clearly, had it been burned or dried out it would not have been good at the time of eating even though it would have continued in existence. Indeed, had it lost its goodness it would probably have continued in existence longer— because it might have not been eaten. The point is that A.2 seems rather to refer, implicitly, to some unspecified features of the steak in question.

The preceding suggests a proposal of analysis like this:

A.2.b1 There is a property φ-ness such that this steak is φ, and is it good that steaks be φ.

A proposal very much like this one was in fact made by Everett Hall in his *What is Value?* (pp. 177 f). A.2.b1 is a special limiting case of:

A.2.b2 There are properties ϕ_1-ness, . . . , ϕ_K-ness such that both this steak is ϕ_1 and ϕ_2 and . . . and ϕ_K, and for every property ϕ_i-ness ($i = 1, 2, . . . , K$) it is good that steaks be ϕ_i.

The crucial difference between A.2.b1 and A.2.b2 is *that*, in the latter, we have a conjunction of K statements of the form

f it is good that steaks be ϕ_1 and it is good that steaks be ϕ_2 and . . . , and it is good that steaks be ϕ_K,

whereas in A.2.b1 there is a nonconjunctive statement of such a form. If the axiological operator expressed with "it is good that" distributes through conjunction, form f would be equivalent to:

f.s it is good that steaks be (ϕ_1 and ϕ_2 and . . . and ϕ_K).

Then if the conjunction of properties is also a property, A.2.b1 and A.2.b2 would be equivalent.

We shall accept here the principle that properties combine by means of logical operations to yield complex properties. But the equivalence of f and f.s is another story. G. E. Moore's famous principle of organic unities stands in the way of that equivalence. According to that principle the value of a whole (e.g., a conjunction) is not identical with the sum of the values of its parts (e.g., its conjuncts). In particular a conjunction can be good even though it has bad or indifferent conjuncts. We shall not inquire into the truth of this principle of Moore's, but we shall strive to reach an analysis of the goodness of particulars in terms of the goodness of states of affairs which is consistent with the principle. Thus, we shall treat A.2.b2 as non-equivalent to proposal A.2.b1.

Obviously, A.2.b2 implies A.2.b1, regardless of whether the number K of A.2.b2 is *1* or greater than *1*. Hence, any lack of sophistication in A.2.b2 is also a lack in A.2.b1. Now A.2.b2 is inadequate as an analysis of A.2. The latter entails the former, but the former does not entail the latter. As we have already noted, an object of kind ϕ may very well have good features that are necessary, but not sufficient, for the object to be a good ϕ-er. Furthermore, an object of kind ϕ may have features that would make it a good ϕ-er and lack every single property needed for being a good ϕ-er. Both situations make A.2.b2 true without making A.2 true.

This suggests that what A.2 asserts is that the balance of good features is greater than the balance of bad features. But we want to make this statement without committing ourselves to an irreducible goodness of features. And this is the real difficulty. Consider, for example, the following suggestion:

A.2.c There are more properties ϕ_1-ness, . . . , ϕ_n-ness such that both this steak is ϕ_1 and . . . and ϕ_n and it is good that steaks be ϕ_i, for $i = 1, 2, \ldots, n$, than properties ψ_1-ness, . . . , ψ_m-ness so that both this steak is ψ_1 and . . . and ψ_m, and it is bad that this steak be ψ_i, for $i = 1, 2, \ldots, m$.

The trouble with A.2.c is that a mere count of properties involved in facts of the form "it is good that steaks be ϕ" and "it is bad that steaks be ψ" is not always sufficient to determine whether the steak in question is good or not. Furthermore, we can immediately see that there is an infinity of ϕ-properties as well as of ψ-properties, and this infinity is of the same magnitude, provided that there is one ϕ-property and one ψ-property. If the steak is ϕ_1, then the steak is ϕ_1' for every property ϕ_1'-ness tautologically equivalent to ϕ_1-ness. For instance, even the single pattern below yields an infinite sequence of logically equivalent properties:

ϕ-ness, (ϕ or ϕ and ψ)-ness, [ϕ or (ϕ or ϕ and ψ)]-ness, . . .

Clearly, then, we cannot assume that the set of all the properties of an object is finite. Nevertheless, it might be suggested that the sets of paired, logically independent properties of a given contingent object are finite. Two properties are logically independent of one another if it is possible for each one of them to have an instance which is not an instance of the other.

Yet even if the set of paired, logically independent properties of an object is finite, we cannot simply count the logically independent good-making properties and the logically independent bad-making properties, unless Moore's principle of organic unities is false. By this principle it is possible that: (1) it is bad that an object x be ϕ, (2) it is bad that x be ψ, and yet (3) it is good that x be both ϕ and ψ. Or, if that is not possible, it is certainly possible that there be a surplus of goodness accruing to an object by its being both ϕ and ψ, over and above the sum of the goodness accruing to it by being ϕ plus the goodness accruing to it by being ψ. And this surplus of goodness will not be taken into account if we restrict ourselves to logically independent properties.

Now it seems safe to assume that

V.E If that p is logically equivalent to that q, then the amount of goodness (or badness) of that p = the amount of goodness (or badness) of that q.

Thus, of any two equivalent properties, we need consider just one. But can we suppose that:

M. 1 Each set of logically nonequivalent properties of a contingent object is finite?

If this were the case we could select one property to represent all those properties equivalent to it. It makes no difference which one is selected. The properties so selected can be called *representative properties*. By M.1 any set of representative properties of a contingent object is finite. Thus, by principle V.E, when of two logically equivalent propositions we consider only one of them we are considering all sources of value, so to speak, but without multiplying by an infinite factor.

If M.1 is true, then the set of goodnesses and the set of badnesses accruing to an object are finite, and there is no logical impossibility in obtaining their sums. But is M.1 true? It does not seem so. Suppose, for example, that there are m persons at a given time in the universe, and choose any extensional property ϕ-ness (e. g., squareness, redness, or any other property that is obviously extensional). Then we have m psychological properties of the simplest belief type: a_i believes that x is ϕ, which we can represent thus:

$$\text{Ba}_1 (\phi)\text{-ness}, \ldots, \text{Ba}_m (\phi)\text{-ness}.$$

But we have m^2 psychological properties of the next belief type: a_j believes that a_i believes that x is ϕ:

$$\text{Ba}_1 [\text{Ba}_1 (\phi)]\text{-ness}, \ldots, \text{Ba}_m [\text{Ba}_m (\phi)]\text{-ness}.$$

These properties are all nonequivalent to each other. The only plausible equivalence is that between $\text{Ba}_i (\phi)$-ness and $\text{Ba}_i [\text{Ba}_i (\phi)]$-ness. A little reflection shows, however, that a person A can very well believe something without believing that A believes it; conversely a person A can believe that A believes something without A believing it, simply because A believes that he himself is not A. In fact this situation shows that in addition to the previous two types of belief-properties we have the following:

Ba_i [he himself believes (ϕ)]-ness, which we may write:
$\text{Ba}_i [\text{Ba}_i{}^*(\phi)]$.[2]

But the interesting thing is that there are psychological properties of the third order:

$$\text{Ba}_i \left\{ \text{Ba}_j [\text{Ba}_k (\phi)] \right\}\text{-ness}, \left\{ \text{Ba}_i [\text{Ba}_j{}^* (\phi)] \right\}\text{-ness, etc.}$$

It is perfectly clear that the properties of these types are different from the properties of second and first orders, when $i \neq j \neq k \neq i$. Consider the properties:

$$\text{Ba}_i \left\{ \text{Ba}_i [\text{Ba}_i (\phi)] \right\}\text{-ness and Ba}_i [\text{Ba}_i (\phi)]\text{-ness}.$$

These properties are not logically equivalent to each other. Suppose that a man A, a psychologist or philosopher, who does not believe that he himself is A, is studying the logic of belief, and writes "A believes that A believes that p" on the first page of his yellow pad, just to put down some consequences. Thus he does not believe that A believes that A believes that p. He goes home, leaving all his notes on his desk. Later on, the man forgets what he did, is brought into his office, which he does not recognize, and on reading his previous notes, without recognizing them to be his, he takes them as evidence for the proposition "A believes that A believes that p," which he believes. Thus, in this case, A believes that A believes that A believes that p, but it is false that A believes that A believes that p.

In general, it seems that there is an infinity of non-equivalent belief properties that an object has, inasmuch as either a given belief property or its negation will be true of the object. Hence, we are still plagued by infinite summations of goodnesses and badnesses.

Of course, we could simply assume that

M. 2 Psychological properties of contingent objects are neither good- nor bad-making.

It might be argued in defense of M.2 that the value of an object depends solely on its objective properties. Yet in many cases, actions are good or bad partly by virtue of beliefs that people affected by the actions have. Indeed, beliefs and other psychological properties are so obviously relevant to values that subjectivistic analyses of value often look plausible. Here again we are touching on an important topic that has to be discussed but that we shall disregard for the time being.

It may also be argued that given the infinite divisibility of time and space, there are infinite sets of temporal or spatial properties, for example, the properties to the effect that an object is not at such-and-such a position in time or space. Thus, in addition to M.2, we need analogous assumptions for other, non-psychological types of properties. But how many types are there?

What we need is, therefore, a general assumption that can do for all infinite types of properties the job that M.1 and M.2 together are intended to do. The following is an excellent candidate:

M. 3 Any set of representative or non-equivalent properties of a contingent object which are either good- or bad-making is finite.

This assumption is actually better than M.2, in that it allows that psychological properties be value-making. At the moment I do not have any satisfactory way of defending M.3. Some considerations that make it plausible at least from the point of view of the values *open to us* are these: the psychological properties form an infinite sequence, but in daily life we are concerned only with the properties of the very lowest orders. Note, for instance, how confusing it is to discuss whether A believes that A believes that A believes that A believes that p entails, or fails to entail, that A believes that A believes that p. It is not a wanton generalization to say that most human beings become dizzy when considering belief properties of the eighth order. For human beings, then, psychological properties which they take to be good- or bad-making are definitely finite in number. Thus, we can weaken M.3 to:

> M.3a Any set of representative or non-equivalent properties of a contingent object which are either good- or bad-making, and which a practical creature can recognize at a given time, is finite.

This principle allows that there be in *rerum naturae* an infinity of non-equivalent value-making properties of an object, but by establishing a finite relevant threshold makes value-thinking viable.

M.3 and M.3a are not the only principles that allow of finite balances of good over badness, or vice-versa. The following is another assumption that serves the same purpose:

> M.41. Any mapping into the real or the rational numbers of the goodnesses accruing to an object by having a given full set of non-equivalent properties yields either a finite sequence or an infinite sequence, the members of which form a convergent infinite series.
> 2. Similarly for badnesses.

This assumption is weaker than M.3. Clearly M.3 entails M.4. But if M.3 is false, it seems implausible that the amount of values accruing to an object should conveniently arrange themselves in a convergent infinite series. It should be noted that the very existence of valuable objects or, instead, the very existence of objects with positive or negative value requires that the balance of the values of a thing be finite. Thus, if there is no convergence of the infinite series there simply is no value *of* the object, even if there are infinite amounts of value *in* it. Now it may be thought that with increasing scientific knowledge we find increasing amounts of value (or disvalue) in objects, and that this discovery suggests that we can go on discovering (or creating) more value, so that, in the objectivistic view of value, there must be an indefinite set of amounts that we may discover. But this statement is no proof of M.4. The finitude of the sets of representative value-making properties, required by M.3, is compatible with there being amounts of value in a given object, which are not recognized at a given time. I, myself, find

M.4 hard to defend unless M.3 is assumed. Thus, I will ignore M.4 and concentrate on M.3 and M.3a as more feasible candidates.

On assumption M.3 or M.3a we can avoid the infinity objection to A.2.c by replacing A.2.c with:

> A.2.d There are more representative value-making properties of this steak ϕ_1-ness, . . . , ϕ_n-ness so that it is good that this steak be ϕ_i, for $i = 1, 2, . . . , n$, than representative value-making properties ψ_1-ness, . . . , ψ_m-ness, of this steak such that it is bad that this steak be ψ_i, for $i = 1, a, . . . , m$.

Unfortunately, A.2.d is still inadequate. There may very well be more representative properties of the steak that are good-making than representative properties of it that are bad-making, yet the steak may still be a bad one, simply because the bad-making properties are weightier or more value-making than the good-making ones. This possibility suggests a further proposal:

> A.2.e Any maximal set of non-equivalent value-making properties of this steak is partitioned into two subsets a and β so that: for every property ϕ_i-ness in a it is good that this steak be ϕ_i, for every property ϕ_j-ness in β it is bad that this steak be ϕ_j, and the sum of the goodnesses of the a-states of affairs (i.e., the states of affairs in which properties in a enter predicatively and the steak in question enters as a subject) is greater than the sum of the β-states of affairs.

By V.E no surplus value contributed by a complex whole is left out, but it is not multiplied by an infinite factor that makes the computation arithmetically unmanageable. By M.3, or even M.3a, the sets a and β are finite.

Now A.2.e does look like a plausible analysis of the goodness of the steak in terms of the goodnesses and badnesses of states of affairs. There is, however, one bothersome thing in A.2.e. Our original statement A.2 made it clear that the steak under consideration was good qua steak, leaving it open whether the same steak was bad qua something else, for instance, qua a gift or qua a cure for a black eye or even qua a cure for a black eye for Jones, who is allergic to fresh steak. Clearly A.2.e does not leave it open whether the steak is bad or not under some other classification. Remember that A.2.e considers *all* the representative value-making properties of the steak. To overcome this weakness we should amend A.2.e to

> A.2.f Any maximal set of non-equivalent value-making properties of this steak is partitioned into two subsets: a and β so that:

for every property ϕ_i-ness in a it is good that all steaks be ϕ_i, for every property ϕ_j-ness in β it is bad that all steaks be ϕ_j, and the sum of the goodnesses of these universal a-states of affairs is larger than the sum of the badnesses of these universal β-states of affairs.

The analysans in A.2.f does not leave it open that with respect to a class a' of objects different from the class a of steaks that we are considering, the value-making properties of our steak may be partitioned differently and the sum of the goodnesses of the new universal a'-states of affairs may be smaller than, or equal to, the sum of the badnesses of the corresponding β'-states of affairs.

But there is an objection to A.2.f as a paradigm of the analysis of the goodness of objects in terms of the goodness of states of affairs. Perhaps all steaks qua main courses of dinners are made good by exactly the same good-making properties. But more general types of objects seem to require alternative sets of value criteria. Meats, for instance, even qua edible and delectable items, do involve different good-making properties. Clearly there are no two sets of non-equivalent, value-making properties as described in A.2.f of all the properties of meats. For example, fresh meats must be juicy, while dry meats must not be juicy. Thus, we seemed to be driven to an analysis of the form:

A.2.g This is a steak of kind K, and any maximal set of non-equivalent value-making properties of this steak is partitioned into three subsets a, β, and γ so that: for every ϕ_i-ness in a it is good that all steaks of kind K be ϕ_i, for every ϕ_j-ness in β it is bad that all steaks of kind K be ϕ_j, for every ϕ_h-ness in γ it is neither good nor bad that all steaks be ϕ_h, and the goodness of these a-states of affairs is greater than the badness of these β-states of affairs.

Obviously, a parallel analysis A.2.g' must be available for one to say, "This steak is bad."

Now A.2.g is not a genuine analysans of statement A.2 in the sense of analysis in which Moore was interested. There is in A.2 no reference to any kind K of steaks, so that the letter K in A.2.g is a schematic letter or a free variable occurring freely or schematically in the alleged analysans, but not in the given analysandum. Thus A.2.g is merely an analysans schema which will yield one or more genuine analysans upon binding or elimination of K. This restriction of K can be accomplished in several ways, particularly

1. by putting an existential quantifier "There is a kind K such that" at the very beginning of A.2.g,

2. by keeping the schematic letter K open for different fillers that specify kinds in different contexts of utterance, and

3. by introducing a free variable K in the analysandum A. 2.

If we existentially generalize A.2.g on K, we find a genuine analysans A.2.g.a. A characteristic feature of this analysis is that given a certain kind K, a given steak may be good; given another kind, it may be bad. But since the kinds in question are not specified in A.2.g.a, there is never an inconsistency in saying of a steak that it is both good and bad. We do in fact say consistently that things are both bad and good; when we do say something of that form we explain ourselves by saying that a thing can be good in one respect and bad in another. So far, then, A.2.g.a is all right. However, it is part of the meanings of *good* and *bad* that once we have fixed the perspective from which we are valuing things, then to say "This is both good and bad" is to assert a self-contradiction. That is, we can specify the relevant perspective of valuation and, so to speak, detach it so as to produce incompatible judgments about the given object. Yet this possibility is ruled out by A.2.g.a: according to this analysans, the value judgment about the given object includes an undetachable aspect: the existential quantifier is part and parcel of the judgment.

If, adopting the second approach, we preserve the schematic letter K open for different specifications of kinds of steak, there is no analysis of *the* property goodness, but there is a multiplicity of analyses: one for each specification of a kind of steak. Each of these analyses will determine one meaning of the word *good*, and their counterparts (when the sum of the badnesses is greater than the sum of goodnesses) determine different counterpart meanings of *bad*. Schema A.2.g.b allows us to specify a respect, find the corresponding meanings of *good* and *bad* and determine that "This is both good and bad" is a self-contradiction. It may be thought that the enormous multiplicity of meanings of the words *good* and *bad* that result from this way of handling the interpretation of the schematic letter K is objectionable. But I am not fully confident of the force of this objection. It would be objectionable to adopt the view that the words *good* and *bad* are enormously ambiguous if the meanings in question were wholly unrelated to each other: obviously the whole point of using the same words in value judgments is to say the same or something similar about the things on which we pass judgments. But the view that analyzes A.2 as A.2.g.b has the great merit of relating very neatly and simply all the meanings of *good* and *bad*: they all have the uniform characteristic of being instances of the property schema represented by the sentence schema A.2.g.b. There is, it seems, a generic goodness expressed by the schema A.2.g.b. This generic goodness is, of course, not analyzable in Moore's sense, but comes as close to being analyzable as is logically possible.

If we follow the third procedure and introduce another free occurrence of K in the analysans, we find that the latter becomes A.2K: "This is a good steak of kind K" or, much better, "This is a good steak qua thing of kind K." On the view adopted through this procedure, we have no general analysis of the meaning of *good* (or *bad*): we have an analysis of the context "good qua things of kind K." We can, of course, adopt a derivative abbreviational rule to the effect that when it is clear what the kind K under consideration is we just say *good* or *bad*. But these words do not acquire by this rule an independent semantic meaning of their own: their independent meaning is purely the syntactical one of serving as economical abbreviations. On this view, the goodness of objects has a syncategorematic character: it is always of the form "... qua ...." One problem here is the understanding of this structure. At any rate, in this view, too, the goodness of objects *simpliciter* turns out to be unanalyzable in Moore's sense, although here too it comes close to being so by virtue of the analyzability of the qua structure in which it appears—provided, of course, that the analyses illustrated by A.2.g.c are complemented with the principle that there are no other contexts or structures in which it appears.

Which of three views is correct or true? This is a very intriguing question. But we shall refrain from groping for answers here. For our present purpose the significant thing lies in that, regardless of which of the three views is the true one, or the best one, they all agree in furnishing a reduction of the goodness (and badness) of states of affairs.

Now it is natural to think that similar schemata can be framed for other statements that predicate goodness of objects as well as for those that predicate goodness of persons. This is particularly evident with regard to statement C.1, "Jones is a good student," in part one above. We can easily formulate an analysans parallel to A.2.g. In the case of C.2, "Jones is a good man," it might be argued that the analysis illustrated by A.2.g fails because, as some philosophers have claimed, to predicate moral goodness of a person is not to predicate goodness with respect to a class. This topic of moral goodness is too large for discussion here. At any rate it is goodness accruing to men by their *having* certain properties, so that the states of affairs consisting of their having such properties are good in the primary sense.

We leave for another occasion the discussion of statements like C.3, "It was good of Jones to come," which *appear* to have goodness as a relation between an action, or a state of affairs, and a person. They raise very intriguing and exciting problems, but we must refrain from the temptation to treat them here.[3]

In conclusion it seems that the goodness (badness) of contingent objects is different from the goodness and the badness of states of affairs. *Perhaps* also the goodness of objects derives from the goodness and the badness of states of affairs. Here we have not established this fact; we have only Socratically experimented with one example. Clearly, if we find a successful analysis of one example, we are close to home. Yet we cannot even claim that we succeeded in finding an analysis of example A.2. We stop here because we have run out of counter-exampling and Chisholmian steam. As is characteristic of Socratic examinations, we end with many more questions than we started with. We are sure, however, that the measurement of values whose viability is an integral part of our very concept of value presupposes assumptions like V.E and M.3, M.3a or M.4.

NOTES

1. In his unduly neglected book *What Is Value?* (London and New York, 1952).

2. This expression "he himself" in "a_i believes that he himself is ϕ" is of a very peculiar type with very intriguing properties. It is called a *quasi-indicator* and has been studied in our " 'He': A Study in the Logic of Self-Consciousness," *Ratio*, Vol. VIII, No. 2 (Dec., 1966); "Indicators and Quasi-indicators," *American Philosophical Quarterly*, Vol. IV, No. 2 (Apr., 1967); and "On the Logic of Attributions of Self-knowledge to Others," *Journal of Philosophy*, Vol. LXV, No. 15 (Aug. 8, 1968).

3. While Professor John Davis was preparing the present volume for the printer, I have examined the apparently relational goodness expressed in "It was good of Jones to come" in "Goodness, Intuitions, and Propositions," to appear in a Festschrift for Charles Baylis, being prepared by Paul Welsh.

The Relevance of Deontic Logic for Ethics

GERHARD FREY

Translated by Rita D. S. Hartman

THE LANGUAGE OF ETHICAL SYSTEMS

ETHICAL-MORAL SENTENCES ARE, according to their grammatical form, either *indicative* or *imperative*. In the first case they contain value predicates, such as *good, bad,* and *evil,* found in such sentences as "It is a crime to kill a human being." The predicate "is a crime" is a value, if this sentence is understood as an ethical sentence and not a juridical one. The second case concerns imperatives, which are frequently connected with obligatory or prohibitory predicates. Thus, we read in the Decalogue: "Thou shalt not kill." This idea could also be formulated by means of the prohibitional predicate: "It is prohibited to kill." Or the imperative form of the eighth commandment, "Thou shalt not covet thy neighbor's wife," may be reformulated by means of an obligatory predicate: "You ought not . . . ," "You may not . . . ," or the prohibitory predicate: "It is forbidden that you . . . ." The latter example shows that the obligatory and prohibitory predicates are *reflexive,* meaning that they are predicates asserted by whole sentences as their logical subjects. Value predicates, on the other hand, may be used both directly and reflexively. One speaks of an evil or of a criminal human being and uses the value predicates directly. One says also, reflexively, for example: "It is mean of you to have stood her up," or "It is decent of you that you don't demand interest of him."

To talk about a person, in direct language, as being evil, bad, good, or decent means to use indirect language as far as one can immediately ask for the reason of this valuation, and then to expect in answer the explanation of the actions of these persons. "This person is good, because he has helped less fortunate people in need." Direct valuations, thus, are based on valuations of actions. "It is good to help less fortunate people in need." Added to this idea is the common maxim: "He who does good deeds is a good person." Primarily, therefore, values are reflexive predicates, for they assert something of action propositions. They are *monadic* if they refer to one action expressed in one proposition: "It is good that . . . ." There are *dyadic* and *polyadic* reflexive predicates which, respectively, refer to two or more action propositions. Thus, *better* is a dyadic reflexive value predicate; it refers to two action propositions. Value predicates can also be used dyadically to the degree that they refer, on the one hand, to an individual and, on the other, to a proposition and, thus, so to speak, express a relation between individual and proposition. "It is not right of you that you defrauded him." The value predicate refers directly to the individual indicated by *you* and reflexively to the proposition stating the action. In many value statements we suppress the reference to the acting subject. Such formulations, as contained in the last example, express the fact that every value predicate refers both reflexively to action statements and directly to acting individuals. In other words what is valued is the action of a certain individual.

In the imperative form, all imperative modes, such as command, prohibition, and permission, can be used. We regard as imperative sentences those which express command, prohibition, or permission, or, eventually, other forms deducible from these. Related to these forms are obligatory sentences formed by *ought*. Imperative sentences should be treated as *triadic* relations between two persons, the imperator who gives the command, the imperandus to whom the command is directed, and the content of the action commanded. If an action is designated by the proposition p which the imperator x demands of the imperandus y, the imperative has the form "x demands p from y." However, in ethics and morals, we are concerned with universal or general norms, not with specific commands, of, or to, individual persons. These commands become ethically relevant only if they agree with, or contradict, universal moral norms or value propositions. Juridical sentences can be expressed as imperatives whose imperator is understood to be the head of state, the legislative body, or the government. In moral statements it does not seem possible to use as imperator unspecified instances, such as *custom*, *habit*, or the like. Only in religious morality is it possible to interpret norm sentences as commands coming from a personal god. As such there appear, for example, the Ten Commandments in the Old Testament.

Ethical and moral sentences, thus, are not imperative sentences, except for those of religious morality, with their reference to a personal god. Imperatives play, in any case, only a secondary role in moral systems. Commands, prohibitions, and permissions are decreed by authorities. But that certain authorities are recognized as such is itself usually subject to certain moral norms. Thus, in many interpretations of the moral system of the Decalogue the fourth commandment is regarded as establishing the norm of parental authority. In a similar fashion certain passages of the New Testament may be interpreted as establishing the norm of authority of the state (Rom. 13). These norms determine that parental or governmental decrees, prohibitions, or permissions must be obeyed. This requirement may lead to genuine moral conflicts. Thus far we have determined that ethics cannot do without imperative sentences.

THE DEONTIC ELEMENTS IN A LANGUAGE OF ETHICAL SYSTEMS

By *deontic*, or deontic logic, we understand the theory of the formal connections of obligatory propositions, which are generally expressed as *ought* propositions. Formally, there is a close relationship between ought and imperative propositions. R. M. Hare[1] has made a very useful distinction. Every statement has two parts: one which expresses the content and another which, generally speaking, expresses the mode. The first, Hare calls *phrastic* and the second *neustic*. In indicative sentences, within our natural languages, the neustic usually does not explicitly appear. Following Frege were Russell and Whitehead, and following them are other writers who have introduced a special assertion sign. Wittgenstein has pointed out that in indicative language we implicitly always mean to assert that the statement is true without expressing as much explicitly. This is the reason that authors schooled in formal logic overlook the neustic in assertory propositions. "It is true that p" is identified with "p." B. Juhos, by the way, has shown that this is owing to a silent agreement, which he calls the positive mode of speech.[2] He indicates that there is also the possibility of agreement on the negative mode of speech, in which every sentence in the indicative mood would be understood as false. It so happens that the natural languages have the rule of positive speech inherent in their nature.

Hare differentiates, at first, only between indicative and imperative neustic. We can, of course, understand the neustic as a linguistic expression which says something about the content of the sentence. If the neustic expresses the indicative or assertion, it means that it asserts that the content statement is true. However, the distinction between indicative and imperative statements, which is taken from grammar, is not sufficient. We shall call *reflexive* forms of language[3] all forms of expressions which refer to, or say something about, content statements, as do indicative or imperative neustic.

In the indicative linguistic field we find different reflexive forms of language. This is not the place to examine thoroughly the different reflexive forms of language. As an example we mention only the so-called oblique modalities, such as *necessary*, *possible*, and *impossible*. "It is possible that p" (formally "Mp"). Here the reflexive element, which corresponds to the assertion sign is expressed by "M," which refers to the content proposition p and asserts something of it.

Accordingly, it is also insufficient to speak only about imperatives. Most natural languages have a special mode which expresses itself, as in Latin, by special endings. Imperative sentences express commands or prohibitions. The imperative mode of permission can, in most languages, be expressed only by a special verb. It is a reflexive verb which refers to an action sentence which asserts: "It is permitted to do p." Beside commands and prohibitions our natural languages have several other deontic expressions, which can be formulated with *ought* or *must*. Here also belongs the *optative* form—the expression of a wish. There are languages, for instance the Gothic, which contain the optative as a special grammatical form. In Gothic the optative is the only grammatically fixed deontic form. In the majority of newer languages, wishes can be expressed only by the corresponding reflexive verbs or the subjective.

What today is called *modal logic* is nothing else but a formalism with one reflexive linguistic element. We do not wish to discuss the question of whether one can present a so-called modal logic purely extensionally without reflexive linguistic elements, as is elaborated in the calculus of strict implication of C. I. Lewis and C. H. Langford.[4] Neither are we interested in the question of why this circumstance is possible. Precisely, a reflexive formalism with one reflexive linguistic element M may be interpreted as modal logic, in the sense of oblique modalities, if we define $M = possible$. If one introduces a second modal predicate, $N = necessary$, then it results that this combination can be reduced to M: $NP = -M-p$. That is, "p is necessary" = "non-p is impossible." This formulation may be introduced as the definition of N. Now it has been noted for some time that under certain conditions these formalisms with a reflexive element, which can be interpreted as modal calculi, can also be interpreted as deontic logic. For we have seen that a reflexive element is contained also in all deontic systems, no matter whether systems of imperatives, of *ought* propositions, *must* propositions, or optatives. If we designate the neustic of the imperative by "!," the imperative itself may be designated by "!p." Designating the reflexive permission predicate by "¡," one can designate the permission itself by "¡p." And again one obtains the formally selfsame definition $!p = -¡-p$; that p is being commanded is equivalent to the statement that —p is not permitted. Introducing the predicate $O = ought$, the *ought* sentence is indicated by "Op." Again, we may introduce a predicate P, for which we do not always have a completely adequate designation in our natural languages. However, if we understand the *ought* sentence as purely obligatory, we can again approximately interpret P by "permission." $Op = -P-p$ has again the same formal structure. Since this structure with one reflexive element (the second is always reducible, by negation, to the first) was originally developed as modal logic, it is understandable that one has tried, again and again, to interpret modal logic, and the logical calculi of strict implication, as deontic systems.[5]

A formalism with one reflexive predicate and a second reducible to it is determined by rules and axioms. For modal logic there are different possible axiomatic systems, all of which can be interpreted in the sense of oblique modalities. The best known are the different formalisms of strict implication developed by Lewis and Langford from S_1 to S_5, all of which can be translated into the form of reflexive predicates.[6] The attempts to develop formalisms can be further developed deontically; therefore, all proceed by changing the formalism with one reflexive predicate axiomatically in such a way that it can be interpreted deontically. Thus, the axiomatic system developed by O. Becker[7]

A1: $\quad N (p \wedge q) \rightarrow Np \wedge Nq$
A2: $\quad Np \rightarrow p$

can be interpreted in the sense of oblique modalities. The transformed axiomatic system,

B1: $\quad ! (p \wedge q) \rightarrow !p \wedge !q$
B2: $\quad !p \rightarrow ¡p$

on the other hand, may be interpreted deontically by imperative sentences.[8]

We have already stated that in ethical-moral systems different kinds of deontic sentences are relevant. We shall understand by *deontic* the general concept of all such non-indicative sentences. Imperative sentences are precisely defined to the extent that they are based on the univocal command by one person (or authority) and unambiguously directed at individual persons. Optative, or wish, sentences, as far as their logical structure is concerned, have practically not been investigated, even though it cannot be denied that they have an ethical significance which should not be underrated.[9] *Must* sentences are concerned with linguistic formulations which are reducible to either imperatives or *ought* sentences. There remain the *ought* sentences which, on closer examination, do not appear as homogeneous. An *ought* sentence may either express what ought to be or what ought to be done. Sentences that express an ought to be are normative and are therefore to be interpreted ontologically, as is shown, precisely, by the axiological investigations of R. S. Hartman. Sentences that express an ought to do, on the other hand, are obligatory sentences. From an ought to do there does not always follow an ought to be. Inversely, if something ought to be we have to tailor our actions accordingly; hence from an *ought to be* follows, generally speaking, an *ought to do*.

DEONTIC LOGIC AND AXIOLOGY

All ethical-moral systems, as we have seen, contain deontic elements of different kinds. They always contain, moreover, norms and values. The latter may be formulated as *ought* sentences. As far as they are normative we use deontic elements for their formulation like, for instance, the reflexive verb *ought*. Deontic elements are used to express norms and values, and are probably necessary for this purpose. So far we have merely made an assertion about the language of ethical-moral systems.

A deontic logic, on the other hand, is a formal system which, in addition to the normative rules of logic, establishes rules for propositions with deontic linguistic elements. We have above indicated a system of axioms B1-B2 which, together with the laws of the logic of propositions, may be interpreted as deontic logic. Such a system yields a sequence of formal theorems which rule normative propositions and, thus, norms and values. For example, deontic propositions are subject in two senses to the law of contradiction. One cannot at the same time be and not be obligated to something: Op and –Op cannot be valid at the same time. It is also impossible at the same time to be obligated to something and, on the other hand, for this obligation to be prohibited: Op and O–p cannot be valid at the same time; the execution would result in contradiction. In our everyday language the forms –Op and O–p are not always clearly distinguished. "Thou shalt not steal"; here it cannot be decided, formally, which of the two cases is meant. Considerations of the text and the context of chapter twenty of *Exodus*, leads us to interpret the passage as prohibition; that is, in accordance with the form O–p. The four deontic forms Op, –Op, O–p and –O–p can also be presented by different value predicates, for instance, *good, not good, bad, not bad*. In the same way one can form four interpretative values from the value pair *beautiful-ugly*. Our everyday languages do not, for all values, contain such pairs of predicates which correspond to the deontic formulations we have examined.

Moreover, deontic logic shows how to deduce new normative propositions from normative propositions, perhaps together with descriptive propositions. On the basis of Axiom B2 we can deduce from the proposition that something ought to be, that it also may be. In the system mentioned it is possible, for instance, to deduce from the proposition that p ought to be and from the proposition that p → q, that also q ought to be:

$$\frac{Op, O\,(p \to q)}{Oq} \qquad (3.1)$$

In the same way it follows that if p may be and p → q is necessary, that also q may be:

$$\frac{Pp, N\,(p \to q)}{Pq} \qquad (3.2)$$

The rules of formal logic are often defined as normative. Obviously, *truth* may be understood as a value. Formal logic, however, presupposes but does not determine the values *true* and *false*. This tempts us to remark that it may be quite impossible to define the concept of *truth* explicitly. Still, formal logic is capable, on account of a common under-standing of the value concepts *true* and *false*, to define the concepts "logically true" and "logically false" and the respective concepts "tau-tology" and "contradiction."[10] All these concepts, however, will have to be viewed as epistemological values rather than as logical values.

All rules have a normative character, no matter whether they are rules of a society, called customs and habits, or laws and decrees of a state; or rules of games or the syntactical rules of language, or, finally, the logical rules which determine thought. The logical rules are norma-tive only in this formal sense. That a norm cannot at the same time be and not be, that I cannot at the same time recognize as valid a value and its negation—these are purely formal, logical norms, which have nothing to do with the content of the norms and values in question. The existence of implicative relations between different value proposi-tions and the possibility of deducing one proposition from another are also purely formal connections for which the values in question are irrelevant.

A deontic logic can be understood as built on a logic of propositions. This prompts most authors, for instance, G. H. von Wright, to assume that the binary logic of propositions is applicable.[11] In constructing a deontic logic on a logic of propositions, one encounters the difficulty that neither imperatives nor obligatory propositions, as expressed, are propositions. An imperative is not true or false but justified or unjusti-fied. It is based on a different value system than are propositions. *Ought* sentences can always be formally interpreted as propositions, if they are not merely imperatives formulated in *ought* form but general *ought* propositions. Even if one did have scruples in this respect concerning obligatory sentences in the sense of ought to do, one can always obtain unobjectionable propositions by switching to existential propositions. To the imperative "Close the door" belongs the existential proposition: "A orders B: Close the door," which may be a true or a false proposition. If one has these scruples even with general obligatory propositions, one can say that to the obligatory proposition "One must not kill" belongs the existential proposition "There exists the obligation: One must not kill," which again, in our moral system, is true. If one knows that one is using existence sentences only, one may, in the formalism, omit the clause "There exists the obligation . . . ." just as in pure logic one omits the assertion sign. This method is also possible when one is using pure value predicates. When looking at the value assertion "It is objectionable to defraud" one can always switch to a kind of statistical existential proposition which says that in our society the great majority of people will accept this value statement.

Thus, it is indeed possible to build a deontic logic on a logic of propositions. To be specific, this logic can only mean a logic of deontic existential propositions. In general it suffices to introduce a deontic predicate as a *functor*; for example, the functor of obligation O as mentioned above. The system of axioms examined above has the following form which, in addition to what has already been said about it, is to be completed by a definition and a rule:

$$B_1: \quad O\,(p \wedge q) \rightarrow Op \wedge Oq$$
$$B_2: \quad Op \rightarrow Pp$$
$$D: \quad Pp = -O-P$$
$$R: \quad \text{From } N\,(p \rightarrow q) \text{ follows } Op \rightarrow Oq$$

It is further presupposed that the axioms as well as all expressions of the form Op, Pp, . . . are propositions. All rules and theorems of the calculus of propositions are therefore applicable to these expressions, including the modal functor N = necessary. On the basis of these presuppositions of assertion and modal calculus, Axioms B_1, B_2, the definition D, and rule R define the functors O and P. As a consequence it can be shown that this formal system is interpretable in such a way that both Op and Pp are existential propositions, of obligatory and permissive propositions, respectively.

The question now is whether these axioms, definitions, and rules have only a formal-logical normative character as do the axioms and rules of pure logic, or whether they include, or may include, axiological significance. If instead of a first-order deontic calculus, like the one just presented, we admit higher-order deontic modes, one obtains a more complex calculus. In that case B_2 may be expressed as an obligation:

$$\text{B2}': \quad O(Op \to Pp)$$

"It ought to be that if p ought to be, p may be." What appears in B2 as a true proposition about obligatory and permissive propositions appears in B2′ as itself an obligatory proposition which, as a matter of fact, is to be understood as true and valid. In such a higher-order calculus may then also appear a proposition like the following:

$$O(Op \to p) \qquad\qquad (3.3)$$

In a first-order calculus one does not have this possibility; neither is there an analogue to it as in the previous example. For the first-order proposition $Op \to p$ is certainly not always true. We can designate B2 and B2′ as frame norms (*Rahmen-Normen*). Also $O(Op \to p)$ can only be formulated in the second-order deontic calculus.

One obtains other frame norms by starting with the definition D. It says that nonprohibition and permission are equivalent. This raises the question whether this equivalence is valid for all systems of ethics and law, or systems of jurisprudence. We can, with respect to moral and legal systems, make three different premises:

1. The equivalence mentioned above: "What is not prohibited is permitted, and what is permitted, is not prohibited."
2. One accepts the concessional principle: "What is not prohibited is permitted." $-O-p \to Pp$.
3. One accepts the interdictional principle: "What is not permitted is prohibited." $-Pp \to O-p$.

In the binary logic of propositions presupposed so far, the theorem of strong contraposition is valid:

$$(-p \to q) \to (-q \to p)$$

If we apply this theorem to propositions two and three above, we get, on the one hand:

$$(-O-p \to Pp) \to (-Pp \to O-p)$$

or, on the other hand:

$$(-Pp \to O-p) \to (-O-p \to Pp).$$

This is to say that, if we presuppose the binary logic of propositions, with its inherently strong contraposition, the principles two and three merge, and only principle one remains.

In intuitionistic logic in which, on the one hand, the principle of the excluded third is not valid, and on the other, the principle of double negation is valid only in a limited way, the forms of strong contra-position do not hold. Only the forms of weak contraposition are valid:

$$(p \rightarrow q) \rightarrow (-q \rightarrow -p) \text{ and } (p \rightarrow -q) \rightarrow (q \rightarrow -p),$$

as against the forms of strong contraposition:

$$(-p \rightarrow -q) \rightarrow (q \rightarrow p) \text{ and } (-p \rightarrow q) \rightarrow (-q \rightarrow p).$$

In order to be able to differentiate between the two points of view presented in propositions two and three above, binary logic cannot be used; instead, we must presuppose intuitionistic logic of propositions. We then can state completely the frame postulates of the two points of view, by positing them as a third axiom instead of definition D:

$$B_3: -O-p \rightarrow Pp$$

"What is not prohibited is permitted." This we shall call the concessional postulate.

$$B_3': -Pp \rightarrow O-p$$

"What is not permitted is prohibited." This we shall call the interdictional postulate.

One could ask in what way such deontic calculi, based on intuitionistic logic, differ from those based on binary logic. Deontic calculi based on intuitionistic logic afford one concessional and one interdictional system which show those differences, with the latter system showing considerably more incisive differences from binary deontic logic. I have already discussed these differences in another article.[12]

We can thus assert, in summary, that deontic logical systems, in the narrow sense, are not axiological. The possibility to posit axiologically relevant frame norms depends on the kind of formalism used. As the example in the preceding paragraph makes clear, this reaches all the way into the assumptions of the logical calculus to be applied.

NOTES

1. R. M. Hare, "Imperative Sentences," *Mind*, new series, LVIII (1949); R. M. Hare, *The Language of Morals* (Oxford, 1952).

2. B. Juhos, "Der positive und der negative Aussagengebrauch," *Studium Generale*, IX, No. 2 (1956).

3. G. Frey, *Sprache-Ausdruck des Bewusstseins* (Stuttgart, 1965), chaps. 1 and 2; G. Frey, "Reflexionsanalysen von Texten," *Studium Generale*, XIX, No. 7 (1966).

4. Lewis and Langford, *Symbolic Logic* (New York and London, 1932).

5. R. Feys, "Expressions modales du 'devoir-être'," *Journal of Symbolic Logic*, XX (1955), 91–92.

6. Lewis and Langford.

7. O. Becker, *Einführung in die Logistik, vorzüglich in den Modalkalkül* (Meisenheim a.d. Glan, 1951).

8. G. Frey, "Imperativ-Kalküle," *The Foundation of Statements and Decisions* (Warsaw, 1965).

9. K. Menger, *Moral, Wille und Weltgestaltung* (Vienna, 1934), where optatives are also dealt with.

10. It need not be elaborated here that all these concepts cannot be defined, within an object language, solely by its formal means. See R. Carnap, "Die Antinomien und die Unvollständigkeit der Mathematik," *Monatshefte f. Math. u. Physik*, XLI (1934).

11. G. H. von Wright, "Deontic Logic," *Mind*, new series (1951).

12. G. Frey, "Imperative-Kalküle," pp. 381–82.

Changes of Value Order and Choices in Time

ROBERT S. BRUMBAUGH

IN THIS DISCUSSION I intend to explore the rules for right choice that follow if there are incommensurable orders of value and if we assume that a "right" choice conserves or increases value or involves infinitely less value loss than any other. The key to this discussion is Robert Hartman's formal model of value orders, which I believe offers the best resolution to a paradox that follows from two of our fundamental intuitions that underlie decision and evaluation.

Ever since there has been discussion of choice, there has been an intuitive conviction that while some values are additively related, others cannot be. There is no cash price, no degree of comfort, that can persuade a Socrates to give up his pursuit of wisdom or a Beowulf his quest for glory and honor.

At the same time we do have to compare all sorts of values in making decisions; and a second intuitive conviction we hold is that "better than" is an asymmetrical, transitive relation analogous to "greater than"—though a Minoan merchant probably would not have formulated his intuitive notion in so abstract a way. This second notion suggests at once that the number series is a suitable formal model for rational comparison and that the alternatives are either such a calculus or a rejection of the relevance of thought to action. If A is better than B, we want to know how much better, better for how many people, and better for how long. And we feel intuitively that these questions make sense.

Now these two intuitive notions, within the formal resources of pre-nineteenth-century mathematics, set up an antinomy that is irreconcilable. For, if we assign numbers on a scale to A and B, a sufficient number of additions of A (reaching A.B+A) will constitute a value total greater than B. If Beowulf—as is the case—values both valor and treasure, the dragon should be able to avoid combat by offering a large-enough treasure hoard as a bribe. Honor is indeed partly measured by gifts, rings, and well-wrought arms in *Beowulf*; but bribery by the dragon would go against Beowulf's character and wreck the epic. A familiar illustration, closer to home than heroes and dragons, is the application of hedonic calculus to the Indians and Joe. The calculus rests on the assumption that the right thing to do is that which produces the greatest excess of increments of pleasure over displeasure, each moment for each person to count as $+1$ or -1. In that case, if the

Indians really enjoy burning Joe alive, that is the right thing for them to do. Nor can we get out of this by a "weighting" which sets Joe's displeasure equal to −n on our value scale. For in that case it is right to burn him as soon as the number of tribal celebrants is increased to n+1. The result is squarely counterintuitive: Joe's life and dignity are simply more valuable than an afternoon of entertainment, however large the house.

As is often the case in dealing with mathematical concepts and models, our intuition is *almost* but *not quite* right. (Compare our intuitive notions of "inside" and "outside" with the precise formulation of these concepts in topology.) And Robert Hartman has seen that if we extend the notion of cardinal numbers to include *transfinite* numbers, the two notions—that values can be ordered and compared by an arithmetical model and that some values are nonadditively related—become compatible. He suggests that there are three value orders, standing in "greater than" relation, that can be represented as having cardinal numbers n, aleph-null, and aleph-one. That does the needed trick as far as the two intuitive notions we have cited go: we keep comparability but without reducibility between orders.

This tension between intuitions is more than a mere abstract analyst's curiosity. Historically poets and playwrights have tended to resolve it by denying the second of the pair—the relevance of calculation to action, while merchants and social scientists resolve it (after vague murmurs about dimensions and standpoints) by calculi that operationally reject the first. Ordinarily, I suppose, not too much damage is done: for ordinarily we are engaged *either* with an impersonal citizen and economic man, or with an epic villain or hero; and the engagement is reflected in our picking the single right-order value scale. But a Leibnizian single plane of finite permutations of property-chains, called "possible worlds," can lead to disaster when it fails to provide for infinite positive and negative changes in value.

By various strategic devices of using the "greater than" relation between transfinite ordinals, then correlating the ordered set with ordinary measures, we can still use simple arithmetical formulae for value comparison on any given level. And this, too, is what we want if the model is to match the properties of our ordinary behavior in discussing and deciding value questions. For among *comparable* alternatives it takes no philosopher, but only information, prudence, and a computer to decide which is more accurate, or more efficient, or least deviant from a consensus of preferences. It does take philosophic insight to decide when, if ever, a high value on one order of scale compensates for a low value on another. Suppose, for example, that we find a way of teaching aesthetic sensitivity to grade-school students that is very interesting for them, but very inefficient because it is expensive and slow. We also have an efficient but deadly program which gets whatever counts as the "right" response to an objective appreciation test cheaply and quickly. The choice here is no longer a "horizontal" measure on a single scale, but involves a "cross-level" one that raises philosophic problems (though of course it also involves all sorts of "horizontal" evaluation). Finally the issue may boil down to whether the value of aesthetic appreciation is measurable by the number of "right" responses on an objective test. The case is very similar here to the problem of tense or aspect in logical inference: usually it is irrelevant, but *if* we cross aspect lines, we need to answer some radical philosophic questions before we can avoid self-referential inconsistencies.

Before going on, however, let me note another very basic ethical intuition: there are times when a single choice or act that does transpose value orders is, in its context, the best and the right one. This intuition involves the introduction of value changes through time, which we will return to presently.

I also think Hartman is right in his use of a principle of plenitude—of ontological complexity—to discriminate his three orders of value. If, as he holds, value is the adequacy of a thing to the appropriate concept, there are indeed three kinds of adequacy and three kinds of appropriateness that are important to distinguish. (There may well be more; I can see a good case for at least five orders rather than three.)

The first case to consider is the match between a thing and the *definition* of its concept. Such a criterion—a definition—isolates a minimal set of essential properties, so that if any is lacking, the concept does not apply. *Systemic value,* the match between definition and case at hand, is always 1 or 0; either this plane figure *is* a triangle or it *is not*. If I erase one of the sides, I have not turned a "better" triangle into a "worse" one, but have turned a triangle into a non-triangle—and I must find a different defining concept to evaluate what this non-triangle now is. This systemic value has the sort of simplicity and exhaustibility that can be represented by finite integers; its order of plenitude is n or k; its parts are tightly conjoined, admitting no omission or variation.

The second case is the match between a thing and the *exposition* of its concept, Hartman's *extrinsic value*. The exposition adds onto the definition of a concept a set of properties which are further specification: these are *not* logically necessary, but *are* necessary in the sense that an instance must have all (or some) of them in addition to the minimal defining set. If we were to identify the definition with an *essence* or *form*, the exposition would become a *type* or *type specimen*.

It seems to me that insufficient attention is given by Hartman to the difference between *form* and *type*. The type is not a minimum but a maximum set: its properties are more specific in the alternatives they exclude, where the form is far more open and permissive; the type admits of degrees of approximation and keeps its relevance as criterion in the fact of omission or transposition of specific characteristics. In fact, Hartman's scheme of extrinsic evaluation resurrects an Aristotelian logic with propositions of "indefinite quantity" to describe degrees of type realization. The instances are "better" as they approach the maximum presented in the exposition.

The most relevant example for an ethical discussion is that of the relation of X as a *human being* to X as a *person* is a social-legal scheme. But the logical relations stand out more clearly if we begin again with the triangle. "A closed plane figure bounded by three straight lines" defines the concept we are applying, but tells us nothing about the respective lengths of side, size of angle, or surface color. But from each of these sets of properties—side length, angle size, and color—the instance must have just one definite set, which excludes all the other alternatives of this quantitative or qualitative spectrum. And not all combinations from different sets are compatible: obviously side lengths and angle sizes co-determine each other. These alternative possibilities for schematization taken together are an exposition of the concept. The logical relations are of three types: (1) The *defining* properties must all necessarily apply; a schema that destroyed any of them would also destroy the identity of the type as triangle. (2) Of the alternative sets of shapes, sizes, etc. *some* item of the set must apply *if* we are to have an existent triangle, not just the pure concept of triangularity. (3) Within each set the presence of any one specifying property *excludes* the others; and between sets it may exclude some others (angle size and side length do stand in this relation; angle size and surface color do not). This schematic triangle is an entity halfway between the realms of systemic and of extrinsic value: it has greater complexity than the pure definition, but in the absence of a context indicating some function, we cannot set up a maximum-to-minimum ordering of the added specifying sets of properties.

A legal "person" offers a case of a type which does permit maximum-to-minimum evaluative ordering. A human being is essentially defined, let us say, by freedom, reason, sensitivity, and creativity. But these do not yet tell us what someone's role, rights, and relations to others are in a schematized society, where his status is specified by custom and law. The best society will then have the maximum properties of individual realization of full humanity, and this is greater when all human beings are recognized as legally equal than when they are not. The person, as opposed to the essence, obviously has an infinitely greater complexity: an adequate description would require an infinite enumeration of compossible properties. This requirement is particularly clear if we consider the various deviations, the partial realizations of the perfect type, the alternative subtypes through which the pure type may be realized, and so on. There is obviously a sense in which history can combine in one system rules and insights that are ethically inconsistent or even ontologically mistaken.

Obviously, the peculiar problems of types and expositions of concepts need much exploration. For ethics, though, we can be satisfied with the distinction between a human being (systemic value) and a person (extrinsic value), and the observation that the latter is infinitely more complex than the former.

On the level of intrinsic value we come to the individual. He adds his own style, interpretation, unique space-time adventures and constructions to the more abstract identity of himself as a person in society; and this continuum of individual adventure is once again infinitely more complex than the person or the type. If we indicate the degree of plenitude of the systemic norm as n and of the extrinsic as aleph-null, the degree of intrinsic value norms becomes aleph-one.

The history of axiology seems to involve an opposition between emphasis on the principle of plenitude and emphasis on the principle of limitation. On the one hand, Hartman suggests that "better than" is equivalent to "ontologically more complex than"; some very interesting results can be calculated directly from the "greater than" relationship in his model. On the other hand, the Platonic tradition has equated "better than" with "more essential than," so that the forms, on the level of systemic value, are more real than their instances and so "better." After at least one reading of the *Republic* we would get the following result: the form is no better if it has instances than if it has not; the instance has no identity, hence no value, if it is not an instance of the form. But the system of the cosmos is better if forms are instantiated: this is an axiological, not strictly an ontological, judgment. Or, to the degree that it is an ontological judgment, it rests on the power of the good to establish cross-level relevance among instances, types, and forms.

The Platonist's point may be introduced into our formal model in the following way. If A is a necessary condition for B, then the value of A is equal to the value of B. This is the principle of limitation. It works differently for the relation of instances to definition and to explication. If to be an authentic individual is impossible without conserving the defining properties of a human being, respect for individuality cannot be greater than respect for humanity. But even though to be an individual requires a human community where one is a person in *a* context of order and law, the principle does not require us to value every detail of the current system as though this were the *only* type of organization that could provide law and order. In fact, combined respect for consistency and law may dictate revising or even rejecting some folkways and subordinate statutes in the interest of a better society.

It is here that the difference between a definition and an explication, between a form and a type, becomes crucial to legal and political discussion. The temptation is to identify the current organization with a *definition* of what it is to be human and to equate every detail of that system with the value of full individuality, or to reject the system as a whole because some properties are inconsistent with such individuality.

If we can establish the limitation relation in such a way that to be an individual necessarily presupposes being essentially a human being and also presupposes being a person in *some* type of social community, though not in any one unique type, it turns out that Hartman's distinction of value orders and the Platonic insistence on orders of limitation are capable of being combined consistently in the model of value types we are trying to set up.

Perhaps we can return now to ethics and to the results that follow from the rule for choice that "a choice ought not to result in an infinite decrease in value." Or, put the other way, "a choice should always conserve or increase value." On any given value scale, as we have said, the question of selecting a larger value is a matter of experience, skill, and prudence; no properly ethical issues are likely to arise. But when a choice reverses the real structure of value orders, the transposition represents an infinite decrease in value over at least a one-choice increment of time (it seems, in this model, that such an incremental infinite loss is corrigible). A morally bad choice thus always involves a mistake in its logic or in its motivation. Through ignorance one may incorrectly *believe* that value orders are not involved as in reality they are; through vice one may *will* that value orders not be related as they are. A third factor here is insensitivity—not perceiving that orders are related as they are or not appreciating their relation. Ordinarily we test the axiological correctness of choices by projecting their consequences: if my decision were repeated, magnified, observed as a rule, what would the consequent, long-range value change with time be? If it would be a transposition of orders, or a reduction to zero, it is in itself bad—not just because of its consequences, but because of its intrinsic contradiction of the axiological order. I think a case can be made for the fact that all types of ethical theory agree on some use of a "consequences over the long run" test as relevant to right choice. They differ in regard to whether unfavorable, long-run consequences show a logical, prudential, or aesthetic defect in the motives of that choice itself. They agree in assuming that choices should increase or at least conserve value through passing time.

It seems to me that three rules, derivable from the model of orders of value, offer axioms for an ethical calculus. Two and one-half of the three sound like Kant; but the final half of the final rule is non-Kantian.

Rule 1. A Choice Must Be Realizable. Not only are there things that cannot be chosen, but they ought not to be chosen. Sheer logical or physical impossibilities are not alternatives with positive value. Perhaps the most interesting case here would be the desire to make x a better F by destroying it as an F altogether. It is not possible to make people better human beings by taking away their freedom and imposing all decisions from external coercion. It is not possible to alter the past. It is not possible for me to jump over the Empire State Building. And so on. But, as my first example shows, logical and temporal entailments are different things. That first example is, of course, logically impossible; but it is temporally possible in the sense that, in the expectation that the consequent will follow, I can indeed affirm and create the antecedent. Unhappily, given time, the pattern "first, A, with the expectation that A implies B; then non-B" is a genuine historical possibility. So the first rule is weaker than a Kantian would want it; things that are simultaneously, not successively, inconsistent with logic, physics, and ethics are excluded. This might, of course, be taken as a definition of choice, not as a rule. But it follows as a theorem from our calculus: an impossibility has a value of 0, hence, it is less than any non-zero alternative.

Rule 2. A Choice Must Be Repeatable in Space and Time without Infinite Decrease in Value. This rule may amount to saying that if there is an atemporal, logical inconsistency between means and ends, there will also be a temporal incompatibility over a sufficient span of time. The reason for this rule is the normal human shortsightedness that forgets the hierarchy of scales of value. When X on S_1 is greater than Y on S_1, the counsel of expediency is to choose X. If it turns out that repetition of X leads to a disaster even on S_1, the reason may be that we forgot to look at another value scale of a different order, S. There is very little deterioration of the environment, and very much financial gain, in disposing of the waste from a paper mill in the Androscoggin River. But there is a reversal of the values of human survival and large dividends involved in the choice, a transposition that shows very clearly under the test of consequences that magnify the transposition involved. More often, probably, the result is not that repetition of X leads to a disaster on the S_1 scale, but that it does reduce value infinitely on the S scale. This rule implies a definition of justice, of a person, and of immortality. In the calculus we are using, the transposition may be either one in which we put arbitrary systemic value ahead of intrinsic, extrinsic value ahead of nonarbitrary systemic, extrinsic value ahead of the entire class of possible intrinsic value, intrinsic value that contradicts all extrinsic value ahead of extrinsic value (logically impossible, but not so temporally; this point holds for the other cases, too), and so on.

Rule 3. On the Level of Intrinsic Value Every Choice Should Be Repeatable without Infinite Loss of Value, but No Choice Should Be Repeated. The necessary condition of individuality is instantiation of a type; a human being with no status, context of rules, or society could not also have individuality. But the converse is also true: an individual has the unfortunate power to choose to be merely a person—predictable, repetitive, entirely typical. There are certainly justifications for this choice: it may be much more comfortable, and we certainly cannot argue that it is unjust or antisocial or inefficient. But to give up authenticity and creativity is to make a choice that does lead to putting value of order aleph-null ahead of order aleph-one. Aesthetic interest diminishes with literal repetition: *literal* here means, not the same in general outline, for that is inevitable and all right, but the same in full, concrete texture, interpretation, and detail. Value of order aleph-one depends on novelty, idiosyncrasy, and adventure; the universe would be the worse without it. True, limitation is its essential condition; but we need plenitude within the boundaries of limitation. If the long-range implications of automation, or teaching machines, or public schools are to destroy and negate the right to style, we had better revise them before we choose to endorse them. The revision takes the form, of course, of a reconstructed type which leaves open the range of aleph-one value. This is the addition to Kant: for a being with aesthetic sensitivity it would be an aesthetic contradiction to choose the dull over the interesting, the painful over the pleasant. Our law of contradiction therefore operates on the level of interests, as well as that of reason and that of will; I would contradict my identity as a human being by acting to reinforce anesthetized dullness.

Formalization has several virtues, not least among them that it provides a way for carrying out Descartes's fourth rule of method, to conduct exhaustive reviews and enumerations. Those activities, in turn,
challenge our imagination to invent and consider cases, to find images,

TABLE FOR CALCULATIONS

#	t−	to	t+	Vc/t
1	S	S	S	o
2	S	S	E	+
3	S	S	I	+
4	S	E	S	−
5	S	E	E	+
6	S	E	I	+
7	S	I	S	−
8	S	I	E	−
9	S	I	I	+
10	E	S	S	−
11	E	S	E	−
12	E	S	I	+
13	E	E	S	−
14	E	E	E	o
15	E	E	I	+
16	E	I	S	−
17	E	I	E	−
18	E	I	I	+
19	I	S	S	−
20	I	S	E	−
21	I	S	I	−
22	I	E	S	−
23	I	E	E	−
24	I	E	I	−
25	I	I	S	−
26	I	I	E	−
27	I	I	I	o

myths, and problems that we might well not have thought of in our
normal, well-ordered chains of ideas that Descartes's third step of
method recommends. So, given the indications we have had of the purpose, limits, and ambiguities of the formalization of value orders, it
may be interesting simply to set out the possibilities of value change
from past through present into future, using Hartman's abbreviations,
I, E, S (see Table for Calculations). The table does not take account of
o values, nor does it take account of "essential" S values; i.e., cases
where S as a necessary condition must be set equal to E or I. The result

is that our Platonic qualifications of Hartman's theory are not adequately represented in the table.

Rows 1, 14, and 27 of the table are simple cases in which value is conserved: an entity preserves or recovers its identity through passage. This fact implies a certain novelty in respect to choices and adventures for row 27, since mere endurance or subsistence (rows 1 and 14) will lead to a loss of intrinsic value. Rows 10 and 19 are bad by any standard; they involve the respective choices to reduce persons to things or to reduce individuals to things. These negative choices point up the need for value orders, which caution us against them. Let S be material efficiency, or abstract ideology, or profit; the higher reading of the course chosen on the relevant S scale has obviously not been balanced against the consequences on the E and I scales, and the result is a permanent value loss. Lines 13 and 25 show a similar pattern, except that the value change is a future consequence, not an immediate concomitant, of the decision. (But it is a consequence of the value criteria by which the decision was made; *consequence* here is a stronger relation than mere historical succession.) Lines 2 and 5 are desirable patterns, in which work with ideas or materials is made relevant to better functioning of the society. (New work with computers in the interest of eventual better information for representative governments would be a case in point here.) Lines 9 and 18 represent new aesthetic insights and interpretations that add value to systemic or extrinsic situations. These insights and interpretations are also desirable. Lines 3 and 12 have the same pattern. Line 6 is the pattern Whitehead had in mind for "social progress," which was to lead to "depth of individuality." Line 15 is a similar pattern of progress, except that here we are readjusting extrinsic rather than systemic values.[1]

We are left with two types of pattern: failures and temporary corrections. Surgery, therapy, and enforced rehabilitation fall under the second of these kinds. Medical treatment may involve the temporary handling of an individual simply as a complex mechanism, a thing. In itself, then, it is bad; but we decide it is good when the only open choices are the I S S or the I S I pattern. Law in its corrective role, again, is good when the *only* alternatives are I E I, I E E, I E S, I S S. But obviously this situation is much more complex than the case of medicine, and our natural temptation to identify the two is a way of evading this complexity. (Line 11 represents another medical alternative, I think, where we can restore effective social and vocational functioning without involving individuality and authenticity positively or negatively.) There is a tempting similarity between correction and education: to treat the individual pupil as a thing to be processed or an anonymous "student" to be informed. But, of course, there are infinitely better patterns open here, such as S E I, E E I, E I I, I I I, and even S E E. (The scheme is complicated because for certain technical purposes—such as curriculum design—we need to think of human potentialities as developing successively into actual characteristics. Thus, nursery-school students need things to play with, and they need gradual socialization leading to group activities proper to kindergarten levels. Empirical studies, though, are beginning to show the extent of value loss when parents and teachers ignore the fact that the I I I pattern is both the best and the most realistic criterion for educational design.)

The analogy with medicine and law suggests that a corrective value pattern may sometimes justify political revolution. But the pure corrective value patterns represent conservation, not progress; and they represent infinitely less desirable alternatives if any of the "progress" value patterns are open. Current political discussion mirrors current discussion of value theory in general, as well as in other specific situations: an antinomy between the principles of plenitude and those of limitation.

The remaining patterns are cases of failure. Failure—pure failure that crosses value orders—is bad. It always involves some mistake about the consequence or the relative importance of the present moment. It can be eliminated by education: education in logic, physics, ethics, and aesthetics. And there is an infinite gain in this elimination when patterns of progress replace patterns of failure.

In working with his model, Robert Hartman introduces operations to indicate the way in which values of different order are themselves valued. I have taken a different direction, trying to see what happens if they are descriptively compared, assuming that at least sometimes their objective types can be determined and agreed upon.

The Sunday *New York Times Magazine* is full of case studies and editorial remarks that show the current importance of cross-type value comparison. Should federal aid be given to parochial schools? Should it be given to the individual children who are pupils in the schools? If so, should it be limited to expenses for their health and safety, not for other phases of their education? Should colleges give students more of a role in policy-making? Should state legislators pass bills making correction mandatory for student protestors? Should we withdraw slowly, quickly, or not at all from our military and political commitments in Vietnam? Is *poverty* a state of affairs, a state of mind, or both; and how is it to be corrected? Or is *correction* the right word?

All of these questions are vivid and so engaging that in our present concerns we are apt to overlook the dry abstraction of such a matrix as my formal parade of 1, S, and E above. But when it is overlooked, value change with time is likely to be a spectacular case of failure rather than a progress pattern.

At this point I am in logical trouble. I need the concept of a state or society as a community of persons which provides production, protection, and education. But if it is essential to a person that he be a human being, what happens to communities that do not recognize the essential humanity of some classes, races, or sexes? Three distinctions are needed to avoid the conclusion that Plato drew: "there are no true states other than this (the ideal) one."

1. The essence of a human being must be understood as a potentiality for realization, not as a fixed and determinate structure.

2. The definition of a state may need to be weakened so that it becomes "an association of one or more actual persons with other human beings."

3. The exposition of the concept of a state may have to have two stages: (a) the criterion, widest possible equality among persons, which selects the maximum quality we will use in ranking; (b) the complex matrix of descriptions by law, class, custom, and so on which establishes how fully and widely *persons* are recognized and *human potentialities* are recognized.

Point three brings out the difference between the state and the triangle on the level of *types*. Where there is a unifying function holding the properties of a type together, the exposition can begin by positing it as a criterion for maximum (*best*) schematization. The same thing is true if we ourselves supply such a function as a criterion. (A stone may turn out to be "very poor" as a hammer, though it is completely "a stone".) Something new gets in here, but Hartman needs it, too: in discussing disvalue as transposition, he says that there are no concepts that serve as normative criteria of an auto wreck, or a mixed brew of sawdust and coffee. Why not?

NOTE

1. The "progress" patterns are interesting in connection with the present "generation gap." Material and social resources, as well as essences, serve as necessary conditions for value realization. Thus, although they are in their non-instrumental role of order S, by the principle of limitation they count as equal to the higher orders that require them. (This situation is the key to much modern political debate: one group of theorists stresses that S and E conditions are *necessary* for realization of intrinsic value; another group stresses that they are *not sufficient*. Both are right.) But with increasing rates of technological and social change, new alternatives keep appearing: what

were once necessary limits now become arbitrary limitations. An older generation tends to begin planning *within* the assumed limits that held earlier; a younger generation, which has seen these limits constantly extended, tends to begin with the assumption that possibilities are unlimited by such lower-order conditions. Shortcomings in logic on either side look like gratuitous errors in ethics to the other. The logical mistake in either case is a failure to see the true "necessary condition" relations that hold; the result is in fact an unintended failure to maximize value; but the cause is ignorance, not vice.

A Value-perspective on Human Existence

WILLIAM H. WERKMEISTER

L ET ME BEGIN with a confession, for the problems with which I intend to deal here attain significance—at least for me—only within the framework of my basic belief that, despite all recent trends to the contrary, philosophy still is, or ought to be, "love of wisdom"; that it must concern itself with the basic issues of human existence—with what it means to be a human being and to live a humanly satisfying life. This point of view is, no doubt, old-fashioned; but it is modern as well. And it leads directly to the problem of values; for we encounter values wherever we must make a decision, and we define ourselves as human beings only in our commitment to values.

It follows from this basic orientation that I am not interested in an analysis of "value language" per se or in the use and classification of "value words." Such matters are of secondary importance. My interests center on the problems themselves as these are encountered in human experience and for the analysis of which words are at best merely useful tools.

Common usage as well as the dictionary identifies *value* with "the quality or fact of being excellent, useful, or desirable." But the ambiguities inherent in such a definition are so grave that the definition itself is confusing rather than helpful in our understanding of values. And the multitude of value theories that have been developed since the days of Hermann Lotze is also bewildering. The spectrum of interpretations ranges from the "emotivism" of DeWitte Parker's final period to the "Platonistic" metaphysics of Münsterberg, from the feeling-centered views of Meinong to the desire-oriented theories of von Ehrenfels and Ralph Barton Perry, from hedonism pure and simple to pragmatism and its emphasis upon the useful, from the intuitionism of Max Scheler to the psychologism of Joseph Kreibig, from the personalism of William Stern to Heinrich Ricket's identification of value and validity—to mention but a few of the conflicting points of view. Is there no end to the diversity of interpretations? Let us take a new look at the human scene.

Nobody seriously doubts, I am sure, that despite the most sophisticated arguments to the contrary we are all empirical realists. We find ourselves in situations in which we respond intellectually, emotionally, and volitionally to a world which in some sense is "out there" and whose character as subsumable under laws is essentially "given." We may explore it and exploit it, and may come to understand it ever more fully.

But the more we do so, the more we realize that our own existence is inextricably interwoven with the reality of that world, that we would not be if the world were not real.

We know all this because of specific constraints intrinsic to our first-person experience itself. In the cognitive sphere these constraints include the given configurations and contents we speak of as *perceptual* experience, and the norms of logic and rational thinking. These essentially *intellectual* aspects of experience are intimately interwoven with the constraints imposed upon our actions that are experienced as hindrances in some situations and as determinants of the course of action in others. And, lastly, we feel the satisfactions and frustrations characteristic in varying degree and quality of our emotional responses to all that we experience. But whatever the experience—be it cognitive, conative, or affective—it is we who have the experience. Strictly speaking, it is I (or you)—the subject who can say "I" to himself—who has the experience, who distinguishes himself from his experience and is able to reflect upon it. This fact is crucial—for value theory no less than for all forms of cognition and for every choice we make or action we pursue. In the field of cognition, for example, where our concern is with propositions—or, better yet, with beliefs—that, presumably, are true, the perceptual and logical constraints provide the needed warranty. We regard a proposition as true (if you insist on using this terminology) if and only if it is what it ought to be in the light of the cognitive constraints. That in some instances the justification is complex, having far-reaching ramifications in chains of reasoning and interrelated perceptions, is no argument against the thesis that all the evidence in its support must be encountered in first-person experience. And it is only because the assertion "There exists a world" is so supported by the constraints intrinsic in that experience that we accept it as "warranted belief." If there is to be cognition at all, then we must affirm or deny something which, because of the perceptual and logical constraints in first-person experience, ought to be affirmed or denied.[1]

When we now turn to the problem of values, we again encounter certain constraints in our first-person experience; but the facts in the case have their own complexities. Our basic question now is, what, precisely, is a value experience? The hedonists give us a simple answer. Since they identify value with pleasure, a value experience (so they maintain) is an experience of a pleasure. But this explanation will not do. In itself a feeling of pleasure or satisfaction is no more a value experience than perceiving alone—i. e., perceiving detached from all affirmation or denial in a judgment—is already cognition. The value experience is complete only when an attitude—be it pro or con—is taken toward what is felt. But such is the complexity of the value experience that the attitude is, or may be, taken not only with respect to the feeling state but with respect also to the object—whatever it be, real or imaginary, simple or complex—that induces the feeling state. The warranty of the attitude is the felt quality of the experience in the same sense in which the warranty of a perceptual judgment is the perception itself. But only feeling and attitude together constitute a value experience.[2] This fact accounts not only for what is valid in value theories for which feeling is basic, and value theories for which attitudes are crucial; but it also accounts for the deficiencies of all such theories, for feelings alone are just that— feelings—and attitudes alone lack warranty.

But if feelings and attitudes together—and only together—constitute value experiences, a further complexity arises from the fact that in a particular situation feeling and attitude may be disharmonious. Either the feeling or the attitude ought not to be what it is. Brentano acknowledged this possibility when he made "right love" and "right hate" the key concepts of his value theory—the "rightness" being in each case certified, as it were, by the appropriateness of feeling tone and attitude for each other. This appropriateness, however, must be intrinsic to the experience itself and must not be a matter of an extrinsic judgment.[3]

Value judgments and judgments of preference add further dimensions to our value experience. A value judgment—"x is pleasing," "y is beautiful," "z is good for you"—lifts the value experience out of the purely subjective realm and adds to it the claim of objective validity. The judgment may, of course, be wrong; but, right or wrong, its warranty is the (actual or expected) value experience plus the nature of the object eliciting the experience *as that nature is understood*. The clause in italics is here crucial. It implies that objectively valid value judgments presuppose warranted or true cognitive judgments, and that a change in our value judgments is warranted when the relevant cognitive judgments undergo a change. When tomatoes were believed to be poisonous, they were valued negatively and were avoided. But when it was discovered that they actually are a rich source of vitamins and minerals, they were valued positively and became a standard item in our diet.

Once we have introduced value judgments and, through them, have transcended the immediacies of value experience, we can extend our valuations and attitudes beyond the objects or situations that directly elicit the experience to objects and conditions that are instrumental in bringing them about. We now value a vast range of objects that engage our social, economic, and political interests. Put otherwise, our social and political institutions but reflect our valuations—as do our economic and cultural activities. We have created this complex pattern of human living because we value certain things and situations; and in creating the pattern we have in effect objectified our valuations.

As previously indicated, judgments of preference add still another dimension to all this—and they do so in at least three different modes. In the first place, preferential judgments may pertain directly to the immediacies of our value experience—as when we prefer a pleasing experience to a painful one, or a less painful one to a more painful one. The warranty of the judgment is in such cases the value experience itself.

The judgment of preference may, in the second place, be concerned with things we value as "instruments" in the chain of conditions that ultimately culminate in a value experience. One thing may be more useful than another for a certain purpose. The term *useful*, however, must here be taken in its broadest meaning—including *efficient, economical, convenient*, and the like. We prefer the more useful to the less useful, the more convenient to the less convenient, and so on. The warranty of such judgments is the facts in the case, and these may be pragmatically ascertained.

More important than the modes of preferential judgments so far indicated is the third type, for these judgments pertain to the levels of human existence and, therefore, to the very nature of what it means to be a human being. We are here at the very heart of all valuations. I have discussed this point in some detail in *Man and His Values* (chap. 5), but it can be stated briefly here: Our value experiences, though interrelated in many ways, differ in essential respects in the feeling-tone characteristic of each level of experience as we pass from the simple sensory pleasures and gratification of appetites to a sense of well-being; the satisfactions of communal living; peace of mind; the joys of creation and enterprise; and, ultimately, the sense of self-fulfillment. If there be any doubt about the differences in feeling tone at these various levels, then consider the respective disvalue experiences: a sensory pain, disturbed communal relations, a troubled mind, the sense of utter frustration— and the differences should be clear. Nobody would confuse the algedonic feeling tone of utter frustration with that of a sensory pain. Also, the objects or situations which elicit the value experience are different at each level. What gives us peace of mind is not the sort of an object that yields gratification of an appetite. And neither do we derive a sense of fulfillment from conditions that give us a feeling of bodily well-being.

But now it is important to remind ourselves that the person who has the value experiences is by no means identical with the experiences themselves; that, on the contrary, the experiences are but the consequences of his interactions with a world—with factors and conditions, that is, upon which his very existence depends. And this means that the various levels of value experience are actually indexes of the extent to which the individual himself is at stake—and is at stake not simply as a living organism but as a person, as a human being. There is a sense, therefore, in which the facts in the case warrant the judgment that those conditions of human existence which involve us profoundly—which give us peace of mind and, ultimately, a sense of fulfillment—are better than those which affect us only tangentially—the sensory pleasures and the gratifications of appetites. And this amounts to the affirmation of an *order* or *rank* of values that ranges from the sensory pleasures at the bottom to the ideal of self-fulfillment at the top. But it is also evident from the facts in the case that the lower levels are in essential respects preconditions of the higher; that together and in multiple variations and interrelations they spell out what it means to exist as a human being.

Life in all its forms is basically dynamic. It is so in its lowest forms where metabolism and multiplication by cell-division are perhaps the only manifestations of its inner drive. But it is so also at all other levels, and it has been so throughout the multiple phases of evolutionary development. Man is but part and product of this expansive drive. His whole sojourn on earth is proof of it.

But that sojourn is proof also of another fact. Freed from total dominance of instinctive drives and responding to the world guided by the first dim light of reason, man began to mold his environment "ever closer to the heart's desire." Determinative of his actions at all times was the realization that he himself was at stake, and that his valued goals but reflected this fact.

As man progressed from that first emergence as a human being to the present, his valuations became embodied in his various patterns of social living and found objectification in his social institutions no less than in his rituals, his mores, and his art. No matter how primitive it was at first, his mode of existence became increasingly cultural, with each culture pattern being but the precipitate of his valuations. But man, being the creator of his culture, was at the same time in a large measure the product of that culture. Born into a given society, the individual was at once confronted with a pattern of valuations and with an *ought* reflecting that pattern. It was expected of him—and it still is— that he conform. His own potentialities and his drive for self-fulfillment —his new insights and his revaluations of existing conditions—led him to modify traditional patterns. Accepting the cultural achievements of the past, he could and did rise above them, attaining ever-higher levels of cultural existence. I am not saying that he always did so, for he did not. Man's cultural development has often been halted and, temporarily at least, has been reversed by a throwback into barbarism. Dachau and the Katyn Forest alone are sufficient proof of this truth. But, despite such reversals, the dynamics intrinsic in human existence—inherent, that is, in man's drive toward the realization of his highest valuations—keep the general line of development open. What will emerge in the end we cannot forsee. We only know that it will be a manifestation of man's highest valuations as he sets himself goals in the perspective of his drive toward personal self-fulfillment. If there be any doubt about it, consider the valuations that inspire the various demands for civil rights in our immediate present.

There is one aspect of human culture which shows most clearly a value-determined development that is essentially free from reversals: man's relentless pursuit of truth in the sciences. Progress is here cumulative and one-directional. The goal is to understand the whole of reality—and to understand it fully. But the cognitive ideal is at once related to more practical affairs—to the development, that is, of a technology that enables man increasingly to use the forces and resources of nature for his own purposes; and this also is an irreversible process determined by human valuations.

Other aspects of human culture, however, are not equally cumulative and progressive. Although they are also precipitates of human valuations, our essentially sensate art and our literature, for example, demean rather than enhance the whole of our existence as human beings. To be sure, violence and eroticism play their part in man's life; but to regard the values underlying them as the alpha and the omega of human existence is to disregard potentialities which raise man above the mere animal and which have already proven their presence and their effectiveness in science and technology—to wit, the potentialities of reason and understanding.

It is obvious, of course, that man's valuations play a part also in the sphere of communal living. In fact, the very idea of a community implies that individuals share and, together, pursue certain values. Where there is no such shared commitment there also is no community. Social institutions in all their diversities are but focal points and embodiments of shared valuations. The difficulties which we encounter here arise from the fact that the valuations reflected in the institutions are largely carry-overs from the past and may no longer be acceptable, or they are valuations of a dominant social class and therefore are not shared by all. In either case, a re-examination of the value bases of the institutions is called for, and the institutions themselves may have to be changed to bring them into harmony with new valuations. The abolition of slavery, the dissolution of colonial empires, the great social and political revolutions of all times reveal the process at work; but so, of course, do the social reforms instituted by legislative action: social security, medicare, desegregation, and countless others here and abroad. All of them reflect judgments of preference that are keyed to the order of rank of values rooted in the levels of human existence previously mentioned. The process may be agonizingly slow and beset with reversals, or it may move with revolutionary swiftness; but, in the course of human history as a whole, it indicates a direction which is progress toward the realization of human freedom and the dignity of the human being as a person who creatively projects and pursues the highest values conceivable within the framework of his culture.

At this point I return to my initial confession—to the belief that the basic concern of philosophy still is the problem of what it means to be a human being and to live a humanly satisfying life. It is crucial that I return to this problem, for the trend of the ideas just touched upon seems to imply that our lives—i. e., the lives of individual human beings —have meaning only as "points of transition," as "bridges to the future," in a process that in itself has only such meaning as we ourselves impart to it; and there is truth in this implication. But it is only a partial truth—and for two reasons.

In the first place, we are integral parts of the whole of reality. Our evolutionary origin is proof of this fact. But that origin is proof also of the further fact that in our human enterprise cosmic reality itself has, as far as we know, achieved its most advanced thrust into ever-new levels of self-manifestation. In a very real sense, therefore, we find ourselves in the vanguard of cosmic evolution, and our projection and pursuit of values thus attain their true significance only in this broader, this metaphysical, perspective.

In the second place, however, we are not only "bridges to the future," cosmic or otherwise. Our lives have meaning also when, in the pursuit of values, we achieve our own self-fulfillment. And here the order of rank of values is again decisive. The search for truth, artistic and technological creativeness, and a sympathetic concern for our fellow men— these and others like them, rather than the sensory pleasures and the gratification of appetites, are the values the pursuit of which gives meaning to our existence. He who is committed to the search for truth, for example, no longer wonders whether his life has any meaning; he knows that it has because truth is intrinsically meaningful. And he who is truly creative also knows, for he finds his life's meaning in what he is doing and, in doing it, finds self-fulfillment here and now, not as a "bridge to the future." And with this example I rest my case.

NOTES

1. For details see W. H. Werkmeister, *The Basis and Structure of Knowledge*, 2d ed. (New York, 1969).

2. W. H. Werkmeister, *Man and His Values* (Lincoln, Neb., 1967), chaps. 4, 5, and 6.

3. For a variety of alternative views see W. H. Werkmeister, *Historical Spectrum of Value Theories*, Vol. I, *The German-Language Group* (Lincoln, Neb., 1970).

2. Problems of Methodology

The Naturalistic Fallacy and Its Different Forms

MANFRED MORITZ

Translated by Dru Ritezel

I

THIS ESSAY DEALS with various forms of the naturalistic fallacy. It employs a distinction that I first must say something about. I have in mind the distinction between ontological statements about values and statements which state how we use value sentences, i. e., statements about value sentences. I can express this idea in another way by saying that I distinguish between a *theory* about value sentences and an *ontology* about values.

A theory about value sentences is a theory about what value sentences mean and about functions that value sentences have or both. There are three main types of theories about value sentences: (1) *objectivistic* theories, (2) *subjectivistic* theories, and (3) *non-cognitivistic* theories. Objectivistic and subjectivistic theories assume that value sentences are statements which are either true or false. Accordingly, one can denote such objectivistic and subjectivistic theories as cognitivistic theories about value sentences.

The situation is different with the non-cognitivistic theories. They do not ascribe cognitive meaning to value sentences. These theories maintain that value sentences have emotive meaning, that they function as prescriptions, as recommendations, etc.

Objectivistic theories about value sentences are generally combined with another theory. These philosophers who assume that value sentences are judgments in which it is maintained that a certain object or certain objects are "equipped" with a "value property" generally assume, in addition, that there are such objects (or that there have been or at least that there can be) which are equipped with such value properties. These theories do not speak about the meaning of value sentences, but they speak about reality; namely, that there exist value properties, that there have been or that there can exist value properties. These are ontological statements. Therefore, I shall call theories of this kind ontological theories about values.

Objectivistic theories about value sentences are generally combined with a *positive value ontology*. That which is called *value objectivism* is most often a combination of (1) an objectivistic theory about value sentences and (2) a positive value ontology. That is to say, *value ob-*

jectivism is a combination of two theories: that value sentences are propositions, and that many value sentences are true. (Value objectivism, of course, implies that there are or can exist value properties.)

An objectivistic theory about value sentences is not always combined with a positive value ontology. An objectivistic theory may be combined with a view which denies that there exist value properties—i. e., with a *negative value ontology*. The error theory consists exactly of such a combination—i. e., a combination of an objectivistic theory about value sentences with a negative value ontology. Value sentences are in this case interpreted propositions which can be either true or false. But, according to the error theory all positive value sentences are de facto false. Only negative value sentences are true (for instance, that this action is not good, that this work of art is not aesthetically valuable, etc).

Subjectivistic and non-cognitivistic theories about value sentences are usually combined with a negative value ontology. They deny that there exist any value properties. If one speaks of *valuational subjectivism*, one is usually thinking of the combination of a subjectivistic theory about value sentences with a negative value ontology.

The situation is similar to that regarding the term *non-cognitivism*. *Non-cognitivism* usually means a theory which is a combination of a non-cognitivistic theory about value sentences with a theory that maintains that there do not exist value properties.

The distinction between a theory about value sentences and a value ontology corresponds to a common distinction. One can ask whether a sentence is true. One can define what the sentence "This is a centaur" means. However, that one can define what this sentence means does not imply that this sentence is ever true. The analytical question "What does this sentence mean?" must be held apart from the ontological question "Is this sentence true?". The situation would be the same if one were to interpret value sentences in the manner that the objectivistic theory about value sentences does. If one maintains that value sentences must be interpreted according to the objectivistic theory, it nonetheless does not follow that any value sentence is true. The aforementioned error theory accepts the objectivistic theory about value sentences. However, it does not combine this theory with a positive value ontology. Vice versa, if one is of the opinion that value sentences are not propositions in which the existence of value qualities is stated, then it is not implied that there are not any such value qualities. Subjectivistic theories maintain that value sentences are propositions, but not propositions which state that there are value qualities. That there are no value qualities does not follow from the statement that value sentences state nothing about the existence of value properties. That there are no value properties is likewise not implied by the statement, which non-cognitivistic theories make, that value sentences are not propositions. (Of course, if value qualities exist, but value sentences do not talk about value qualities but are used in some other way, we need other terms to describe value qualities.)

So much for the distinction between theories about value sentences and value ontologies. This distinction is fundamental for the following exposition.

II

I shall now go on to deal with the naturalistic fallacy. Instead of referring to the *naturalistic fallacy*, I shall refer to the *axiological fallacy*, and I shall give the reason for the change in terminology later on.

G. E. Moore introduced the name *naturalistic fallacy* in *Principia Ethica*. Moore uses the term *naturalistic fallacy* to denote two stated fallacies, as far as I can see. I shall call these two fallacies the axiological fallacy in its form pertaining to theory about value sentences (or, in short, in its sentential form) and the axiological fallacy in its form pertaining to value ontology (or in its ontological form).

In addition to these two forms there is a third one which G. E. Moore has not dealt with: the axiological fallacy in its descriptivistic form. (As far as I can see, certain philosophers use the term *axiological fallacy*, or *naturalistic fallacy*, in this third meaning, which differs from Moore's use of it.)

Finally, it would be suitable to recognize a fourth type: the axiological fallacy in its general form.

First, I shall give an exposition of the first two forms of the axiological fallacy. For this reason I shall present a simple objectivistic value ontology and a similarly simple objectivistic theory about value sentences as follows:

A. Assume that there are non-axiological properties in the world. Non-axiological properties are *natural properties* and *metaphysical properties*. There may exist additional non-axiological properties, but for our purposes it is irrelevant.

Natural properties are, for example, physical properties. But even psychological and sociological properties are natural properties. Examples of a psychological relational property are, for instance, "to be liked," "to be willed," "to be commanded," etc. Examples of sociological properties are "to be liked by group G," "to be commanded in a given society S," etc. Examples of metaphysical properties are "to be commanded by God," "to be willed by God," to be commanded by the pure, practical Reason," etc.

B. Assume further that there exist value (axiological) properties in the world. Whether or not there are other properties, which are non-axiological, need not be discussed here. It is enough for the present argument that one assumes that there exist value qualities.

C. Assume finally, that a person P confuses a non-axiological property with a value property. There are two possibilities: P can confuse a natural property with a value property, and P can also confuse a metaphysical property with a value property.

1. If, for example, a philosopher says that the property "to be pleasurable" is the same as the property "to be good," then there is an occurrence of such a confusion. A value property is being identified with a natural property. This is the axiological fallacy in its ontological form.

2. The axiological fallacy (in its ontological form) occurs in the same way if one confuses a metaphysical property with an axiological property. The person who maintains that the property "to be commanded by God" is the same as the axiological property "to be good" commits such a fallacy.

In the same manner I shall present an objectivistic theory about value sentences. It assumes that terms (predicates) must be divided into axiological and non-axiological terms. Non-axiological terms are natural predicates and metaphysical predicates. (Whether or not there are other non-axiological terms in addition to these is left open.)

The axiological fallacy in its sentential form has a similarity with the fallacy in its ontological form. An axiological fallacy in its sentential form occurs when an axiological predicate is confused with a non-axiological predicate. Instead of saying "an axiological fallacy occurs when a value predicate is confused with a non-axiological predicate," one often says "the person who defines a value predicate with non-axiological concepts commits the axiological fallacy (in its sentential form)." Moreover, whether one defines value concepts with natural concepts or does so with metaphysical concepts, one commits the axiological fallacy (in its sentential form).

Moore himself does not draw a distinction between these two forms of the axiological fallacy. Both are classed as naturalistic fallacy. But the examples which Moore gives of the naturalistic fallacy are examples of both types of the axiological fallacy.

The axiological fallacy in its sentential form consists either in the confusion of two predicates with one another or in the assumption that two concepts have the same meaning. The axiological fallacy in the sentential form is a special case of this confusion of two concepts. Its special trait consists in that the two concepts (according to Moore) are used to denote properties which have "different ontological status."[1]

According to Moore value concepts can only be defined with value concepts; non-axiological concepts can only be defined with non-axiological concepts. Other value concepts can, according to him, be defined with the help of "to be good." But "to be good" cannot be defined either with value concepts or with non-axiological concepts.

When a philosopher says that an argument contains the axiological fallacy in its ontological form, he assumes that the objectivistic value ontology is true. Only a philosopher who accepts the objectivistic value ontology can say that an axiological fallacy in its ontological form has occurred. When one says that a certain philosopher P has committed the axiological fallacy in its ontological form, one is making the following statements: (1) There are non-axiological properties and there are value properties. (2) The philosopher P has identified these properties with one another. He has assumed that there are only non-axiological properties. (3) It is a fallacy to identify these properties.

It follows from this logic that the statement that the axiological fallacy (in its ontological form) has occurred is not without assumptions. It assumes that the objectivistic value ontology is true. This is seen in statement (1). It contains a short formulation of the objectivistic value ontology. If one maintains that the objectivistic value ontology is false, then one cannot object to the claim "Here is an occurrence of the axiological fallacy (in its ontological form)." If a philosopher makes the statement that this fallacy has occurred, his statement is not independent of his view about value ontology.

This truth can be illustrated with the help of the error theory. A philosopher who accepts the error theory cannot use as an argument against a certain philosophical view, "Here is an occurrence of the axiological fallacy (in its ontological form)." The error theory maintains that there are no value properties. If a philosopher maintains that there are no value properties, he cannot maintain that non-axiological properties have been confused with value properties.

III

A philosopher who accepts the error theory could, however, say that the philosopher P has committed the axiological fallacy in its sentential form. The error theory maintains that value sentences are used to state the fact that value properties exist. The error theory maintains, therefore, that value predicates are used to denote value properties. Consequently, a subscriber to the error theory can raise the objection against, for example, Mill, that he has committed the axiological fallacy (in its sentential form). The objection is that Mill has a fallacious theory about how "to be good" is in fact used.

A subscriber to a non-cognitivistic theory about value sentences cannot state that the axiological fallacy (in its sentential form) has occurred. Subscribers to a non-cognitivistic theory usually combine this with a negative value ontology. If a non-cognitivist accepts this combination, then he cannot object against another philosopher P, that P has committed the axiological fallacy (in its ontological form). As soon as one denies that there are value properties, then consequently one cannot maintain that the philosopher P has confused a value property with a non-axiological property. If there are no value properties, then they cannot be confused with something else.

It is not necessary to say much about the axiological fallacy in its sentential form after what I have said above. The objection, "philosopher P is committing the axiological fallacy (in its sentential form)," consists of three propositions.

A. Value predicates are used to denote value properties.
B. The philosopher P has interpreted (defined) the value concept as a non-axiological concept.
C. It is fallacious to define concepts which are used to denote value properties by concepts which are not used to denote value properties.

The comment which was made concerning the axiological fallacy in the ontological form can be repeated here, *mutatis mutandis*. The statement that an axiological fallacy (in its sentential form) has occurred assumes that the objectivistic theory about value sentences is true. To be sure, if one maintains that value concepts are not used in the way in which the objectivistic theory about value predicates maintains, then one cannot object that philosopher P has interpreted expressions used to denote value properties as concepts which do not denote value properties.

(It should be noticed that not only objectivists can negatively state "philosopher P has interpreted value concepts as concepts which denote natural or metaphysical properties." Objectivists can certainly raise such an objection. But the same objection can also be raised by a subscriber to a non-cognitivistic theory. I call such an objection "the axiological fallacy in its general form," and I shall deal with it further on. "The axiological fallacy in its general form has occurred" can be stated by both objectivists and non-cognitivists.)

The archenemies of the objectivistic value theory are subjectivism and naturalism. Moore has, in general, directed his criticism (that they commit the naturalistic fallacy) toward these theories. Moore could not direct this objection toward the non-cognitivistic theories. There are two reasons why that was impossible. (1) When Moore developed his theory about the naturalistic fallacy, the non-cognitivistic theory had not yet been presented. At any rate, he did not know of any such theory. (2) The non-cognitivistic theory does not define value concepts with non-axiological concepts. That is not, of course, to say that—according to the non-cognitivistic theory—value concepts have another function than to denote something. Therefore, one cannot object to the non-cognitivistic theory that it defines value concepts with non-axiological concepts.

While Moore introduced the term "naturalistic fallacy" in *Principia Ethica*, it is not mentioned in *Ethics*, which was published only nine years later. This omission is very surprising, for a large portion of *Ethics* consists of critical comments against subjectivistic, naturalistic, and metaphysical theories.

I do not know why Moore, in *Ethics*, has not cited the axiological fallacy against subjectivistic and metaphysical theories. I can only guess at the reason for this. The reason could be that it must seem paradoxical to say that metaphysical theories, which are just antinaturalistic theories, should commit the "naturalistic" fallacy.

Moore's terminology allows the following proposition to be formulated: "the naturalistic fallacy occurs even in non-naturalistic theories." For example, "theological ethics ("to be good" is "to be commanded by God") contains the naturalistic fallacy."

Moore's term *naturalistic fallacy* has led to misunderstandings. It has been puzzling how a non-naturalistic or downright antinaturalistic point of view can contain the naturalistic fallacy. Several philosophers have not only been puzzled over this situation, but they also have maintained that it would be fallacious to state that non-naturalistic theories have committed this fallacy, which they considered to be an objection to Moore's theory. This objection rests upon a misunderstanding. In order to avoid it, I have introduced the term *axiological fallacy*.

It is unsuitable for Moore to use the term *naturalistic fallacy* in both its forms, but it is not *fallacious* from the point of view of the objectivistic theory about value sentences. Subjectivistic, naturalistic, and metaphysical value theories (*definist theories*) have a common characteristic, according to the objectivistic theory: they confuse value terms with non-axiological terms, and they confuse value properties with non-axiological properties. This characteristic is to be found in naturalistic value theories, among others. This fallacy can easily be denoted as the naturalistic fallacy. It seems unsuitable to say that the same fallacy could occur in antinaturalistic (metaphysical) theories of value, but it is not fallacious.[2]

IV

I shall now deal with the third form of the axiological fallacy. I have called it "the axiological fallacy in the descriptivistic form." To state "P has committed the axiological fallacy in the descriptive form" means "P has interpreted a value term as a descriptive term, and this interpretation is fallacious," or that "P has defined a value term with descriptive terms, and this definition is fallacious." According to the non-cognitivistic theory, value terms are non-descriptive terms.

If one maintains that a given philosophical theory commits the axiological fallacy in the descriptivistic form, then one assumes that the non-cognitivistic theory about value sentences is correct. Only if one maintains that it is correct, that value terms are non-descriptive terms, one can maintain that it is fallacious to say that value terms are descriptive terms. If the non-cognitivistic theory were wrong, then the axiological fallacy in the descriptivistic form would not necessarily be a fallacy.

Subscribers to the non-cognitivistic theory about value sentences criticize objectivistic, naturalistic, subjectivistic, and metaphysical theories about value sentences. All of these theories assume that value terms are descriptive terms. They assume that value sentences are either true or false.

A subscriber to the non-cognitivistic theory about value sentences can then say that even Moore has committed the axiological fallacy (in the descriptivistic form). He has interpreted value terms as descriptive terms. Value terms certainly should denote properties of a special kind (non-natural properties). But Moore assumes that these terms are used in order to denote properties.

Occasionally, subscribers to a non-cognitivistic theory accuse other theories about value sentences of committing the naturalistic fallacy. If they were consistent, they could not use *naturalistic fallacy* with the same meaning as Moore. A subscriber to the non-cognitivistic theory cannot say (without being inconsistent) that a philosopher has committed the axiological fallacy (in the ontological form). Since he himself (normally) denies that value properties exist, he cannot maintain that another philosopher is confusing value properties with non-axiological properties. Neither can a subscriber to the non-cognitivistic theory accuse someone of having committed the axiological fallacy in its sentential form. Since a non-cognitivist denies that value terms are descriptive terms, he, consequently, cannot criticize a theory, which interprets value terms as descriptive terms, of confusing a descriptive value term with some descriptive, non-axiological term.

A non-cognitivist, however, can raise the objection against certain theories that they have interpreted value terms as descriptive terms. Sometimes non-cognitivists say in such cases that these theories have committed the naturalistic axiological fallacy. But in this case "axiological fallacy" must mean something other than our use of "axiological fallacy" (in the sentential form or in the ontological form). From a terminological point of view, one ought, therefore, to distinguish the descriptivistic form from other forms of the axiological fallacy.

V

Objectivistic and non-cognitivistic theories about value sentences have a common characteristic: both say that value predicates have a different character, a different function, a different nature than other (common) predicates. Both can object that theories which deny that value predicates have a different function than common predicates commit the axiological fallacy. *Axiological fallacy*, however, is then used with a fourth meaning. I earlier termed the axiological fallacy in this fourth sense "the axiological fallacy in its general form." "Philosopher P has committed the axiological fallacy (in its general form)" means "P interprets value terms as common descriptive predicates, and this interpretation is fallacious." If one raises the objection that the axiological fallacy (in the fourth form) has occurred, one need not say, in a positive way, how value terms ought to be interpreted. One need not say that value terms ought to be interpreted as the objectivistic theory about value sentences interprets them. Neither need one say that value terms are to be interpreted as a non-cognitivist interprets them. What one may say is merely that value terms have another character than non-value terms, and that philosopher P has overlooked this point.

If a philosopher says that the axiological fallacy in the general form has occurred in the theory T, then one cannot, from this statement alone, decide whether he is a subscriber to an objectivistic or a non-cognitivistic theory about value sentences. Both theories maintain that value terms are not common descriptive terms. However, if one considers the fallacy to be determined by the fact that value terms are being regarded as common descriptive terms (while it is maintained in reality that they are indeed descriptive terms, but not common descriptive terms), then one is a subscriber to the objectivistic theory about value sentences. The fallacy consists in one's having interpreted or defined non-natural descriptive terms as common, natural, metaphysical, etc. In this way, the sentence in which the axiological fallacy in its sentential form has occurred can be understood as a variant of the sentence in which the axiological fallacy in its general form has occurred. The sentence "The fallacy in its general form has occurred" is transformed into the sentence "The fallacy in its sentential form has occurred," when it is maintained that the fallacy does not consist in the fact that non-natural terms are considered to be descriptive terms, but are considered to be common descriptive terms. On the other hand, the sentence "The axiological fallacy in the general form has occurred" is transformed into the sentence "The axiological fallacy in the descriptivistic form has occurred," when one adds to this that the fallacy consists in the fact that, on the whole, value terms are not understood as descriptive terms because they are not descriptive terms at all. The claim that the fallacy in the sentential form and in the descriptivistic form, or both, have occurred can, therefore, be considered as a variant of the claim that the axiological fallacy in the general form has occurred.[3]

VI

There is a well-known saying in philosophy: "*Ought* does not follow from *is*." This is an aphoristic way to formulate a sentence, which can be formulated in the following supplementary way: "*Ought* sentences cannot be deduced from *is* sentences." Or in an even more detailed way: The sentence "x ought to be A" does not follow from any sentence such as "A has such and such properties." That something is one's duty cannot be deduced from the statement that P suffers from need. That it cannot be deduced, of course, does not imply that the sentence "One ought to help the needy" would be incorrect. Neither can recommendations, imperative sentences, etc., be deduced from such statements.

The proposition "*Ought* sentences cannot be deduced from *is* sentences" is closely related to the proposition that one must not commit the axiological fallacy. It is related with the proposition that value terms must not be confused with common (e.g., natural) terms.

That there is a near relation between the two propositions can be shown as follows: According to a certain type of the non-cognitivistic theory, value sentences are to be understood as recommendations, as prescriptive sentences, as imperative sentences, etc. According to this theory value sentences are some sort of *ought* sentences.

The view that value predicates (value terms) cannot be defined with common (non-axiological) predicates can be formulated even as: "Value sentences cannot be defined with non-value sentences (factual sentences)."

If one holds the view that value sentences are some sort of *ought* sentences, then one can "translate" the proposition that value sentences cannot be defined by factual sentences as *ought* sentences cannot be defined with non-*ought* sentences (*is* sentences), and, consequently, *ought* sentences cannot be deduced from non-*ought* sentences.

Thus, it is shown that there is a close relation (if not identity) between the proposition that one must not commit the axiological fallacy and the proposition *ought* sentences cannot be derived from factual sentences (*is* sentences).

NOTES

1. Moore does not employ the terminology "different ontological status." I am using it in this context, and believe that it correctly reconstructs what Moore himself intended to say.

2. If Moore had said "the naturalistic fallacy consists of the fact that *natural* properties are confused with value properties," then it would, of course, be fallacious to say that a subscriber to a metaphysical theory about value sentences has committed the naturalistic fallacy. A subscriber to a metaphysical theory about value sentences does indeed interpret a value concept as a non-axiological concept. But he does not interpret it as a natural concept. According to Moore, the naturalistic fallacy does *not* consist of the fact that a value concept is interpreted as a natural concept, but of the fact that value concepts are interpreted as non-axiological. Consequently, it is correct (although unsuitable) to say that antinaturalistic *and* naturalistic theories commit the naturalistic fallacy. If the term *axiological fallacy* is employed instead, then one can say both naturalistic and antinaturalistic value theories contain the axiological fallacy. Then the pseudoparadox that antinaturalistic value theories contain the naturalistic fallacy does not arise.

3. Mr. Bengt Åke Hoff, of Lund, has imparted a series of critical observations to me, which he had directed against an earlier version of this paragraph. I owe many thanks to him for these and other valuable observations.

The Place of Values in the Integration of Knowledge

OLIVER L. REISER

IN THE REALM OF PHILOSOPHY there is no area more important and difficult than the field of values. The diversity of the points of view in this domain is abundantly demonstrated in *New Knowledge of Human Values.*[1] Everywhere the lack of unity and the resulting confusion are obvious. With his usual thoroughness, Robert Hartman has surveyed the multiplicity of theories and has discussed the variety of ethical theories that confront mankind.

Some of the crucial issues in the field of ethics arise from what is termed the *dichotomy of facts and values,* i.e., the dualism of *judgments of fact* and *judgments of value.* A severe test of my own *Cosmic Humanism* confronts us when we try to determine whether such a world view can transcend this dualism. The purpose of this article is to overcome this seemingly paralyzing opposition. If we are successful, we then have reason to reject the so-called naturalistic fallacy. It is surely no fallacy to pass from facts to values, provided it can be done properly.

We could begin a discussion of this problem almost anywhere: with Bertrand Russell's statement that the field of values is closed to science;[2] or the view of Robert M. Hutchins that science is more suited to the determination of means than to the determination of ends;[3] or the dictum of the positivists that value preferences, if considered in relation to the past, are *cultural anthropology,* and if considered in relation to future needs and desires, are only wishful thinking;[4] or the pronouncements of the clergy who claim that moral principles are outside the scope of science and belong to the domain of religion. This is a strange assortment of individuals to be found in the same camp. They all agree on the inability of reason to build a science of ethics, but they agree about little else.

To get the full nature of the problem before us, let us state more explicitly the several aspects of the alleged dualism. The natural and social sciences (physics, biology, chemistry, psychology, etc.) deal with the *is*ness of the world of facts, while the normative sciences (logic, ethics, aesthetics, etc.) deal with the *ought*ness of a world of preferences and values as objects of human desires.

An example of such dualistic thinking would be that although natural science can tell us how to get to the planet Mars if we want to go there, it cannot tell us whether man should go to the other planets of the solar system. Again, natural science tells us whether smoking cigarettes is (or is not) a causative factor in producing cancer (or science will give us a probability statement of the statistical correlation between the two), but it cannot tell us whether we should (or should not) stop smoking. Our inability, up to the present, to resolve this dualism, i. e., find the answer to the problem of *ought*ness in the *is*ness of things, seems to be responsible for a number of resulting difficulties. For example, one consequence of the fact-value dualism is that it appears to support the cultural relativism of those anthropologists and sociologists who can find no final and universal standards, though they can sometimes discover trends. Thus, by implication, if Nietzsche extols the tough virtues of the superman, and Jesus praises the virtues of love, charity, and mercy—who is "right"? Is it possible to prove that any preferred values are "better"? This, indeed, is a bewildering and demoralizing condition in a world that urgently needs rebuilding. And what is the way out?

My own scheme for the organization of knowledge as a basis for a resulting social program was first presented in my address before the Foundation for Integrative Education at the University of New Hampshire workshop in 1948, which was subsequently printed in the booklet *Issues in Integration.* The "temple of knowledge" approach was later used in my book *The Integration of Human Knowledge* (1958).

In this scheme there are three levels of inquiry: (1) the *formal foundations of knowledge* (logic and scientific method, semantics and epistemology); (2) the pillars of the temple, namely, the *special or natural sciences* (physical, biological, and social sciences, aesthetics, and science of religions); and (3) the level of *philosophical synthesis* (social planning and guidance, world philosophy and wisdom). The first level corresponds to what C. D. Broad termed *critical analysis of concepts*; and the third, to his enterprise of *speculative synthesis*.

The problem we are concerned with here is the question of how to get from the second to the third level, which is the problem of going from *facts* (what is) to *values* (what ought to be). But if it is true, as it seems to some of us, that there already are value commitments in scientific methods as employed in the natural sciences, then there is no inherent dualism, or dichotomy.

If we are correct in holding that the practitioner of scientific methods assumes ethical obligations, such as the desire for truth (passion for facts), objectivity and honesty in the presentation and interpretation of data, and so on, then the only difference between generalizations of the second and third levels is in the area of application. Because proposed principles in the field of "wisdom and social guidance" are broader and more general in scope, they are more controversial. The statement that "democracy is a better form of government for human beings than fascism or communism" is no different in principle from the statement that "biological evolution is more adequate as an explanation of the origin of species than the doctrine of 'special creation' of *Genesis*." If this is correct, the distinction between the field of values and the field of facts is not fundamental—it is a distinction that serves momentary or utilitarian purposes or both, but not long-range inquiries, whether in science or in philosophy.

Having set aside the dualism of science and ethics, we are now in a position to state theses which summarize and extrapolate our above point of view:

1. Our first general observation is that values are facts and facts are of value. Facts are of value, because a knowledge of facts helps us solve human problems, i. e., they enable man to survive and enrich his existence. Of course, knowledge is valued for its own sake as well as for its utility.

2. Values are entirely natural products of man's psychosocial evolution, and as such they are modified as our knowledge increases. Values are phenomena to be studied and understood like any other phenomena. A survey of the evolutionary process demonstrates that whereas in biological evolution "natural selection" operates as an ordering principle directing organisms toward greater adaptiveness for survival ("teleonomy"), in psychological development ideological factors operate in relation to consciously conceived goals and values. Morality must, therefore, evolve to keep pace with new circumstances and new knowledge of a changing world.

3. We humans never begin or carry on existence with a tabula rasa of values. Man, whether he be scientist, poet, peasant, or philosopher, begins with emotional and valuational commitments which are implicit in the facts of organic existence, i. e., man's biological constitution and cultural heredity. Because of this inescapable inheritance, we all want a measure of biosocial security, balanced with more or less novelty and adventure.

4. Science involves ethical commitments and goals no less than religion, politics, art, education, and other phases of human enterprise. The notion of the scientist as scientist is a product of an abstraction. The objectivity of science is itself an ethical imperative. The scientists of Nazi Germany may have prided themselves on their "ethical neutrality"—until it was too late. Whether we have taken a side or not, we are on a side in every important social issue, even if it is only the side of non-resistance.

5. Judgments of fact and judgments of value are not necessarily ex-

clusive of each other. When a judge says to a vicious criminal, "you are an evil man," this evaluation may be true both as a judgment of fact and as a judgment of value—it may be both true and right. When an ethicist says, "it is good that men should develop their potentialities," his statement is both morally sound and logically defensible. Indeed, we hold that it may be possible to show that every judgment of fact presupposes prior value judgments, and conversely. There is here a feedback between facts and values which resembles the servomechanisms of cybernetics.

6. Historically what were once only value preferences have occasionally become matters of social fact; and, conversely, what were once facts may have disappeared from the human scene. Thus, social security, public hygiene, etc., which were once ideals to be realized, are now (in some parts of the world) matters of fact. On the other hand, organized fascism is now socially extinct in those parts of the world where it formerly flourished. Our values help to determine the facts, at least some of the psychological and social facts. True, in some areas, such as the physical and biological sciences, "reality is not so damned plastic after all," as William James confessed in later years. Nonetheless, it is also true that alternatives are sometimes set up as exclusive of each other (either, or), which in fact are not exclusive. To say that we can have either security or adventure, but not both, is to set up a false antithesis: perhaps we *can* have some of both. Such mutually satisfying values may be described as complementary—they are *syntropic*.

7. If we completely understood the nature of the facts and the logic of events implicit in factual situations, we could frequently resolve conflicts which otherwise are unresolvable except by force. Thus, if one could demonstrate that happiness is incompatible with selfishness, as Erich Fromm asserts in his book *Man for Himself*, or that "race prejudice" is not only based on false beliefs but will ultimately lead to injury to the supposedly "superior" race, it should be possible to persuade reasonable men to abandon self-injurious beliefs. This principle can be generalized.

8. To resolve problems which involve conflicts of beliefs and associated values, we must try to find more inclusive value systems. Thus, loyalty to mankind provides a higher plateau than, e. g., loyalty to capital or labor, loyalty to this or that nation, race, or religion. Sometimes, however, higher loyalties can be fostered only through the media of existing institutions and values. Thus, excessive nationalism is a social evil, but international friendship can be created only through existing nations. In other cases (for example, human slavery and re-

ligious fanaticism), the institutions may have to be combatted directly, or even destroyed outright.

The frame of a Cosmic Humanism is one in which the greatest mass of significant facts becomes the supporting foundation for the maximum fulfillment of human values. The problem is to achieve the optimum combination of factual knowledge and value satisfactions. The problem is that of finding the greatest personal freedom and variety consonant with the least social standardization—a problem in the "calculus of variations" which perhaps only our computer technology society can solve. But we now have what it takes.

9. The problem of the modern world is to create planetary objectives, universal values for all humanity. This creation would provide the local frame for a Cosmic Humanism within which a limited cultural pluralism of diversifications could be protected. The process of choosing new ends and creating new values, as previously indicated, must maintain continuity with the fact-finding process. The choices should favor those alternatives which promise results maximally advantageous to all affected by the consequences of the choices. In general, social and ethical progress has moved toward the fabrication of more inclusive societies, historically from *family units*→ *tribal societies*→ *villages*→ *city-states*→ *nation-states*→ *world community*. In this process, differences of races, religions, nationalities, and social classes are gradually being transcended into higher ideological integrations.

10. At any given stage in the process of human evolution particular problems will loom large and demand solution. The present moment in psychosocial evolution is a stage in which several issues are of overriding importance, e. g., the threat of atomic war, of overpopulation and mass starvation, environmental pollution, and the immense problem of unifying the whole of humanity into some sort of single, interthinking group.

Here man's knowledge of his own possibilities is a powerful tool for his own progress. We need research on human potentialities and an integration of the resulting knowledge about man's creative capacities. Somehow the subjective drives toward new freedoms through "consciousness expansion techniques" must be harmonized with the requirements of a progressive world community. What Preston Harold in his book *The Shining Stranger* terms the "authority ego" must provide a substitute for the coercions of social authoritarianism.

Perhaps we have here the answer to the challenge of cultural and ethical relativism. In an evolutionary framework social values will change; they are relative; but they are relative to something—in the case of ethical values they are relative to the greater fulfillment of the present peoples of the world and to the welfare of future generations of mankind.[5] Thus, increasingly and progressively, our social world becomes a self-integrating plurality of cultures which moves forward in the convergent march of humanity toward what William Hocking called the "coming world civilization."

At the present magnetic moment in human history the one new electrifying technology for the program of planetary education which these ideals call for is available in the global communications satellite systems, such as the *Project Prometheus-Krishna*.[6] Here is the next challenge and opportunity for our electromagnetic society.

NOTES

1. Abraham H. Maslow, ed., *New Knowledge of Human Values* (New York, 1959).

2. Paul Arthur Schilpp, ed., *The Philosophy of Bertrand Russell* (Evanston, Ill., 1944).

3. Hutchins, *The Conflict in Education in a Democratic Society* (New York, 1953).

4. Richard von Mises, *Positivism, A Study in Human Understanding* (Cambridge, Mass., 1951).

5. A methodology for handling decisions in the field of ethical-social problems, which gives the equivalent of an "objective theory of values," is outlined in my article "Religion from the Standpoint of a Scientific Humanism," appearing in the symposium *Religion in Philosophical and Cultural Perspective*, edited by J. Clayton Feaver and William Horosz (New York, 1967).

6. See my *Cosmic Humanism* (Cambridge, Mass., 1966).

The Use and Abuse of Normative Definitions

WAYNE A.R. LEYS

As THE STORY of Western moral philosophy is usually told, the systematic search for normative definitions began with Socrates, who discovered that common moral judgments were vague and incoherent. Aristotle says that Socrates undertook to deal with this problem by "seeking the universal in ethical matters and fixing thought for the first time on definitions."[1] A man's failure to square all his approvals and disapprovals with 'a single definition was regarded as a defect needing correction.

Many of the post-Socratic philosophers offered definitions which, they believed, would correct moral mistakes and confusions: "Justice is every man doing what he is best fitted to do" (to serve the common good); "*Good* means *pleasant* and *evil* means *painful*"; "The only absolutely good thing is the good will" (the will to do one's duty); "The good is self-realization"; "Our duty is to seek the greatest happiness of the greatest number"; etc.

Each of these definitions met with vigorous objections from philosophers who preferred other definitions and, in our time, not a few theorists are convinced that common moral deliberations are not improved by the proposal of definitions. Definitions have been damned as oversimplifying moral problems. Instead of applying rigid definitions and replacing vague terms, some contemporary philosophers recommend a study of cases. Others would do some defining but insist that final moral judgments cannot be simple applications of definitions. Both of these strategies seem to leave normative studies in a radically unsystematic condition.

Robert Hartman has tried to retain the systematizing use of definitions by showing that the trouble with the classical philosophers resulted from the overworking of certain definitions. Hartman believes that the word *good* can be given a definition that will clarify its many uses; but after *good* has been defined, there remains the problem of defining the objects, situations, attitudes, activities, and relationships to which the words *good* and *bad* are applied. It is by inquiry concerning the objects that can be judged *good* or *bad* that definitions may be expected to make possible the comparison of values which are now incommensurable and logically independent.

Although I have some doubts about the extent to which value studies can become scientific, this essay can be read with Hartman's assumption that various value sciences will eventually correct vague and incoherent value judgments. The skeptical thrust of the paper is a questioning whether, in the case of moral judgments, a single mind can react to all of the values involved.

As previously mentioned, Western philosophers have treated vague and inconsistent moral opinions as indications of errors to be corrected. The correction could, presumably, be accomplished by a single person, a moral agent, a self legislating for itself. This is the assumption which I wish to call into question by contrasting it with legal practice.

In the theory of law, vagueness and inconsistency are interpreted as indicative of difficulties to be resolved, but not necessarily of errors to be corrected. It is generally recognized that legislators sometimes deliberately employ vague language. What this observation means to the legal theorist is that a power of choice is being conferred by the legislator upon someone else. Judges and juries, administrative agencies, and executives thus are given rule-making authority.

I have been especially interested in the delegation of rule-making power to administrative agencies because it was so clearly explained by the late Ernst Freund of the University of Chicago law faculty. In his book *Administrative Powers over Persons and Property*,[2] Freund identified incompletely defined directives as the legal basis of administrative discretion. In our system of government legislators were supposed to have the rule-making powers. Judges and executives were supposed to apply the rules rather than make the rules. Yet, it was obvious that administrators did have legislative power. The source of their discretion Freund found in statutes containing what he called "indefinite terms."

> A statute confers discretion when it refers an official for the use of his power to beliefs, expectations or tendencies instead of facts, or to such terms as "adequate," "advisable," "appropriate," "beneficial," "competent," "convenient," "detrimental," "expedient," "equitable," "fair," "fit," "necessary," "practicable," "proper," "reasonable," "reputable," "safe," "sufficient," "wholesome," or their opposites. These lack the degree of certainty belonging even to such difficult concepts as fraud or discrimination or monopoly. They involve matter of degree or an appeal to judgment.[3]

Freund then tried, rather unsuccessfully, to identify the different degrees of discretion. He also sought to identify the circumstances that justified a delegation of rule-making power. In this connection he mentioned the complexity of some matters and the newness of certain problem areas.

There are a number of areas in which Freund's conception of the functions of expert administrators has seemed plausible: safety in mines and factories, the allocation of routes in aviation, and the protection of the public in the sale and distribution of new chemicals and drugs. Yet, even in these areas the delegation of legislative power has often appeared to be less a search for an intelligent policy than a way out of legislative deadlock. In such fields as labor law our legislators have clearly "passed the buck," sending disputes to administrative agencies, not because of ignorance but because of unwillingness to agree on a compromise between opposed interests.[4]

Whatever the reason for delegating the power of choice, the legislators typically identify the person or organization to which power is given, and they limit that agent's choice by indicating more or less specifically (1) the type of activity to be regulated, (2) the purpose to be served, and (3) the procedure to be employed. In the United States, where judicial review limits much legislative power, the courts have declared against "roving commissions." Health commissioners, who have virtually dictatorial power for dealing with health hazards, are supposed to have no power to lay down rules to prevent unfair competition.

The officials to whom rule-making power is delegated make some choices on the basis of empirical study of the facts. For example, testing showed that television stations operating on the same frequency interfered with each other if they were separated by less than 220 miles. Research has established a "scientific" basis for many other administrative determinations. But what is more pertinent to our present inquiry is the delegated choice which defines normative terms that are not references to simple fact.

Take the word *safety* as an example. Absolute safety would mean complete absence of danger to life and limb. If manufacturing, transportation, and medication were required to be absolutely safe, there would be no manufacturing, transportation, or medication. The specialized regulatory agencies issue rules regarding safety, taking into account such considerations as the statistical frequencies of various kinds of accidents, the urgency of the need for services, and costs in relation to available income. They may also be influenced by popular opinion or the zeal with which partisans insist upon their contentions. Occasionally, no doubt, decisions are arbitrary, justified merely by a deadlocked legislature that has referred a hotly disputed question to a duly authorized arbitrator who has tossed a coin.

Another interesting set of definitions are those relating to *fairness* and *unfairness*. When a legislature asks an agency to define *fairness* in trade, in labor relations, or in race relations, some of the legislators may have well-defined concepts of *fairness*, but they do not all have the same concept. Other legislators may not have clear concepts. They may only be aware that there is some sort of trouble and that complainants are expressing their displeasure with the word *unfair*. The administrators may never develop an intensive definition of *fairness*. They may merely construct a list of practices to which they attach the word *unfair*.

Apologists for a legal system may contend that the vagueness of delegated power and the broadness of discretion vary according to the competence and reliability of those to whom the delegation is made. Thus, trustees are sometimes limited only by such indefinite injunctions as to "exercise ordinary prudence." Professional men are licensed to perform their services according to "accepted accounting practices," "the best interests of the patient," or "reasonable care and diligence." By contrast, less competent and less trustworthy people are often confronted by detailed regulation and constant supervision.

The extent of delegated discretion is, however, sometimes a historical accident, and I am not here trying to defend or attack existing institutions. My immediate purpose is to show that vague words do get into legislation, not merely by inadvertence or mistake, but in some cases by design. The effect (and, very often, the purpose) is to let someone share with the legislators the process of evaluation and rule-making.

When we turn from the directives of legislators to the writings in normative ethics, we immediately notice that there is less attention to the division of decision-making power. Who is making or enunciating the rules? Who is doing the defining? A book like Kant's *Metaphysics of Morals* seems to have an Olympian point of view. The author seems to think that he is speaking for all rational men and, when he gets into his casuistry, he seems to be stating complete definitions. Bentham's *Morals and Legislation*, similarly, seems to be addressed "To Whom It May Concern."

In making this comparison I am not assuming that legislative practice should be a model for moralists, but the comparison does highlight a neglected topic in studies of "the moral point of view." What is the competence of the person who moralizes? And does he ever delegate to his reader the task of specifying what is desirable? In spite of much recent talk about democracy and sharing, how often is a discussion of duties and obligations divided into phases or units that are assigned to different decision-makers?

To explore the possibilities here, let us contrast three jobs or predicaments in which one may take "the moral point of view." This typing of situations will make sense only in societies that have specialization of labor and complex organization. My excuse for concentrating on the predicaments of such societies is that they are the places where "the moral point of view" has been most vigorously attacked as nonsense.

One situation in which people discuss moral problems may be called "the agenda-maker's situation." The agenda-maker may be a citizen who feels some sort of distress or he may be a person who feels constrained to make a survey with the idea of allocating resources, time, and manpower so that no important moral problem is neglected. Teachers who are charged with the moral instruction of the young often find themselves in the role of official worrier, but there are also other occupations that believe they should needle complacent communities.

Agenda-makers have done their work when they persuade their listeners that "here is an area of life where someone needs to do something." They identify an area from which distress signals are coming and to which people are not giving much attention. They do not have to operate with precise definitions. They can talk vaguely about the evils and wrongs of war, poverty, and racism. They may even weaken their case if they offer a well-defined ideal or prescription. Their use of indefinite language leaves to aroused listeners the task of pinpointing evaluations.

A second and different predicament is that of the specialist, the man who has familiarized himself with one aspect of life or one activity in society. He knows better than most people how to diagnose and prescribe within the field of his specialization. Within that field he knows what is important and what is unimportant, what is right and what is wrong. The scale of values that is appropriate in his work and experience may be very different from the scale of values of other specialists in other fields. A diplomat and a local politician are both in government, but the career man in the foreign service probably has strong convictions on subjects that scarcely interest the local politician. A nutritionist and a speech correctionist may both work with children; yet, if the nutritionist specializes in the dietary diseases of poor children and the speech correctionist works with stammerers in affluent families, they may be expected to be sensitive to different values.

One of the difficulties of specialists' taking the moral point of view is that they often assume that their kind of problem is always on the agenda, and that what is urgent in their kind of service is always urgent. Architects and city planners who solve transportation problems, for example, notoriously neglect many things that citizens regard as more important than quick, safe transportation.[5]

Specialists are better equipped to define criteria than to define the whole duty of man. They contrast sharply with unspecialized citizens who have many interests, and with executives and politicians who have to "live with" all sorts of specialists and their services. The "generalists" who must coordinate the expert services are in a third type of predicament. It is a predicament that breeds the greatest skepticism concerning the definition of moral problems and the definition of moral solutions.

Acquainted with the criteria and well-defined ideals of many specialists, the consumers, the coordinators, and the budget-balancers tend to discount the claims of specialists. Their philosophical and theological advisers argue against strict application of the specialists' definitions. Neatly defined moral requirements are treated as prima facie statements of what ought to be done, binding only if "other things are equal." (W. D. Ross's way of stating the matter.) Or they reject definitions altogether, trusting their intuitive, unanalyzed assessment of the total moral situation, as the Reverend Joseph Fletcher did in his *Situation Ethics*. Or they trust their impulsive acts, as Sartre did in his resistance days.

When "the moral point of view" is articulated by men in this third predicament, value theory tends to become an antitheory. The Socratic quest for wisdom seems to culminate in unutterable and, possibly, irresponsible whimsy. The agent is so intent on defining his choice in viable action terms that he denigrates all specialized insights. The executive's task of translating and coordinating purposes in plans of action becomes opportunistic, guided by chance hunches.

I realize that the agenda-maker, the specialist, and the executive do not add up to an adequate typology. Nevertheless, their contrasting points of view may suggest how moralizing in a complex society can make use of both indefinite and well-defined moral terms.

If I may use a medical analogy, we can idealize medical science and imagine a practitioner who (1) detects any and all symptoms of pathology, (2) knows exactly which treatment will arrest or correct each condition, and (3) makes the best possible judgment of the treatment's costs and side effects. But in a complex, specialized society the specialist does not go around detecting symptoms. The initial detection of symptoms is done by patients who feel pain or by general practitioners and routine examiners. The third function, the over-all judgment that the patient will be better off as a result of correcting pathology (1), is, at times, determined in consultation.

A theory of valuation must reckon both with the objects valued and the evaluators. Evaluators do not all have the same opportunity to become acquainted with the objects valued. Thus, no matter how expert scientists may become, a society will still depend upon ordinary citizens to give the distress signals that indicate areas about which somebody ought to be doing something. Voting upsets, sabotage, apathy, restlessness, and violence may be no more precise than the medical patient's cry of "Ouch!" Yet there are so many possible tasks to which specialists may be devoted that vague distress signals continue to be the first promptings of uneasy consciences.

The courses of action that conceivably can correct a "bad" situation are so numerous and their repercussions on other aspects of life are so many that here again the specialist with his precise definitions may not be acquainted with all the facts that would be reacted to in an ideal evaluation. I conclude that agenda-makers and coordinators can be expected to continue to use *good* and *bad* with reference to objects that will not be precisely defined. Is it possible for the theory of moral values to recognize that "indefinite terms" may be used for good reasons and, at the same time, facilitate communication with the specialists whose insights expand the limits of human action?

NOTES

1. Aristotle, *Metaphysics*, 987^b2.
2. (Chicago, 1928).
3. *Ibid.*, p. 71.
4. See W. A. R. Leys, "Ethics and Administrative Discretion," *Public Administration Review*, III (1943), 10–23.

5. The specialists who did the staff work for the President's Commission on National Goals outlined what they regarded as the most urgent and unavoidable programs in each of their respective fields (see *Goals for Americans* [Englewood Cliffs, 1960]). An economist totaled up the cost of all these programs and showed that the cost of the recommended programs far exceeded the funds likely to be available for many years to come.

The Possibility of a Pure Phenomenology

PAUL WEISS

Pᴿᴱᴶᴜᴅɢᴍᴇɴᴛs ᴀɴᴅ ᴀᴄᴛɪᴠɪᴛɪᴇs qualify our attempts to know. Nothing less than a long and difficult process of voiding the conditions which make us attend only to certain items, and then in challengeable ways, will bring us to the stage where we actually know what is real. Until then we cannot be sure just what is unaffected by us and what is not.

Mystics and Eastern thinkers try to free themselves from their daily conditions. Some claim to have escaped from every limited situation; if so, they have lost contact with whatever is in the world with themselves. Freedom from all arbitrary limitations should not require a rejection of the world in which we live. If it does, the price is too high. When we are asked to make sacrifices, it is always wise to ask if we are not giving up too much for what may not prove to be good enough.

Instead of trying to detach ourselves from all that is about, it is better simply to accept what is encountered. One can then reasonably suppose that changes, normally intruded into what is confronted, will then be avoided. Some men, consequently, have tried to lose themselves in unsophisticated encounters, where anything and everything whatsoever was allowed to impinge, leaving for later the attempt to describe precisely what they underwent or confronted. Such men have made an effort to become pure phenomenologists.

A pure phenomenologist tries to look at anything and everything without blinkers and without illusions, without loss, distortion, modification, or addition, and then report what he discovers. He is not concerned with phenomena only, if by *phenomena* we mean simply the appearance, the surface, the presented face of things. Nor is he content to deal solely with the immediately sensed, with mere experience. He wants to accept everything in the very guise in which it is confronted, free from prejudgment, categorization, criticism, or theory, whether they are valuable objects or not, useful or useless, trivial or important.

The pure phenomenologist thinks that whatever is present can be known truly, if one takes a truly catholic, open-ended, neutral approach to it. Only after one attends in innocent honesty is one able, he thinks, to classify, judge, and use properly. Such a pure phenomenologist is hard to find, though a number of contemporaries take themselves to fit the category. No one of the three great phenomenologists, at any rate—Hegel, Husserl, or Peirce—can be correctly said to have been occupied with attending to whatever is present. All of them confined their phenomenological investigations to only some of the available material. But a full phenomenology is just as receptive to substances as it is to objects of intention, to daily objects as it is to what lies behind them, to mathematical forms as it is to sensuous qualities, to constant forces as it is to transient particulars. It prejudges nothing; it welcomes every fact and every kind of experience.

Hegel interested himself mainly in large-scaled items, cosmic in range and historically important, but devoid of interiority. His phenomenology traversed the history of Western civilization with brilliance and ingenuity; but it rarely stopped to attend to anything encountered by man in the course of daily life, or even to note what, if anything, was revealed about man or whatever else there was, or both.

Husserl, instead, occupied himself with what he could separate off from the world of practical affairs. It was his conviction that ability to consider something in abstraction from existence or without regard for its usefulness was identical with an ability to consider it as freed from all relation to these. This belief ignores the fact that the abstracted is incipiently concretized. Even when we attend only to the properties of a triangle, we continue to confront the triangle as that which is or can be spread out in real or imagined space.

Peirce, in contrast with the other two, concentrated on the main types of presented content, and then only as far as these types could be distinguished formally. His was a rational phenomenology which attended primarily only to the possible classes into which encountered content could be placed.

A pure phenomenology aims far beyond the interests of these great innovators. Ready to accept everything without prejudice, it refuses to impose divisions, to introduce classifications, to set up hierarchies, or to qualify what it faces. Where the momentary and the persistent intersect or intertwine, or are involved with one another in any way, it reports the fact, and does not, for the sake of some theory, place one against the other. The here and the there, the good and the bad, the hard and the yielding, the rational and the textured, the surface and the depth, the given and the taken, the confronted and the intrusive— all are acknowledged in the same spirit of openness. Pure phenomenology seeks that virgin state where things are taken for what they are, and not for what we would like them to be or do.

Some men have tried to arrive at the pure phenomenological position by taking drugs. But they ended by neglecting what was in fact encountered. Soon they immersed themselves into another realm where they could not distinguish the knower from the known and could not, therefore, possibly know what had been altered by the knower's presence.

Drugs and other agencies bring one close to the kind of problems which beset mysticism without yielding any of the truths mysticism claims to have reached. A more hopeful method would involve vigorous acts of self-criticism and reconstruction. But these make us reject some things that are, in fact, encountered; they also introduce new conditions which affect what they enable us to know.

Few encountered objects are steady or permanent. All have depth and nuance, fluctuating and vibrating in countless ways. They appear—which is to say, they surface, come out into the open, but not as sundered from their source. All are rooted in a darker region whose power we feel and whose nature we faintly glimpse. Most undergo change constantly and last for but a short time. The pure phenomenologist must allow what he confronts to advance and to recede, to fade off and to pass away without hindrance. He can hardly do more than live with and through what happens; he surely has no time to examine all of the objects. Indeed, he has insufficient time to examine more than one or two with care. Most of what he confronts at one time slips away before he can dissect even a part of it. And any report that he writes about what he discovers will be presented at a time when what he noted is no longer there in that very guise.

We are, of course, not without some reliable knowledge. All of us at times do somehow manage to avoid intruding our needs, aspirations, and purposes into things. We do not always work; we are not always engaged in serious, practical activities. Play takes us away from the workaday world. When frolicsome, spontaneous, and unconfined by rules, it allows us to ignore the normal uses of things. But even it must take some account of the contours and capacities of things, and keep in accord with our intentions. To free ourselves from even these limitations, we would have to sink ourselves deeper into what we confront. We would have to be willing to live aesthetically, doing no more than remaining attentive to the different textures of things as they flow past or into us, without our subjecting them to any conditions, practical or otherwise. Ours would be an *aesthetic apprehension* of what was sensuously encountered—roughness or smoothness, the dark, the light.

An aesthetic apprehension occurs in a context. That context is bound on one side by attentive men, and on the other by a continuum of changing qualia. The men, no steadier than the qualia, slip unreflectingly from simple enjoyment to appreciation, participation, and dramatization. They come closest to accepting items in enjoyment, since contents are then not qualified by a conceptual framework. In appreciation they go further and make use of a standard in terms of which items can be ordered as more or less agreeable, desirable, or interesting.

Through participation, they share in the rhythms and tensions of that which they aesthetically apprehend, to make themselves once again united with it in an intimate way, but now while in control of themselves and the manner in which they are united with it. Finally, in dramatization they sharpen the continuities and discontinuities, the similarities and differences, the accords and discords which the different aesthetically apprehended items have with respect to one another and perhaps with them.

These different stages pass so imperceptibly into one another that it is customary to speak of aesthetic apprehension as though it were a simple act in which surfaces were all subjected to one simple kind of unreflecting acceptance. But in all of them one is active. Men affect all content, no matter how accepted. What they confront makes its own distinctive contribution to the result, but only because a man gives himself to it and thereby colors it. This coloring can be distinctively individual or common to a number. He who has delicate fingers feels differences where another feels none. Both can feel something to be wooly, glassy, woodish. Though one will note and stress what the other does not, both can rightly be said to enjoy, appreciate, participate in, or dramatize common generic features.

There are men who have only minimal interests or gifts of acceptance, but they, too, appreciate some things. To be able to do nothing but enjoy, they would have to lose themselves entirely in the sensed immediacy of experience, without intruding anything of themselves. But only those who are completely passive could achieve this state. Even when immersed in an experience where they can distinguish neither themselves nor anything else, in which item slides into item without break, they make an impression on whatever they confront.

A content can sink below consciousness just as surely as it can be a constituent of some more complex whole, or serve to order and evaluate other items. In speaking of it in these ways we treat it as though it were neutral to the different roles. But it is neutral only in abstraction from its actual functioning. It is either operating below consciousness as a condition for a grasp of something else, as a constituent of some more complex entity, or as an instrument for deliberately mastering something else. Each mode entrains its own conditions; otherwise there would be no distinguishing of those ways of functioning. One might, of course, argue that the content lies inert beyond these different approaches, but then the question arises about how it can be known.

Experience is too kaleidescopic to permit one to be a pure phenomenologist in any other sense than that of merely undergoing encounters, without knowing or understanding what is undergone. If we are merely to sense, we must restrain ourselves. If we are to know any part of what we sense, we have to fix it for a while and continue to keep it before our consciousness. What then remains steady and persistent will be open to a possible exploration, while what recurs with sufficient frequency will permit the checking of our descriptions and judgments. In both instances, what we will face will be conditioned by us and our approach to it. In any case, both will be found to have endless details, nuances, and relations, which no man has sufficient time or great enough resistance to boredom to examine.

No one can take account of every facet of even one of the things that he might confront. Yet if he neglects anything, he inevitably selects the remainder, and cannot, so far, be open to whatever there be. Even he who sets himself to attend to every phase and facet of what was encountered, and thus to what was neglected by one who concentrated only on the common and constant, would have to deal initially with some items rather than with others. There is no escaping some selection, whether one attends only to the constant and common or is willing to take account as well of what is neither.

It might be objected that nothing is so simple or harmless as the enjoyment of items one after the other, without bias. Putting aside the question whether the fact that something has been fastened on does not give it a role it did not have before, there is the act of noting what is undergone or faced. This noting carries the imprint of individual past experiences, associations, interests, needs, and desires. The past and the future intrude upon the present to make it at once a consequence and a condition. Detached, neutral observation of what is simply present may be possible to a camera. It is beyond the power of a man, unless it be within his power to have a passive eye and no convictions.

In the rough commerce of every day we do not question the emphases which are commonly placed on things by the mature members of our society. Yet those emphases are affected by our beliefs, concepts, and language. Because all of us behave in somewhat similar ways toward similar objects, all of us unreflectingly read something of the traditional grammar, expectations, and common memories into the thing confronted. Inevitably and readily we suppose that what we commonly affirm is both veridical and objective. But what we express, severally and together, evidently tells us more about ourselves than about that of which we speak.

The size of some of these difficulties can be reduced. It is possible to attend to the common fact that certain items occur, or that they have a certain degree of unity, distinctness, vividness, and the like. Or a constant, pervasive dimension of experience might be isolated and studied at leisure. Our three great phenomenologists—Hegel, Husserl, and Peirce—did something like that. As far as they succeeded in focusing on what was constant and common they became phenomenologists, but of only a part or a dimension of what there was before them. None, of course, was a pure phenomenologist to begin with, even of this limited area, since he first had to select out the desirable part or dimension. The common assumption of these philosophers—that they did not add anything in the course of their attending and did not compromise the being or the nature of what they neglected—they never justified.

A good phenomenologist is a narrow one. Restricting the content of his experience, he does not succeed in obtaining unqualified material. Yet he necessarily modifies whatever he confronts. His items are all products, mediated immediacies.

A phenomenologist would like to stay with his items for a considerable time. At once impersonal and open-minded, he tries to report what he sees—and nothing more. If he backs up a virtue of persistence with that of forethought and supports sensitive observations with analysis, he should be able to minimize what he unreflectingly adds. But he will not be able to compensate for all the changes he introduces unless he somehow is aided by forces not within his power to control.

If, instead of trying to get to the position where we have nothing but aesthetic content, we were to attend to a daily object, we would bypass a pure phenomenology of experience. But we will not then have escaped from the fact that our confronted content was qualified by us at least in the sense of having been picked out, isolated, focused on by us—a state it obviously did not have apart from us.

A pure phenomenology, at best, can be carried out only with respect to some aspect of things, or with respect to some items, and then only after it has moved away from what is simply enjoyed or experienced. It gets to the immediate by starting from daily life and attending only to portions of it. Inevitably it raises the question of whether there is a desirable method for obtaining data and of what must be done to heal whatever distortions the getting of it introduces. An indication of how the establishment of a workable method for collecting data might be accomplished can be obtained from a look at the position of some philosophical linguists.

It can be said that every approach we take is from the perspective of a language which, if it distorts, will do so unwittingly and beyond our realization, since the distortion will affect whatever we say and whatever we acknowledge. This thesis, I think, is somewhat incoherent. Those who offer it believe that there are ways of using language so as to say what is the case. Otherwise they would not be able to tell us that language does or does not distort and that all are trapped within it. Were it not possible to escape the conditions imposed by one's language, no truth could be stated which holds when one uses another language, or when one leaves language behind to observe or to make. But then it cannot be true that language is purely conventional and that when we use it we reveal nothing of what is the case. Every language, of course, is conventional in its roots, distinctions, vocabulary, and grammar. But these limitations can be known. If we could not know them we could not know that language was subject to them. But if we know them, we can in principle compensate for them. What we confront gives us an opportunity to determine whether or not we falsify it when we speak of it, if we are able to know what we bring to it. And if we cannot find out what we bring to it, we cannot claim that its effect is good or bad, or even that there is one. In a similar way, without supposing that we can directly know immediacies, we cannot come to learn what things are like apart from our involvement with them.

Socrates: On the Interpretation of His Ignorance

GOTTFRIED MARTIN

Translated by Rita D. S. Hartman

IN THE PLATONIC DIALOGUE *Theaetetus*, Socrates says: "As the world in general have not found me out; and therefore, they only say to me, that I am the strangest of mortals and drive men to their wits' end: *atopotatos eimi kai tous anthropous aporein*" (149 A). At this point Socrates relates that he is the son of a midwife, and what he reports is doubtlessly true. So one may suppose that also the phrase itself is a true report and that it was not Plato who coined it in order to characterize his master, but that it comes from Socrates himself, either provoked by him in others or coined by him.

The word *atopotatos* is not easy to translate. The root contains *topos*, place, location. It is preceded by an alpha privativum; the ending is the expression for the superlative. In paraphrase one might say: "there is no place to put me in, there is no location to fit me in." In order to maintain the spatial core in the translation one could say: "I am the most eccentric (meaning opaque) of all humans." Just as difficult to translate is *aporein*. *Poros* is the fording place of the river, the trail over the mountain, the voyage over the sea. It is preceded, again, by alpha privativum. Again, one could say in the paraphrase: "I cause people to lose their way." Here, too, one is tempted to maintain the spatial image. Perhaps one could translate the entire phrase: "I am the most eccentric of all humans and cause people to lose their bearings."

If we suppose that Plato has correctly characterized his master with this phrase or, better still, in my opinion, that Socrates has characterized himself in this manner, then every interpretation of Socrates will soon be confronted with certain limits. How can an interpretation make a person understandable who himself holds that he is not understandable, who sees himself as out of place, as opaque? Here an interpretation can do nothing more than make intelligible the unintelligibility Socrates claimed for himself, make transparent his self-proclaimed opaqueness.

We have taken a Socratic word as historical testimony. If one looks for further evidence one soon finds that the Socrates of the Platonic dialogues at times stands for the historical Socrates and at times is the mouthpiece for Plato's own philosophy. The Socrates of the *Republic*, except in the first book, is certainly not the historical Socrates. A lengthy study of mathematics, a lengthy study of philosophy—that is not the life and philosophizing of Socrates; it is Plato, the head of the Academy. Such a distinction between the historical Socrates and the spokesman of Platonic philosophy is perhaps not impossible even though, up to this day, it has never been thoroughly pursued. Yet even today one can count with general agreement if one limits himself to extreme situations. I choose the Platonic dialogue *Laches* and regard it as evidence of a genuine Socratic conversation.

Laches is a conversation between Socrates and two famous Athenian generals, Laches and Nikias. The two generals must know what bravery is, and, thus, to Socrates' question "What is bravery?" (190 D) there follows immediately the answer "To stand firmly and not to yield one's place in the battle line" (190 E). But the logical examination of this answer soon shows that it cannot be correct, for the bravery of a horseman is different, and there is bravery in sickness, there is bravery in politics, or at least there should be. So one must look for a better answer. The new answer does not hold up under logical investigation either, and every answer proposed proves inadequate. The dialogue thus ends with the resigned conclusion: we have not found what bravery is.

This exchange of question and answer, of suggestion and investigation, is built up as a brilliant game, and it has been compared as of yore with the Attic comedy. One must assume that the poetic creativity of Plato has an essential part in the form of the dialogue. One must not imagine Plato to have used shorthand while listening to the actual dialogue. For it is unlikely that a conversation so rich in striking climaxes, so spirited, so fluent and consistent would actually have occurred. On the other hand, one can readily assume that the poetic form Plato gave the dialogue has made its actual meaning even more transparent.

Seen from the systematic point of view, the dialogue contains two fundamental problems—the meaning of the question "What is bravery?" and the meaning of the aporetic assertion "We did not find what bravery is." As to the meaning of the question, it is almost impossible to imagine that Socrates did not ask such a question, and that he was not the first to ask "What is bravery? What is virtue?" These questions have become so natural to us today that it is difficult to understand that there was a time in which they were not asked. But who could have asked this way before Socrates? Certainly not the poets. But neither the philosophers. Thales does not ask "What is water?" Pythagoras does not ask "What is number?" Parmenides does not ask "What is being?" They did not ask such things, nor could they. Aristotle was the first who recognized the significance of this kind of question. He examined the problem, and came to the conclusion that, aside from some experiments,

Socrates was the first to ask questions in such a way (*Metaphysics*, 1078^{b}13).

The significant thing is not the question itself, but the answer Socrates expects. What answer does he expect to the question "What is bravery?" If one says he expects a definition of bravery, one is not quite incorrect, of course; but one answers in terms of the later development of Aristotelian logic, and such an answer presupposes a situation of logic which for Socrates did not exist. Thus, one has to look for a formulation which leads to the early beginnings of logic. Perhaps one could say that Socrates expected a logical determination of bravery. But even this statement would presuppose too much of a logical formation at his time. Maybe one should say that Socrates expected a verifiable determination of bravery. This was, indeed, the meaning Socrates had in mind—that the answer to be given to the question "What is bravery?" could be verified, and that it could stand up to the verification.

But if the question "What is bravery?" has this emphasis and this urgency, how can one understand that Socrates at the end says resignedly, "We did not find what bravery is"? Pedagogics know the Socratic method. According to it, the teacher should not lecture on ready conclusions but should induce the pupil, by his agility of asking questions, to find the answer spontaneously by himself. The prime example of this method has always been the passage in *Meno* where Socrates elicits from a slave completely ignorant of mathematics one of the most important results of mathematics then known: that the diagonal of the square is incommensurable with its side or, speaking arithmetically, that the square root of 2 cannot be a fraction. It may be doubted whether Meno's questions represent a good example of the Socratic method, pedagogically speaking. But in *Laches* there can be no question of this method, for there is no result of the conversation, neither through Socrates' questions nor the generals' answers. Many interpreters, however, believe that the dialogue seems to deal with the Socratic method in a more subtle manner, and that Socrates does know what the right answer is, that he knows what bravery is. The conversation, then, has as its aim to introduce the participants into the method of such a question and the method of verification of the answer, and Socrates would then expect that the participants in the conversation, with such preparation, would later spontaneously find the correct answer. The interpreters in question are able to find sense in such a conversation only if it leads to the correct answer, and this ability naturally presupposes that there is a correct answer and that Socrates knows it. These interpreters find the question meaningful only if it leads to an absolute and definitive answer.

But is this assumption necessary? Would it not be possible that even Socrates himself does not know an absolute and definitive answer and that the Socratic conversation nevertheless contains a meaning? (I will clarify the meaning of such an interpretation in a later example.) In the dialogue *Theaetetus*, Socrates posits the question, "What is science?" (145 E). It is true, one may suppose, that in this dialogue, Plato lets his master express Plato's own thinking; that is, specific Platonic considerations. The dialogue starts with a mathematical example which treats a very subtle problem, the solving of which belongs to the greatest results of Greek mathematics at the time of Plato. Nothing in the dialogue indicates that Socrates possessed such far-reaching knowledge, and nothing indicates his appreciation of the significance of such mathematical results. This reasoning is Plato and wholly Plato. Certainly, Plato's question "What is science?" is based on the old Socratic question "What is bravery?" And, indeed, the Platonic question carries on the Socratic quest. However, the Platonic question is significant only if science as such is elevated to be the grand aim of all inquiry; and, again, there is no indication that it was for Socrates. It was Plato who elevated science to this grand position. Science, however, can exist only if it continuously reflects upon itself; and, thus, the question "What is science?" becomes a question that must necessarily be asked again and again. Here it becomes clear that the question is necessary, even though an absolute and definitive answer does not exist. It is true there have been many, too many, who knew with irrevocable assurance what science is, but none of the answers given with such irrevocable assurance has stood its ground. Plato's question, then, "What is science?" proves to be a question that is necessary, even though an absolute answer is not known, and may not exist. If science reflects upon itself it fulfills a task which cannot be completed, and ought not even to be completed. From this observation it becomes understandable that even the Socratic question "What is bravery?" remains uncompleted.

It is advisable to check this interpretation by a second dialogue. I choose the dialogue *Euthyphro*. Euthyphro is a priest, and Socrates meets him early in the morning on the Agora. Socrates is on his way to court to defend himself against the accusation which has been directed against him. Euthyphro has denounced his own father for murder. Socrates starts a conversation and asks immediately, "What is piety?" (5 D). It would be good for Socrates to know the answer for just this very day he has been accused of impiety. Surely Euthyphro is the right man to give a correct answer. As a priest he must know what piety is, and he is convinced he does know. He surely would not have accused his own father if he were not sure that it behooves a pious man to accuse even his own father of the sin of impiety. To Socrates' question "What is piety?" Euthyphro answers, therefore, without hesitation, "It is pious to prosecute the evildoers" (5 D). But Socrates can easily show that this answer will not bear scrutiny. Euthyphro without hesitation gives a second determination, "Pious is what finds favor in the eyes of the gods" (7 A). But also this second answer cannot measure up to Socrates' objections, and so fares every answer Euthyphro suggests. Finally, Euthyphro removes himself from further investigations by pretending to be in a great hurry. And, thus, even that conversation ends negatively; what piety is could not be determined.

Therefore, in this conversation we also find the two fundamental moments: Socrates demands a verifiable definition of piety but such verifiable definition is not being found. It is perhaps in the nature of the subject of the conversation that here both moments appear with particular clarity. Hegel has shown, in his *History of Philosophy*, that in the demand for a logical definition of bravery or of piety, the individual rises up against the unlimited power of the polis. Up to then, the polis had ordained what bravery is and what piety is; and the individual had, without contradiction, acknowledged the dictates of the polis. Now the individual examines all these decrees before the judgment seat of his own reflection; only that is valid which can stand the scrutiny of his own insight. This confrontation between the individual and the polis appears in dramatic forms. Socrates asks, "Even war, do you really believe the gods war against each other, and have dreadful hatreds and battles and all sorts of fearful things like that, as the poets tell of, as good artists represent in sacred places; yes, and at the great Panathenaic festival the robe that is carried up to the Acropolis is all inwrought with such embellishments. What is our position, Euthyphro? Do we say that these things are true?" (6 B). But Euthyphro answers without hesitation, "Not only these, but even many others." Here the confrontation appears very sharply. The thinking individual asks, "Is all this really true?" The priest answers, in the name of the polis, "All this is really true and many other things as well." Here we see what power the demand for logical determination has.

But, also, the negative result of the dialogue becomes more understandable. Who would really be so bold as to say, with absolute finality, what piety is? Here it becomes clear that the penetrating question of Socrates has also the task to destroy false securities, to expose self-righteous certainties, which are only too often found in piety. Thus, there are positive aspects in both the thematic question and the negative result of this dialogue.

This interpretation is derived from premises of interpretation which have found almost general acclaim in the last decades. It finds support, moreover, when we turn to the *Apology*. In the *Apology* the question of historical credibility can be decided with more certainty than in the Socratic dialogues. There is no doubt that Socrates was accused and sentenced. It is also certain, therefore, that he defended himself in an oration. That Plato was present during the trial is said explicitly, and must be understood as obvious anyway. It is not necessary that the *Apology*, as Plato has written it, is a literal transcription of the defense oration. It is unknown when Plato wrote the *Apology*. It can hardly be later than 390 B.C., maybe even earlier—that is, less than ten years after the trial itself. This was a short span of time, under Athenian circumstances; the Platonic dialogues, in so far as they are retold by Plato, presuppose much longer intervals of time after which, according to the presupposition of each dialogue, their reproduction takes place. One must assume with certainty that Plato worked over the *Apology*, again and again recomposing it. And probably he elaborated the decisive moments in the written reproduction with more distinctness and meaningfulness than did Socrates in the spoken delivery.

In the *Apology*, Socrates' ignorance plays a significant role. Socrates tells of Chairephon, his lifelong friend who had died not long before the trial, and whose brother was still alive and was present at the trial. Chairephon had gone to Delphi and had asked the oracle if there was someone who was wiser than Socrates. Pythia had denied that someone was wiser (21 A). This tale is peculiar and yet trustworthy, and as good an expert on Greece as Wilamowitz-Möllendorf regards it as truthful. Doubtless, then, Socrates must have been known throughout both Athens and the country. The latter fact may well be assumed, and in Athens, Socrates must have been known to everyone at the time when Aristophanes wrote about him in his bitter satire *The Clouds*.

Socrates finds the answer of Pythia peculiar. Thus, he wants to find out in his conversations with statesmen, with poets, with workers, whether they are wiser than he himself. He finds, in these conversations, that the others believe they know something, but do not really know it. Socrates does not know anything either, but he does not believe that he knows it; he knows that he does not know it (21 D). In this connection occurs a remark which throws light on the Socratic dialogues and their interpretation: "Those present, namely, assume, whenever I succeed in disproving another person's claim to wisdom in a given subject, that I know everything about that subject myself" (23 A). But Socrates does not claim such knowledge to be his; he knows that he does not know.

Returning from this Socratic self-interpretation in the *Apology* to the Socratic dialogues, the supposition that Socrates knows what bravery is is indeed prohibited. Thus, starting from the Socratic self-interpretation in the *Apology*, one has to read, in my opinion, the text of the Socratic dialogues exactly as it is written. During the conversation one really does not find out what bravery is, and no one has a right to substitute an answer which Socrates consciously hides. That the other moment in the Socratic dialogues, the demand for logical determination, does not appear in the *Apology* is, in my opinion, completely understandable from the situation of the *Apology*.

If one wants to understand the Socratic dialogues, and through them Socrates himself, he has to combine the two fundamental moments in question. The process of critical examination gets its true significance only if it is not terminated with an absolutely definitive answer. And the fact that none of the answers holds absolutely must never lead to skepticism, a skepticism which would surrender the search for truth. The realization that we have not discovered what truth is must be followed by the understanding every Socratic conversation ends with: Tomorrow we shall search again.

3. Types of Value
INTRINSIC VALUE

Psychotherapy and the Value of a Human Being

ALBERT ELLIS

ALMOST ALL MODERN AUTHORITIES in psychotherapy believe that the individual's estimation of his own value, or worth, is exceptionally important and that if he seriously denigrates himself or has a poor self-image, he will impair his normal functioning and make himself miserable in many significant ways. Consequently, one of the main functions of psychotherapy, it is usually held, is to enhance the individual's self-respect (or "ego-strength," "self-confidence," "self-esteem," "feelings of personal worth," or "sense of identity") so that he may thereby solve the problem of self-evaluation (See references: Adler, 1927, 1931; Ellis, 1962, 1966; Ellis and Harper, 1967; Kelly, 1955; Lecky, 1945; Rogers, 1961).

When an individual does not value himself very highly, innumerable problems result. He frequently will focus so intensely on what a rotten person he is that he will distract himself from problem-solving and will become increasingly inefficient. He may falsely conclude that a rotter such as he can do virtually nothing right, and he may stop trying to succeed at the things he wants to accomplish. He may look at his proven advantages with a jaundiced eye and tend to conclude that he is a "phony" and that people just haven't as yet seen through him. Or he may become so intent on "proving" his value that he will be inclined to grovel for others' favors and approval and will conformingly give up his own desires for what he thinks (rightly or wrongly) they want him to do (Ellis, 1967; Hoffer, 1955; Lecky, 1945; Nietzsche, 1965). He may tend to annihilate himself, either literally or figuratively, as he desperately tries to achieve or to please (Becker, 1964; Hess, 1966; Watzlawick, 1967). He may favor noncommitment and avoidance, and become essentially "nonalive" (May, 1967). He may sabotage many or most of his potentialities for creative living (Gardner, 1964). He may become obsessed with comparing himself to others and their achievements and tend to be status-seeking rather than joy-exploring (Farson, 1966; Harris, 1963). He may frequently be anxious, panicked, terrified (Branden, 1964; Ellis, 1962; Coopersmith, 1968; Rosenberg, 1962). He may tend to be a short-range hedonist and to lack self-discipline (Hoffer, 1955). Often he may become defensive and thus act in a "superior," grandiose way (Adler, 1964; Anderson, 1962, 1964; Low, 1967). He may compensatingly assume an unusually rough or "masculine" manner (Adler, 1931; Maslow, 1966). He may become quite hostile toward others (Anderson, 1964; Low, 1967). He may become exceptionally depressed (Anderson, 1964). He may withdraw from reality and retreat into fantasy (Coopersmith, 1968; Rosenberg, 1962). He may become exceptionally guilty (Ellis, 1967; Geis, 1965). He may present a great false front to the world (Rosenberg, 1962). He may sabotage a number of special talents which he possesses (Coopersmith, 1968). He may easily become conscious of his lack of self-approval, may berate himself for having little or no confidence in himself, and may thereby reduce his self-image even more than he has done previously (Ellis, 1962; Ellis and Harper, 1967). He may become afflicted with numerous psychosomatic reactions, which then encourage him to defame himself still more (Coopersmith, 1968; Rosenberg, 1962).

This list is hardly exhaustive since almost the entire psychotherapeutic literature of the last fifty years is more or less concerned with the harm an individual may do himself and how badly he may maim or destroy his relations with others when he condemns himself, makes himself feel guilty or ashamed about his acts or inactions, and otherwise lowers his self-image. This same literature illustrates the corollary proposition almost endlessly; namely, that when a human being somehow manages to accept, respect, and approve of himself, in most instances his behavior changes remarkably for the better: his efficiency considerably improves, his anxiety, guilt, depression, and rage lessen, and he becomes much less emotionally disturbed.

An obvious question therefore presents itself: If the individual's perception of his own value, or worth, so importantly affects his thoughts, emotions, and actions, how is it possible to help him consistently to appraise himself so that, no matter what kind of performances he achieves and no matter how popular or unpopular he is in his relations with others, he almost invariably accepts or respects himself? Oddly enough, modern psychotherapy has not often posed this question—at least not in the form just stated. Instead, it has fairly consistently asked another, and actually almost antithetical, question: Since the individual's self-acceptance seems to depend on (1) his succeeding or achieving reasonably well in his society and on (2) his having good relations with others, how can he be helped to accomplish these two goals and thereby to achieve self-esteem?

Self-acceptance and self-esteem may seem, at first blush, to be very similar; but actually, when they are clearly defined, they are quite different. Self-esteem—as it is fairly consistently used by Branden (1964), Rand (1961, 1964), and other devotees of Ayn Rand's objectivist philosophy—means that the individual values himself because he has behaved intelligently, correctly, or competently. When taken to its logical extremes, it "is the consequence, expression and reward of a mind *fully* committed to reason" (Branden, 1965; italics mine); and "an *unbreached rationality*—that is, an unbreached determination to use one's mind to the fullest extent of one's ability, and a refusal *ever* to evade one's knowledge or act against it—is the *only* valid criterion of virtue and the *only* possible basis of authentic self-esteem" (Branden, 1967; italics mine).

Self-acceptance, on the other hand, means that the individual fully and unconditionally accepts himself whether or not he behaves intelligently, correctly, or competently and whether or not other people approve, respect, or love him (Bone, 1968; Ellis, 1962, 1966; Rogers, 1961). Whereas, therefore, only well-behaving (not to mention perfectly behaving) individuals can merit and feel self-esteem, virtually all humans are capable of feeling self-acceptance. And since the number of consistently well-behaving individuals in this world appears usually to be exceptionally small and the number of exceptionally fallible and often ill-behaving persons appears to be legion, the consistent achievement of self-esteem by most of us would seem to be remote while the steady feeling of self-acceptance would seem to be quite attainable.

Those psychotherapists, therefore, who think and practice in terms of their clients' achieving a high measure of self-esteem or of highly conditional, positive self-regard are clearly misguided. What they had better more realistically aim for would be to help these clients attain self-acceptance or *un*conditional positive regard. But even the very term *unconditional positive regard*, which was originally coined by Carl Rogers (1951, 1961), tends to have misleading overtones, since, in our culture, we usually regard someone positively because of a good thing that he has done, for some beauty or strength of character he possesses, or for some talent or particular achievement. Rogers, however, really seems to mean that the individual can be accepted, and can accept himself, without reference to *regard* or achievement; or that, as I have noted elsewhere, he can accept himself just because he is he, because he is alive, because he exists (Ellis, 1962, 1966, 1968, 1971; Ellis and Gullo, 1971).

It is mainly philosophers, and existentialist philosophers in particular, who have honestly and determinedly tackled the problem of human value and who have tried to determine what the individual can do to see himself as a worthwhile being even when he is not behaving in a notably competent, successful, or supposedly deserving way. Among these philosophers, Robert S. Hartman has led all the rest. No one has given more time and thought to the general problem of value than he; and no one, to my knowledge, has come up with a better explication of intrinsic value, or a human being's worth to himself, than has Hartman.

According to Hartman's theory "value is the degree in which a thing fulfills its concept. There are three kinds of concept—*abstract, construct,* and *singular.* Correspondingly, there are three kinds of value: (1) *systemic* value, as the fulfillment of the construct, (2) *extrinsic* value, as the fulfillment of the abstract, and (3) *intrinsic* value, as the fulfillment of the singular concept. The difference between these three concepts is that a construct is *finite,* the abstract is *denumerably infinite,* and the singular is *non-denumerably infinite*" (Hartman, 1959, p. 18).

By sticking to these highly original and well-delineated concepts of value, Hartman is able to concentrate upon the exceptionally important idea of intrinsic value and, by its use, to prove, as well as I have ever seen anyone prove, that the human individual is fully and unconditionally acceptable in his own right, as a unique and singular person; that he always has value to himself, as long as he is alive; and that his intrinsic worth, or self-image, need not depend in any way on his extrinsic value, or worth to others. Hartman gives several reasons why an individual may invariably accept himself, or consider himself good or valuable in spite of his talents and achievements or lack thereof. These reasons include:

1. A thing is good if it fulfills the definition of its concept. A "good man," therefore, is a person who fulfills the definition of a man—that is, one who is alive, who has arms, legs, eyes, a mouth, a voice, etc. In this sense a Martian might well not be a good man; but virtually every alive Earthian would be (Hartman, 1967a, p. 103).

2. "It is infinitely more valuable, in the strictly defined sense of infinity, to be a morally good person than to be a good member of society, say a good conductor, baker, or professor. To be sincere, honest, or authentic in whatever one does is infinitely more important that what one does" (Hartman, 1967a, p. 115). As long, therefore, as a man is sincere, honest, and authentic—as long as he is truly himself—he has great intrinsic value, no matter what his fellowmen may think of him.

3. Man can think about an infinite number of items in the universe and he may think *that* he is thinking about each of these items. He can also think that his thoughts about his thinking are being thought, and so on ad infinitum. Hence he is essentially infinite—"a spiritual *Gestalt* whose cardinality is that of the continuum. This cardinality, however, is that of the entire space-time universe itself. The result of this axiological proof of the value of man is that every individual person is as infinite as the whole space-time universe" (Hartman, 1967a, pp. 117–18). In any axiological system, therefore, man's intrinsic value is above all other values, and he must be conceived of as being valuable or good.

4. "Being is extensionally the totality of all beings. Intensionally, it

is the totality of all consistently thinkable properties: it is that than which nothing richer in properties can be thought. But if Being is this totality, then by the definition of good given by the Axiom, Being is good. For if Being is the totality of all consistently thinkable properties, its goodness is the secondary property defined by this totality—good is a property of the set of properties that define Being" (Hartman, 1967, p. 119).

5. If man does not accept the intrinsic value of a human being as more important than his extrinsic value to others, if he does not learn that "intrinsic value has nothing to do with what a person does, but only with what he is," he will not see the injustices that he does to himself and others, will lose out on life and love, and will create a world of death and desolation. Pragmatically, therefore, for his own self-preservation and happiness, he had best fully accept the premise that he is good because he exists (Hartman, 1960, p. 22).

6. "I have moral value in the degree that I fulfill my own definition of myself. This definition is: 'I am I.' Thus, in the degree that I *am* I, I am a morally good person. Moral goodness is the depth of man's own being himself. That is the greatest goodness in the world" (Hartman, 1962, p. 20).

7. "Who gives me my definition of myself? Of course, nobody can give me the definition of myself but myself. So, I defined man as *the being that has its own definition of itself within itself.* ... Now, then, I know I am human if I have my own definition of myself within myself. What then is the property I have to fulfill to be a good myself? Precisely this: to be conscious of myself, to define myself—for to define myself, to be conscious of myself—that *is* the definition of myself. *The more, therefore, I am conscious of myself, the more, and the more clearly*, I define myself—the more I am a good person." All one has to do, then, to be good, is to be conscious of himself (Hartman, 1962, p. 11).

8. "This is the important thing, you cannot fully be systemic or extrinsic unless you are fully intrinsic, fully yourself. In other words, the moral man will also be a better accountant, pilot, or surgeon. The value dimensions are within each other. The systematic, the social, and the human envelop each other. The human contains the social, and the social the systematic. The lower value is within the higher. The systemic is within the extrinsic, and the extrinsic within the intrinsic. The more fully you are yourself, the better you will be at your job and in your social role, and in your thinking. Out of your intrinsic being you summon the resources to be anything you want to be. Thus, the intrinsic, the development of your inner self, is not a luxury. It is a necessity for your own being yourself in all three dimensions" (Hartman, 1962, p. 31).

9. "Man as personality, as intrinsic value, is in a dimension which makes him not more valuable—for the intrinsic value is not comparable —but incomparably valuable in comparison to the whole extrinsic world, the physical universe. This world is *nothing* compared to the intrinsic value of one person" (Hartman, 1962, p. 95).

10. Extrinsic value of an individual depends on his fulfilling an abstract concept of what a human being should be, while intrinsic value depends on his fulfilling a singular concept. His intrinsic or personal value, therefore, cannot be measured in extrinsic terms; and he is, consequently, good within his own right, as a singular person (Hartman, 1959).

11. "A person's arrival in the world is a cosmic event because of the unlimited possibilities of the human person" (Hartman, 1967b, p. 2). Consequently, if the world has any value, the person and his existence should have as much or more value.

12. "Once one starts with the axiom of value, namely that value is richness of properties, then, since man is an infinity of properties, it is impossible to say that he may be bad. All thus depends on the definition of 'good,' and this is a definition in value theory which has to be accepted or else a new value theory has to be designed" (Hartman, 1967b, p. 3).

Although these arguments of Hartman may not be definitive or unchallengeable, they certainly provide much useful material which any bright and philosophically oriented psychotherapist may use to combat his clients' overwhelming fears that their traits and abilities are far from ideal, that many people whom they encounter more or less disapprove of them, and that therefore their intrinsic value, or self-worth (which they importantly correlate with their extrinsic value, or worth to others), is abysmally low. I have used Hartman's kind of existential arguments with self-deprecating clients for a good many years now, and I have usually found that they work rather well. For if a disturbed individual insists that he is worthless and hopeless, it does not take me very long to show him that this "fact" is really an hypothesis and that although he may think he can substantiate it with some kind of evidence, he actually cannot. Since, moreover, his stubbornly maintaining this hypothesis inevitably leads him to dismal results, he had damned well better give it up—and he usually, at least to some degree, does.

As Hartman himself notes, however, especially when he admits that a man's accepting himself as a good person "all . . . depends on the definition of 'good'," the basic argument in favor of the theory that man has intrinsic value and that he cannot possibly be worthless is essentially tautological and definitional. There is really no empirical evidence to back (or confute) it, and it looks very much as though there never will be any. True, it has a strong pragmatic appeal; for if the opposite point is made, and it is held that man in general or a man in particular is bad or unworthy of his own or others' respect, dire consequences will ensue. Therefore, he had bloody well better accept his "goodness" rather than his "badness," if he is to survive long and happily.

I am hardly opposed to this pragmatic argument, as I doubt any effective psychotherapist would be. The trouble, however, is with the inelegance of the philosophic premise that goes with it. Granted that man's thinking of himself as bad or worthless is usually pernicious and that his thinking of himself as good or worthwhile is more beneficial, I see no reason why these two hypotheses exhaust the possibilities of useful choices. I believe, instead, that there is a third choice that is much more philosophically elegant, less definitional, and more likely to conform to empirical reality. And that is the seldom-posited assumption that value is a meaningless term when applied to man's being, that it is invalid to call him either "good" or "bad," and that if educators and psychotherapists can teach people to give up all "ego" concepts and to have no "self-images" whatever, they may considerably help the human dilemma and enable men and women to be much less emotionally disturbed than they now tend to be.

Must man actually be a self-evaluator? Yes and no. On the yes side he clearly seems to be the kind of animal who is not merely reared but is also born with strong self-evaluating tendencies. For nowhere in the world, to my knowledge, does civilized man simply accept that he is alive, go about the business of discovering how he can enjoy himself more and discomfort himself less, and live his century or so of existence in a reasonably unselfconscious, nondamning, and nondeifying manner. Instead he invariably seems to identify and rate his *self* as well as his *performances*, to be highly ego-involved about accomplishing this and avoiding that deed, and to believe and feel strongly that he will end up in some kind of heaven or hell if he does the "right" and eschews the "wrong" thing.

Take, for example, the extremely permissive, hedonistic-oriented people of Polynesia and, especially, of Tahiti. The Polynesians, as Danielsson (1956, 1961) reports, are still pleasure-seeking and careless, are outspoken in sex matters, are premaritally free, have erotic dances, delight in sexual games, practice free love without legal weddings, and are fairly free extramaritally; and in the not-too-distant past they also practiced polygyny and wife-lending, danced in the nude, engaged in sexual intercourse in public, had pleasure houses for young people, permitted periodic sexual liberty, and encouraged deflowering ceremonies.

At the same time, however, the Polynesians have many tabus, the violation of which makes them feel utterly ashamed and self-hating. To this day, for instance, they seriously adhere to circumcision rites when the male reaches puberty; they have separate eating and sleeping houses; and they cling to rigid division of work between the sexes. In the past, moreover, they have practiced sexual privileges based on birth and rank, obligatory marriage of widows, ritual continence, the forbidding of women to concern themselves with religious matters, and the isolation of females during periods of menstruation. Religiously and politically they have been very strict: "The Polynesian chiefs and nobles would certainly never have been able to maintain their provocative privileges in the long run if they had not had an effective support in religion. According to the Polynesian religious doctrine they were descended from gods and were thus holy and unassailable. . . . The Polynesian gods required sacrifices, on many islands even human sacrifices. Nothing, therefore, was easier and more natural for a devout chief than to get rid of all troublesome persons by sacrificing them. . . . In Tahiti the most powerful rulers were always carried by a servant when they wanted to go anywhere, for if they touched the earth the owner would not be able to tread on it in future . . . . Certain Hawaiian potentates were so holy that subjects had to stop working at once, throw themselves flat on the ground and remain in that position so long as the rulers were in sight; so in order not to paralyze the food supply the rulers inspected the fields by night. Most Polynesian chiefs could not eat with their families, and on certain islands they were actually so full of mana that they could not eat at all, but had to be fed" (Danielsson, 1956, pp. 52–53).

General discipline in Polynesia, moreover, has been and still, to a considerable degree, is based on exceptionally ego-raising and ego-debasing rules: "Polynesian ethics were certainly far from being as charitable as the Christian, and what was permitted a chief was often forbidden to his subjects, but on the other hand the existing rules were infinitely better observed than they are with us. The cause of this strict discipline was, of course, that public opinion in the small Polynesian communities or tribes had a strength and importance which even a newly arrived schoolmistress or a curate in a remote country district can hardly imagine. Public disapproval was in Polynesia simply intolerable, and there was as a rule no possibility of moving to another district or island on account of the enmity between the different tribes. Good behavior was therefore a primary necessity . . . . Although contrary views have sometimes been expressed, the Polynesians were not moral anarchists, but rather slaves of custom" (Danielsson, 1956, p. 55).

I have quoted at length here to show that even among one of the most sexually permissive and easy-going groups of which we have knowledge, rules and rites of "proper" conduct are the norm rather than the exception, and humans become so ego-involved in following these rules and so ashamed to break them that they literally hurt or kill themselves and easily permit themselves to be severely punished or sacrificed when they flout these publicly approved regulations. If there ever was a culture in which practically all the members did not similarly denigrate themselves and bring severe emotional or physical penalties on their own heads for engaging in "wrong" or "bad" behavior, I have never heard of it and would be delighted to learn about it.

The reason, I believe, for this practically universal tendency of man to put himself down, as well as to rate some of his ineffective performances negatively, is his biological predisposition to be what we call self-conscious. Certainly many of the lower animals (especially the mammals and primates) seem to be somewhat aware of "themselves," in that they "know" or "learn" that one kind of behavior (e. g., going where food is likely to be) is more "rewarding" or "reinforcing" than another kind of behavior (e. g., randomly exploring their environment). But these lower animals act much more instinctively than does man, meaning that they "think" about their actions much less than he does; they rarely, if ever, appear to think about their thinking; and it is probably impossible for them to think about thinking about their thinking. In the usual sense of the word, therefore, they have no "selves," and are not particularly aware that "they" are responsible for their own "good" or "bad" acts and that, consequently, "they" are "good" or "bad" individuals. In other words, they are only to a limited degree, if at all, what we call ego-involved in their performances.

Man, on the contrary, not only has a strong "self-awareness" or "ego," but he also has an exceptionally strong, and I again think innate, tendency to tie it up with his deeds. Since he is a thin-skinned and highly vulnerable animal (as compared, say, to the rhinoceros, which can be quite careless about its behavior and is not likely to suffer ill effects) and since he relies so heavily on cognition rather than instinct for his survival, it is greatly to his advantage that he observe and appraise his actions to see whether they are satisfaction- or pain-producing and to keep modifying them in one direction or another. Unfortunately, however, just as he protectively rates his performances in relation to his own survival and happiness, he also dysfunctionally tends to rate his self; and he thereby almost inevitably does himself in.

Let me graphically illustrate this human tendency with a typical case of *rational-emotive psychotherapy*, which is a system of therapy based on the hypothesis that people become emotionally disturbed by foolishly rating or giving report cards to their selves as well as to their deeds. Mr. Richard Roe comes to see me because he is terribly depressed about his work and because he frequently becomes enraged at his wife and acts cruelly to her when she has her minor lapses of decorum. I first show him, perhaps in a session or two of psychotherapy, how and why he is making himself depresed. At point A, an *action* exists—he is not doing well at his work and his boss is consistently bringing his poor performance to his attention. At point C—the emotional *consequence*—he is becoming depressed. Quite wrongly he concludes that the action at point A is causing his disturbed emotional reaction, or consequence, at point C: "Because I am working inefficiently and because my boss is displeased and may fire me, I am depressed." But if A really caused C, I quickly show him, magic or voodoo would exist: for how can an external event (his inefficiency or his boss's disapproval) cause him to think or to feel anything?

Obviously, Roe is doing something about these outside actions to make himself suffer the consequence of depression. Probably he is first observing these actions (noticing that his performance is inefficient and that his boss is disapproving) and then reflecting on them (thinking about their possible effects and appraising how he would dislike these effects). Moreover, he is appraising these possible results in a highly negative way. For if he were not noticing his poor work or if he were appraising it as a good thing (because it would enable him to get fired from a job he really did not want), he would hardly feel depressed. In fact, he might feel elated!

It is almost certain, therefore, that Roe is signaling, imagining, or telling himself something at point B (his *belief system*) to produce his depressed reactions at point C. Most probably, he is first telling himself a *rational belief* (point rB): "I see that I am working inefficiently and that my boss may fire me; and if he did, that would be unfortunate. I certainly wouldn't like being fired." This rB belief is rational because, in all probability, it would be unfortunate if he were fired. He would then (1) be without income, (2) have to look for another job, (3) possibly have to put up with a displeased wife, and (4) perhaps have to take a worse or lower-paying position; etc. There are several good, empirically ascertainable reasons why it would not be pleasant if he were fired. Therefore, his rB hypothesis that it would be unfortunate for him to keep working inefficiently is a sane, verifiable proposition.

If, moreover, Roe held rigorously to his rB conclusion, he would most probably never feel depressed. Instead, he would feel the *rational consequences* (rC) of displeasure, disappointment, sorrow, regret, annoyance, or feeling of frustration. These are all negative emotions but are far from the feeling of depression. In order to make himself feel the *irrational consequence* (iC) of depression, he would almost certainly have to add to his rational belief an inappropriate, self-defeating, self-denigrating *irrational belief* (iB): "If I keep working inefficiently and am fired, that would be awful. I couldn't stand his disapproving of me and firing me. Not only would that action show that my work is poor, but it would also conclusively prove that I am pretty worthless; that I can never do well on a job like this; and that I deserve to be poor, unloved, and otherwise punished for the rest of my life for being such a slob!"

Roe's irrational belief is inappropriate for several reasons: (1) it is definitional and unverifiable. However unfortunate his working inefficiently and his being fired may be, it is only "awful," "terrible," or "catastrophic" because he thinks it is. Actually it is still only unfortunate or inconvenient. (2) It is an over generalization. Because he doesn't like being fired hardly means that he can't stand it. Because his work is inefficient does not prove that he, a human being, is no good. Because he now works poorly is not evidence that he will always do so. (3) It is a non sequitur. If he really were a worthless individual who could never succeed at any job, why should he deserve to be unloved and punished? Being thus handicapped, he might well be said to deserve an unusual degree of love and help from the rest of us less-handicapped humans. What just person or deity would ever condemn him for having been born and reared to be deficient? (4) It almost invariably leads to dreadful and even more unfortunate results than those which Roe may naturally derive from his inefficient work behavior. For if he thinks it awful to be disapproved of and cannot stand being dismissed, he will probably make himself so anxious that his job efficiency will deteriorate rather than improve, and he will stand even less chance of keeping his job. Moreover, if his boss lets him go and he concludes that, therefore, he is worthless, he will tend, on future jobs, to act as if he were unable to perform, and he will bring about his self-fulfilling prophecy—he will not do well and will be dismissed again (thereby falsely "proving" his original hypothesis).

As a rational-emotive psychotherapist, therefore, I will clearly show Roe what his rational beliefs and irrational beliefs are; I will try to help him discriminate his sensible rB from his foolish iB hypotheses; and I will indicate how he can keep his rB appraisals of his performances and feel rational consequences (sorrow, regret, displeasure, increased effort to work more efficiently) and to minimize or eliminate his iB appraisals and their irrational consequences (feelings of panic, depression, increased inefficiency, etc.).

Similarly, I will explain and help change Roe's feelings of rage against his wife. I will show him that when her actions, at point A, are inconsiderate, impolite, or unjust, he is probably first signaling himself the rational belief, "I don't like her behavior; I wish she would change it; what a nuisance!" At point rC, he is consequently experiencing the rational consequences—that is, emotions of dissatisfaction, disappointment, frustration, and annoyance. At point iB, he has the irrational belief "Because she is acting badly, I can't stand it. She is a horrible person. I'll never be able to forgive her for acting like that. She deserves to suffer eternally and to be eventually roasted in hell for the awful way she is treating me!" He, consequently, at point iC, feels the irrational consequences of rage and self-pity. If I can induce Roe to retain his sensible rB hypotheses and to surrender his condemnatory iB hypotheses, he will tend to feel displeasure but not rage, and he will probably have a better chance of helping his wife change her unpleasing behavior.

The main point here is that the actions that occur in Roe's (or anyone's) life at point A do not cause or make him feel depressed or enraged at point C. Rather, his thoughts, appraisals, and evaluations—his beliefs at point B—create these feelings. To a large degree he has a choice at point A about what he will feel at point C regarding the actions or agents in his life—as long as he thinks about his thinking, challenges some of his iB conceptions and conclusions, and returns to his empirically based rB hypotheses. Being, however, born and raised a human, he easily and naturally tends to make a magical jump from rB to iB conclusions; and, much more often than not, he confuses his self, his total personality, with his performances, and he automatically evaluates and rates the former along with the latter. Consequently, he very frequently ends up by damning himself and other people (that is, denigrating his and their intrinsic value) rather than merely appraising the efficacy or desirability of his or their performances (his and their extrinsic value). He thereby gets into all kinds of needless difficulties, or emotional problems, with himself and with others.

Again, I ask: Must man be a self-evaluator? And again I answer: Yes, to some degree he must, since it is biologically and sociologically almost impossible for him not to do so. In terms of self-preservation, if he did not constantly evaluate his performances, he would soon be dead: for before he can safely drive a car, climb a mountain, or cultivate a certain kind of food, he had better know how competent he is likely to be in these respects, else he will maim or kill himself. So, to survive, he really has to assess his deeds and his potentials.

Self-appraisal, moreover, has distinct advantages as well as disadvantages. If you (unempirically and unscientifically) rate your self, your being, as "good," "great," or "noble" when you succeed in love, work well on your job, or paint a fine canvas, you will tend, at least for awhile, to be much happier than if you merely rate your performance in a similar manner. If you (unrealistically) appraise your girl friend or your wife as being a "glorious," "marvelous," or "goddess-like" person when you (more accurately) really mean that she has some highly desirable and pleasing traits, you will also tend to feel ecstatic about your relations with her. Man, as May (1967, 1969) has strongly pointed out, largely lives with demons and deities, and it is silly to think that he does not gain much by doing so.

But is it really worth it? Does man absolutely have to rate himself as a person and evaluate others as people? My tentative answer to both these questions, after spending a quarter of a century busily engaged as a psychotherapist, writer, teacher, and lecturer, is no. Man has an exceptionally strong, inborn, and socially acquired tendency to be a self- and an other-appraiser; but by very hardheaded thinking, along with active work and practice, he can persistently fight against and minimize this tendency; and if he does, he will, in all probability, be considerably healthier and happier than he usually is. Instead of strongly evaluating his and other people's selves, he can pretty rigorously stick to rating only performances; instead of damning or deifying anyone or anything, he can adhere to reality and be truly demonless and godless; and instead of inventing demands and needs, he can remain with desires and preferences. If he does so, I hypothesize, he will not achieve utopia (which itself is changeless, absolutistic, and unrealistic) but he most probably will achieve more spontaneity, creativity, and satisfaction than he has ever previously achieved or presently tends to attain. Some of the main reasons for my espousing man's taking a non-evaluative attitude toward himself (while still evaluating many of his traits and performances) are as follows:

1. Both positive and negative self-evaluation are inefficient and often seriously interfere with problem-solving. If one elevates or defames himself because of his performances, he will tend to be self-centered rather than problem-centered, and these performances will, consequently, tend to suffer. Self-evaluation, moreover, is usually ruminative and absorbs enormous amounts of time and energy. By it one may possibly cultivate his "soul" but hardly his garden!

2. Self-rating only works well when one has many talents and few flaws; but, statistically speaking, few are in that class. It also tends to demand universal competence. But, again, few can measure up to such a demand.

3. Self-appraisal almost inevitably leads to oneupmanship and one-

downmanship. If one rates himself as being "good," he will usually rate others as being "bad" or "less good." If he rates himself as being "bad," others will be seen as "less bad" or "good." Thereby he practically forces himself to compete with others in "goodness" or "badness" and constantly feels envious, jealous, or superior. Persistent individual, group, and international conflicts easily stem from this kind of thinking and feeling; and love, cooperation, and other forms of fellow-feeling are minimized. To see oneself as having a better or worse *trait* than another person may be unimportant or even beneficial (since one may use his knowledge of another's superior trait to help achieve that trait himself). But to see oneself as being a better or worse *person* than another is likely to cause trouble for both.

4. Self-evaluation enhances self-consciousness and therefore tends to shut one up within himself, to narrow his range of interests and enjoyments. "It should be our endeavor," said Bertrand Russell, "to aim at avoiding self-centered passions and at acquiring those affections and those interests which will prevent our thoughts from dwelling perpetually upon ourselves. It is not the nature of most men to be happy in a prison, and the passions which shut us up in ourselves constitute one of the worst kinds of prisons. Among such passions some of the commonest are fear, envy, the sense of sin, self-pity, and self-admiration" (Russell, 1952).

5. Blaming or praising the whole individual for a few of his acts is an unscientific overgeneralization. "I have called the process of converting a child mentally into something else, whether it be a monster or a mere nonentity, *pathogenic metamorphosis*," Jules Henry declared. "Mrs. Portman called [her son] Pete 'a human garbage pail'; she said to him, 'you smell, you stink'; she kept the garbage bag and refuse newspapers on his high chair when he was not in it; she called him Mr. Magoo, and never used his right name. Thus he was a stinking monster, a nonentity, a buffoon" (Henry, 1963). But Henry failed to point out that had Mrs. Portman called her son, Pete, "an angel" and said to him, "you smell heavenly," she would have equally converted him, by the process of pathogenic metamorphosis, into something he was not; namely, a godlike being. Peter is a human person who sometimes smells bad (or heavenly); he is not a *bad-smelling* (or heavenly smelling) *person*.

6. When human selves are lauded or condemned there is a strong implication that people should be rewarded or punished for being "good" or "bad." But, as noted above, if there were "bad" people, they would already be so handicapped by their "rottenness" that it would be thoroughly unfair to punish them further for being "rotten." And if there

were "good" people, they would already be so favored by their "goodness" that it would be superfluous or unjust to reward them for it. Human justice, therefore, is very badly served by self-evaluations.

7. To rate a person high because of his good traits is often tantamount to deifying him; conversely, to rate him low because of his bad traits is tantamount to demonizing him. But since there seems to be no way of validating the existence of gods and devils and since man can well live without this redundant hypothesis, it merely clutters human thinking and acting and probably does much more harm than good. Concepts of god and the devil, moreover, obviously vary enormously from person to person and from group to group; they add nothing to human knowledge; and they usually serve as obstructions to precise intrapersonal and interpersonal communication. Although it is possible that people who behave stupidly and weakly may derive benefits from inventing supernatural beings, there is no evidence that those who act intelligently and strongly have any need of them.

8. Bigotry and lack of respect for individuals in their own right are consequences of self- and other-evaluation. For if you accept A because he is white, Episcopalian, and well educated and reject B because he is black, Baptist, and a high school dropout, you are clearly not respecting B as a human—and, of course, are intolerantly disrespecting millions of people like him. Bigotry is arbitrary, unjust, and conflict-creating; it is ineffective for social living. As George Axtelle has noted, "Men are profoundly social creatures. They can realize their own ends more fully only as they respect one another as ends in themselves. Mutual respect is an essential condition of effectiveness both individually and socially. Its opposites, hatred, contempt, segregation, exploitation, frustrate the realization of values for all concerned and hence they are profoundly destructive of all effectiveness" (Axtelle, 1956). Once you damn an individual, including yourself, for having or lacking any trait whatever, you become authoritarian or fascistic; for fascism is the very essence of people-evaluation (Ellis, 1965a, 1965b).

9. By evaluating an individual, even if only in a complimentary way, one is often trying to change him or trying to control or manipulate him; and the kind of change envisioned may or may not be good for him. "Often," Richard Farson notes, "the change which praise asks one to make is not necessarily beneficial to the person being praised but will redound to the convenience, pleasure or profit of the praiser" (Farson, 1966). Evaluation may induce the individual to feel obligated to his evaluator; and to the degree that he lets himself feel compelled or obligated to change himself, he may be much less of the self that he would

really like to be. Positive or negative evaluation of a person, therefore, may well encourage him to be less of a self or of a self-directed individual than he would enjoy being.

10. Evaluation of the individual tends to bolster the Establishment and to block social change. For when one gives himself a report card he not only becomes accustomed to telling himself, "My deeds are wrong, and I think I'd better work at improving them in the future," but also, "I am wrong, I am a 'no-goodnik' for performing these poor deeds." Since "wrong" acts are largely measured by societal standards, and since most societies are run by a limited number of "upper level" people who have a strong, vested interest in keeping them the way they are, self-evaluation usually encourages the individual to go along with social rules, no matter how arbitrary or foolish they are, and especially to woo the approval of the powers-that-be. Conformism, which is one of the worst products of self-rating, generally means conformity to the time-honored and justice-dishonoring rules of the "Establishment."

11. Self-appraisal and the measuring of others tends to sabotage empathic listening. Close and authentic relationships between two people, as Richard Farson points out, are often achieved through intensive listening: "This does not merely mean to wait for a person to finish talking, but to try to see how the world looks to this person and to communicate this understanding to him. This empathic, non-evaluative listening responds to the person's feelings as well as to his words; that is, to the total meaning of what he is trying to say. It implies no evaluation, no judgment, no agreement (or disagreement). It simply conveys an understanding of what the person is feeling and attempting to communicate; and his feelings and ideas are accepted as being valid for him, if not for the listener" (Farson, 1966). When, however, one evaluates a person (and oneself) as one listens to the other person, one is usually prejudicedly blocked from fully understanding him, seeing him as he is, and uncompetitively understanding and getting close to him.

12. Person-rating tends to denigrate human wants, desires, and preferences and to replace them with demands, compulsions, or needs. If you do not measure your selfness, you tend to spend your days asking yourself, "Now what would I really like to do, in my relatively brief span of existence, to gain maximum satisfaction and minimum pain?" If you do measure your selfhood, you tend to keep asking, "What do I have to do to prove that I am a worthwhile person?" As Richard Robertiello has observed, "People are constantly negating their right to take something just purely because they want it, to enjoy something simply because they enjoy it. They can hardly ever let themselves take anything for pure pleasure without justifying it on the basis of having

earned it or suffered enough to be entitled to it or rationalizing that, though they enjoy it, it is really an altruistic act that they are doing for someone else's good. . . . It seems as if the greatest crime is to do something simply because we enjoy it and without any thought of doing good for anyone else or of serving an absolute need in us that is essential for our continued survival" (Robertiello, 1964). Such is the folly born of self-deservingness!

13. Placing a value on a human being tends to sabotage his free will. One has little enough self-direction in the normal course of events!—since even his most "voluntary" activities are significantly influenced by his heredity and environment; and when he thinks that one of his thoughts, feelings, or actions is really "his," he is ignoring some of its most important biosocial causes. As soon as one labels himself as "good" or "bad," as a "genius" or as an "idiot," he so seriously stereotypes himself that he will almost certainly bias and influence much of his subsequent behavior. For how can a "bad person" or an "idiot" determine, even to a small degree, what his future actions will be, and how can he work hard at achieving his goals? Moreover, how can a "good person" do non-good acts, or a "genius" turn out mediocre works along with his outstanding ones? What asinine, creativity-downing restrictions one almost automatically places on himself when he thinks in terms of these general designations of his selfness!

14. To give a human an accurate global rating is probably impossible for several reasons:

a. The traits by which he is to be rated are very likely to change from year to year, even from moment to moment. Man is not a thing or an object, but a process. How can an ever-changing process be precisely measured and rated?

b. The characteristics by which a person is to be evaluated have no absolute scale by which they can be judged. Traits which are highly honored in one social group are roundly condemned in another. A murderer may be seen as a horrible criminal by a judge but as a marvelous soldier by a general. A man's qualities (such as his ability to compose music) may be deemed fine in one century and mediocre in a later age.

c. To rate a human globally, special weights would have to be given to each kind of positive and negative action that he performed. Thus, if a man did a friend a small favor and also worked very hard to save a hundred people from drowning, his latter act would normally be given a much higher rating than his former act; and if he told a lie to his wife and also battered a child, his second deed would be considered much more heinous than his first. But who is to give an exact weight to his various deeds, so that it could finally be determined how globally "good" or "bad" he is? It might be convenient if there existed on earth some kind of St. Peter, who would have a record of every single one of his deeds (and, for that matter, his thoughts) and who could quickly assess him as a potential angel or as hell-bound. But what is the likelihood of such a St. Peter's (even in the form of an infallible computer) ever existing?

d. What kind of mathematics could we employ to arrive at a single, total rating of a human being's worth? Suppose an individual does a thousand good acts, and then he fiendishly tortures someone to death. Shall we, to arrive at a general evaluation of his being, add up all his good acts arithmetically and compare this sum to the weighted sum of his bad act? Shall we, instead, use some geometric means of assessing his "goodness" and "badness"? What system shall we employ to "accurately" measure his "value"? Is there, really, any valid kind of mathematical evaluation by which he can be rated?

e. No matter how many traits of an individual are known and employed for his global rating, since it is quite impossible for him or anyone else to discover all his characteristics and to use them in arriving at a single universal rating, in the final analysis the whole of him is being evaluated by some of his parts. But is it ever really legitimate to rate a whole individual by some (or even many) of his parts? Even one unknown, and hence unevaluated, part might significantly change and, hence invalidate the final rating. Suppose, for example, the individual is given (by himself or others) a 91 per cent general rating (that is, is considered to have 91 per cent of "goodness"). If he unconsciously hated his brother most of his life and actually brought about the early demise of this brother, but if he consciously only remembers loving his brother and presumably helping him to live happily, he will rate himself (and anyone but an all-knowing St. Peter will rate him) considerably higher than if he consciously admitted his hatred for his brother and causing this brother needless harm. His "real" rating, therefore, will be considerably lower than 91 per cent; but how will this "real" rating ever be known?

f. If an individual is given a very low global rating by himself and others—say, he winds up with a 13 per cent general report card on himself—it presumably means that (1) he was born a worthless individual; (2) he never possibly could become worthwhile, and (3) he deserves to be punished (and ultimately roasted in some kind of hell) for being hopelessly worthless. All of these are empirically unverifiable hypotheses which can hardly be proved or disproved and which tend (as stated above) to bring about much more harm than good.

g. Measuring a human being is really a form of circular thinking.

If a man is "good" because he has "good" traits, his "goodness," in both instances, is based on some kind of value system that is definitional; for who, again, except some kind of deity is to say what "good" traits truly are? Once his traits are defined as being "good," and his global "goodness" is deduced from his specific "goodnesses," the concept of his being globally "good" will almost inevitably prejudice one's view of his specific traits—which will then seem "more good" than they really may be. And once his traits are defined as being "bad," the concept of his being globally "bad" will almost inevitably prejudice one's view of his specific traits—which will then seem "more bad" than they really may be. If the "good" traits of a person who is rated as being globally "good" are prejudicedly seen as being "more good" than they really are, one will keep seeing him, by prejudice, as being "good," when he may not actually be. Globally rating him, in other words, includes making a prophecy about his specific "good" traits and rating his specific traits as "good" includes making a prophecy about his global "goodness." Both these prophecies, in all probability, will turn out to be "true," whatever the facts of his specific and general "goodness" actually are; for "goodness" itself can never accurately be determined, since the entire edifice of "goodness" is based, as I have said, on concepts which are largely definitional.

h. Perhaps the only sensible way of making a global rating of an individual is on the basis of his aliveness: that is, assuming that he is intrinsically good just because he is human and alive (and that he will be non-good or non-existent when he is dead). Similarly, we can hypothesize, if we want to accept redundant and unnecessary religious assumptions, that an individual is good because he is human and because Jehovah, Jesus, or some other deity in whom he believes accepts, loves, or gives grace to all humans. This is a rather silly assumption, since we know (as well as we know anything) that the individual who believes in this assumed deity exists, while we have no way of proving the existence (or non-existence) of the deity in which he believes. Nonetheless, such an assumption will work, in that it will refer back to the more basic assumption that a human is globally "good" just because he is human and alive. The trouble with this basic concept of general human "goodness" is that it obviously puts *all* humans in the same boat—makes them all equally "good" and leaves no room whatever for any of them to be "bad." Consequently, it is a global rating that is not really a rating, and it is entirely definitional and is rather meaningless.

i. The concept of giving any human a general or global evaluation may be an artifact of the inaccurate way in which almost all humans think and communicate with themselves and each other. Korzybski

(1933, 1951) and some of his main followers, such as Hayakawa (1965) and Bourland (*Time* magazine, 1969), have pointed out for a good many years that just as pencil$_1$ is not the same thing as pencil$_2$, so individual$_1$ is hardly the same as individual$_2$. Consequently, generalizing about pencils and about individuals is never entirely accurate. Bourland has especially campaigned, for the last decade, against our using any form of the verb *to be* when we speak about or categorize the behavior of a person. Thus, it is one thing for us to note that "Jones has (or possesses) some outstanding mathematical qualities" and another to say that "Jones is an outstanding mathematician." The former sentence is much more precise and probably "truer" than the latter. The latter sentence, moreover, implies a global rating of Jones that is hardly warranted by the facts, if these can be substantiated, of Jones's possessing some mathematical qualities. If Korzybski and his followers are correct, as they in all probability (at least to some degree) are, then global terms and ratings of humans are easily made (indeed, it is most difficult for us not to make them) but would better be fought against and transformed into more specific evaluations of their performances, talents, and traits. Such generalized (or overgeneralized) grades exist (since we obviously keep employing them), but it would be much better if we minimized or eliminated them.

j. All of man's traits are different—as apples and pears are different. Just as one cannot legitimately add and divide apples and pears and thereby get a single, accurate global rating of an entire basket of fruit, so one cannot truly add and divide different human traits and thereby obtain a single, meaningful global rating of a human individual.

What conclusions can be drawn from the foregoing observations and deductions about psychotherapy and human value? First, that self-reference and self-evaluation are a normal and natural part of man. It seems to be much easier for him to rate his self, his being, as well as his performances, than it is for him only to assess the latter and not the former.

When man does appraise himself globally, he almost invariably gets into trouble. When he terms himself "bad," "inferior," or "inadequate," he tends to feel anxious, guilty, and depressed, to act below his potential level of efficiency, and to falsely confirm his low estimation of himself. When he terms himself "good," "superior," or "adequate," he tends to feel forever unsure of maintaining his "goodness," to spend considerable time and energy "proving" how worthwhile he is, but still to sabotage his relations with himself and others.

Ideally, it would seem wise for man to train himself, through rigorous thinking about and working against some of his strongest inborn and environmentally bolstered tendencies, to refuse to evaluate himself at all. He had better continue, as objectively as he can, to assess his traits, talents, and performances, so that he can thereby lead a longer, pain-avoiding, and satisfaction-filled life. But, for many reasons which are considered in detail in this chapter, he would better also accept rather than rate his so-called self and strive for the enjoyment rather than the justification of his existence. According to Freud (1963), the individual attains mental health when he follows the rule "Where id was, there shall ego be." Freud, however, did not mean by *ego* man's self-evaluating but his self-directing tendencies. According to my own views (Ellis, 1962, 1966, 1968, 1971) and the principles of rational-emotive therapy, man attains maximum understanding of himself and others and minimum anxiety and hostility when he follows the rule "Where ego was, there shall the person be." By *ego*, of course, I mean man's self-rating and self-justifying tendencies.

For man, as an individual living with other individuals in a world with which he interacts, is too complex to be measured, or given a report card. He may be legitimately "valued," in the sense of accepting and abiding by the empirically determinable facts that (1) he exists, (2) he can suffer satisfaction and pain while he exists, (3) it is usually within his power to continue to exist and to experience more satisfaction than pain, and (4) it is therefore highly probable that he "deserves" to (that is, would better) go on existing and enjoying. Or, more succinctly stated, man has value because he decides to remain alive and to value his existence. Observations and conclusions other than those based on these minimal assumptions may well be foolishly egocentric and fictional, and in the final analysis human—all too human, but still essentially inhumane.

REFERENCES

Adler, Alfred. *Understanding Human Nature*. New York, 1927.
———. *What Life Should Mean to You*. New York, 1931.
———. *Social Interest: A Challenge to Mankind*. New York, 1964.
Anderson, Camilla. *Saints, Sinners and Psychiatry*. Portland, Ore., 1962.
———. "Depression and Suicide Reassessed," reprint from *Journal of the American Medical Woman's Association* (June, 1964).
Axtelle, George E. "Effectiveness as a Value Concept," *Journal of Educational Sociology*, XXIX (1956), 240–46.
Becker, Ernest. *The Revolution in Psychiatry*. New York, 1964.
Bone, Harry. "Two proposed alternatives to psychoanalytic interpreting," in Emanuel F. Hammer, ed., *Use of Interpretation in Treatment* (New York and London, 1968), pp. 169–96.
Bourland, D. David. "Language," *Time* (May 23, 1969), p. 69.

Branden, Nathaniel. "Pseudo-Self-Esteem," *Objectivist Newsletter*, III, No. 6 (June, 1964), pp. 22–23.

————. *Who is Ayn Rand?* New York, 1965.

————. "Self-esteem," *Objectivist*, VI (Mar., 1967), 1–17; (Apr., 1967), 5–10; (May, 1967), 8–10; (June, 1967), 1–4; (Sept., 1967), 5–8.

Coopersmith, Stanley. "Studies in Self-esteem," *Scientific Monthly*, CCXVIII, No. 2, (Feb., 1968), pp. 96–106.

Danielsson, Bengt. *Love in the South Seas*. New York, 1956.

————. "Sex Life in Polynesia," in Albert Ellis and Albert Abarbanel, eds., *The Encyclopedia of Sexual Behavior* (New York, 1967), pp. 832–40.

Ellis, Albert. *Reason and Emotion in Psychotherapy*. New York, 1962.

————. *Sex Without Guilt*. New York, 1965a.

————. *Suppressed: Seven Key Essays Publishers Dared Not Print*. Chicago, 1965b.

————, with Janet L. Wolfe and Sandra Moseley. *How to Prevent Your Child From Becoming a Neurotic Adult*. New York, 1966.

————. "Psychotherapy and Moral Laxity," *Psychiatric Opinion*, IV, No. 5 (1967a), 18–21.

————, and Robert A. Harper. *A Guide to Rational Living* (Englewood Cliffs, N.J., 1967b).

————. *Is Objectivism a Religion?* New York, 1968.

————, and John M. Gullo. *Murder and Assassination*. New York, 1970.

————. *Growth Through Reason*. Palo Alto, 1971.

Farson, Richard A. "Praise Reappraised," *Encounter*, No. 1 (1966), pp. 13–21, reprinted from *Harvard Business Review* (Sept.-Oct., 1963).

Freud, Sigmund. *Collected Papers*. New York, 1963.

Geis, H. Jon. "Guilt Feelings and Inferiority Feelings: an Experimental Comparison," Ph.D. dissertation, Columbia University, 1965.

Harris, Sydney J. "A Man's Worth is Not Relative," *Detroit Free Press*, Dec. 12, 1963.

Hartman, Robert S. *The Measurement of Value*. Crotonville, N.Y., 1959.

————. "Sputnik's Moral Challenge," *Texas Quarterly*, III, No. 3 (Autumn, 1960), pp. 9–22.

————. *The Individual in Management*. Chicago, 1962.

————. *The Structure of Value*. Carbondale, Ill., 1967a.

————. Letter to Albert Ellis, June 27, 1967b.

Hayakawa, S. I. *Language in Action*. New York, 1965.

Henry, Jules. *Culture Against Man*. New York, 1963.

Hess, John L. "Michelin's Two Stars Lost, Paris Chef Shoots Himself," *New York Times*, Oct. 14, 1966, 1, 3.

Hoffer, Eric. *The Passionate State of Mind*. New York, 1955.

Kelly, George. *The Psychology of Personal Constructs*. New York, 1955.

Korzybski, Alfred. *Science and Sanity*. Lancaster, Pa., 1933.

————. "The Role of Language in the Perceptual Process," in R. R. Blake and G. V. Ramsey, eds., *Perception* (New York, 1951), pp. 170–202.

Lecky, Prescott. *Self-consistency*. New York, 1945.

Low, Abraham. *Lectures to Relatives of Former Patients*. Boston, 1967.

Marston, Albert R. "Self Reinforcement: The Relevance of a Concept in Analogue Research to Psychotherapy," *Psychotherapy* (Winter, 1965), p. 2.

Maslow, Abraham H. *The Psychology of Science*. New York, 1966.

May, Rollo. *Psychology and the Human Dilemma*. Princeton, 1967.

————. *Love and Will.* New York, 1969.

Nietzsche, F. W. In H. J. Blackman, ed., *Reality, Man and Existence: Essential Works of Existentialism.* New York, 1965.

Rand, Ayn. *For the New Intellectual.* New York, 1961.

————. *The Virtue of Selfishness.* New York, 1964.

Robertiello, Richard. *Sexual Fulfillment and Self-Affirmation.* Larchmont, N.Y., 1964.

Rosenberg, Morris. "The Association Between Self-Esteem and Anxiety," *Psychiatric Research,* I, (1962), 135–52.

Russell, Bertrand. *The Conquest of Happiness.* New York, 1952.

Watzlawick, P., and others. *Pragmatics of Human Communication.* New York, 1967.

Humanistic Approaches to the Study of Human Life

CHARLOTTE BUHLER

ABRAHAM MASLOW, THE MAIN FOUNDER of the American Association for Humanistic Psychology (AAHP), has played an outstanding role in relating management in a new way to psychology. In his preface to the Japanese translation of his book *Eupsychian Management* of 1967, Maslow expresses the view that under certain "synergic" conditions, ". . . the good of the individual, and the good of society can come closer and closer to being synonymous rather than antagonistic. Eupsychian conditions of work," he goes on to say, "are often good not only for personal fulfillment; but also for the health and prosperity of the organization, as well as for the quantity and quality of the products or services turned out by the organization."

It is this assumption upon which our cooperation rests. We want to study those conditions of human development and of human relationships which, it is to be hoped, are optimal for the individual and society in general and for organizations more specifically.

As far as my own work is concerned, I have found three approaches that are important for an adequate understanding of people and an ability to help them:

1. The study of human lives in biographies as well as in case histories. In these studies we can get an idea of the total structure of human life, its up-and-down movements, its development in behavior, inner experiences, and production.

2. The study of those problems of human life which have become the specific concern of humanistic psychology; that is, the problems of *values* and *goals* in human life, with the desired result being self-realization. These problems require a penetration beyond biographical and case studies which can be accomplished only in detailed interviews, actually sometimes only in psychotherapy.

3. The study of people through *sensitivity training or psychotherapy group practice*. The participation in such groups effects an *experience* that seems to be irreplaceable by any other means. Communication, self-understanding, and understanding of others are here experienced in a unique way. Taped records of such sessions make them available as research material.

Thus far, case studies dealing with the complete life of an individual have not been widely accepted among psychologists, primarily because of the enormous bulk of material involved in such undertakings. And for those who are willing to surmount this difficulty, there is still wide disagreement on how to go about it. I would suggest three approaches to solving the problem—*statistical*, *biographical*, and *developmental*.

In the statistical approach certain behaviors, functions, or productions are studied with groups of people in respect to age distributions and possibly also in respect to social and educational correlations. Thus, the question "In which age are people the happiest or the unhappiest?" or the question "How do people of various ages and various social groups spend their leisure time?" may be studied statistically with the help of questionnaires, interviews, or tests. Pressey and Kuhlen's *Psychological Development Through the Life Span* (1957) is a widely known example of this type. Another example is the excellent study of Bernice Neugarten, *Personality in Middle and Later Life* (1964). In this type of study the individual is seen only as the member of a group and only in a fraction of his life.

In contrast to the statistical approach, the biographical approach is concerned with a single individual in the total context of his development, with emphasis on the characterization of the individual personality and his life style, partly in terms of psychoanalysis, sociology, and the concepts of Henry Murray. An example of this approach is Robert White's *Lives in Progress* (1952), in which one life history is presented and analyzed from the point of view of its dynamic, emotional, and social aspects.

The development approach considers the whole of one life under various systematic aspects, one of which is the *biological maturation process*. This process may be combined with *psychosexual* and *ego development aspects*, as found in the work of Erik Erikson (for example, his *Identity and the Life Cycle* [1959]); with *educational aspects*, as found in the work of Robert Havighurst (*Developmental Tasks and Education* [1952]); with *sociological aspects*, as in the work of Williams and Wirth (*Lives Through the Years* [1965]); or with *self-realization*, as in my own work (*The Course of Human Life: A Study of Goals in the Humanistic Perspective* [1968]).

All these approaches are of relative merit, and used correctly, complement each other. Although I have found it useful to integrate some of the other findings into my own investigations, I consider my main objective to be the study of self-realization toward fulfillment within a developmental frame of reference.

I have applied systematic considerations to the organization of life data, beginning with an evaluation of the degree to which the course of an individual life is influenced by biological facts, essentially *age* and *reproductivity*. Another organizing principle that I have established is concerned with the idea that *behaviors, inner experiences,* and *productions* represent three different facets of life and that each of them requires different methodological approaches by the psychologist. Karl Buhler (1967) spoke in this connection of the three aspects of psychology. It has been one of my main endeavors to relate these three aspects in such a way that the life cycle could be seen as a unit to which behaviors, inner experiences, and productions, each in a different manner, contributed essentially.

A third systematic consideration was in regard to the establishment of appropriate *time segments* that would best facilitate the handling of life-cycle data. There are several possibilities in handling time segments. There is the arbitrary, mechanical choice of a time unit, such as the subdivision of the total length of life into units of five- or ten-year periods, which is being used in all statistical studies. Then there is the possibility of applying the opposite principle by distinguishing units as they seem to appear as natural subdivisions in an individual life history, as in the case in White's *Lives in Progress,* in which the man Hartley Hale is discussed in part one from early childhood to the end of college, in part two from age twenty-three to thirty-three, and so on. Yet another possibility is to use a general scheme for subdivisions, or periods, that are marked by the sequential development of certain fundamental functions or behaviors.

In those theories using the schematic method, progressive aging seems to underlie the behavioral sequence. Havighurst's assumption of either stages or developmental tasks and Erikson's assumption of eight stages of the development of self are good examples of theories setting up schematic steps of psychical development. In my own theory the study of the underlying biological scheme is combined with a theory about the stages of self-realization, which I saw centralized in the continuity of human beings' goal-setting. From their beginnings, human beings seem constantly in pursuit of something. Pursuit was also seen by Freud and his followers as the most fundamental trend of human behavior and development. At first defining it as pleasure, he and his followers later conceived of it more scientifically as a release of tension or a tendency toward *homeostasis.*

Homeostasis as a goal was argued against as early as 1939 by Kurt Goldstein, who pointed out that the healthy human being—in fact, the healthy living being generally speaking—has an innate liking for a certain amount of tension which prevails in all his pursuits. Thus, the goal of release of tension is only relative and temporary. In a study entitled "Basic Tendencies of Human Life" (1959), I myself projected the fact that homeostasis cannot be conceived of as a goal. Homeostasis is simply a state, a comfortable condition, which for the healthy person, who wants to be active and who does not mind a certain degree of tension, is not only desirable but necessary. In fact it has been shown in modern research on creativity that the most creative individuals like the tension of unresolved problems and, not infrequently, set up problems for themselves to resolve (Eiduson, 1962; Getzels and Jackson, 1962).

What then is the ultimate goal of the humans' pursuit? The humanistic psychologists agree essentially on this point. Goldstein and Maslow speak of self-actualization; Karen Horney and Erich Fromm, who on this point as on others deviate strongly from their psychoanalytic beginnings, call the goal self-realization, which is the most frequently used term in humanistic psychology. I myself tried to define this pursuit as *intentionality* directed toward *fulfillment*. This fulfillment would be experienced essentially through self-realization. Also, Rollo May (1958) thinks of intentionality's being given and effective from the outset of an individual's life. This concept leads back to Brentano and Husserl.

The questions of where and how this intentionality is given and how it operates have usually not been answered. I think of it as a *core system* in the individual that operates in different strengths and to different degrees of consistency in each individual. The presence of a more or less consistent directive in people was suggested to me through the study of biographies and *clinical case* materials.

All people desire something, even though they may not always be certain of the particular thing or things they want or to what degree they want them. Nonetheless, they know they want "something," or ought to. Some people, of course, have specific, well-defined goals toward which they strive. As I see it there are four basic tendencies of human striving (C. Buhler, 1959): *need satisfaction, self-limiting adaptation, creative expansion*, and *upholding of the internal order*. Optimal interaction of these tendencies brings about that self-realization that is experienced as fulfillment, which implies a satisfaction of needs and creative accomplishments that result from an individual's adaptation to given situations and his upholding of an inner, more or less hierarchical order. This order is the order of values that Allport and Maslow also conceive of as being more or less hierarchical. But it is, of course, only the exceptional case and the exceptional development in which the satisfaction of needs and the pursuit of accomplishments are integrated without conflict.

Biographical and case history studies have helped me to set up the schematical frame for the stages of the development of self-realization.

There are biographies and cases of people who, toward the end of their lives, declare themselves as essentially fulfilled. Their development seems, in many examples, to have proceeded in a certain order. While their childhood may have differed, all were essentially healthy children, brought up in an adequate environment, who were interested in various things, although usually they were not conscious at that point of a particular, life-long goal.

In adolescence, we find the individual beginning to move toward self-realization and becoming aware of life as a whole and the various goals to pursue. This pursuit might be started tentatively and experimentally; and conflicts of direction, which originated in childhood, become distinct and may even reach a climax in this period.

In early adulthood we find this individual becoming more or less definite and specific with respect to long-range goals if he has been able to integrate his tendencies somewhat successfully. If he is an all-around self-realizing person, he would seek need-satisfying goals in his personal life as well as in his occupation; that is, in his marriage and in his career. Judging from the results of psychotherapy, this integration causes the most widely spread problems and conflicts.

Most people assess themselves repeatedly from early life. They question how bright they are, how strong, how popular, how good. At certain times people assess their lives as a whole. This happens often in adolescence, but most frequently in later adulthood. In later adulthood, in their fifties and sixties, people are assessing both their past and their future lives. A person may have had by now some of those experiences which Maslow calls peak experiences. He may have had what he feels to be successes and failures in bringing his best potentials to materialization. He may feel there is hope for fulfillment, or else there is only resignation or even despair. This period, then, may be decisive for how he will live the final stages of his life. Accordingly, old age may be spent by this person in rest or resignation or in renewed or continued efforts in the direction of an ultimate fulfillment. These five phases represent an optimal scheme. As the word *optimal* indicates, this is not necessarily the average, nor even a frequent development. But it may be used as a standard by which to measure the actually frequent deviations from and disruptions of a regular development.

It is, of course, not possible in the context of this presentation to go into details of these deviations and disruptions, but I should like to spend a little time with the discussion of that phase which presents at the moment such extremely difficult problems to everyone interested in human development as related to society and culture. It is the goal problem of many of our present youths.

Youth, which I define as normally the period of tentative and experimental goal-setting, appears at the present in a still undefined
percentage as a period of rebellion against goal-setting, either against
goal-setting within the frame of our given culture, or even against all
goal-setting as such. "Our attitudes," says the sophomore coed Elizabeth
Crosby, "are more an emphasis on relationships, and sex is bound up
in this" (R. Jones, 1967). With the emphasis on relationships, the emphasis on self-realization is given up or at least diminished.

It seems that the recent development of civilization has led to a
widely spread confusion regarding life's goals and values. People now
have such serious doubts about the validity of authorities and traditions
that they seek the counsel of psychologists and psychiatrists. "People,"
says the psychiatrist Allen Wheelis (1958), "don't come any more as
much as they used to with neurotic problems of the previously known
types, but they come with the question of 'Who am I? How do I find
myself. . .' ," which Wheelis calls the quest for identity.

The present outburst of these problems has historically conditioned
causes, which lie in the problems of our time. But underlying these
general societal problems are the specifically chronic problems of young
people. The acute problem is the present rebellion against all established authority. It is a movement which, as we know, extends over
the whole world. It leaves every individual with the problem as well as
the responsibility of complete self-determination. This brings me to the
second subject which I mentioned at the beginning of this paper and
about which I shall now talk briefly.

An adequate understanding of people's motivation in living and
working is possible only if one understands their beliefs and their
values. In the present revolutionary movements I see several issues.
There is the general rebellion against authority caused by the Establishment's abuse of its power, as exemplified by its leading youth into
wars, and its failure to defend its injustice and selfishness, as exemplified
by its hypocrisy regarding morality, religion, and an over-all concept
of life.

Another issue follows in the wake of the first. It is the strong feelings
held by this generation regarding unfairness, injustice, and repression
in the world particularly as these wrongs affect those underprivileged,
not only economically and culturally but also physically and mentally.

A third issue seems to me the most relevant in the context of the
work we are planning here. It is that shift of emphasis regarding goals
of human life, from goals of self-realization and bringing-out of one's
best potentials to goals of human relationships. I mentioned earlier the
statement of the coed Elizabeth Crosby, quoted in *Time*: "Our atti-

tudes are more an emphasis on relationships, and sex is bound up in this." Not too long ago I saw *Hair,* a play in which relationships with emphasis on sexual freedom, called "love," are presented as the essence of life. Convictions and goals are ridiculed. Also the relationships are in no way based on personal merits or even preferences. They are kept impersonal, and the consistent mass cult is called "tribal." Disturbing to me more than the play itself was the reaction of the audience, which was predominantly enthusiastic—and not exclusively on the side of younger people.

What does this kind of reaction mean? These young people and all who acclaimed them are enthusiastic in their determination to be free from any rules and regulations. In the play an older couple come on the stage and, after questioning the young people, declare that they are all for the kids' doing as they please, as long as they don't hurt anybody. All right. But what do the kids want? They want sex, called "love," and self-expression of feelings without obligations, self-limitations, or goals. Unfortunately, today many youths are not goal-determined even to that degree, but are simply alienated and isolated (K. Keniston, 1960).

One would hope that this excessive form of freedom-seeking would soon pass from the youth movement or at least remain limited to small groups, for we still have the general, over-all picture of a rebellious youth, with large numbers of them ready to stand up for newly emphasized ideals—a youth that does not simply turn away from society but tries to reform it, a youth ready to work for more justice, more equality, more relationships, and more honest self-expression. These are important and valuable objectives. With these values and goals they actually assist that movement which motivates those of us who foster group therapy and sensitivity-training.

It seems, as was mentioned earlier, that this present youth's predominant value is more that of helping others than that of self-realization. I do not, of course, think that these goals are mutually exclusive. On the contrary, in the more recent thinking about meaningfulness of life by Frankl (1969), Maslow (1962), and others, self-transcendence has been worked out as that orientation which makes life most meaningful; and an important form of this self-transcendence materializes in self-dedication to others. This present youth's asking for closer relationships, with more self-expression and more helpfulness, may be considered to lie in the same direction as modern psychotherapists' endeavors in group therapy and sensitivity-training.

Herewith I come to my last point, to what I called the third approach to the understanding and helping of people, namely group therapy and sensitivity-training. Some people still think of these techniques only in terms of their being less expensive and therefore more widely usable than individual therapy. But I think most of us who have actually worked in these areas have recognized that with these methods completely different things can be accomplished than in individual therapy.

These accomplishments lie in the direction of newer, deeper relationships between people, which cannot be equally satisfactorily established in individual therapy, because the mutuality of the contact is conditional to and instrumental in bringing about new ways of reacting to each other. In individual therapy a patient can be freed in his self-expression, can become more honest, more feeling, more open. But he needs the response from others to experience the impact of free communication—the communality of problems, conflicts, and needs, and the response of others to himself.

At this point we can combine the ideas of the modern concern for human relationships with the emphasis on group procedures as the most effective means to further relationships. And if anything is suited to enhance simultaneously the benefit for society as well as that for the self-realizing individual, it is to be found in these procedures. I agree with Maslow that if anything at all can help mankind to survive, it is psychology, and specifically it is the work in group encounters.

REFERENCES

Buhler, Charlotte. "Theoretical Observations about Life's Basic Tendencies," *American Journal of Psychotherapy*, XIII, No. 3 (1959).

———, et al. *The Course of Human Life: A Study of Goals in the Humanistic Perspective*. New York, 1968.

Buhler, Karl. *Die Krise der Psychologie*, 3d ed. (Stuttgart, 1967).

Eiduson, Bernice T. *Scientists: Their Psychological World*. New York, 1962.

Erikson, Erik H. *Identity and the Life Cycle*. New York, 1959.

Frankl, Viktor E. *The Will to Meaning*. New York, 1969.

Getzels, Jacob W., and Philip W. Jackson. *Creativity and Intelligence*. New York, 1962.

Goldstein, Kurt. *The Organism*. New York, 1939.

Havighurst, Robert J. *Developmental Tasks and Education*. New York, 1952.

Jones, Robert. "Twenty-five and Under: The Man of the Year," *Time*, LXXXIX, No. 1 (Jan. 6, 1967).

Keniston, Kenneth. *The Uncommitted: Alienated Youth in American Society*. New York, 1960.

Maslow, Abraham. *Eupsychian Management*. Tokyo, 1967.

———. *Towards a Psychology of Being*. New York, 1962.

May, Rollo et al. *Existence: A New Dimension in Psychiatry and Psychology*. New York, 1958.

Neugarten, Bernice L. et al. *Personality in Middle and Later Life*. New York, 1964.

Pressey, Sidney L., and Raymond G. Kuhlen. *Psychological Development Through the Life Span*. New York, 1957.

Wheelis, Allen. *The Quest for Identity*. New York, 1958.

White, Robert W. *Lives in Progress: A Study of the Natural Growth of Personality*. New York, 1952.

Williams, Richard H., and Claudine G. Wirth. *Lives Through the Years: Styles of Life and Successful Aging*. New York, 1965.

Philosophy of the Living Spirit and the Crisis of Today

FRITZ-JOACHIM VON RINTELEN
Translated by Rita D. S. Hartman

W E SHALL DISCUSS a philosophy of the living spirit or, better, the spirit in its role in life in the crisis of today. We shall deal with it in the following manner. (1) We must ask ourselves what kind of spiritual situation we are faced with. We can speak, on the one hand, of the superiority of a highly successful radical rationalism and, on the other, of the historical relativization of previous spiritual allegiances. The results are shown (2) in the inner foment and discontent of a part of the young generation. This point forces us (3) to confront the inner relation between spirit and life and thus, again, to understand man in relation to the whole of existence.

Thus is posed the philosophical question of whether there is still something we acknowledge as binding man, not only externally but also intrinsically. This question concerns (4) meaning and (5) value. Is not—to paraphrase Gabriel Marcel—a commitment necessary for man's inner life in order for him not to sink into spiritual alienation? "Are we not today in an age of perfect means but confused [values] ends?" asked Einstein. In this question (6) history can be our teacher; and this fact leads us, as our final subject, to the encounter of cultures. Is it not the case that in them the spirit unfolds itself for us as a living spirit, in its creations, also its great variety, yet in time-transcending significance?

1. We stand impressed before the immense progress of natural science and its results, which we recognize in particular fields, even though these sciences are in a continuous process of change. It is precisely the leading scientists of physics, such as Heisenberg, Pascual Jordan, von Weizsäcker, and the earlier Planck, who point out the limits of physical cognition. The physicist Heitler (Zurich) reminds us that "the human person is not merely a physico-chemical system." An uncritical identification of model and reality is, according to Heistermann (Berlin), illegitimate.[1] And, according to the astronomer J. Meurers, "the power of special physical methods must be transcended." Otherwise, he says, they will lead us "into disaster."[2] The psychiatrist Frankl (Vienna) says that the different disciplines often defend their insights, which in themselves are valid, with a single-minded absolutist claim. The specialized

truth is simply transferred, by such "terrible generalizers," to the whole, who then, *pars pro toto*, know only the "nothing-but."[3] The biologist Oepen (Marburg) also speaks of the ever-present danger of overemphasizing partial aspects.[4]

However, who would be so foolish as not to recognize the incredible significance of mathematics, especially for modern technology and for the mechanics of engines in particular? But this realm, according to Heistermann, means merely a secondary world which needs the "human function of an ordering superstructure."[5] This problem leads us to something even more decisive, the answer to which is the task of philosophy.

In the history of the humanities—rather than in systematic philosophy —we observe a direction toward *historical relativism*, that is, the widely accepted notion that everything is subject to historical change. According to Huber (Zurich), this idea actually means an "absolutization of the historical process."[6] These ideas go back to Dilthey and especially to Troeltsch who, after all, recognizes a transitory "meaning totality" in each epoch. No one can deny that different epochs, cultures, and times have looked for very different aims of life, which often were in conflict with each other and, without doubt, were strangely dependent on economic factors. For each of them something different was "significant" (Rothacker), which gave each epoch its own character.

But this thought has now been intensified to time-bounded momentaneity. May we still dare the experiment of gaining a certain time-transcending horizon beyond the historical moment? Is not this, precisely, the task of philosophy? Only thus can we gain intellectual power. "The most dangerous thing," says Chesterton, "is the modern philosopher without norms."

2. It is in this situation that for a long time the younger generation has been invoked. Often the old generation is unable to say anything meaningful to the young because, through the events and upheavals of the last decennium, it is spiritually, though not necessarily intellectually, weakened. But formal intellectualism, though in itself successful, and total questioning of a normative sense of life do not convey an inner mandate. They are unable to contribute anything to human existence and, consequently, result in personal despiritualization. Not without reason, therefore, philosophers have been discussing, for some time, subjects such as "existential alienation" and personal "inauthenticity."

What remains? To succumb to one's own calculated advantage, one's comfort, the exploitation of technical knowledge, while the irrational drives surging more and more into the foreground—for let us not believe in an apparent absence of conflicts—unless we are ourselves party to the enrichment of knowledge and technical advancement, a privilege granted to only a very few. So, as Hans Freyer says, we lose ourselves in the hectic "busybody seriousness of perfect fools, the particular is all-important, the whole nonsense."[7] In constant restlessness the eye gazes into the future, always aiming for the new, because the pure present leaves us unsatisfied and all that went before is declared outdated. In this sense one has spoken of an intoxication by progress.

It is true, of course, that in our time there has been steady and unprecedented progress in the knowledge and utilization of the natural forces. But, according to Ortega y Gasset, this progress is one-sided; and Eduard Meyer has said, not without reason: What builds up, tears down; what tears down, can build up. That is to say, any one-sided development brings about a counter-movement. It is this which has announced itself, though somewhat hazily, in the younger generation.

What is the reason? In view of the situation characterized above, we must speak of an emptiness of human existence, a lack of meaning, a crisis of sensibility, a vacuum of significance, which is widely spread and felt throughout the young generation, especially since we ourselves do not seem to be able to grasp more than marginal zones of life. Again, with Frankl, we find an "existential vacuum" about which he conducted thorough experiments both in Vienna and in the U.S.A.[8]

The everyday humdrum of a guided and utterly empty existence results in a feeling of being lost, of being forsaken. There is a bored dissatisfaction with everything that is offered. One reduces everything to the ridiculous, says H. Köhler. There is nothing to anything, nothing is true, everything is permitted. To repeat an expression often uttered by youth, "Everything is senseless." This is spiritual sell-out, intellectual abdication. But we have only ourselves to blame. At the International Congress of Philosophy (Vienna, 1968) we were reminded of this by the gentlemen from the East. And in a student paper in Würzburg recently were these characteristic sentences:

> We scream, until the world is reeling . . .
> Until she recognizes why we have to yell.
> We are the generation without morals because we are honest,
> We are the generation without ideals because
>   we cannot believe in anything,
> We are the generation without meaning,
> Lost in emptiness. We are
> Fear's laughter over the unspeakable.[9]

Existential philosophy has from its beginning discussed the fundamental anxiety in the face of *nothing*. But this is not really what concerns this youth. Rather, we see in it rebellion, pure and simple, against the conditions of public, mechanized, manipulated life, wherever on earth. However, there is no consciousness of its true reason, namely, lack of meaning.

History teaches us that, in the long run, such a state of behavior is not possible; it means dissolution. From this point of view, let us read again the letters of Seneca about later Rome, where there were great technical achievements like the building of the Colosseum and the thermal baths of emperors. Thus, we have today a colossal surge toward freedom, against regimentation, and as we said before, manipulation, together with willingness of devotion so typical of youth. However, as Eduard Spranger has pointed out, this condition also includes the possibility of the dominance of power hunger, ambition of dynamic resolve, and, at the same time, normless determination, which, as we experienced in 1933 and are experiencing again, can turn toward questionable goals with incredible dedication, thereby turning away from rationality toward hyper-emotionality. This state can easily be mistaken as something profound, but it has no spiritual content. Plato, in his letters and in the *Republic* (VI, 354D, 560 ff.) says that "democracy is dissolved through a certain boundlessness of freedom . . . and this is the beautiful and marvellous beginning of tyranny"—the beginning of the intolerance of tolerance.

Against this idea we say: It depends entirely on what the new is that is being striven for as against the old, especially if precedence is always given to *becoming*, in ever increasing, steady swiftness. Thus, the "new" in the Germany of 1933, with its radical impatience, was given precedence, and those who opposed it *out of time-transcended experience and insight* were at that time judged reactionary, backward, outdated, and calcified. What hitherto existed was regarded, in such times, say Huxley, as "antiquated pieces of furniture." One is, says Heinemann (Oxford), *rerum novarum cupidissimus*. One tries to separate, says Brun (Dijon), "the death of a world from the birth of a new one."[10] I would like to answer, however, that in the dynamic of every becoming there must be, as something static—a meaning, a significance; just as in everything static there must be something dynamic. Goethe gave the classic formula for this condition in *Urworte Orphisch*: "*Geprägte Form, die lebend sich entwickelt*" ("Prepatterned form in life itself unfolding"). There must always be a form which gives sense to a life process. What counts is the content striven for and the quality of the striving. These things are what man at all times, true to his character, has aspired to; otherwise he would have lost his inner equilibrium, become victim to ambiguity, and fallen into what Roig Gironella (Barcelona) has called (at the Congress of Philosophy in Vienna, 1968) the *desesquilibrio y claudicación* so typical for our time.

3. So much for our critical exposition. We shall now try to gain a positive orientation. Is there not, as a reaction to the remarks made above, an even newer movement in the offing, a new point of view? This is clearly being stated in the cooperative work of twenty-one nations, *Human Existence and Modern World* (1967), edited by Richard Schwarz. On all sides, says the American mathematician Morgan, there arises the question of the reinstatement of the "integral man." The "plundering of human existence," as Radhakrishnan formulates it, "has to be overcome."[11] In the last instance, it seems, we have to be guided in our decisions in life by time-transcending insights which, of course, cannot be demonstrated sensually-empirically, nor are they of a purely formal nature without content. As a reaction there has awakened again the need to differentiate the essential from the inessential, the decisive from the peripheral, the higher from the lower, the valuable from the valueless.

According to the physicist von Weizsäcker, science alone (natural science, that is) is unable to fill the vacuum.[12] The well-known physician Krehl, therefore, demands the "mutual complementation of natural science and spiritual life."[13] At the same time we are striving, with Georg Simmel, to go "beyond mere life" and "to incorporate past and future into the present." This may be the starting point of a new, present-day movement in philosophy. Our task thus seems to be to combine spirit and life in a living reality, to combine them in harmony in spite of their tension, to weigh their respective claims so that they do not pass each other by, for otherwise an emotional dynamic will spill without limit and use the calculating abstract intellect for the power-hungry world of instinct. Hermann Hesse lets Plinio Designori say, in his *Glass Bead Game*: "You are on the side of the highest development of spirit. I am on the side of natural life."[14] Does the one exclude the other? We reiterate with W. Grenzmann: "He who loses himself in the senses is guilty in the spirit. He who wants to be pure in spirit loses the connection with nature."[15] The unity of both ensures richer and more intense reality, a relation to true Being.

This is not the occasion to weigh these ideas more precisely. Let us only say that *spirit* is to be understood as personal, humanely thinking activity. Its contents are presupposed as objective meaning-contents. Nicolai Hartmann adds here the understandable difference of the supra-individual, age-determining "objective spirit" and the "objec-tivized spirit" as spiritual creation, even in the past. On the other hand, one also speaks of spirit as the classic *logos*, as the decisive spiritual order, "the spiritual element" even in nature which, in the words of the physicist Heitler, we strive to emulate. Life itself is basis and bearer of the spirit, and its inner movement makes possible what we call the spiritual—so that we may not get frozen in rigidity.

Turning to human spiritual life we have to appeal to the whole human being; for "lack of totality is the core of the crisis of modern man," to speak with Morgan (U.S.A.). In this sense, Leo Gabriel directs his efforts toward an all-embracing contemplation of an integral spiritual understanding, a spiritual integral in genuine closeness with reality, in order not to get caught in barren, formal abstractions.[16] Thus, man, in his intellectual strivings, would not be understood *exclusively* by the quantitative determination of physical processes, a procedure which, according to Thielike (Hamburg) is illegitimate. It would mean an "extroversion of the *humanum*."[17] Man has his own original inner *selfhood*, source of creativity; and this selfhood, according to Werkmeister (U.S.A.), is the "core and basis of all valuing." As such the human person is not merely a functional wheel in an impersonal, organizational mechanism. If he limits himself to this role, then, according to the sociologist Schoeck, man becomes a "mechanical motor" to be steered and manipulated by others. This brings about an improverishment of true humanity which, in the long run, history punishes by death—as history itself teaches.

Today our task is to discover again the complete, the total man; as was said before, his integral level, so to speak, must be found if we want to penetrate into his spiritual life. What is demanded is not only very important extrinsic knowledge but also the inner concentration, the connection of spirit and life, of *logos* and *bios*, spirit in its total fullness. It arises from the inner core of man (see the author's *Der Aufstieg im Geiste*, 1970); and its painful and widely felt loss is lamented by Erich Heyde (Berlin). This core is the realm of inner confrontation of body, soul, and mind. It connects, overarchingly, the extremes of only abstract formalism and spiritless irrationalism. Let us think back upon what was said about the younger generation. Here it is that the rise and fall of the conflict of the inner hierarchies of the human being are raging.

In this inner region also resides the creative, constructive spontaneity which is the original existential ground of human personality. It presupposes an atmosphere of *freedom*, which, among other scholars, is recognized by the physicists Pascual Jordan and Heisenberg.[18] This fact poses another question: Will it be possible for the gifts of the spirit, in their mission of fulfilling life and acquiring transparent understanding of meaning, to penetrate to essential insight in the sense of Husserl?

Against this question there arises the easily understandable objection: If this were the case, would this achievement be verifiable in any strict sense? In the sense of exact natural science, of course not. The conditions of exact, scientific proof have, in ever increasing measure, methodically restricted what should be regarded as proof. Can we then transfer this strict concept of proof to an answer explaining human existence and its inner order of life without losing its meaning? And, what is even more decisive for us, is it not possible to find a justifiable procedure on the basis of insight? Otherwise, frankly, all we can do is show up the factually discernible pure power of life, and one could speak of an ethically valuable attitude or adjustment only in the sense of shortest momentaneousness. This thesis implies the tremendous danger that only ambition for power—understood in the widest sense of the word— and for self-assertion can be validly recognized.

Precisely here philosophy has an ordering, scientific responsibility, demanding a critical analysis bound to experience, but of the totality of life, in order to penetrate to decisively valid phenomena, thus saving us from self-deception and emotional affection. Such insights are, according to Heitler, by no means the product of subjective thinking nor, as against Mohr (Freiburg), mere subjectivity—which would be a bold assertion anyway since, according to Mohr, the so-called exact sciences "can only deal with a narrow section of the world."[19] We are here confronted with the reality of life and, with Nicolai Hartmann, "being assailed from the Outside." It is true, we are bound, in all our answers, to the categorial and sensorial possibilities of human cognition, as shown up by critical idealism; but the conformation to the data of life's reality must be confirmed and justified over and over again.

4. From our observations we draw the conclusion that our present situation compels us to ask what *is* our intimate understanding of *meaning (Sinn)*?[20] Is not this question the original a priori of all philosophy, to the degree that it raises questions and attempts answers, in order not to lose itself in an infinite horizon? One can, of course, on the basis of a definite methodological position—for method creates and determines the subject matter—declare that the quest for meaning is meaningless, as did Schlick, and as Mohr (Freiburg) does today with respect to science. It is striking that humanity up to now has never been satisfied with limiting methods but has always looked beyond to fullness of meaning for inner enrichment. This is the reason for its cultural creativity. The mere fact of life and its preservation does not seem to be sufficient.[21]

What then do we understand by *meaning*? First, its conceptual content, which is unequivocal and not in itself incongruent (which is different from contradictory). Meaning, according to Eduard Spranger, is not graspable by the senses. It includes a content which signifies something specific and, hence, is distinguished from everything else. This content can manifest itself in anything, not only in conceptual assertions, but also in actions, conduct, even in concrete pictures. Michelangelo's *The Creation of Man*, for example, proclaims the idea that through the pointed Finger of God the spark of the spirit is being transmitted to the young human being awakened to life. Thus, sense can become *Prosopon*, spiritual countenance—let us say, of Being as such and as basis of our *Existence*. Buytendijk says that man is put into the "web of meaning" of all nature and environment, in order to fulfill an even higher meaning. And Heitler speaks of the "inner core of nature," the "inner being of the organism."[22]

Meaning and *concept* must be distinguished. The concepts of different languages only partly correspond to one another; they do not have the same content of meaning (see Wittgenstein). It is, for example, impossible to find in Japanese a word corresponding in meaning to the English *person*; but the sense of the word is also affirmed there. In German the word *Sinn* has a specific significance, the idea, namely, that an action is significant, makes sense, if it fulfills a worthy aim or serves the common good.

5. With this notion we transcend the aspect of pure being, which states the factual, the inner so-called law, and deal with the value aspect. He who does not see this point talks past the reality of life and history. Therefore, the well-known words of Nietzsche: "The world revolves around the inventors of values—its discoverers, I would say—soundlessly it revolves." Heinemann (Oxford), therefore, formulates the following: "The order of values is the problem on the solution of which depends the life and death of nations." What is the specific peculiarity of the value aspect?[23] It is not only the word, *Wert, valeur, value, valore, valor*, but the common meaning of the term that counts. As against mere assertion, the valuable is an attitude which *affirms* something the realization of which is, or ought to be, *striven* for. Everyday we find ourselves in such a situation.

A further characteristic moment of the value phenomenon consists, in my opinion, in the feature of *qualitative intensification*, as against quantitative increase or addition. I can, for example, execute a value pregnant with meaning in a social effort for another person, either in a trivial manner or by risking my own life, as in saving a shipwrecked person, or, as I experienced it, when a young person endangered his own life by rescuing children from the upper floor of a burning house during an air raid in wartime. Here we see clearly the increasing degree of a given value content. We also know sufficiently that the aesthetic value in works of art has been realized historically in very different degrees of quality. But decisive is *what* it is that through its content conveys inner satisfaction and a sense of life's meaning.

It has been recognized, even though sometimes very obscurely, that we are striving for something which has value owing to its inner quality (*Eigenwert*, intrinsic value), as the examples mentioned demonstrate. It is something which, with Kant, is affirmed for its own sake. Or else we speak of something which serves a further purpose and is of use (utility value, relation value, instrumental or extrinsic value). The orientation toward mere extrinsic use for the individual and for the community is of a very relative and controversial value. Let us only think back to the time in Germany from 1933 on, when we were taught what was "useful" for the community and the individual.

A heroic action against the abuse of power, as we have experienced it, can be without effect, that is, useless, yet have its own value within itself. I could observe how, when my friend Professor Huber and the brother and sister Scholl in Munich were condemned to death by the National Socialists, some students incriminated them even more completely than justified, unfoundedly and unwarrantedly, for their own benefit, while others exposed themselves to danger, not for the sake of their own advantage, but simply in order to defend them courageously. Or the following experience which I will here relate. In August, 1918, at the front at Harbonnière before an attack, my comrades were ordered to dig in. When the attack started, a strong, older soldier threw a younger nineteen-year-old soldier, who had been at the front only eight days, out of the hole the younger one had dug for himself. The young soldier consequently lost his life, while the older one remained unharmed. This was useful for the older soldier with his greater war experience, but it was base in attitude, and negative in value. Soon thereafter I saw how a seriously injured soldier was carried out of the danger zone by another who lost his own life in the act. This was of high value in itself, in the fullest sense, completely independent of the particular situation. On the other hand, obviously, values of utility are of great significance, as those of economic goods which have each their impersonal value quality but, at the same time, serve the community and, thus, the high development of human existence and its intrinsic values.

There are also impersonal intrinsic values of human vitality, as they are felt in modern sports movements; and, thus, they serve as bases for the development of human activity, in spite of some misuse. Presupposed here is the qualitative perfection, or fulfillment, of the naturally given. Earlier ages spoke of an *agathon* or *bonum*. I wish to say, however, that the closer a value is to *human existence*, the higher the rank of intrinsic value (*Eigenwert*) to be ascribed to it. It represents, as personal value, an appeal to the human person in whose value character we may penetrate in different dimensions of depth. One has spoken many times in history of hierarchies of value, as did Scheler and Nicolai Hartmann. It can hardly be denied that the ethical level of character is of a higher value dimension than the aesthetic, as is clearly seen in moments of great stress. For the religious person, the religious value of confrontation with God is the highest; but it affirms and includes, at the same time, the other value realms, especially the ethical.

Examining values accordingly, we note a *dynamic-vertical* axis of meaning which beckons to ever-increasing richness of fulfillment, as well as a *status-horizontal* qualitative axis of each order and its meaning content. As in all intellectual endeavors we must strive to determine the essential content which demands to be realized. Without such orientation we lack guidance and are confronted with a "system" devoid of all systematic order.

There remains one decisive observation still to be made. Our valuations refer to concrete events of *real* life, each in its individual form. This is the reason why we are not only concerned with abstract ideas and concepts. It leads to confusion to use the word *real* only for things and, to speak again with the physicist Heitler, to consider only "external existence as real" and to limit reality to this definition. After all, Descartes spoke of the *res cogitans*. If reality were purely material, all intellectual relations would become subjective illusions without any degree of reality. No, concretely valuable surrender, as well as value-negation, can gain an incredible importance in reality in moments in which an intellectual value content, or a disvalue, becomes reality. To this statement must be added that the precise degree of intensity of the value in the moment of fulfillment cannot be displayed in its abstract concept but only in its actual completeness, which is why, in this connection, we speak of a completely *real value* (*Realwert*) and propose a *value realism*. It is a remarkable fact that we know fully the meaning of the value of truth, the law, of dedication, and experience them in our inner existence only when we are confronted with them concretely in either their affirmation or denial. It is this which must be emphasized, and we must no longer consider ideological superstructures alienated from reality.

But does not the emphasis on each individual value lead to complete *relativity*? We shall ask ourselves that question again in connection with the history of culture. Here it shall only be mentioned that we become conscious of the limit of possible fulfillment in every particular case. At the same time, however, valuing is directed toward a transcending goal, a perfection which, as a *supra-individual* norm, stands as an example before our eyes. The situation in which we find ourselves compels us, especially in conflicts of value, to decide under our own responsibility, but not arbitrarily. This is the topic of so-called situation ethics. Let us think, for example, of the fundamental values of honesty, truthfulness, and compassion, as against cheating, sanctimoniousness, and mendacity —frequent sins of our time found even, and especially, in the so-called intellectual circles—or of the value of social devotion which so strongly determines our age and was strikingly formulated by Schleiermacher as "growing into the community and growing out of the personality" (*"Hineinbidlung in die Gemeinschaft und Herausbildung der Persoenlichkeit"*). This attitude is, with Thielicke, not neutral to value but of unconditional intrinsic value, even though it is often disdained. The American philosopher Fridjof Bergmann said in his communication (in the section "Ethics and Philosophy of Value") at the International Congress of Philosophy in Vienna, 1968: "The world is . . . much richer and denser than we sometimes imagine, not a collection of neutral objects."[24]

Let us then summarily formulate our position: The meaning of human existence and its innermost task is found in the active, spiritual-intellectual completion of life's events. In these events, out of an existential attitude, comprehensive, partially transtemporal fundamental values—namely, intrinsic values (*Eigenwerte*)—must be concretely realized in different forms and in individual intensities, in degrees of fulfillment with respect to depth or height. The extrinsic or utility values must be directed toward the intrinsic values. Everything depends on the question of whether such spiritual fullness of meaning (*Sinngehalte*) can still find a genuine echo in this age and within each one of us. One may well say: "Tell me your value goals and I shall tell you who you are." The same can be said of every age.

6. Thus, we are confronted with our last question. We are largely influenced today by so-called historicity, meaning here not the specific existential philosophy. Everything, one says, is in the last instance determined by the changeability of the historical process, hence also, of course, value-thinking, which depends on one's own changeable position or norms. But is there not, up to a certain point at least, a homogeneous human structure, a structure of man, as Aldrich (U.S.A.) affirms? Margaret Mead, the well-known American investigator of different cultures, also says: "We may expect ultimately to identify in human beings an original nature which has a very definite form or structure, and possibly systematic individual differences which may be referred to constitutional type within that original nature."[25]

No complete renunciation of the *humanum* is possible, no matter how undeveloped or stunted the knowledge of it, or, to follow Scheler, how great the prevailing value blindness. The experiences of recent times have given us the insight to understand that the primary demands to be met are universally human, indeed, simply humanitarian demands. We are justified, therefore, in calling a crime (even in the political life) by its right name. If there is no overarching sense and performance of value in history, then history becomes, as Schopenhauer says, a chaos of fighting cats (*ein Wirrwar von Katzbalgereien*). The logic of value, as it was outlined above, helps, in my opinion, to answer the question of the connection between historicity and supratemporal meaning. Why? Because it includes the rich variety of value concretions with their respective degrees of fulfillment. Do we not have here, then, fundamental values not bound to particular times, so that we can speak of a kind of essential value constancy? We can grasp such phenomena only if we consider what is common and not what is divisive in history and cultures, no matter how great the variety in which it manifests itself.

Let us mention a few illustrative examples. The leading investigator of Zen Buddhism, Suzuki, says that in the Japanese culture the values of faithfulness, self-sacrifice, responsibility for oneself, piety, benevolence, and devotion were required at a time when they had no relation whatsoever with the European culture. The Zen master Dogen (who died in 1253) writes: "Everything evil is not effective, with all living beings have deep compassion, . . . have charity, not hate" (*Shotogenzo Shoji*).[26] These same requirements were valid in the European culture, even though with another coloration and background. In the Hindu *Upanishads* we read of the highest value of completion or perfection through being self (*kaivalya*), freedom of the self and absolute love (*Katha Up.*). The *Bhagavad-Gita* (fourth century B.C.) knows exaltation, wisdom, goodness, and holiness. Lao-tzu (sixth century B.C.) writes: "The higher person strives for the complete, because the good is, and does not lean on external things. Only the material contains utility, the non-material effects essence" (*Tao Te Ching*, No. 11). Such innumerable examples of different cultures could be added; for, as Garcia Maynez (Mexico) says: "There is a common fund in the convictions about value."[27]

I, therefore, maintain that out of inner responsibility we cannot pass by the fact that there are supratemporal, fundamental values which have different historical manifestations and that not everything valuational is relative. Eduard Spranger believes that one has always to look for the "ultimate sense" and the values of the human community. But they appear, I would say, in different breadth of variation in their historical realizations, according to the spiritual horizon that carries them.

This insight makes understanding and true tolerance possible. It does not consist in the freedom not to have an opinion, which historically would mean dissolution. Rather, the openness and understanding required for other cultures, times, and opinions presuppose that they are carried by persons wrestling with themselves. There has probably never been a time in which love has not been affirmed. But even in our own historical past we can show up the variations of classical *eros*, Christian *agape*, humanitarian charity, and social concern, all of which have a common core of meaning but do have distinct dimensions of depth.

Even in the aesthetic realm certain fundamental supratemporal features of quality can be ascertained. Thus, the director of the Academy of Art in Munich, Preetorius, at the beginning of the century found in the flea market of Paris innumerable small Chinese drawings, some of which he took with him. They turned out to be of insuperable quality and value, and have today an artistic value of the very highest level. He confessed, however, that he had never known anything of Chinese art. The level of quality of the aesthetic, we conclude, expresses itself in the various art styles. The values of architectonics certainly are conditioned by the actual situation, tradition, and social structure. But this does not mean that the breadth of variation of which we spoke is absolutely relative. Rather, I would say, it is of a limited relativity. Thus, we can speak of fundamental value as a meaning independent of temporality. In this sense writes W. Rudolf in *Der kulturelle Relativismus* (1968): "The validity of cultural relativism . . . is limited." There is something "interculturally valid"; there are "value shadings and decisions with intracultural reference."[28]

It is true, one could object, that I have not sufficiently emphasized the disvaluable in history and its large debit side, which might make every quest for historical meaning illusory. We are reminded of the words of Shakespeare about history in *Henry IV*:

> The happiest youth, viewing his progress through,
> What perils past, what crosses to ensue,
> Would shut the book, and sit him down and die.
>
> Part 2, act 3, scene 2, lines 54–56

But in order to rise from desperation, let us cast another glance at the partial conquests of this situation so humiliating for man, at the positive, the meaningful, and the valuable to be discovered in each historical hour, its concretion of value, and, hence, that in which lifts up cosmic anxiety to the joy of being. The past speaks to us in its actions, its achievements in different degrees, as in the creations of a Dante, Shakespeare, Pascal, Calderon, and Goethe in the modern age. Of course, we always view these accomplishments in our own time-bound perspective, but at the same time in sublimation above our own situation. If we lose this point of view, the past becomes irrelevant and completely meaningless for us. If not, we have a positive attitude toward it and we are then face to face with a philosophy of the "living spirit," the human spirit which, both philosophically and historically, seeks to comprehend life in its various realizations and the spirit as normative content in intrinsic unity. It overcomes, on the one hand, the exclusive valuation of the physical, vital powers and, on the other, limits the calculating formalism of reason, no matter how successful the latter in its own field.

The spiritual life is manifest in different forms in cultures, in history, as well as in daily life. We have been given a compass which shows us to what degree in the historical hour, in the rich weave of interrelations, of choices and selections, a realization of basic human values has come about, and which rank was assigned to them, or whether devaluation and abandonment of value have occurred. In this sense we have to take and do take a position toward life every day. Not to acknowledge this obligation would mean fooling ourselves every day.

Today's events demand of philosophy a realistic approach, which includes, of course, a binding recognition of the secure results of natural science. But beyond this requirement the philosophical question about the sense and value of life is being asked. It is not sufficient, when we speak of the living spirit, or the spirit inherent in life, to content ourselves with general, conceptual abstractions, disregarding the particulars which include, precisely, the intensified degree of height and dimension of depth of the respective value realization. The latter is a synthesis of the particular and individual with the universal supraindividual core of being and meaning, of historicity and intellectual normativeness, of life and spiritual order. This combination seems to me of decisive importance. Aspects of meaning and value become realized in very different, often enriching variations and in different degrees. At the same time they manifest general normative principles of human conduct. Every age needs a deeply felt task and challenge to the human person, which alone make possible the human encounter. May our age, too, be granted the great thought which will enable it to live to the fullest.

NOTES

1. W. Heitler, "Das Bild des Menschen als Objekt der Naturwissenschaft," in Richard Schwarz, *Menschliche Existenz und moderne Welt. Ein internationales Symposium*, I (1967), 724; W. Heistermann, "Mensch und Maschine," *ibid.*, p. 788.

2. "Die Naturwissenschaft im geistigen Spannungsfeld der Gegenwart," in Schwarz, I, 718.

3. V. E. Frankl, "Tiefenpsychologismus und dimensionale Anthropologie," in Schwarz, I, 342, 346; "Aphoristische Bemerkungen zur Sinnproblematik," *Archiv für die gesamte Psychologie* (1964), pp. 336 f.

4. "Utopie und Wirklichkeit der Steuerung von Genen durch den Menschen," *Weltgespraeche*, I (1967), 33.

5. Schwarz, p. 794.

6. G. Huber, "Spiegelungen des Menschen in der gegenwärtigen Philosophie," *Festschrift G. Hug* (1968), p. 642.

7. See "Probleme der menschlichen und geschichtlichen Existenz in der modernen Welt," in Schwarz, II, 666.

8. *Ibid.*, I, p. 346. Cf. L. v. Bertalanffy, "Meaninglessness," *The World of Science and the World of Value: Challenges of Humanistic Psychology* (1967), p. 336.

9. H. Koehler, *Christliche Existenz in säkularer und totalitärer Welt* (1963), p. 86. See Schwarz, II, 664; *Nunc et semper*, II (1968), 6–7.

10. F. Heinemann, "Die Menschheit im Stadium der Absurdität," in Schwarz, I, 240. Jean Brun, "Für eine Entmythologisierung der Entmythologisierung," *Kerygma und Mythos*, VI (1968), 203.

11. G. Morgan, "Die Krise in Amerika und die Menschlichkeit des Menschen," in Schwarz, I, 115. Sarvepalli Radhakrishnan, "Menschsein als Idee und Verwirklichung in Indien," in Schwarz, II, 236.

12. "Das Weltbild des Atomwissenschaftlers," *Aral-Journal* (Spring, 1968).

13. *Pathologische Psychologie*, VIII (1930), 30.

14. *Das Glasperlenspiel*, I (1946), 148.

15. "Das Selbstverständnis des Menschen in der modernen Literatur," in Schwarz, I, 522.

16. See his work *Integrale Logik* (1965).

17. See E. Schwarz, *Wissenschaftliche und menschliche Existenz*, I, 111; II, 834, 846.

18. "Der Beitrag der Naturwissenschaft zum Problem der Willensfreiheit," in Schwarz, I, 737.

19. H. Mohr, *Wissenschaft und menschliche Existenz* (1967), p. 18.

20. The German word *Sinn* has no exact English equivalent. It is being translated, depending on the context, by "sense," "idea," "meaning," "significance." [Trans.] See also von Rintelen, "Sinn und Sinnverständnis," *Z. f. philos. F.*, II, No. 1 (1947), pp. 69–83; J. F. Heyde, "Vom Sinn des Wortes 'Sinn'," in *Sinn und Sein: Ein philosophisches Symposion*, ed. R. Wisser (1960), pp. 69 f.

21. See L. v. Bertalanffy, "Meaninglessness," pp. 338 f.

22. "Über das innere Wesen der Naturdinge," *Z. f. Ganzheitsforschung*, XII, No. 1 (1968), p. 16.

23. F. Heinemann, "Auf der Suche nach Sinn in einer zerbrochenen Welt," *Neue Rundschau* (1949), p. 35. Also, von Rintelen, "Der Wertaspekt," *Z. f. philos. F.*, XIX, No. 1 (1965). "A Realistic Analysis of Values," *International Philosophical Quarterly*, IV, No. 3 (1964). "El Carácter del Valor," *Rev. Nord-Este*, VII (1965), 7–38.

24. "Doubts Concerning Some Fundamental Assumptions of Contemporary Ethics," *XIV. International Congress of Philosophy* (Sept., 1968).

25. "Personality," *Nature, Society and Culture* (1953), p. 117. See Schwarz, "Probleme der menschlichen und geschichtlichen Existenz in der modernen Welt," II, 717.

26. See D. T. Suzuki, *Mysticism: Christian and Buddhist* (1967), pp. 36 f.; H. Dumoulin, *Zen* (1959), pp. 168 f.

27. Maynez, "Vom Wesenssinn des Rechtes," *Sinn und Sein*, p. 604.

28. P. 267.

Kant and the Problem of World Peace

PAUL ARTHUR SCHILPP

I DOUBT WHETHER any thinking person can be found today who would question the assertion that the most important problem facing mankind in the second half of the twentieth century is the problem of world peace. For the first time in the history of the human race mankind actually possesses the weapons which make the annihilation of the human race possible (whether or not probable). What is more: we are told, on highest governmental authority, that the U.S.S.R. already has enough such weapons to destroy mankind twelve times and the U.S.A. can accomplish the same feat twenty-five times! What no one is telling us is who is going to be around to do it the second time after the successful achievement of mankind's annihilation the first time.

It is facts such as these that make the problem of world peace the predominant issue of today—recognized as such by every President of the United States from Eisenhower on. It is also true, however, that practically no one in a position of governmental authority believes that philosophy could, even conceivably, have anything of significance to contribute to this problem—much less that it might have some really valid answers. And, as regards philosophers by and large, such judgment may not be far from the truth. For it does seem to be the case that most of them today appear to be so exclusively concerned with language, semantics, and grammar that they have no time left for any considerations of the problem of "to be or not to be." Apparently they seem to think that this problem should be left to poets and dramatists, à la Shakespeare.

As much as two centuries ago, however, there existed a philosopher who not only dealt with this problem of world peace, but seemed to think that it was of the utmost importance for mankind; namely, the great Sage of Königsberg, Immanuel Kant (1724–1804). And in the April 2, 1965, issue of *Time* magazine, there appeared the statement: "Edgar Faure, France's scholarly ex-Premier, dates the first serious, non-utopian version (of an international organization) from 1795, when Immanuel Kant developed a plan for world peace." It is a telling remark: Crediting the great Kant, they do not quote a philosopher, but a former premier of France.

True, almost every student of philosophy reads and respects Kant's *Critique of Pure Reason*. His second critique, the *Critique of Practical Reason*, is not only much less read but seems to hold in most philosophi-

cal students' minds a position of rather minor importance. Such a judgment is, of course, contrary to the relative importance assigned by Kant
himself to his first two critiques, as I tried to prove over thirty years ago
from Kant's own writings.[1] Even in the *Critique of Pure Reason* itself
we find Kant's statement concerning the "superiority which moral philosophy has over all other occupations of reason,"[2] a statement sufficiently clear and straightforward that one should think it could leave
no further doubt for any open-minded reader. John Silber has recently
demonstrated the fact that Kant gave us "The Copernican Revolution
in Ethics"[3] as surely as in epistemology.

Still fewer students of Kant seem yet to have realized the greatness of
the insight and the prophetic character of the ideas of Kant's small
treatise of 1795, *Zum Ewigen Frieden (Concerning Eternal Peace)*, published when Kant was seventy-one, in which he carries the ethical and
socio-political principles inherent in his larger works to their logical
conclusion as regards mankind's problems of war and peace—problems
which, as we have already seen, in the meantime, turned out to be the
problems *sine qua non* concerning the very existence of man on this
planet.

Within the brief compass of one essay it should at least be possible to
sketch some of Kant's major ideas on this important subject and briefly
to show how these ideas are indeed rooted in Kant's ethical views and
convictions. Moreover, I trust that, by the end of this paper, the reader
may realize that this discussion is not merely an academic exercise in
philosophical exhumation, but has something terribly important to say
to men who live in the space age.

In the very opening sentence of the tract, Kant reveals himself not
merely as a man of the world, but as one who—even in beginning a treatise on so serious a subject as the problem of war and peace—has not forgotten his humor. He calls the reader's attention to the fact that the title
of his tract, *Zum Ewigen Frieden*, reminds him of the satirical inscrip-
tion on a Dutch innkeeper's sign which not merely bore the same name
but also had a graveyard painted on it!

But the very same opening sentence also raises the question of whether this title is—or is not—applicable "to men in general, or particularly
to heads of state" (the latter "never tire of war"), or "perhaps only to
those philosophers who are dreaming the sweet dream of peace";[4] in
the long respected philosophical fashion, he leaves the question unde-
cided. And then he turns to entering a *caveat*—just in case anyone should
find his tract dangerous, not to say treasonable—that, after all, no ruling
statesman takes the philosopher or political theorist seriously anyway.
The ruling statesman can well afford, therefore, to let such theorists play

their harmless game. Was Kant trying to disguise the bitter seriousness of his treatise by this tone of gentle irony? Or was he really attempting to disarm his opponents in advance? One must not forget, in this connection, that the Prussia of Kant's day was a rigidly authoritarian state.

An ironical approach on Kant's part comes to light, by the way, once more later in the tract—in fact, in a second "Addition," which he entitles "A Secret Article Concerning Eternal Peace," Kant develops and advocates the idea that whenever any states are ready to go to war, it would be wise if the statesmen were first to consult the philosophers on the conditions and requirements of "public peace." But, inasmuch as much consultation would obviously appear humiliating to statemen, "in their great wisdom," this article will be kept secret:

> Hence the state will solicit the philosophers silently [by making it a secret] which means that it will let them talk freely and publicly about the general maxims of the conduct of war and the establishment of peace (for they will do it of their own accord, if only they are not forbidden to do so). . . . This does not mean that the state must concede the principles of the philosophers have priority over the rulings of the jurist (the representative of governmental power); it means that the philosopher be given a hearing.

Today's ruling statesmen do not even bother to give philosophers so much as a hearing. The closing paragraph of this secret article also is worth quoting:

> It is not to be expected that kings philosophize or that philosophers become kings, nor is it to be desired, because the possession of power corrupts the free judgment of reason inevitably. But kings or self-governing nations will not allow the class of philosophers to disappear or to become silent, but will let them speak publicly, because this is indispensable for both, in order to clarify their business. And, since this class of people are by their very nature incapable of forming gangs or clubs, they need not be suspected of carrying on propaganda.

These comments are still appropriate one and three-quarter centuries after they were written. Or can anyone imagine any government in power either consulting philosophers or taking them seriously?

The tract itself consists of the following sections: the main body of the text is divided into two main parts, the first of which contains six "preliminary" articles giving the negative conditions for the establishment of peace among states; whereas part two gives the three "definitive articles," specifically so named by Kant. These are followed by two "Additions," the first of which treats of "The Guarantee of Everlasting Peace," while the second—which was added by Kant only in the second edition of his tract—is the one called "the secret article." These additions, in turn, are followed by an "Appendix," which, in its turn, has two parts, the first of which treats of the "Disagreement between Morals and Politics in Relation to Everlasting Peace," while the second discusses the "Agreement between Politics and Morals According to the Transcendental Idea of Public Right and Law." The tract ends on Kant's insistence that everlasting peace "is no empty idea, but a task which, gradually solved, steadily approaches its aim"; namely, that of making real "a state of public law" by "an infinitely gradual approximation."

We turn now to the content of the tract. The six "preliminary articles" read as follows:

1. No treaty of peace shall be considered to be such, which is made with the secret reservation containing the material for a future war.
2. No independent state, large or small, shall be acquired by another state through inheritance, exchange, purchase or gift.
3. Standing armies shall in time disappear.
4. The state shall not contract any debts in connection with the foreign affairs of the state.
5. No state shall interfere by force in the constitution and government of another state.
6. No state at war with another shall permit any acts of warfare which must make mutual confidence impossible in time of future peace: such as the employment of assassins, or poisoners, the violation of articles of surrender, the instigation of treason in the state against which it is waging war, etc. These are dishonourable strategems. [What, by the way, would be the reaction of the CIA to this article?]

These six conditions are, obviously, interrelated and depend, for their final justification, upon the tract as a whole. But every one of them describes practices which not merely existed in 1795, but which still exist today. One thing should be clear, even from these "preliminary articles," namely, that Kant was questioning state absolutism of any kind, a dangerous thing to do in a monarchical state. The fact is that even today most so-called peace treaties are hardly anything more than armistices, a fact to which Kant himself returns in the very last sentence of his tract where he refers to the "peace-makings falsely so-called because they are just truces."[5] Under such conditions, he says, any lasting peace obviously is impossible. Kant himself clearly puts his finger on the underlying difficulty of the problem when, at the very end of the comments on the first "preliminary article," he writes: "But if, according to the enlightened ideas of political prudence, the true honor of the state consists in the continual increase of its power by any means whatsoever, then my reasoning will, of course, appear academic and pedantic."[6] Is not Kant, with this sarcastic stroke, saying that peace can be had only at the price of giving up the veritable craze for power? And, if so, is he not flying directly in the face of all so-called "good people"—even today—

who keep insisting that only the *power* of deterrence can keep the peace?

At the same time, Kant is no idle utopian dreamer. He introduces the second major part of *Zum Ewigen Frieden* with these words: "The state of peace among men who live together is not a natural state; for the natural state is one of war, i. e., if not a state of open hostilities, still a continuous threat of such. The state of peace must therefore be established." Is this not hard-headed realism and facing of the facts, however unpleasant? In fact, the same philosopher, in our tract, makes not merely the most plausible but the most insistent demand for a federation of all the states of the world as the only ultimately feasible condition of creating, maintaining, and preserving world peace. In his 1793 essay, "Concerning the proverb: That may be correct in theory, but is no good in practice," Kant is frank enough to mention the possibility that "a condition of universal peace" could, conceivably, "produce the most terrible despotism," with the whole world united under one head and no chance at all of throwing off the yoke. Whatever else, Kant is no rosy-hued, wild-eyed utopian idealist. He keeps his feet quite solidly on the ground, even politically.

Perhaps it could be said that Kant was first, last, and always concerned with the fullest possible development of the autonomous moral personality as the real goal of man, a goal which he realized could be achieved only by way of the establishment of a universal rule of law, and that only such a universal rule of law could guarantee universal and eternal peace.

Such an idea, he had written in 1784, in his *Ideen zu einer allgemeinen Geschichte*,

> may seem utopian [yet] it is the inevitable escape from the distress into which human beings bring each other. It must force the states to the resolution [however difficult a pill it may be for them to swallow] to which savage man was forced equally unwillingly, namely: to surrender his brutal freedom and to seek calm and security under a lawful constitution.[7]

And earlier, in the same paragraph, Kant had said:

> Through the wars, through the excessive and never realized preparation for them, through the want which hence every state even in the midst of peace must feel, nature drives man to make attempts, at first quite inadequate, to leave the lawless state of savages, and to enter a league of nations; where each state, even the smallest, may expect his security and his rights—not from its own power or its own legal views, but alone from this great league of nations, from a united power, and from a decision according to laws adopted by the united will.[8]

It is very clear, then, that Kant is looking for a firm basis of law for international order.

His first definitive article for an eternal peace reads: *"The civil constitution of each state should be republican."* Why "republican"? I think the answer is reasonably clear. What Kant is after is constitutional government, i. e., a constitution established according to well-defined laws which represent the consent of the citizens. Every student of Kant knows of his everlasting emphasis on freedom under law. Such a republican constitution, Kant says, is "founded on three principles. First the principle of the freedom of all members of a society (as men). Second, the principle of the dependence of all upon a single common legislation (as subjects); and third, the principle of the equality of all (as citizens)."

Real freedom has to take the freedom of all other free men into consideration constantly. And the only laws which are possible to such free men are such as result from agreement by consent of the citizens. Morally free and autonomous men—and nations—can maintain peace only by recourse to the widest possible organization under law, so that only a truly international government really can preserve the peace.

In his 1793 essay ("Theory and Practice") to which reference has already been made, Kant pays his emphatic respect to all those who put their trust for peace into the so-called Balance of Power. There he says:

> An enduring universal peace by way of the so-called balance of power in Europe is—like Swift's house, which, having been perfectly erected by a master-builder according to all the laws of equilibrium, which, as soon as a sparrow came to sit on it, collapsed—a mere phantom.[9]

Surely Kant could not have said it more pointedly or more emphatically.

Let us move now to Kant's second definitive article, which, for our purposes, really contains the heart of the message. It reads: *"International Law shall be based upon a Federalism of free states."* By "free states," Kant obviously means states with a republican constitution, states, that is to say, which depend upon lawful relations based on the consent of the governed.

In the second paragraph Kant begins the discussion of the second consent of the governed.

> We look with deep aversion upon the way primitive peoples are attached to their lawless liberty—a liberty which enables them to fight incessantly rather than subject themselves to the restraint of the law to be established by themselves; in short, to prefer wild freedom to a reasonable one. We look upon such an attitude as raw, uncivilized, and an animalic degradation of humanity. Therefore, one should think, civilized peoples (each united in a state) would hasten to get away from such a depraved state as soon as possible. Instead, each state insists upon seeing the essence of its majesty (for, popular majesty is a paradox) in this, that it is not subject to any external coercion . . . .

In view of the evil nature of man, which can be observed clearly in the free relation between nations (while in a civil and legal state it is covered by governmental coercion), it is surprising that the word *law* [*Recht*] has not been entirely banned from the politics of war as pedantic, and that no state has been bold enough to declare itself publicly as of this opinion . . . . States as such are not subject to a common external coercion. There is not a single case known in which a state has been persuaded by arguments reinforced by the testimony of such weighty men to desist from its aggressive design . . . .

In short, the manner in which states seek their rights can never be a suit before a court, but only war. However, war and its successful conclusion, victory, does not decide what is law and what is right. A peace treaty puts an end to a particular war, but not to the state of war which consists in finding ever new pretexts for starting a new one. Nor can this be declared strictly unjust because in this condition each is the judge in his own cause . . . .

Nevertheless, reason speaking from the throne of the highest legislative power condemns war as a method of finding what is right. Reason makes [the achievement of] the state of peace a direct duty, and such a state of peace cannot be established or maintained without a treaty of the nations among themselves. Therefore, there must exist a union of a particular kind which we may call the pacific union which would be distinguished from a peace treaty by the fact that the latter tries to end merely one war, while the former tries to end all wars forever. This union is not directed toward the securing of some additional power of the state, but merely toward maintaining and making secure the freedom of each state by and for itself and at the same time of the other states thus allied with each other. And yet, these states will not subject themselves . . . to laws and to the enforcement of such laws.

It can be demonstrated that this idea of federalization possesses objective reality, that it can be realized by a gradual extension to all states, leading to eternal peace. For, if good fortune brings it to pass that a powerful and enlightened people develops a republican form of government which by nature is inclined toward peace, then such a republic will provide the central core for the federal union of other states. For they can join this republic and can thus make secure among themselves the state of peace according to the idea of a law of nations, and can gradually extend themselves by additional connections of this sort . . . .

On the other hand, a concept of the law of nations as a right to make war is meaningless; for it is supposed to be a right to determine what is right not according to external laws limiting the freedom of each individual, but by force and according to one-sided maxims. Unless we are ready to accept this meaning: that it serves people who have such views quite right if they exhaust each other and thus find eternal peace in the wide grave which covers all the atrocities of violence together with its perpetrators. For states in their relation to each other there cannot, according to reason, be any other way to get away from the lawless state which contains nothing but war than to give up, like individual men, their wild and (lawless) freedom, to accept public and enforceable laws, and thus to form a constantly growing world state of all nations (*civitas gentium*) which finally would comprise all nations. But states do not want this, as not in keeping with their idea of a law of nations, and thus they reject in fact what is true in theory.* Therefore, (unless all is to be lost), the positive idea of a world republic must be replaced by the negative substitute of a union of nations which maintains itself, prevents wars, and steadily expands. Only such a union may, under existing conditions, stem the tide of the law-evading, bellicose propensities in man, but unfortunately be subject to the constant danger of their eruption.[10]

I believe it is safe to say that what Kant actually desires as his "positive idea" is a government of nations, an actual comprehensive world state, as his final goal. But, inasmuch as people are just not ready to accept a comprehensive world state (world government), we will have to be satisfied with the "negative substitute" of an ever expanding federation of nations, which will try to prevent war by restraining man's hostile tendencies and by trying to get the nations to act under law instead of merely on the basis of national self-interest. But he realizes in the end that, after all, the "substitute" leaves us with the constant danger of the outbreak of new wars, so that, although he is willing to grant that federalism is better than nothing, it actually cannot guarantee peace or prevent war. On the other hand, we have already seen that he realizes also that an actual world government raises the possibility of a worldwide dictatorship and that it may, therefore, be wiser to aim at federalism.

The other point which stands out so clearly in Kant's second definitive article is his straightforward insistence that war is contrary to the moral law. A "law of war" for Kant is a contradiction in terms. What is right can, according to him, never be decided by victory in war, since moral consciousness condemns war and makes peace a matter of duty.

In his third definitive article, "*The Cosmopolitan or World Law shall be limited to conditions of a universal hospitality*," Kant undertakes briefly to discuss the place and function of the world citizen in a peaceful world. Universal hospitality shall be accorded to all men—as visitors

---

*After the end of a war, at the conclusion of a peace, it would not be improper for a people to set a day of atonement after the day of thanks so as to pray to heaven asking forgiveness for the heavy guilt which mankind is under, because it will not adapt itself to a legal constitution in its relation to other nations. Proud of its independence, each nation will rather employ the barbaric means of war by which that which is being sought, namely the right of each state, cannot be discovered. The celebration of victory, the hymns which in good Old Testament style are sung to the Lord of Hosts, contrast equally sharply with the moral idea of the Father of mankind; because besides the indifference concerning the manner in which people seek their mutual right, which is lamentable enough, they rejoice over having destroyed many people and their happiness. [Can anyone imagine any victorious nation setting aside such a "day of atonement"?]

—by all peoples. Visitors—yes; but conquerors—no! Conquest and colonialism, to say nothing of imperialism, are contrary to world order.

It is amazing, moreover, to note how—as long ago as 1795—Kant was acutely aware of the shrinking of our planet. So much so, in fact, that he states here that a violation of law at one point is bound to be felt everywhere on the planet. Kant's urging of real world citizenship seems to imply the concept of human equality everywhere. Here is the way Kant puts it in the concluding paragraph of his third definitive article:

> The narrower or wider community of all nations on earth has in fact progressed so far that a violation of law and right in one place is felt in all others. Hence the idea of a cosmopolitan or world law is not a fantastic or utopian way of looking at law, but a necessary completion of the unwritten code of constitutional and internal law to make it a public law of mankind. Only under this condition can we flatter ourselves that we are continually approaching eternal peace.[11]

Without actual world law, Kant is saying, we are not even *approaching* peace; world law is a sine qua non of world peace.

So much for the major body of Kant's tract. It may be interesting, in this connection, merely to note parenthetically that the two Additions plus the Appendix are approximately one-third longer than the text proper. However, that, too, seems to be the way of philosophers.

In his first Addition, Kant argues that it is nature itself which offers the guarantee of eternal peace—although, by the time he comes to the last paragraph of the section, he admits that "the certainty [that eternal peace will come to pass] is not sufficient for us to predict such a future in any theoretical sense. But for practical purposes the certainty suffices and makes it one's duty to work toward this not merely chimerical end."[12]

How does nature offer such a guarantee? Kant replies: "Nature's [even] mechanical course evidently reveals a teleology: to produce harmony out of the very disharmony of men even against their will."[13] Nature has made it possible for human beings to live anywhere on earth, and by war, she has driven them all over the globe and has forced them into more or less legal relationships.

But "war itself does not require a special motivation, inasmuch as it seems to be grafted on human nature." In fact, "it is even considered to be something noble for which man is inspired by the love of honor . . . . Even philosophers will praise war as ennobling mankind."[14] How, then, "does nature guarantee that what man ought to do according to the laws of freedom, but does not do, will be made secure regardless of this freedom by a compulsion of nature which forces him to do it?" Kant answers his own question by insisting that nature suffices to this end at all three levels of constitutional, international, and world law.

1. At the (internal) *constitutional* level, "if internal conflicts did not compel a people to submit themselves to the compulsion of public laws, external wars would accomplish the same purpose." True: "the republican constitution is the only one which is fully adequate to the rights of man, but it is also the hardest to create and even more difficult to maintain. . . . But now nature [itself] comes to the aid of this revered, but practically ineffectual, general will which is founded in reason." It is only necessary, Kant says, "to organize the state well (which is indeed within man's ability) and so to direct these [even] selfish forces against each other so that one balances the other . . . . Consequently, the result for reason is as if both selfish forces were non-existent. Thus man, although not a morally good man, is compelled to be a good citizen." Kant goes even farther: "The problem of establishing a state is solvable even for a people of devils, if only they have intelligence, though this may sound harsh." "Such a problm," he writes, "must be solvable. For it is not the moral perfection of mankind, but merely the mechanism of nature, which this task seeks to know how to use in order to arrange the conflict of unpacific attitudes in a given people in such a way that they impel each other to submit themselves to compulsory laws and thus bring about the state of peace in which such laws are enforced . . . . In short, we can say that nature wants irresistibly that law achieve superior force."[15]

2. At the *international* level the very "idea of a law of nations presupposes the separate existence of many severally independent states. Such a situation in and of itself constitutes a state of war." But, Kant goes on to say, "it is the desire of every state, or of its ruler, to enter into a permanent state of peace by ruling if possible the whole world. But nature has decreed differently. It employs the differences in language and in religion to differentiate peoples." And these differences, in turn, "occasion the inclination toward mutual hatred and the excuse for war; yet at the same time they lead, as culture increases and men generally come closer together, toward a greater agreement on principles for peace and understanding."[16]

3. At the level of *world law* it is mutual self-interest which, according to Kant, does the trick. The *commercial spirit*, "which sooner or later takes hold of every nation," "cannot co-exist with war." (How one wishes this really were so.) And "inasmuch as the power of money is perhaps the most reliable among all the powers subordinate to the state's power, states find themselves impelled . . . to promote the noble peace." "It is in this way that nature guarantees lasting peace by the mechanism of human inclinations,"

although, as we have already seen, Kant admits that the "certainty is not sufficient" for prediction.

Kant's second Addition, the "secret article" concerning everlasting peace, we have already discussed. We may then turn our attention, finally, to the Appendix to the tract. The Appendix is, as a matter of fact, in length just short of the length of the original major part of the piece. It is divided into two halves, dealing respectively with, first, the disagreements between morals and politics in relation to everlasting peace, and, second, the agreements, of which the former is by far the longer section (as one might expect).

Much of the Disagreement section is concerned with the "serpentine turnings of an amoral prudential doctrine" of the politician who uses sophistical maxims to gain his predetermined ends, such as: "Act first and explain—or excuse—as best you can afterwards" [the U-2 incident]; or "Never admit any guilt (for anything which may have gone wrong) on your own part: always find a more or less convenient scapegoat" [the *Pueblo* incident]; or the famous maxim "Divide and conquer!" [Britain in India]. "It will be well," Kant says, "to uncover the fraud with which such persons deceive themselves and others, and to discover the highest principle from which the purpose of everlasting peace is derived and to show that all the evil which stands in the way of eternal peace results from the fact that . . . the political moralist subordinates his principles to the end, i. e., puts the cart before the horse, and thereby thwarts his own purpose of bringing politics into agreement with morals."[17]

According to Kant, practical philosophy can be harmonized within itself only if in tasks of practical reason we start, not from the material, but from the formal principle, from the principle, that is to say, "which relates to freedom in one's relation to the outside world" as laid down in the Categorical Imperative: "So act that you could want the maxim of your action to become a universal law, regardless of the end." For, "as a principle of right," this formal principle "possesses absolute necessity." This principle of the moral politician is an ethical task "which is now desired not only as a mere physical good, but also as a condition resulting from the recognition of duty."[18]

> . . . the a priorily given general will (within a nation or in the relation between nations) alone determines what is right amongst men. At the same time this union of the will of all . . . can be the cause within the mechanism of nature which produces the intended effect and thus effectuates the idea of law.
>
> Thus it is a principle of moral politics that a people should unite into a state solely according to the natural-law concepts of freedom and equality. This principle is based upon duty. . . .[19]

[In order to achieve the desired result] there is required first of all an internal constitution of the state which is organized according to the pure principles of right and law, but then also the union of such a state with other states, either neighboring or more remote, for the purpose of settling their controversies legally (in analogy to what a universal state might do).

But "political maxims must *not* proceed from considering the welfare and happiness to be expected from their being followed; . . . such maxims must be derived from the pure principle of duty under natural law (from the *ought* the principle of which is given a priori by pure reason) regardless of what might be the physical consequences thereof."[20]

Consequently, Kant comes to the conclusion that "no conflict exists objectively (in theory) between morals and politics. Only subjectively, in the selfish disposition of men . . . such a conflict may remain. . . ."[21]

In fact, he goes so far as to assert that "the moral principle in man is never extinguished, and reason, which is capable pragmatically of executing the ideas of natural law according to this principle, is steadily on the increase because of the progress in culture . . . ."[22] One only wishes he could agree with this all-too-optimistic view of the increase of reason.

According to Kant we must "assume that the pure principles of right and law have objective reality in the sense that they can be realized . . . . [In fact] true politics cannot take a single step without first paying homage to morals"—in which case the contemporary, twentieth-century modern man may be pardoned if he wonders whether there are any "true politicians."

But Kant goes on to insist that "the [natural] right of men must be held sacred, regardless of how much sacrifice is required of the powers that be. It is impossible to figure out a middle road, such as a pragmatically conditional right, between right and utility. All politics must bend its knee before the [natural] rights of men . . . ."[23] (How greatly Eleanor Roosevelt would have enjoyed this Kantian remark while she was engaged in her great task of helping to write the U.N.'s *Universal Declaration of Human Rights.*)

The final section of the Appendix is entirely concerned with a discussion of what Kant calls "the formal quality of publicity" in the use and exercise of public law. "Without publicity," he writes, "there cannot be justice . . . and hence also no right, since that is only imparted by justice." "This quality provides a criterion which is easily applied and a priori discoverable through reason. . . ." Kant therefore announces the following statement as "the transcendental formula of public law: 'All actions which relate to the right of other men are contrary to right and law, the maxim of which does not permit publicity.' This principle should not only be considered as ethically relevant . . . , but also as juridically relevant."[24] We have, in this statement, one of the best ethical justifications for the freedom of the press and all means of public communication. (See Bryce W. Rucker, *The First Freedom*, Carbondale, Ill., 1968).

When, in the last part of this section, Kant comes to apply this principle to international law, he says:

> The fact that the maxims of international law are not compatible in principle with publicity constitutes a good sign that politics and morals do not agree [in this area] . . . . For the basic condition of the possibility of a [true] law of nations is that there should exist a lawful state . . . . We have seen that a federative state among the states which has merely the purpose of eliminating war is the only lawful state which can be combined with the freedom of these states. Therefore the agreement of politics with morals is possible only within a federative union. . . . All political prudence has only one lawful ground upon which to proceed, namely to establish such a union upon the most comprehensive basis possible. Without this purpose, all its arguments are unwisdom and camouflaged injustice.[25]

I do not see how Kant could have stated his insistence that peace is possible only under universal law and such law is conceivable only in federal union of all existing states more clearly or more emphatically. World rule, i. e., world government, under one universal law is the *sine qua non* of universal peace, then.

But even this late in his tract, Kant has not forgotten much of the burden of his ethical theory. He writes: "Both charity for other men and respect for the right of others is a duty. But charity is only a conditional duty, whereas respect for the right of others is an unconditional, and hence absolutely commanding duty."[26]

As an "affirmative principle of public law" he finally proposes the following formula: "All maxims which *require* publicity in order not to miss their purpose agree with right, law, and politics." This principle, he asserts, "is a transcendental formula [since it can be stated] by excluding all empirical conditions of happiness as material of the law, and by merely taking into account the form of universal legality."[27]

Here, all too briefly, I have tried to delineate the ideas and at least the major arguments contained in Kant's famous tract on *Zum Ewigen Frieden*. It is—at least in my humble judgment—a remarkable document, which, with all its faults (and it would be silly to deny that it has faults), even after a century and three-quarters, still is one of the most profound analyses of the problems of war and peace ever penned by man.

Long before the atom, hydrogen, or cobalt bomb, Kant saw with great lucidity that, so long as more than one nation laid claim to absolute national sovereignty, peace among nations—as, indeed, among individuals—could be maintained only by everyone's living under law. But it is the very essence of the claim to national sovereignty to acknowledge no law above that of the nation. Consequently, the claim to national sovereignty can result only in international anarchy. And international anarchy is precisely what we have today. We have a so-called World Court; however, not only are its decisions not binding on any nation, but neither can a problem even be brought before the court without the initial consent of the contending parties. Consequently, as far as the world's major and most powerful nations are concerned, the World Court might as well not exist.

And even the United Nations are, as often as not, the dis-United Nations, as we have had all too much opportunity to observe during the last twenty-four years. Do not misinterpret this statement; as things stand at this moment, I am a strong and staunch supporter of the United Nations (in harmony with the principle that, if a community cannot have a church, it should at least have a saloon!). But the fact remains that the U.N.—just because it is not an actual federation of nations and governments under one universal world law—has neither the ability nor the power to enforce its will against the major governments of the world. (This is to say nothing of the initial requirement that only "peace-loving" nations were invited to join the U.N. The *definition* of "peace-loving" in the Dumbarton Oaks preliminary statement reads: "Any nation having declared *war* on one of the Axis-powers by March 25, 1945.")

The fact remains that—aside from the Utopian dream of all men loving each other (a worthy dream, but not one to be realized in our lifetime, I am sure—for example, one need only recall the scurrilous language used by supposedly "good Christians" during the presidential campaign of 1960)—peace among nations depends upon the enactment, use, and enforcement of universal law. And such enforcement requires an enforcing universal agency, which obviously, only an actual, honest-to-goodness world government can be. That such a world government needs to be a federation, if the relative fredom and independence of the federated states are to be preserved, Kant also saw clearly 175 years ago.

Thus, I find myself in complete agreement with Carl Joachim Friedrich (of Harvard), when he says that Kant "has given us the most coherent, viable, and comprehensive philosophy of peace which the bourgeois world has [yet] produced."[28]

That mankind as a whole is not very likely to listen to Kant's not merely good but, from my point of view, necessary advice is best demonstrated by the fact that, although his tract was published 175 years ago, it has, thus far, hardly made a dent on mankind's thinking and still less on our actions. So much the worse for mankind! Even philosophers, by and large, have paid almost no attention to it. Perhaps the title *philosopher* is a misnomer: perhaps we are not "lovers of wisdom" after all.

Notes

1. *Kant's Pre-Critical Ethics* (Evanston, 1938, 1960, 1966), esp. pp. 10–14.

2. *Critique of Pure Reason*, trans. by Norman Kemp Smith, 2d ed. (London, 1933), p. 658.

3. The title of his essay in *Kant-Studien*, LI (1959–60), 85–101.

4. All references to *Zum Ewigen Frieden* are to Karl Vorländer's 2d ed. (1919); my translation.

5. *Ibid.*, p. 55.

6. *Ibid.*, p. 6.

7. *Ideen zu einer allgemeinen Geschichte, Immanuel Kant's Werke*, ed. Ernst Cassirer (Berlin, 1922–23), IV, 159; see also *Zum Ewigen Frieden*, pp. 56–57.

8. *Ideen zu einer allgemeinen Geschichte, Immanuel Kant's Werke*, p. 159; see also *Zum Ewigen Frieden*, p. 56.

9. *Zum Ewigen Frieden*, p. 63.

10. *Ibid.*, pp. 17–21.

11. *Ibid.*, p. 25.

12. *Ibid.*, p. 34.

13. *Ibid.*, p. 25.

14. *Ibid.*, p. 30.

15. *Ibid.*, pp. 31–33.

16. *Ibid.*, pp. 33 f.

17. *Ibid.*, pp. 42–44.

18. *Ibid.*, pp. 44 f.

19. *Ibid.*, p. 46.

20. *Ibid.*, p. 47.

21. *Ibid.*

22. *Ibid.*, p. 48.

23. *Ibid.*, pp. 48 f.

24. *Ibid.*, p. 49.

25. *Ibid.*, p. 53.

26. *Ibid.*, p. 54.

27. *Ibid.*, p. 55.

28. Carl Joachim Friedrich, *Inevitable Peace* (Cambridge, Mass., 1948), p. 21.

Happiness: Intrinsic or Extrinsic?

BERTRAM MORRIS

I TAKE MY SUBJECT to be the question of how to construe *happiness* in human life, not as the particulars of good fortune or of an apt or fitting action,[1] but in relation to a kind of life at which men may aim. This aim may be seen in the use of *happiness* as in "the pursuit of happiness" rather than in its use as in "the happiness of meeting my friend in the market" or in "the happiness of having taken my raincoat to the mountains." Although the suggestion of success, aptness, or fitness may be pertinent to happiness in life, as referring to the particulars of life it does not conform to the broadened use. Pursuit of happiness is not consummated by an incident of life or by a lucky event of fortune. The question remains as to what, if anything, would constitute a consummation which would turn the pursuit into a realization. If the end of the pursuit were to be realized, it would no doubt have to be described either as a substantive or an adjective.

Were it a substantive, it would be capable of being denoted. Then it would be an object of desire which could be recognized and enjoyed, such as a red apple or a yellow buttercup. Yet it is clear that no namable object satisfies the demands of happiness. We must be wrong then in suggesting that it is an object of desire or else that we are using *desire* in a peculiar sense when we say men desire happiness as an object to be attained. It is true that we may say we desire (as the object of happiness?) peace and prosperity. The expression may well be correct even though what linguistically are nouns actually are not that. If *peace,* for example, means absence of warfare, or something tantamount, it signifies either a negation or a kind of activity. Neither, however, is properly designated as a substantive. Consequently, the significance of the term shifts from that of a substantive to that of an adjective, for it is in truth a modifier of action rather than an identifiable object to be obtained. Happiness does not consist of a feeling, a mood, or any other identifiable state of consciousness, or an object capable of being possessed.

If we persist in using *substantive* in this context, it is more appropriately used in such an expression as "substantive action," which is opposed, say, to "formal action." Or more pointedly, if we regard "peace and prosperity" as the "object" of happiness, then the object really turns out to be a gerundive. *Peace* means "peaceful activities" and *prosperity,* a "life of prospering." The positive content is, then, the *peaceful arts,* through which men carry on the business of life. The adjective at least excludes the arts of warfare, which certainly are not part of human happiness. If happiness is "the blank pages of history," it is so, not because it is a life without felicity, but because its aim is not to create an empire over which a people subject others to their rule.

If we may agree that happiness signifies the practice of the peaceful arts, there is still the question of how these arts are related to one another and what the place of the artisan is to his art as well as to other artisans. The language appears somewhat quaint for today; yet it is, I think, worth keeping because it can be instructive both of a certain standard of happiness and of a certain criticism of industrial society. The quaint view may be suggested by two quite different manners of speaking of a man's relation to the arts. The one is associated with the Puritan's view and the other with the engineer's. Together they make for an interesting combination. The Puritan spoke of it as a man's "calling," the practice of which defined for him a special place in the world as well as a special relation to God. This assured him of an expression of a personal commitment as well as guaranteeing his being part of a benevolent plan designed by God. The engineer's view is couched in the phrase "instinct for workmanship," which is a secular version of the Puritan "vocation of man." Whatever the "instinct" is, it gets expressed through man's designing tools and machines, and in consistently employing them to satisfy his needs. Means and ends thus become mutually adapted to each other, and concern is as much for the one as for the other. Workmanship comes to have a kind of value of its own such that the adjective *happy* is applicable at least to the workman. Both views suggest a fittingness of man in the scheme of things. The question is whether a vocation of an expression of instinct is sufficient for the definition of happiness.

Can a man who practices his vocation be happy in a world torn by strife and shot through with misery? Possibly a person can be happy in a world otherwise given over to strife and misery, but it seems more than inhuman for a man to be happy under such circumstances. It would seem odd under these circumstances that a person could be happy, even if he were engaged in the practice of healing body or soul. However much one may be committed to his vocation, his life is inevitably bound up with the life of others and their pursuits. To be happy in the midst of unhappiness is a sordid affair, if not a contradiction in terms. Happiness suggests a kind of consistency in life, a kind of productivity, in which the arts support one another in a more or less complete way.

Some arts, therefore, are contrary to this kind of life. Death-dealing arts or those that cripple and maim others, physically or mentally, are contrary to it. And in general the practice of any art that aggrandizes a person at the expense of others appears contrary to it. Hence, although there may in a sense be a kind of instinct of workmanship employed in picking pockets or in inducing people by skillful means to buy what they neither want nor need and which may actually be known to the purveyors to be harmful—such arts surely do not satisfy the happiness principle. Unless artisans are a sort of jolly Robin Hood gang, their expertise only further degrades them from realizing the kind of peaceful pursuit that rightly satisfies the happiness principle. I find then that in practicing my art my pursuit is interdependent with others pursuing their arts. Since men cannot live alone, neither can their happiness be in themselves alone, for happiness is not divisible, even if the activities that sustain it are.

Must it not then be that it exists only in all people, or else in no one? The all-or-none test is a stringent one. If it appears too stringent, we may wish to appeal to one less so, even though a line of demarcation becomes difficult to draw. But since we say a person can be "happy" or "supremely happy," and since "annoyances" are not usually regarded as a serious deterrence to happiness, a less stringent test may be appropriate.

We may reasonably conclude that as long as there is not widespread misery in the community in which a person lives, he may find his happiness in pursuing a vocation or in expressing workmanship suited to carrying on the life of the community. Suitability is a matter of the relations of activities to one another, so that they support one another, or at least do not annul one another. At best, it suggests common ends to be pursued, or at any rate, ends which do not cause debilitation and frustration. Thus, whatever is fit for human life must not be degrading or inhuman, and it surely cannot be defined apart from one's relations to others. Apart from others, a person may be a Nero or a Don Quixote, but not a happy man.

The same is true of the arts or of particular callings in themselves, since apart from the larger community they have no intrinsic value and, therefore, lose their virtue. Why, for example, architecture? Or why teaching? The architect's art is good for making buildings or the teacher's art for educating students. But then we have to ask whether buildings or education is good per se. As we examine these questions, we come to see that we cannot convincingly say that an art or calling is good in and of itself. The arts do not store up well; for as soon as we make something precious of them, they become museum pieces. Then they may be good as history, but not as activity, and, consequently, not as life.

If an art is not properly termed good in itself, possibly there is another element associated with it that may make it good and, therefore, serve to make a man happy. The most likely candidate is pleasure, for it is not only said by many to be the chief good in life, but is even said by some to *be* the happiness principle. Does pleasure and pleasure alone taken in activity confer value upon it? Do we seek pleasure? If so, does it amount to happiness as the principal end of life? These are all old questions of value theory, which we need not rehash. Clearly, whatever the value of pleasure, it is not the same as happiness. One does not say, "I am supremely pleasure" (or even "pleased" or "pleasured" or "pleasant") in the sense in which one says "I am supremely happy." The reason is that pleasure is not an activity, and possibly not even the quality of an activity in such cases of the pleasures that are a relief of pain or the warmth of the sun or of the coolness of a mountain breeze. Happiness, however, is an activity of a certain kind, save for that abnormal state in which one may be said to be "slap-happy."

The conclusion is irresistible: pleasure and happiness are not the same. Consequently, if pleasure is the chief end of life, then happiness cannot be; and if happiness is the chief end, then pleasure cannot be. Also, something is wrong, or at least something is concealed, in the utilitarian principle that interprets the "greatest happiness of the greatest number" as equivalent to "the maximization of pleasure" (or "the minimization of pain"). Pleasures cannot add up to happiness, mostly because pleasures cannot be added, but primarily because, if they could, they still would neither be nor produce happiness. The addition does not yield a sum, even though we may speak of a day or a time of "many pleasures" or of "a short-lived pleasure" or "count your pleasures," etc. Even if we could somehow add the pleasures of a whole life, the sum, however great, cannot equal happiness. We still need to distinguish a life of pleasure(s), which may be phrenetic, from a happy life, which cannot so be. The additive interpretation of the happiness principle simply will not do.

Possibly a different interpretation of the alternative to the additive may save the principle. The most likely one would then be that some kind of organization of life activities is required in order to maximize pleasure(s). Accordingly, the maximization of pleasure would be a function of, say, the harmonization of activities. Thus, a selective principle would be introduced, which, instead of being a selection of pleasures, would be a selection of activities, the consequence of which would be the maximum pleasure. Clearly, a virtue of this interpretation is that it makes much more sense to choose one's activities than to choose pleasures. One may choose to be an architect, but one does not choose the pleasures of being an architect. In the one case, choice may be based upon good reasons; in the other, it cannot be. Authentic issues of life are engendered in the former; there are no such issues in the latter because pleasure cannot serve as a selective principle. "Choose to be an architect" is directive; "choose pleasure" is not. According to this interpretation, the hedonic principle appears non-functional in comparison with another principle which is functional.

The functional principle that needs to be substituted for the hedonic is that of the fitness, or suitability, of activities for promoting the life processes. The *organization* of such activities is their suitability for promoting the end, which is nothing other than life itself.

The means by which life is sustained are the peaceful arts. Thus, we are led back once again to declaring that the happiness principle is the life principle, or that happiness is just life well lived. Moreover, we are led to conclude that a well-lived life is reflected in the arts of man as far as they support one another, and, thus, it is a life that also includes the men who are their agents. The dynamics of the arts, the clashes they produce, and the possible means for resolving the clashes are complex matters the understanding of which calls for elucidation far beyond the present, limited discussion. Yet, there is a question about the relation of happiness to the various arts that is central to our discussion and should not be ignored: how can happiness, which is regarded as being an intrinsic value, be defined by the arts, the values of which are regarded as being extrinsic? In other words, how can the whole as an intrinsic value be defined by its components, none of which possesses such value?

Before considering the question in relation to the arts, we may profitably consider it in relation to the human virtues. Why should one be continent or kind or honest or brave? The reply, of course, may be that each is good in and of itself, or at least that some of the virtues are. The simple answer is that they are *right*, and that is an end to the matter. Of course, the shift from *good* to *right* is not inconsiderable. Although it complicates the question, it does not, I think, alter the final outcome, for the use of these terms in this context may actually be synonymous. Virtue or morality may very well be good in and of itself, or right, and not be susceptible of any proof. But the same is not true of virtues; for virtues are qualities of men, not things in themselves, and they may conflict with one another. An incontinent act may be justified, but not an incontinent man. The same may be true of an unkind or dishonest or cowardly act, but not of a man with these traits. If it is true that one virtuous act does not make a virtuous man, is it also true that one wicked act does not make a wicked man? The latter statement is subject to question, not because a wicked act is so bad in and of itself as because, as with contaminated food, it may contaminate all the other actions of a man. A coward becomes dishonest and unkind and incontinent and so forth. This line of reasoning, however, supports the allegation that goodness or badness is either a quality of the whole or is justifiable, or the reverse, by reason of its relations to some of its qualities.

If happiness is a function of the virtues taken together as a whole, then as one virtuous act does not make a virtuous man, neither does one virtue make a happy man. Happiness then becomes an affair of the relation of the virtues to one another, and indeed the virtues have virtue by reason of their relationships to one another. Vice, too, is then a question of the clashing and annulling of actions rather than an intrinsic quality of an act itself. Kant acknowledged that fact in appealing to the principle of autonomy as opposed to heteronomy, but the resultant formalism prevented him from defining concrete duties that would not violate his a priori stricture. Rejecting empirical considerations, he could not successfully advance morality beyond the formal stage.

When the language of morality is shifted from *goodness* to *rightness*, either rightness is equivalent to the moral point of view itself, and, thus, refers to all morality, or it is meant to refer to particular acts, and then their fitness is an affair of how various acts "fit" with one another in human life. The shift in terminology thus appears insignificant, for *goodness* is also either a quality of the whole or of the relationships of the various acts or sets of acts to one another in human life. "Sets of acts" may "writ large" be conveniently regarded as the arts of man, for it is these that give shape to men's lives. In short, they define *culture*, a distinctive form of social life. Moreover, it is not unreasonable to define *happiness* as a well-functioning culture; that is, as the arts, as far as they support one another. This is the good life, which has no other end beyond it.

We are prepared now to state more clearly the paradox of happiness as a supreme value, and the sense or senses in which it may be said to be *intrinsic* or *extrinsic*. The paradox I wish to clarify is how to understand happiness as an intrinsic value when the values of each of its components are extrinsic. The preceding discussion was meant to provide a clearer notion of what happiness is and of its components. I wish now to draw the appropriate conclusions.

The first conclusion is that happiness is the end of life, not as an attainment when life is finished, but as the good life itself. This is, of course, a rigorous, prescriptive statement, which could never be fully realized in practice. If a person's life contains frequent alterations between happiness and unhappiness it is more one of despair and frustration than of the good life that happiness is supposed to be. The crux, then, is, not the length of life, but its quality. To judge its quality is a matter of judging its components in relation to one another. The preceding discussion has indicated these to be (1) the activities of life, (2) the virtues, and (3) pleasure.

1. Activities are purposeful and thus are structured and therefore analyzable. Given a purposeful activity, it is successful, or not, to the extent its purpose is realized. But, as we have seen, the arts, which are the formalization of these activities, are not self-justifying, any more than, say, the art of making pancakes is self-justifying. The rationale of the arts, as we have seen, consists in the mutual support they supply to one another. This is so whether the arts are the practical arts or the fine arts. Otherwise, the practical arts are miserably utilitarian and the fine arts are escapist, and both are a source, not of happiness, but of sheer relief. The relationships of the arts in primitive society may actually offer a better clue about the life of happiness than do the arts of contemporary, sophisticated society.

2. Virtue is an indispensable component of happiness, because it prescribes a humane way of pursuing the arts. In its absence the arts are destructive of one another, instead of being supportive. Thus, dishonesty, brutality, avarice, and the like, in institutional activities as well as in single activities, lead to tragic conflict, with all its horrendous consequences. I am not suggesting that the particular virtues required in one epoch are those necessarily required in another. In fact, contemporary moral analyses show the opposite: if the humane qualities are to be realized, morals require redefinition concomitant with the changes of the technologies of man. Virtues dissociated from the arts produce only moralism.

3. Although some pleasures are harmless, some are not. The only way they can be judged as values, positive or negative, is in context. Pleasures never do appear alone; and although the causes of them may be obscure and varied, their occurrence depends upon other activities, and likewise their values. Otherwise they are a gift; and were they to occur in this manner, they would not qualify as values. Except as they figure in a kind of momentariness, and, thus, are not really values, pleasures can be valued only in relation to activities with which they are conjoined and with the virtues that are appropriate to such activities.

There seem to be no other components of happiness, unless we propose to add the material goods of life, which, however, do not constitute another component of life but rather are themselves the products of activities. They do raise questions about justice, and to that degree they pertain to the virtues of the activities as well as to the activities themselves. There is no doubt about the necessity of material goods. The problems they raise are not different from those that are raised in connection with activities, virtues, and pleasures, unless they are dissociated from these, in which case the problems are unintelligible and, therefore, insoluble. Either the elements of happiness are in the context of the good life or happiness is an illusion.

The final question, then, is whether happiness itself is an art. If it is not illusion, then it would seem to be an art. And if it is an art, it is either different from the other arts or identical to them. If it is different, then it needs to have some subject matter. But if its subject matter is happiness, and happiness is the good life, and the good life is the arts taken together and perfected, then happiness too must just be the arts so conceived. Then the art of happiness is not different, but the same as they. Yet, there still lurks a doubt about whether it really is the same. Aristotle believed there was such an art, and he called it politics. The question in these terms is what exactly is meant by politics.

My final suggestion is that politics is nothing but the art of harmonizing the arts. Its subject matter begins and ends with the arts. There is no superior art called "harmony" or "perfection" from which politicians derive rules to which the arts along with their agents must be subjected. There are only the life processes themselves which are thwarted or which are served by the arts. When they are served, men, in association, are happy; and when they are thwarted, men are unhappy. Happiness, then, is the intrinsic value of which all its components are extrinsic. The paradox remains as a godlike one: happiness is the good *of* man, not the good *for* man, but it is only the good for man that is the good of him. Otherwise happiness is illusion.

NOTE

1. See David L. Perry, *The Concept of Pleasure* (The Hague, 1967), pp. 68–72.

A Defense of Unique *as an Aesthetic and Value Predicate*

JOHN WILLIAM DAVIS

THERE ARE AT LEAST a few philosophers, aestheticians, and critics who attribute significance to the notion that works of art are unique and who defend *unique* as an aesthetic predicate, but why they do so is sometimes difficult for other philosophers to understand. Mary Mothersill, in confessing her failure to understand, suggests the possibility that when philosophers and others say that every work of art is unique, what they have in mind is something not very clearly formulated:

> "A painting is what it is. No mere description can be an adequate substitute. It is unique." "My musical experience is peculiarly mine. If I attempt to convey it, what I say can only be an approximation to what I feel. It is unique." ... What it comes to is that a work of art is, as a matter of fact, hard to describe, and that no description, as a matter of logic, is identical with the work itself.[1]

It seems to me to come to more than that, for if this is all there is to it, then Mothersill is right: the philosopher's claim that every work of art is unique has no relevance for aesthetic judgment or appreciation. Difficulty of description is not peculiar to works of art. Even cars, horses, and trees are hard to describe, except in a very general way, unless one has the training and the technical vocabulary to make explicit their many parts and features. One can just as easily say, "A car, a horse, or a tree is what it is. No mere description can be an adequate substitute. It is unique." Obviously philosophers must have something more in mind.

Critics do not usually speak of the uniqueness of "works of art" in general, unless they are also philosophers, but neither does the car fancier, the judge of horses, nor the tree authority speak of the uniqueness of cars, of horses, or of trees. The critic discusses individual novels, paintings, or symphonies;[2] the judge of horses evaluates particular draft horses, riding horses, harness horses, and so on. Critics and judges do occasionally refer to individual works or particular horses as unique.[3] But when they do we expect them to show us how these particulars differ from others of their type. They have the technical vocabulary, training, and experience to make explicit forms of sound and color, shades of meaning (in the case of works of art), or gaits, hands, and colors (in the case of horses), which, though we may perceive them, we find hard to describe. The observations in each case are implicitly, if not explicitly, comparative, but usually in a weaker sense, it is said, in the case of an artwork. And this weakness appears to point to a difference between aesthetic evaluation and others of the kinds mentioned. The criteria used by the judge of horses (or of cars, chickens, roses, or apples) are clear-cut standards accepted by authorities as requirements of a class. If a judge were to refer to a particular draft horse—a Clydesdale or a Belgian—as being unique, we might expect that it was far superior to others in the group in meeting the standards of its breed, but we should not expect the judge to be treating it as the only one of its kind, a unit class.

In the case of the art critic, however, there is much debate about whether the critic's evaluation of the work of art is one of comparison, as in the case of horses, or is more autonomous, with each work of art being judged by its own standard and in a class by itself. I think it likely that critics do both, but not always with clear recognition that the two kinds of evaluation are quite different and involve two different kinds of value, extrinsic and intrinsic. Following Robert S. Hartman, we shall define *value* in terms of concept fulfillment, and say that a thing—whether horse, artwork, or anything else—is good if it has all the properties of its concept. More formally, "Value is the degree in which a thing possesses the set of properties corresponding to the set of predicates in the intension of its concept."[4] Extrinsic and intrinsic value thus involve the fulfillment of two different kinds of concepts: *analytic*,[5] or general, and *singular*.

Extrinsic value is the value of an empirical thing which fulfills an analytic concept. It is the value of a thing in comparison with others of its kind. The intension of an analytic concept arises from the abstraction of the common properties of a group of things; and since such abstractions, theoretically, can be continued, *ad infinitum*, "the intension of the analytic concept consists of a denumerable infinite—and indefinite—number of attributes,"[6] and its intensional structure is characterized by the transfinite number ℵo. It should be understood that an empirical thing does not have all the attributes of its concept in order to be a member of the class designated by that concept. A painting, for example, may not have all the properties of the concept *painting*.[7] It could be lacking in unity with little apparent plan or control of contrast ranges, fit neither for the home nor a show, and still be a painting (but not a good one).

Intrinsic value is the value of a thing that fulfills a singular concept. It is the value of a thing considered as unique. Obviously, a singular concept, or proper name, is not a concept in the usual sense, for it is not a mental entity that grasps together the common features of several things. It is rather "a 'unicept,' an experiential entity representing one thing in its uniqueness."[8] Here the "concept" and the thing are one, and the "thing is not thought at all but experienced in the actuality of its total being"[9] or "concreteness." In such experience, as in artistic creativity and aesthetic appreciation, it seems to me, there is a fusion not only of "concept" and thing but of the thing and the agent, and the extent to which the experience forms one uninterrupted whole, or *Gestalt*, is the extent to which the thing fulfills the intension of its singular concept. Such a whole is a new creation. It follows that the intension of the singular, in contrast to the analytic, concept is a continuum and consists of a non-denumerable rather than denumerable infinite of attributes. It has the characteristic number $\aleph$ 1.[10] It is this kind of valuation for which the artist strives to create an object (and which he may experience in creating such an object), an object that facilitates an appreciation of itself in its uniqueness.

Where there is a lack of clear-cut, generally accepted criteria and a lack of agreement concerning the nature and types of value, the two kinds of evaluation are easily confused. It is a confusion, in Hartman's terms, of exposition with description or depiction, a confusion of comparative goodness with uniqueness, a confusion of extrinsic with intrinsic value.

Moreover, I shall argue in disagreement with aestheticians who hold to one of the traditional theories of criticism (*imitation, instruction, expression*, and *autonomy*) that the critic need not, and ordinarily would not, limit himself to one type of evaluation, as long as he clearly distinguishes between the two types. Proponents of these theories are apt to argue that the critic must in judging aesthetic value take one approach and not the other. In general, the imitation, instruction, and expression theories hold to an extrinsic approach: imitation, instruction, or expression, it is said, is the function which works of art meet, more or less. There are, thus, certain fixed standards which apply to works of art—either faithful representation, worth of lesson, of sincerity, spontaneity of expression. The autonomy theory, on the other hand, emphasizes that every work of art is unique and is to be judged by its own standards. The expression theory is in agreement with the autonomy theory that works of art are unique, although it rejects the view that there are no standards which apply to all artworks alike.

Much of the judgment of a critic is in practice, I think, comparative. A novel is compared with other novels, a symphony with other symphonies, a painting with other paintings, somewhat in the way a horse is compared with other horses. And just as a judge does not apply the standards of apples to dogs, or dogs to horses, or even Thoroughbreds to Standardbreds, so a critic does not apply the standards of paintings to novels, or novels to symphonies, or even symphonies to waltzes. The artwork is, first of all, expected to meet the requirements of its type. It is either a good, fair, or bad example of its kind. Also, artists learn certain techniques of execution, and critics are quick to point out their failures. A painter, for example, may make awkward use of shapes, colors, or contrasts. Some elements of his work may call undue attention to themselves, and his painting may lack properties which the critic regards as necessary for its particular style or tradition. Yet all of this, for the most part, is concerned with an extrinsic evaluation of the artwork. The critic judges the work in terms of the properties which he attributes to its class.[11] For some theories this type of judgment is one of aesthetic value, but it is hard to see why unless aesthetic value is to be defined merely as the value of artworks, which implies that even their economic value is aesthetic. *Aesthetic value* is, however, generally regarded as an intrinsic value; in Hartman's terms it is the application of the category of intrinsic value to an individual thing. It seems clear that comparative value, the value of the object as measured by its possession of properties which it shares with other members of its class, is not an intrinsic but an extrinsic value. No competent aesthetician, I should think, would regard the standards for collies or quarter horses as standards for intrinsic values, so why should analogous standards for novels or paintings be regarded in a different way? This is not to say that prize-winning dogs and horses are without aesthetic merit, for some certainly have it. The exact relation between aesthetic value and the merit of such prize winners is not clear, but I should suggest that aesthetic value in the case of show dogs and horses can best be understood as that which belongs to the class, or form, of which the prize winner is the best example, or specimen. In the case of grand champions, the best in the show, etc., it is not the individuality or uniqueness, of the winner that is prized, but the uniqueness of the form which the winner best exemplifies; and in this case the winner becomes a singular prototype, paradigm, or model, of all grand champions. The kind of thing, rather than the thing itself, is the object of intrinsic value. A particular Tennessee Walker, for example, may take top honors at a show, but its merit in this instance lies in its excellence as an example of its breed and not in anything peculiar to itself. If there is intrinsic valuation, it is of the form (breed) which the particular horse best exemplifies. But apart from the show, obviously, the horse may be valued as an individual in terms of its own uniqueness.

I should think that the confusion which is so much apparent in art theory results in part from the failure to distinguish between the intrinsic value which is attributed on the one hand to a form, a tradition, a style within a tradition, all of which are repeatable, and on the other, a variation within a style, or the work itself, considered as unique, and unrepeatable. It is the uniqueness in each case that is the intrinsic value. But when the work is judged according to how well it exemplifies a style, or form, which it shares with other works, then the judgment is extrinsic and not intrinsic. All told, the critic must distinguish between three, possibly four, things: (1) the uniqueness of the individual work, (2) the uniqueness of the form, tradition, style, and so on which the work may express, (3) the success or "correctness" of the work in expressing the form, and (4) the "technique" or "skill" of the artist, or the combination of the last two items. There are, as a matter of fact, several classes or subclasses here, all of which may be intrinsically valued, and in terms of which the object may be extrinsically valued.[12] Just as a particular animal may be valued extrinsically as an animal, dog, working dog, boxer, so a particular artwork may be valued extrinsically as "art," painting, painting in the tradition of impressionism, painting with the impressionistic style of Renoir.

The basic difference between the judging of show animals and artworks lies in the greater emphasis given to common forms in the case of animals. The animal is judged entirely in terms of its possession of properties which characterize a prized form; but in art, more emphasis is given to the individual work, for the form prized may be that which is unique to the work. The forms which it shares with others of its type may be of secondary importance. But what is meant by *form*? By *form* we shall mean the essential unity, or intelligible structure, recognizable when the characterizable qualities of a thing are experienced in certain ways. For our purposes we shall distinguish between two different types of forms, those which can be common to a group of particulars[13] and those which are peculiar to individuals in their individuality. Forms of either type can, of course, be novel, but only the former can be repeated. Some newnesses are repeatable, but the newness of an individual in its individuality is not, and so the uniqueness of an individual artwork is not. Newnesses which are repeatable are the first occurrences of forms which will later be common to at least two particulars, for example, the initiation of a new tradition or a new style within a tradition.

One could argue, of course, that only forms that are repeatable are really forms, and there certainly seems to be a difference between a form peculiar to an individual and the forms it shares with particulars of its class. Perhaps the difference is that repeatable forms are abstractions definable in terms of properties which several particulars have in common. The connotations of the concepts of such forms—analytic, or general, concepts—are discursive (and the number of their terms is potentially infinite but denumerable). On the other hand, the unrepeatable form of a particular in its particularity is a "form" in a special sense, a *Gestalt*, and it corresponds to a singular concept. For the individual itself serves as its form, and such form is not thought but experienced in its concreteness. The connotation of the concept of such a form is non-discursive, a continuum (and the number of its terms is nondenumerably infinite).

To be sure, both the individual form and the repeatable form are unique, but the uniquenesses are on different levels, the concrete and the abstract; on the one hand is the uniqueness of a concrete thing; on the other hand, the uniqueness of a *class* of concrete things. It seems paradoxical that several things could have a uniqueness in common. But uniqueness (or novelty?) is not a defining characteristic of either a thing or a class of things. It is, as Robert S. Hartman shows, "on a higher logical level than are the properties of the thing that is called unique. The thing is unique because it has all the properties it has. But the property 'having all the properties it has' is not itself one of the properties the thing is said to have."[14] In much the same way, a class, or repeatable form, is unique because it has all the properties it has. In short, both the individual in its individuality and the particular considered as the first instance of a repeatable form are novel or unique. The uniqueness is not a property of either, but a property of the properties of both. It is, thus, a second-order rather than a first-order property. In the case of a non-repeatable form (the individual in its individuality) these properties are non-discursive and form a continuum. And in the case of a repeatable form (that common to a group of particulars) these properties are abstracted and common and, hence, discrete. They are not, however, seen as discrete when one appreciates the uniqueness of the common form, for in such an experience the connotation of the common form becomes non-discursive and thus a continuum. In this case we have the phenomenological insight, the Aristotelian *hyle noeté*.[15] But this is an intrinsic value of a class seen as a whole. The "best" specimen of a class is still an extrinsic value, unless prized intrinsically.

As we mentioned earlier, in the judging of show animals and artworks, there is a difference with respect to the emphasis given to common form and individuality. Why this difference in emphasis? Obviously the prized animal forms—the standards for the breeds—are set in advance, and failure to conform is treated as an imperfection. Any characteristic which tends to draw attention to individuality, to novelty, detracts from the form. Moreover, development of a new breed, new form, is difficult and may take years, and recognition of new breeds is relatively infrequent. On the other hand, while there are certain general standards for paintings, and while there are certain prized traditions and styles (analogous to breeds), novelty is both expected and prized. Here almost any kind of conformity in excess, even one's mannerisms and habits, may on occasion be treated as imperfection. The artist must, of course, follow the rules of his medium; he cannot, for example, successfully work with water colors in the way he does with oils, and he almost always will be following a certain tradition or style; but unless he is merely trying to produce an exact copy of some earlier work, or exploiting a successful technique through mass production, a new creation is his goal—but not just any new creation. He does not work for the sake of novelty alone. He could get something new by haphazardly throwing paint at a canvas, and the results would occasionally be of aesthetic interest. Children and chimpanzees (and even philosophers) sometimes accidentally become "successful artists" by acting in this manner. Perhaps some "pop" artists do. Such accidental "artworks," regardless of their aesthetic value, are, of course, unique, but we may have difficulty appreciating their uniqueness. The artist ordinarily strives, not merely for something new, but for something which facilitates an appreciation of itself in its newness; and such a work is usually, not an accident, but the result of an intense involvement of the artist with his subject matter. The successful artist is one who has the skill to provide the conditions necessary within the work for us to appreciate the work in its uniqueness. Such appreciation on our (the layman's) part usually requires the artist's having achieved a harmony between novelty and conformity, between particularity and repeatable form, between newness and tradition. A too abrupt break with tradition may mystify or even repel us, as for example in "late modern" art (abstract expressionism, pop, op and kinetic art, happenings, environments). But if the work facilitates an appreciation of its own uniqueness, it must have certain qualities or properties which are, I think, the purely aesthetic qualities, or "aesthetic aspects," of artworks: unity, balance, grace, and beauty—qualities which apparently are out of fashion, if not irrelevant, in some forms of late modern art. These so-called aesthetic aspects of an artwork are those properties which facilitate intrinsic valuation, an appreciation of the work's uniqueness.

I suspect, however, that aesthetic perception and enjoyment (as scientific creation) are not ordinarily a matter of looking and seeing. Aesthetic qualities, such as unity and beauty, are probably like uniqueness and good, not first-order, but second-order properties, the property of properties; and some may even be third-order, the property of properties of first-order properties. In any case, where there is intrinsic valuation, or aesthetic appreciation, of an object there must be, I think, considerable imaginative interplay between the object valued and the valuer. Thus, intrinsic valuation for both the artist and the person who fully enjoys his work is an act of creativity. And just as the artist's mannerisms and habits may obstruct his creativity, so may the habits, preconceptions, and prejudices of the viewer frustrate aesthetic appreciation, or intrinsic valuation. Our need to interact with nature in such a way that life processes are sustained inclines us to a pragmatic view of things: to see things instrumentally and extrinsically as representatives of classes and not as instances of novelty, or as things existing uniquely and in their own right.[16] But if we are to enjoy intrinsic value and to participate in creativity we must break our habitual responses and involvements and continuously take fresh, imaginative looks at our world.

I should like to stress that anything may be valued intrinsically, that is, as unique, but circumstances are such that few things are valued to any great extent in this way, for either the object is deficient in aesthetic quality or the perceiver's orientation is unsuited for aesthetic experience. To many of us a leaf is a leaf, a tree is a tree, and a girl is a girl; but for the poet, the painter, the lover they may be priceless, infinitely valuable, worth the whole world. Most of us, unfortunately, are simply insensitive to intrinsic value, or uniqueness. We are unaware of the wonders that often flood the souls of artists, mystics, and lovers. There have been moments, perhaps, when each of us has caught a glimpse of intimate reality, but an individual is seldom able to appreciate fully the uniqueness of several persons and things, including his own, in his lifetime. All too often we are blind and deaf to the uniqueness of even those persons closest to us.

Much of the late modern art, which seems to have broken with tradition, and some of which lies on the borderline between art and non-art, encourages us to take a new, unfettered look at our world. In giving us a *minimal object*, an *odd assemblage*, an *environment*, the artist solicits a creative, totally involving experience; and the total aesthetic "object" which emerges is the creative, intrinsically valuable experience.[17] Thus, modern art leads us to take a fresh look at ordinary, usually non-aesthetic, even unattractive, things; to see, as it were for the first time, a pile of sand, a grass mound, a box of washing powder. Many of us are, of course, simply mystified, for we are unable to break our habits of seeing things either as parts of a system or as instances of general concepts and not as individuals.

Perhaps such demands upon our (layman's) imagination, reflection, and senses, if met, will help us to understand that anything can be valued intrinsically and aesthetically, and that in such valuing the value to be prized is the uniqueness of the thing.

NOTES

1. Mary Mothersill, " 'Unique' as an Aesthetic Predicate," *Journal of Philosophy*, LVIII, No. 16 (Aug. 3, 1961), p. 437.

2. He does not discuss novels, paintings, or symphonies in general but *this* novel, *this* painting. Otherwise he is not a critic but a non-aesthetic extrinsic evaluator, or expert. This evaluation may be part of a "critic's" job, but it is not the "critical" part.

3. There is a difference between *individual* and *particular*. In reality there are only individuals. A particular is the individual seen (thought) as an instance of a general concept, as a schema. See Robert S. Hartman, "Singular and Particular" in *Critica*, II, No. 4 (1968), pp. 15–45.

4. Robert S. Hartman, "The Logic of Value," *The Review of Metaphysics*, XIV, No. 3 (Mar., 1961), p. 389. See also the Foreword to the present book—Wieman's "The Philosophy of Robert S. Hartman."

5. Kantian term.

6. Hartman, "The Logic of Value," p. 393.

7. According to Richard Clarke (professor of art, University of Tennessee), a painting, technically speaking, is either a depiction or an articulation of feeling in terms of the geometric and empirical properties of color-shapes. A color-shape is a visually observable plane entity. Geometric properties: axial width, axial length, width-to-length ratio, area, location, orientation (axial or edge), contour (regular, irregular, curved, straight). Empirical properties: hue (red, orange, yellow, black, etc.), tone-value (range between black and white), saturation, actual texture (pigment-material thickness), differentiation (implied texture achieved through subdivision of color-shape into parts), transparency, surface luster of pigment material.

8. Robert S. Hartman, "Value Theory as a Formal System," *Kant-Studien*, L (1958–59), 300.

9. Ibid.

10. "The continuum nature of the singular follows not only from its logical and psychological but also from its phenomenological nature. Each thing appears in diverse aspects not only to different persons but also to the same person in different modes of perceiving, remembering, expecting, etc. The singular thing *in itself* is the totality of all these aspects. As there is a denumerable infinity of such aspects, and as each aspect in turn contains an infinity of facets, the totality of all these aspects and facets, in their possible permutations, is of the cardinality of non-denumerable infinity." Hartman, "The Logic of Value," pp. 408–409.

11. This, I think, is what happens in practice. Ideally, the critic would be concerned with this kind of evaluation only preliminarily, if at all.

12. There are many interesting questions here: for example, what is the difference between extrinsically valuing a particular as a member of a class whose form is intrinsically prized and merely extrinsically valuing a particular?

13. Hartman's "schemata." "The schema is that within each individual thing which has the common properties expressed in the concept, it is the thing as instance of the concept, as a particular. The totality of all these

schemata . . . is the extension of the concept" ("Singular and Particular," pp. 16–17).

14. Robert S. Hartman, "Sputnik's Moral Challenge," *Texas Quarterly*, III, No. 3 (Autumn, 1960), p. 15.

15. *Hyle noeté*: the ideal individual, any statement used as axiom. See Robert S. Hartman, *The Structure of Value* (Carbondale, Ill., 1967), p. 202.

16. See Iredell Jenkins, *Art and the Human Enterprise* (Cambridge, 1958), and "Aesthetic Education and Moral Refinement," *Journal of Aesthetic Education*, II, No. 3 (July, 1968).

17. See David M. Levin, "More Aspects to the Concept of 'Aesthetic Aspects'," *Journal of Philosophy*, LXV, No. 16 (Aug. 22, 1968), p. 488.

Expressiveness in Visual and Verbal Art

DAVID POLE

CHILDREN OF THE IMAGINATION, like "all our fathers," worship stocks and stones; for what else is the *David* of Michelangelo but a block of inanimate marble? So, too, the reclining *Venus* of Titian or Brunelleschi's Church of Santo Spirito are only concoctions, artifacts of stone and plaster or canvas and pigment and the like. But, of course, to art lovers and connoisseurs they are infinitely more. Expressiveness in objects of sense seems rather as spiritual grace has been thought of—as something never wholly or properly their own, descending and investing them, yet visibly and miraculously manifest.

I confine myself to only one sort of aesthetic excellence, one thing that we widely praise in works of art; nothing I shall say precludes the recognition of many others. There exist, so some theorists tell us simply enough, a third class of property to be found in things not traditionally taken account of, so-called tertiary qualities, over and above those familiar "primary" and "secondary" qualities (a problematic distinction, irrelevant here). Verbally, if you like, the suggestion may pass as a harmless one; every adjective can stand for a property. More must be at stake, however; and, at least phenomenologically, we shall be told, the account simply answers to the facts. We do just find all these things and "see" them: we "see" respectively grandeur, serenity, or dignity in St. Peter's, in a Brunelleschi arcade, or in St. Paul's dome in London. (Complex balance, or what we call "form," is something we find too; this consideration, however, would belong to another inquiry.)

And they are all, at least prima facie, "out there"; they are, one must stress, qualities of those objects, not, certainly, emotions either aroused in us, or, still less, putatively attributed to their original designers or makers hundreds of years ago. The latter can be summarily ruled out; no such question need ever enter our heads. And for the former the objections are barely less familiar: a man looking at a rival or a colleague might see him unhappy, see "visible" wretchedness written all over him; and, far from sharing it, might secretly enjoy his discomfiture. We first "see" something, which we then may respond to, and respond in different ways without "seeing" anything different.

Now first the main point, which I shall put barely and boldly; doubts and reservations can follow. It is this: expressive things are typically characterized in terms whose primary application is elsewhere. We look at stone or ferroconcrete and call it *bold*. We ascribe *gaiety, serenity,* and the like to colonnades and façades, terms, in the primitive sense, applied to people, their actions, and so on. The ascription, at least on the face of it, must seem odd, somewhat as if one should ascribe *color*, *taste*, or *smell* to the square root of nineteen. "The gesture of the two-wide embracing one-storied colonnades of Ionic columns is irresistible" (Professor Pevsner's description of Park Crescent, Marylebone, London).[1] Mr. Mumford, comparing an embassy in a foreign city to the problem facing "a lecturer from another country addressing a foreign audience," goes on to say:

> Our London embassy presents a cold unsmiling face, a face unfortunately suggesting national arrogance and irresponsible power . . . . One has yet to be persuaded that this blank, bureaucratic-military mask is the true face of America.[2]

Before proceeding, I must pause to take stock; one possible basic objection to my whole approach, to this whole way of presenting the problem, would be the mere denial of its starting-point; that secondary status, namely, that I have made the hallmark of aesthetic vocabulary (not all such vocabulary, perhaps, but a large and significant part of it). Let the critic have the floor, then, and speak. Now surveying some number of facades, suppose we find them to share some common feature, some "visible" quality, which Mumford, perhaps, labels "arrogance." But our critic will advocate another course; we are, henceforth, neutrally, to call it Q; and again what Pevsner calls "reticence" (ascribing it to Wood's excellent Corn Exchange in Bristol), which we shall refer to as Q', and so on. All these qualities, it may be objected, are those that a learner might well have trouble in picking out—I mean, in default of those imaginary helps that our secondary, "metaphorical" language supplies. Such questions, however—questions, that is, concerning a priori conceptual distinctions—are not to be settled by appealing to differences in individual psychology; some learners will be quicker, some slower. And, as things in fact stand, there exist some terms that most of us do master, and without any great difficulty, which, on the face of it, are primarily "aesthetic," terms, for instance, such as *elegance* and *grace*.

These issues, I fear, are far-reaching, and not to be settled out of hand; but broadly, the case is as follows. We can coin terms in any field we please, an easy course, always available. We can *ad hoc* postulate qualities, unique, irreducible qualities, hardly explanatory perhaps, but serving at least to stop the mouths of questioners—or such questioners as prefer words to explanations. Not only qualities, incidentally: we shall also need unique relations, unanalyzable relations, which soon follow. But, I take it, the rule here, one for which we can cite authorities going back to Ockham, is, briefly, the fewer the better. At least before resigning ourselves we may look about us for alternatives; I mean, before submitting meekly to lie down with so decidedly unattractive a thesis and from it, all too probably, engender more offspring resembling their parent.

But what else might one offer by way of an answer, or urge against such a permissive linguistic policy? Well, at least we can nibble at corners, though most likely, I fear, educing on the other side with every new difficulty, a new ad hoc proviso to meet it. The qualities in question, one may argue, are strangely unstable and shifting, and hence, perhaps, calculated to arouse suspicion. (Very well, we meet the answer, so they may be. Why not? They form a special new sort of quality.) Or take the "arrogance" we "see" in a façade and call expressive, or that we "see" in someone's bearing, or impatience in a gesture. Now its source, we are to note, lies further back; these things, first of all, are states of mind. (Very well—so the quality Q, the unique tertiary quality, may, in its own unique way, resemble ordinary arrogance or impatience, which is given and must be accepted, a sheer matter of fact, after its fashion, perhaps, it may be added, somewhat as certain sorts of sounds, usually shrill sounds, are said to resemble bright colors.) And so on. Let us raise whatever difficulty we like: an ingenious enough apologist, on such lines, will always find some countermaneuver to deploy and win, if not a paper victory, at least a stalemate.

But, as I said, nothing prevents our looking for alternatives, alternatives less roundabout and more economical, which if we find them, we shall plainly have a reason for preferring. Now the alternative I propose is, I think, a fairly obvious one: precisely to reverse our critic's maneuver. He reads words like *boldness, arrogance* (that is, terms that as applied to works of art prima facie might otherwise count as derivative), on the analogy of pure aesthetic terms, that is, of non-derivative terms such as *elegance* and *grace*. And, on that basis, he sets out to coin and put in currency a whole new aesthetic vocabulary. Now we can precisely proceed in the reverse direction; reading *grace* or *elegance* on the analogy of those derivative terms, of terms like "aesthetic arrogance" and the rest; reading them, in other words, as expressive, and therefore looking behind them for qualities of another sort, those, on this view, that they will serve to express.

First of all, let us look closer at the former: *graceful*, at least in one very obvious way, is unlike *yellow* or *noisy*, which are qualities simply "met" in experience. To call something graceful, at least in normal contexts, is to praise it; *graceless* and *inelegant* are terms of disparagement.

One can say so in general and pretty confidently, I repeat, barring special qualifications or contexts and, further, without pre-committing ourselves to any one theory of value. These are truisms, however one goes
on to account for them, that any theory of value whatever must start
from; we stand so far, I hope, on non-controversial ground. But what of
our would-be new-found qualities? They suggest strange analogies. "Desirable yellow"—as opposed perhaps to its complementary, "undesirable
blue"—seems a curious quality merely to meet and wholly know in experience; or is that, perhaps, a further sheer fact? We do merely value or
condemn such things—further evidence, if so, of what I spoke of, I mean
the monstrous self-multiplication of ad hoc postulates.

But to pursue my suggested alternative: rather than *grace* I shall start
first of all with its converse, which I take to be *awkwardness*, eminently
an aesthetic or "visible" quality, though doubtless a negative one (for
words such as *ugly*, of course, no less than *beautiful*, are used for expressing distinctively aesthetic views). As to *awkwardness*: we "see" it in
movements in arms and legs, their restriction or jerking, and again in
the stiff carriage of bodies, as plainly as one could desire, and possibly
as painfully. But, we ask, what lies "behind" that impression, its non-
aesthetic *archetype* (I shall call it), that we set out to look for? The question virtually answers itself. The very word *awkwardness*—and indeed
arrogance, too—functions equally naturally in either role as describing
either a quasi-sensible aesthetic impression, or something practical, a
kind of bearing or performance, at least an attempted performance; in
fact, often enough, both at once. What lies "behind" awkwardness, that
is aesthetic awkwardness, is of course plain clumsiness; it is bodily ineptitude. And, I am led to reflect, it would have been hard to hit on an
unhappier example of a would-be pure tertiary quality as subsisting
apart in its own aesthetic realm.

Grace of movement is nowadays perhaps admired, or at least explicitly spoken of, more often in women than in men; and yet it has, perhaps, its masculine counterpart. Whatever holds the twentieth century,
or fails to hold, we often find women novelists of earlier times praising
in their male characters a quality called "military bearing." Traditionally man governs and fights, while woman presides over domesticity.
And small things can be seen as significant. The performance of easy
tasks, absurdly easy, which we hardly call "tasks," such as taking a few
steps across a room, lifting something and putting it down again, may
suggest likely performance or failure faced with harder ones. Grace of
movement suggests sureness and gentleness, the doing of whatever needs
doing, but with no commotion, no strain or the like. The poet Richard
Lovelace who, one recalls, "loved honour more," and protested to his

Lucasta—who may or may not have been reassured—that otherwise he could never have loved her so much, affirms that he embraced yet more fervently "a sword, a horse, a shield," which was evidently admirable and very masculine. But consider a woman's typical tasks, perhaps tending a baby, moreover, importing life, not death. We might here prefer a different sort of touch. Grace, again, is to be connected with poise, the latter being less movement than readiness to move, therefore promptly, towards any occasion. The word functions like *awkwardness* either practically or aesthetically; that is, it names either the actual state of readiness or again the vivid quasi-visual impression, the "visible" appearance of it. Doubtless language may blur these distinctions, which remain possible, nonetheless, and for these purposes, important. That impression, precisely—the impression of present alertness, quiet and vivid—is what theorists call a "tertiary quality." Further, our main point: underlying the aesthetic judgment, the aesthetic impression (impressions being intuitive judgments), what we meet is an ordinary judgment, a judgment, one might add, in which Thomas Gradgrind himself could have found nothing to object to—though he perhaps, or his modern disciples, might prefer to arrive at it otherwise, less "intuitively" probably, by EEG measurements of tension. Now, similarly, with the quality of grace: "forced gracefulness" is virtually a contradiction. It is one, like the quality of mercy, that can never be strained. It presupposes a state of mind, and with it a state of musculature, all carrying, of course, their obvious practical implications. They are things that we recognize "intuitively," and, lastly too, recognizing them, generally value.

Here other related notions converge or overlap: add to *grace* the suggestion of reserve, add the consciousness of worth, and it becomes *dignity*. Still more of the same makes it *arrogance*. I take *elegance* for sophisticated grace, at least in social contexts, something probably acquired, less simply spontaneous, a shade nicer. On the other hand, applied to scientific or mathematical theories, the term suggests apparent and visible economy, as where different things, that look totally disconnected, fall together, fall aptly into place, as if it were on purpose to suit us. True, grace itself suggests economy, but never what we call "rigid economy"; grace, rather, carries a little further, with a hint of amplitude, even space to spare, something like leisureliness. Again, in inanimate things—in arches, pediments, lanterns and the like—gracefulness is still closer to poise, the suggestion being here of exact balance, at once near the edge as it were, yet very safe, a stance whose felicity lies in the combination of economy and ease.[3]

All I have done so far, in fact, amounts to little more than expanding on certain suggestions of Professor Gombrich's:

For there is indeed such a thing as "physiognomic perception" which carries strong and immediate conviction. We all experience this immediacy when we look into a human face. We see its cheerfulness or gloom, its kindliness or harshness, without being aware of reading "signs." Psychologists such as Heinz Werner[4] have emphasised that this type of "global" and immediate reaction to expression is not confined to the reading of human faces and gestures.... These reactions testify to the constant scrutiny with which we scan our environment with one vital question: "are you friendly or hostile?" a "good thing" or a "bad thing"? It may be argued that the answer to this question is as basic to the survival of any organism as are the answers to the questions of other perceptual probings, such questions as "what is it?", "where am I now?", "how do I get from here to there without bumping into things?"[5]

"Behind" tertiary qualities, it seems—or anyhow one class of them, those we call "expressive," including not only *boldness* and *arrogance* but also *elegance* and *grace*—we find other things of a different sort, such as skills, dispositions, and the like. One example, taken from *King Lear*: Lear, returning from hunting and finding Kent disguised as a poor man, waiting in his hall, asks him who he is—"A man, Sir," Kent answers (characteristically)—and what he wants: "Service." The dialogue proceeds:

> Lear: Who wouldst thou serve?
> Kent: You.
> Lear: Dost thou know me, fellow?
> Kent: No, Sir. But you have that in your countenance which I would fain call master.
> Lear: What's that?
> Kent: Authority.
>
> Act 1, scene 4, lines 24–30

The authority Kent "sees" in Lear's countenance is, even literally, physiognomic,[6] yet, it seems, not something different in kind from the visible "arrogance" manifest, according to Mumford, in the façade of the embassy in Grosvenor Square. Kent reports an immediate impression, something "seen" and not "contemplated" or dwelt on. The aesthetic attitude, theorists tell us, is contemplative; Kent here is eminently practical. The judgment he makes, or pretends—but only half-pretends —to make in the character he is playing, is briefly this: Lear, he says, is a man to be obeyed. Such impressions, doubtless, are notoriously deceptive; it remains true that the greater part of our practical conduct, especially under pressure of time, inevitably rests on them. And it remains astonishing what complexities of feeling and attitude a really intuitive observer can "read," reliably and at once, in looks and movements. Kent, to repeat, passes a practical judgment, to qualify it further, an "intuitive" practical judgment, not one (presumably) he would offer or be able to verify or do anything like demonstrate. (I shall henceforth drop the quotation marks enclosing *intuitive*, for, I think, to handle the word we no longer need forceps.) So-called physiognomic perception is in reality not perception at all, but nearer judgment, intuitive judgment. Its objects are not sensible, but mental—namely, skills, dispositions, and the like. It is in fact intuitive judgment, but based on a present perception. We may call it, in a certain sense, "confused perception"; but the word *confused*, here, need imply no disparagement. Doubtless clarity, in appropriate theoretical contexts, is something we value, along with rigor, precision, and above all consistency. Nothing follows elsewhere. The flat surface of a looking glass, for instance, is not only hard but virtually impossible to distinguish focally, to see separately from whatever it happens to reflect. So here, too, we find a kind of confusion, one of course which need involve no intellectual confusion. And it is something we deliberately create; we should be worse off, not better, without it.

So-called physiognomic perception runs together two distinct kinds of object—those of sense perception, faces and facades, and others that, we say, lie behind them—which properly speaking consists in this. We infer these from those, or rather we quasi-infer them. For (among other qualifications to follow) strictly to speak of an "inference" you need two things—evidence and conclusion; they are first distinguished and subsequently related. Here, precisely, we take everything at once. Let us more accurately say that, if that quasi judgment were a true one, we should infer it; we should do so, in other words, if it were not holistic and intuitive but explicit. In the case before us, what we find is this. The latter presence is less inferred than "sensed" or "felt"; the two things are not identified separately. It is that failure that, in certain aesthetic theories that have gained considerable currency, is called "fusion," fusion of percept and concept, for instance, or alternatively is obscurely hinted at in Elisco Vivas's paradoxical references to "felt meanings" in poetry and the like.

In a façade, it seems, we "see" arrogance; menace, in storm clouds. Phenomenologically, at least, theorists insist, we experience such impressions "objectively"; we experience them as qualities of things. Certainly, if so, they are tertiary qualities. But it might be truer to say, in somewhat Sartrean language, that we experience them as qualities haunting things—a further something about them, but neither explicitly distinguished nor firmly grasped.

Of these two kinds of object, to repeat, one is merely thought of, but suggested by the other, actually perceived. And a further confusion is this: it is quasi-inferred, not only as present, but also (at least most often) as good or bad; or, if not most often, for obvious reasons it is such impressions that chiefly interest us. Thus, in our example, fitness to command is something we have reason to value; and we found similarly that poise and grace of movement import valuable qualities. There are, then, properly, two judgments and essentially separate, but all grasped in a single impression—one of value, the other of existence—of something, that is to say, both as present and as good. But we find that our aesthetic impressions distinguish neither one from the other, nor yet the synthesis of both from their common basis in things literally perceived.

Professor Hospers, writing of what he calls "expression"—I think, the same thing is what I have been calling "expressiveness"—refuses to identify it with beauty. Expressive things, he points out, in a simple argument, but surely conclusive, are often not beautiful but ugly.[7] He himself speaks of "whining adagios," mentioned by Hanslick; but simpler examples might serve. Awkward movements are expressive and ugly, their ugliness and expressiveness being indeed exactly proportional. Our appraisal of what we "see," of the so-called "tertiary quality," reflects our appraisal of its archetype; or rather, more accurately, it is simply one and the same thing. Admiration for appropriate skills— or, conversely, its reverse in the case of their opposites, say, physical ineptitude or clumsiness—makes part of a single impression and one precisely which contains in itself no distinction between what I see and what I "see." Thus, we naturally find things at once expressive and ugly, where, judging intuitively, we judge what they express to be objectionable or bad, that is, where we "feel" it to be antipathetic.

It follows, too, that various people's judgments will differ and not only because they first differ, although of course they often do, as to what sorts of non-aesthetic things are good and bad. But further: a voice, for example, that I hear as authoritative, as firm, a better judge may hear rather differently, as pitched a little too shrill, perhaps, as straining after authority, not quietly or confidently possessed of it.

I have spoken so far of skills, dispositions, and the like, of different sorts of mental quality to be found "behind" aesthetic impressions. But, let us note, our argument need imply no such restriction; it requires nothing more than a further object of thought, one whose presence we first "infer" and then secondly respond to favorably or unfavorably, approve or condemn. Tools and instruments, for instance, have functions to fulfill, which they do well or badly; we commend or condemn them accordingly. Those, so far, of course, are "straight" practical judgments. Now in aesthetics we conversely seek vivid impressions and seek no further; viewing instruments too, then, we may judge on occasion, not how they function in fact, but how they look. It would be nonsense to say—

what perhaps no functionalist ever seriously said, or literally meant—
that a perfectly functioning building is *eo ipso* beautiful. But suppose
that a building looks "visibly" functional, that the impression is immediate and strong: now our stance changes; to say that is certainly to
make on its behalf an aesthetic claim. For we are now judging what we
"infer," what we quasi-infer, in what we immediately see; and at least
minimally we should prefer it to look not shaky or top-heavy, but firm
and stable. For underlying the aesthetic preference, here as before, there
exists a practical one. Anything else apart, we have, in Professor Nowell-
Smith's terminology, a pro-attitude to buildings that stand up.

Let me add a last kind of expressiveness, rarely recognized as such,
namely this: where theories in science or mathematics are recommended, as they often are, of course, in aesthetic terms, as *elegant* or *beautiful*, not only as *valid* or *true*, then their aesthetic excellence, one must
insist, is in fact a form of expressiveness. Theory, doubtless, no less than
practice, has its own values, intrinsic values—theoretical power, rigor,
coherence. It may have them, however, without showing them—I mean,
without making them visible or obvious; but where the clothing, as it
were, expresses the body, where the mere form of the theory vividly reveals its own workings, we shall find not only such theoretical values,
but aesthetic value too. Similarly, a last case, with a sportsman: say a
cricket batsman, who not only stays in and scores—our primary, as it
were, "practical" evaluation—but one whose strokes, whose very movements, also express their own function, as he cuts or drives with vividly
"visible" command. Now here once again, on the same principles as before, an aesthetic appraisal supervenes.[8]

Kent's concern, I said, when he read authority in Lear's looks, is not
primarily aesthetic. He does not dwell on the impression for its own
sake—yet, in saying so I find myself pausing. For surely the words Shakespeare gives him, with their brusqueness, their vivid aptness, hint at
more. We are made momentarily, before the dialogue hurries on, to
notice and enjoy the possibility of a face that "has that something in
it" that one naturally obeys; it is at least a first budding of the aesthetic.
Now once we remove practical pressures, the unremitting requirements
of action that drive us hourly on, the rest follows; spontaneously a
purely aesthetic interest will open up.

To repeat, Kent's interest is practical; but where our interest is strictly
aesthetic, no practical question arises. Indeed, if it did, there may be
nothing "there" for it to judge. The "wide-embracing gesture" of Park
Crescent, described by Pevsner as "irresistible," is immediately and visibly "seen"; and gestures, of course, bona fide gestures, do certainly express attitudes, hostile, friendly, or neutral. But what of a terrace of

houses? Bricks and mortar, certainly, are not friendly or hostile—a point, let us note, on which the admirer of Park Crescent need be under no illusion. Nor can Lear's countenance, his face or bearing itself—though it may have authority "in" it—be fit or unfit to command. One passes a make-believe judgment, and is unlikely to mistake it for a real one. A judgment that becomes, roughly speaking, "if that *per impossibile* were gesture, it would then be a warmly open and friendly one." Toy guns, to take an analogy, are made to play with, not fight with, and are assessed for their merits accordingly. Further, play is an activity *sui generis*, yet an activity that in default of the notion of real guns—those that kill people—would be inconceivable.[9]

Art, once again, is both continuous and discontinuous with life. We can either merely dwell in impressions, or seek alternatively to clarify or transform them. They are, of course, fallible, and accordingly call for clarification, though not generally for practical purposes, and under the pressure of the moment, beyond a certain "reasonable" point. Perfect clarity, certainly, is one thing to aim at; it is not the only thing. Let us recall another no less requisite, and still for practical purposes, a strong sense or sure intuition of qualities immediately "seen." But once we leave practical preoccupations behind, two developments lie open beyond them. We can dwell in impressions for their own sake, now seeking mere heightened sensitivity, which has become pure aesthetic sensitivity; or, alternatively, we can seek for sheer clarity, clarity and intelligibility for their own sake, proceeding, in other words, into the alternative region of pure theory. Neither serves any practical purpose—neither pure science, nor pure art; both, then, are in that sense gratuitous; and both are valuable.

I spoke earlier of better judges and worse. Let us return to our earlier example, the would-be "authoritative" voice, the voice that different hearers hear differently, that rings true in my ears but not in yours. That, though so far a practical issue, brings us to the edge of problems that are more specifically aesthetic. First of all, in an instance like this, we need not differ in our primary attitudes in those we may call preaesthetic. We both want to see power in good hands—firm, competent, and trustworthy hands. But turn next to the corresponding quasi-judgment, now an aesthetic judgment. Parallel differences, of course, appear, which naturally we should like ways of resolving. Now those, in one sense, we inevitably lack; there can be no *experimentum crucis* or the like. But that, of course, is anything but exceptional, by no means confined to aesthetics; most fact-statements state only probabilities. The weather forecast, for instance, predicts rain; but of course the non-appearance of rain does not show that the forecaster was wrong. He went on the evidence, perhaps rightly; it was indeed highly probable. True, this failure, along with similar predictions which subsequent events prove false, might certainly have some tendency to show that the forecaster is wrong. So far, then, the judgment we have been speaking of, concerning someone's fitness to command, whether based on the sound of his voice or on other, solider evidence, is no different in principle. In theory, you may say, it could be put to the test, if the owner of the "authoritative" voice, presently gaining a position of authority, were to succeed or fail. But the test, plainly, is anything but decisive: success or failure, notoriously, is contingent on a thousand factors; and winners (we generally observe) are wonderfully lucky. But, at least, verification-ists will insist, we still know what to "count," what to reckon, in such cases, as confirmation or disconfirmation, as relevant evidence.

Hence, the next step, it may seem, is the dubious one; we pass from judgment proper to what I have called quasi-judgment. To those quasi-judgments—judgments which precisely are no longer practical—their truth or falsity no subsequent event can be relevant; no question of that sort can arise. Therefore nothing, it would seem, even tends to confirm or cast doubt upon them. Suppose we say so; it is doubtless a possible way of speaking. So that whatever I hear as authoritative is *eo ipso* "authoritative to me." It is, nonetheless, not the only one, nor in point of fact how we ordinarily talk. I may after all still be what we call a bad judge; and in regard to that possibility, why should evidence be lacking? True, it can only be evidence, strictly speaking, of my practical judg-ment, rather than my aesthetic judgment, my judgment of authority in people, for instance. Set the two things side by side, however: the anal-ogy between them is pretty striking, and if there are differences as well, who is to declare their logical relevance self-evident? It seems that cer-tain statements, certain judgments, are to be allowed; they pass and gain the status of being "meaningful." (Or "science" by a line of "demarca-tion" is distinguished from inferior non-science: presumably inferior, for otherwise what interest attaches to the demarcation?) What we still need to know will be principles that lay down for us just where to draw the line—what principles, and again, how to justify them.

Unless here, as elsewhere, one simply "decides": one can draw it, if he likes, precisely here. Those judgments are empirical and meaningful; these others are pseudo-judgments, void of content. What follows? We on our side can "decide" differently, using the same logical prerogative, or existential prerogative, which is one way of settling philosophical difficulties. Indeed, verificationists show wonderful ingenuity in devis-ing different sorts of strong as against weak, and direct as against indirect verification, so as to let in and keep out just what they want. Ingenuity, I fear, cannot make it less dogmatic; and with a dogmatist the right course is to steal his clothing. Answer a dogmatist according to his dogma, lest he be undogmatic in his own conceit. We answer then that we are verificationists too, but more thorough, more comprehensive verificationists. We take account, not only of "direct" and "indirect" verification as hitherto recognized, but also of "secondary indirect verification" (or "oblique verification") hitherto overlooked.

But after all, I shall doubtless be asked, what is this new method, this "secondary indirect verification"? I have already said. One treats the pure aesthetic judgment as if it were practical, intuitively practical, ignoring extraneous information, judging not what the thing is, but how it looks; so far there is nothing peculiar to aesthetics. The judgment "those clouds look like rain" is intelligible, surely, and may be true, yet concerns appearances, only appearances. Further, I should not withdraw it, should not judge otherwise, even though I may happen to know that nothing but perfect weather lies ahead. I know it, perhaps, by special divine revelation or by private radio communication from the stratosphere. I may say that a man sounds authoritative, that any competent judge would agree, though I myself know him, from some special acquaintance, in fact to be singularly foolish and vacillating, incorrigibly timid and inept.

Larger issues, I fear, lurk behind; and I can only indicate roughly where they lie, can point out the appropriate area, not properly explore it. All empirical findings presuppose judgment, and judgment itself not empirical; you must recognize green things where you see them, to test empirically whether some substance, perhaps immersed in acid, turns green. We assign individuals to given classes, which seems not to be hard. Not in that instance, certainly, but elsewhere the case changes. What are we to say of an "inflationary trend" or "negligence" (Professor Wisdom's example) or—something that may matter in its own way, whose classification may matter, at least, as determining its liability to import duty—a "work of art"? Decisions here, or judgments, are less straightforward. Or is neurosis rightly classified as disease?—"Mental illness" says Dr. Szasz, a shade dramatically perhaps, "is a myth."

We must go further; such judgments often presuppose others, too, and others that differ in kind. We have to do with interpenetrating dimensions; notions can, so to speak, cross our ordinary logical boundaries. Thus, streams of energy are like streams of water—like them, yet radically different. Or light that travels (Mr. Toulmin's example), and travels in straight lines, is like a traveling vehicle or a flying stone. Certain questions that in the old context we ask naturally and legitimately

—the question "traveling fast or slowly?", "a stream of energy flowing or damned up?"—remain equally appropriate here, and they are carried over automatically into the new. But, no less evidently, others are ruled out. That latter stream, for instance, carries with it no quantity of sand or sediment, nor flows between low or lofty banks. We have here a new judgment of likeness, if you like a new sort of class intrusion, though one that embraces or straddles other radical differences. From one perspective the damming-up of energy and of water are things of the same kind, though a kind that also cuts across others. Again, in regard to the whole procedure: the legitimacy of models and metaphors yields questions enough to argue over, both in detail and in general. What we lack, and inevitably lack, is any short or simple way of settling them.

Children's stories paint a world in black and white. At least they used to; nowadays (I believe) psychology has got hold of them. And it seems there remain sophisticated theorists whose logical perspective is much the same; who long to hear a clear, conceptual bell that either strikes—suppose we only hit hard enough—or else fails to. They long for "decision procedures," for answers that are final and unquestionable. We may indeed wish for them, but our actual searching inevitably proceeds mostly among shifting shades of grey. It seems that the harder balance to hold involves recognizing ideals as ideals, neither merely relinquishing them, nor mistaking them for accomplished realities. Precision, like economy and completeness, has its place among regulative principles, among ideals. And, meanwhile, all those problems remain and confront us obscurely and actually, which we must either blindly legislate out of existence, or else accept and make the best of as they are. But to go further: different questions arise at different levels. We can ask, for instance, first and generally, whether energy (or whether libido) may be conceived on the analogy of a stream, or light can be conceived as the kind of thing that travels. Now say that we answer affirmatively. To do so straightaway lets in a whole new range of questions that could never arise otherwise. Suppose someone looks tired or inert. Now given this new way of thinking, we shall naturally ask other questions in turn. Is his energy, his real energy, dammed up, in technical language "repressed"?—and if so we next ask "Repressed by what?" Or is the original supply, the source or spring, in some way deficient? So much in general. Turn now to specifically aesthetic judgments or quasi-judgments; we shall find that the formal analogy holds, indeed holds exactly. To ascribe *arrogance* or *authority* to a facade means to treat it, roughly speaking, like a person, to assess it after the manner of a man's looks, his voice or bearing. And that is the first step, one, however, that easily gets taken for granted, though without it the rest would be nonsense; it would be no less nonsense to apply the term "authoritative" to a building than to call it, say, the square root of nineteen. Now the initial "seeing-as" plainly involves a certain exercise of imagination, and here already it must be possible to fail.

Two distinct steps are involved, to repeat: we first see a façade as a face, which we can then see as authoritative or arrogant. The former is imaginative "seeing-as"; the latter is, basically—and odd as the account may sound—a judgment of class-inclusion. Now not all such issues, once again, can be plain sailing; they may or may not be decidable out of hand. Some, perhaps, we must also acknowledge, may never be decidable at all; and everywhere we shall find a certain indeterminate fringe. Both, nonetheless, are things belonging intrinsically to rational thinking —the one at all levels, the other at all but ground level. Moreover, both are often presupposed—the first, indeed, not often but always—in any final appeal to empirical facts. Now take this sort of question comprehensively. To expect simple procedures for settling them would be naïve. And again, in default of such procedures, it would be, not naïve, but wrong-headedly sophisticated to dismiss them as meaningless.

As to intuitive perception, if only to make it clear that we need to go deeper into these regions than merely de facto psychology, let me add this: we are speaking of something that lies in our nature as rational beings, something intrinsic to it, not accidental. I need not speak of omniscience; I leave that on one side. I speak, then, of fallible beings, learning progressively, and ignore, too, some would-be progressive learner, one in whose mind new truths start out independently, say, like cards in a card index; each one, in other words, is wholly self-contained and self-sufficient. For it is a description that no fact can answer to, inasmuch as each item is, as it were, bound to point to and admit of modification by others still perhaps to follow; in brief, any one suggests others. What remains is as follows. Everything, each single object, among those passing before us incessantly, perhaps in the daily perceptual stream, can never totally focus our attention which, once again, would be a feat only for omniscience. Each one, then, will carry its suggestion of others, suggestions half-clinging to it, and "coloring" it, which are then grasped intuitively, grasped as things lying "behind."

Now any mere exercise of our faculties, let us say—though these, I must grant at once, are large issues, and issues impossible properly to explore here—is its own end and justification. To act is to choose to act, and what we choose ceteris paribus we think good. We may be wrong, doubtless—wrong in any instance. But the presumption necessarily is otherwise; not everyone can be perennially fooled. And so much is necessary, an ineluctable assumption, for thought to be possible at all. Next then, if their mere exercise is good, their fuller exercise will be proportionately better; and art, in one aspect at least, if the previous argument proves acceptable, exercises certain of our faculties—namely, our intuitive faculties—to their fullest.

A couple of final points—points, I hope, that we can deal with more briefly: expressiveness, I have implied, is pervasive. Watching, walking, or talking, we make intuitive judgments all the time. Now works of art differ, of course, but differ in degree, not in kind; they differ, more specifically, in their vividness or concentration of expression. In poetry, it has often been remarked, words seem, as it were, charged or even surcharged with meaning, far beyond their ordinary quota; and visual art, too, presents objects that seem fuller, richer than mere objects, as if they had acquired a new depth, indeed a new dimension of depth. It is a difference that is essential, certainly, one, so far as possible, I do not wish to play down. Here, however, I shall not seek to explore or account for it, not, certainly, that it need be unintelligible or inexplicable. But the analysis of particular effects, the means of heightening particular impressions, I take to be the proper business of art criticism and literary criticism, not the business of the philosophy of art, though the fact, which paradoxical or not, certainly is a fact—that their effects can seem positively more vivid in their "aesthetic" presentation than its archetype, the thing itself—might repay exploration on another occasion.

Lastly, a point dwelt on, and not only dwelt on but fully and brilliantly illustrated, by Professor Gombrich. Expression presupposes a context; we bring expectations to works of art, that is, to particular works, holding comparisons at least implicitly in readiness, normally, no doubt, unconsciously. Now we see them accordingly then, say, as reticent or exuberant, as joyful or calm; and with a different background or set of expectations, the expression, too, may startingly differ.

The difficulty is certainly real, but I think more practical than theoretical. First, as to works from some alien culture, wholly alien prehistoric works, for example: they have, in fact, I have very little doubt, been often quite wildly misjudged. And, of course, if we come to judge them better, it is by learning more of their background, the culture to which they belong. With conscious innovators, however, the case differs, with innovators like Caravaggio or Wordsworth, who were still part of the culture they rebelled against. And as such they felt themselves rebels. True, there must be some things, some aesthetic effects, that history has all but obliterated. Thus, for instance, early baroque nowadays, to our eyes, can never be quite what it presumably was to its contemporaries. We compare it, unlike them, to what followed and not what proceeded, not to mannerism or the renaissance, but to high baroque—that is, to just the same sort of effect carried further. For us, then, inevitably, its impact, its emphatic drama, will partly be muted. At most we can hope and strive, with historical aids, progressively to approximate to an appropriate point of view, which we do more or less anyway in all sorts of historical study. Or alternatively, what seems to be the sole obvious alternative—which some theorists, in ethics, too, appear to revel in as perfect freedom, though one might rather think it perfect meaninglessness, making responsible freedom impossible—we can give ourselves leave to see anything as anything.

Notes

1. N. Pevsner, *Buildings of England* (London, 1952), II, 348–49.

2. L. Mumford, *The Highway and the City* (London, 1964), pp. 148–49. Looked at less "physiognomically," the facade of Saarinen's building presents an odd combination of weighty, angular forms with restlessness and movement.

3. The encyclopaedic Mr. Sparshott has assembled a whole series of interpretations of grace (cf. *The Structure of Aesthetics*, 1963, pp. 75–76). The authorities agree in finding it expressive of qualities of character and the like; but Schopenhauer, who happily thought of seeking light on gracefulness by way of its opposite—"wooden stiffness" or "meaningless bustle" as he calls it—has the truest account, it seems to me. He speaks of "every position" as "assumed in the easiest, most appropriate, and convenient way." Reid, I should say, is near the point, but not quite on it, in speaking of "Perfect propriety of conduct and sentiment, in an amiable character." For, I think, other things would seem to express amiability more clearly, for instance *charm*, though doubtless charm and grace go naturally together. But by "propriety of conduct" he most likely means its fitness for practical purposes, which would be a natural eighteenth-century usage; and if so his account is pretty near our own. Spencer echoes Schopenhauer's attention to "meaningless bustle," stressing economy; but having got to that point, he gets no further. Mechanical and mathematical economy, in human movement at least, is the very antithesis of grace; for it implies a tense and rigid self-control, whereas grace can always afford to overflow. "Good will, like grace," says Halifax, "floweth where it listeth," and so too of visible gracefulness.

4. Heinz Werner, *Einführung in die Entwicklungs Psychologie* (Leipzig, 1956). [Gombrich's note.]

5. E. H. Gombrich, *On Physiognomic Perception* in *Meditation on a Hobby Horse* (London, 1963), pp. 47–48.

6. Though commentators make *countenance* mean, not just *face*, but more generally *bearing*, the verb *to countenance* in *Macbeth* (Act 2, scene 3, line 81) means simply *face* or "look in the face," *confront*; and other examples abound, for instance, what of "A countenance more in sorrow than in anger"? The question two lines earlier had been, "Then saw you not his *face*?" Nothing, however, in the present argument turns on the point.

7. J. Hospers, *Meaning and Truth in the Arts* (Chapel Hill, 1946), p. 70.

8. I have attempted no examples from literature which raise large problems of their own, and problems I cannot adequately explore here. Language, roughly, in virtue, not only of its visible or audible forms, but also of its syntax and vocabulary acquires a kind of quasi-publicity. We have, at least in a certain sense, one object, more accessible, "colored" by others less so, that lie "behind" it. And clearly we have pro and con attitudes to ideas and emotions that language is made to express. Or sometimes, without actually sharing them, we feel bound to take them seriously, nonetheless—often, too, certainly, admiring the extreme vividness of their expression itself.

9. See L. Wittgenstein, *Philosophical Investigations*, sec. I, 282.

EXTRINSIC VALUE

Welfare: Some Philosophical Issues

NICHOLAS RESCHER

I. MAN'S WELFARE

THE WORD *welfare* derives its meaning from the original sense of "having a good trip or journey" and conveys the idea of traveling smoothly on the road of life. The idea of the general welfare correspondingly relates to what is for the public, or common, good, *pro bono publico*, as the Romans put it. One dictionary defines *welfare* as the "state of faring, or doing well; state or condition in regard to well-being: especially conditions of health, happiness, prosperity, or the like." On the negative side welfare contrasts with the no longer common conception of *illfare*, of having one's affairs fare ill. It is, thus, clear that welfare is bound up with the essentials of a man's well-being, especially those within the range of application to which we have become accustomed by such presently current terms as the "welfare state" or a "welfare worker."

The "welfare of a person" has a plurality of components, since welfare is a thing of many dimensions. Preëminent among these are his physical welfare (health), his material welfare (prosperity), and even his spiritual or psychological welfare (state of mind or mental health). Physical health, material circumstances, and mental and emotional well-being are the definitive elements of welfare. The dictionary definition cited above is rather misleading with respect to happiness. Happiness, clearly, is not a component of welfare, but its goal. One feels that the man whose welfare is in good order, who is healthy, prosperous, and secure is—or ought to be—happy, being possessed of what general consensus regards as some of the principal requisites of a happy life.

Significant complexity affects the concept of welfare through its psychological dimension which raises a whole host of ramifications. Where physical and material welfare alone are in question, the issue is a substantially simpler one, since these desiderata can be assured for a man in isolation, without overt reference to his significant human interrelationships. There is, however, the whole sector of a man's relation to his fellows, in the sphere of personal and close-range interactions (in family contacts, professional interactions, friendships, and social interactions). As a social animal a man's own welfare is bound up with that of others. Welfare is a matter of the basic requirements of well-being, and man is so constituted that he cannot achieve this condition without reference to the condition of others.

II. Yardsticks for Welfare

It seems to me important to stress that the determination of the extent to which the welfare of a person is achieved is an objective issue. This leaves open the question of the criteria to be used—the yardsticks for measuring welfare. It is clear that the multidimensionality of welfare will necessitate use of a variety of criteria.

Before one considers this issue itself, a preliminary remark is in order. Satisfaction of these various criteria is not part of the meaning of *welfare*, any more than the meaning of *acid* or of "pressure front" has a part in the behavior of the litmus paper or of the barometer we use for its determination. The criteria are not definitional components of the meaning of *welfare*, but instead they represent tests for assessing the degree of a person's welfare.

The principal criteria by reference to which the degree of realization of a man's welfare can be measured are as follows:

A. Physical Health
  1. life expectancy
  2. physical condition (vigor, adequacy of functioning, absence of pain, etc.)
  3. external normality (absence of disfigurement or disability)
B. Mental Health
  1. capacity to act effectively along chosen lines in chosen directions (outside controlled, limited, or institutional contexts)
  2. satisfaction with himself and his circumstances (absence of abnormal fears, animosities, etc.)
C. Material Prosperity
  1. income
  2. negotiable wealth (money, gold, negotiable securities)
  3. possession of goods (fixed and moveable)
D. Environmental Assets
  1. availability of goods
  2. availability of services
  3. availability of amenities
  4. quality of the environment (physical and natural, cultural, economic, public health, etc.)

A long commentary could—and ideally should—be written about each of these items, but we shall simply note them and pass on.

III. Who Is to Judge?

A key issue regarding welfare is posed by the question of who is best qualified to make assessments about welfare. Who is the best judge of a person's welfare? The exploration of this problem will make possible the clarification of basic aspects of welfare itself and will at the same time point the way towards some of the very difficult issues involved with the concept of welfare.

There is present in most of us a deep-rooted feeling that no one can better judge the considerations involved in a person's affairs—and above all those regarding his own being—than the man himself. This sentiment is supported and fortified by extensive exposure to the liberal democratic principle that people are themselves necessarily the best judges of their interests.

Fundamental to this issue is a distinction between subjective states on the one hand and objective conditions on the other. Whether a man *"feels* cold" or "is worried" or "feels well and healthy" are all subjective matters, in contrast to whether it *"is* cold" (relative to what the man is accustomed to) or whether he "has cause for worry" or whether he "is actually in good health," all of which are objective conditions that can obtain without reference to anybody's subjective feelings. Now this distinction is critical for our present problem. A subjective state is best judged by a person himself—no one else is in a better position to make judgments about it. But whether that person finds himself in a certain objective condition is best judged by persons with the clearest heads and the greatest quantity of relevant information at their disposal, and this need by no means be the subject himself.

A person's welfare is a matter of objective conditions, not of his subjective state. His physical condition, his material prosperity, his mental health—all these are objective circumstances that can be as well (or better) known to others as to himself—his family doctor, his legal advisor, etc. For the condition of his welfare—unlike a fleeting feeling of contentment or happiness or elation—is not a subjective psychological state that the subject himself is, in the very nature of things, best fitted to judge. Welfare is not a matter of the psychological feelings but a question of the extent to which certain objective circumstances are realized—circumstances generally regarded representing requisites for the achievement of happiness in the contemporary life environment.

A clear sign that people are not to be regarded as automatically the best-qualified judges of their own welfare is provided by the case of the intellectually immature or abnormal—viz., children and madmen. It would be patently inappropriate to regard all such people as invariably competent to judge in matters of their own welfare. And this fact shows, at any rate, that it is not in the inevitable nature of things that people should be qualified to make judgments in this area. (Note that there is no doubt that children and madmen are the best judges about whether they feel discomfort or pleasure, and whether they are happy or miserable.)

The fact is that judgments of welfare are matters of (objective) knowledge and not matters of (subjective) feeling. Thus, whether a person's welfare is in better—or worse—shape than it used to be is an issue about which others may be better informed than he—his physician, his attorney, his accountant, etc. Welfare is a matter of objectively determinable circumstances, and thus makes room for the entry of expertise.

What has been said here regarding the welfare of an individual holds true also for that of a group. The members of a group need not themselves be infallible authorities in matters of their own welfare. The "foreign" doctor or economist or anthropologist may well know better than the "natives" themselves that existing conditions are somehow detrimental to their welfare and that their state of welfare would be increased by some change in their *modus operandi*.

Recognizing that the external observer may be in a better position to make an assessment of welfare than the subject himself, it must be stressed that it is the subject himself, however, that is the center about which these considerations revolve. Welfare considerations are not to be made from some abstract, depersonalized point of view. Welfare certainly has its idiosyncratic involvements—the subject's own tastes, inclinations, personality makeup, physical constitution, etc., are indispensable reference points for welfare considerations. Welfare judgments will thus be not subjective, but subject oriented: they require objective information about the subject. In this regard welfare judgments are typified by medical judgments regarding one's state of health. Just as the patient himself is the definitive authority about "how he feels," so the subject is the definitive authority about whether or not "he feels content and happy." But this subjective element settles the question of welfare no more than that of health. Neither in regard to state of health nor in regard to state of welfare are feelings definitive indicators of objective conditions. In both cases expert information provides the crucial basis for judgment. But this information is, in large measure, not a matter of information of general and universalizable sort, but one of specific data regarding the characteristic makeup of the particular individual at issue.

Dangers inhere in welfare judgments made by outsiders on a subject's behalf. The dictator, the foreign sociologist, and the government official are all prone to make horrible blunders when they tell themselves (and others): "I know what's best for the people here." This misconception of fact can lead readily to cynical abuse or to myopic paternalism. There is no doubt that the man who makes decisions regarding the welfare of others is in a position of power, and it is but too well known that power corrupts. But to say all this is to say no more than that welfare judgments—like all judgments—can be made badly. We insist upon our paradigm of the medical or economic or legal counselor. Here too, mistakes can doubtless occur—but in many or most cases are no more likely to come from a well-trained, well-informed, and systematic outsider than from the subject himself.

IV. RESPONSIBILITY FOR WELFARE

Who—apart from the man himself—is responsible for a person's welfare? It is clear that other people can be both legally and morally responsible for a person's welfare. The basis for this statement can be natural: as a parent is responsible for the welfare of a young child, or the child for that of an aged parent. Or the basis can be contractual: captain, for crew and passengers; general, for his troops. There are also borderline cases, e.g., a host and his guest. In final analysis the relationship is always contractual in its generic nature—either by an overt contract or by a "social contract," given implicitly by the rules of the society. Even the scope and nature of parental responsibility are defined by societal arrangements.

One important question in this area is: Under what circumstances and to what extent are others (morally) entitled to interfere when a person neglects his own welfare? Obviously such entitlement exists in a substantial way in the child-parent case—at any rate in our culture. But what of other cases? The answer seems in general to reside in the principle that persons are entitled to interfere in regard to someone's welfare when his welfare is systematically connected with theirs so that his neglect of his own welfare endangers their interests (their welfare, their rights, etc.). The key example here is represented by the collective welfare issues, where one man's welfare is bound up with that of others. Examples include the man who neglects his health on a crowded ship or who lets his house become a fire hazard in a crowded town.

Such collective welfare issues are especially prominent in modern society. We are all living on a crowded ship. This fact puts great stress on the collective sector of welfare. The conditions and circumstances of our common environment are clearly an area of legitimate public responsibility—air- and water-pollution control, public health, crime control, etc. And the area at issue here not only includes the prevention of negative but also the promotion of positive aspects of natural and created environment—e. g., through the provision of services like television, transportation, and communications.

What demands for the promotion of his welfare can an individual reasonably make upon his society? No a priori answer is possible. The range of legitimate demands depends crucially upon: (1) custom, and (2) law. These criteria create a basis for legitimate expectation and claims. Thus, the answer to our question hinges in significant measure upon what the society decides it should be. But this decision is not just a matter of fiat. It is definitely limited by what society can afford. But not just this, but (as was already said) the society's own decisions and decrees may well limit (restrict) society's commitment, not because of stinginess, but because it espouses a conception of "the good life" for man that itself delimits the range of what others can and should do for a person's welfare and to what extent he should "fend for himself." A society thus has at least two legitimate grounds for not doing something on behalf of one of its members' welfare:

1. that it cannot afford the requisite action;
2. that taking the requisite action would be against the best interests of people in general (by destroying initiative, rendering people too dependent, impeding or undermining socially desirable behavior patterns, etc.).

When an individual makes otherwise reasonable-seeming demands upon the society to act in support of his welfare, the society can legitimately decline on either of these grounds.

How far is a society responsible for welfare of its constituent individuals? It is certainly not reasonable to view society as standing *in loco parentis* to people, with virtually open-ended responsibilities (at least not with the parental concept predominant in the West). In this sphere society should at most play the role of a parent of last resort: relationless orphans or those who pose an excessive or impracticable burden for their natural guardians—the insane, handicapped, or illegitimate.

It is advisable to differentiate between first-line and second-line responsibility for welfare. The person who has first-line responsibility is himself to assure welfare of his subject; the person with second-line responsibility merely helps his subject to care for his own welfare, which may mean the creation of opportunities, a climate for initiative, a fruitful environment, etc. A parent has first-line responsibility, but a society in general has only second-line responsibility for the welfare of its members (except perhaps for special categories—the insane, disabled veterans, etc.).

V. Goals Beyond Welfare

A good part of the discussion prior to this point has been devoted to an attempt to clarify the nature of welfare. The time has now come to criticize it, to confront the question: Is welfare all? The issue of social goals beyond welfare deserves careful consideration. Does the welfare-centered society represent an ultimate ideal, or is it to be viewed as an interim stage enroute to more significant objectives?

It is important to recognize that welfare has a certain minimality about it. The components of welfare represent great, indeed almost indispensable assets to "the good life," but all the same, they furnish no more than the beginnings of such a life. The good life is something whose range extends far beyond the core issue of welfare. The man whose cultural horizons are narrow, whose physical environment is unattractive, or whose government is despotical may not actually suffer in any of the dimensions of his welfare—indeed, he personally may conceivably even be every bit as "happy" as though he lived otherwise. Nevertheless we could not qualify his as being "the good life." Welfare is only the foundation of such a life; it is not the structure itself. Physical health, material circumstances, and mental and emotional well-being are enormous—perhaps even indispensable—aids toward a meaningful and satisfying life, but they are not in themselves sufficient for this purpose. The components of the good life must extend far beyond considerations of welfare.

What things are in a person's best interests? Certainly his own welfare. And unquestionably also the welfare of others—his own family, his colleagues, his fellow citizens, and so on toward mankind at large. But a person's best interests go beyond the issue of welfare for self and others. As already mentioned, they include such matters as educational and cultural opportunities and attainments, attractiveness of physical surroundings, pleasantness of natural environs, and openness and orderliness of social and political arrangements—all these represent areas of a man's best interests that go beyond the minimalities of welfare for himself and others.

Certainly in the case of an individual it is obviously appropriate and desirable that he should have life goals that extend beyond his welfare and that of his kindred. When one contemplates the wide range of desirable human achievements and accomplishments it is quite clear that most of them do not lie within the restricted confines of welfare.

A man's being educated (along other than vocational lines), for example, or his taking an intelligent interest in the arts are not matters that affect his welfare, but do all the same represent important human desiderata. Of the seven deadly sins (pride, greed, lust, anger, gluttony, envy, and sloth) at most three—viz., greed, lust, and gluttony—have a direct and immediate connection with material welfare.

The situation with regard to social welfare is exactly analogous. Welfare has to do with the material requisites for a satisfying life. But this very focus on the material is the key indicator of the limited and restricted scope of the whole issue of welfare. A people can enjoy a good standard of living, material prosperity, a good standard of public health, etc. and yet be lacking in education, culture, artistic and scientific creativity, and the good manners and decencies that make for a civilized life. A society whose welfare is in a salubrious condition can all the same lead a low, degraded, and in some respects impoverished existence. To set up welfare as *the* social goal is folly. Welfare is all very nice as far as it goes, but it is certainly incomplete. The Biblical dictum that "man doth not live by bread alone" can be applied to welfare also. (Though, of course, this is not to say that he who lacks bread—or other requisites of welfare—is in a position to devote himself to these "higher" matters.)

Again, for the individual person there are, or should be, important goals beyond welfare. Examples of such goals include attaining the respect of his fellows and the love of some among them; pride of achievement in some areas of activity, vocational or avocational; and appreciation of man's accomplishments in art and science. The achievement of such goals lays the basis for a legitimate view of oneself as a unit of worth. And a significant and general lack in these regards is indicative, not necessarily of any diminution of welfare, but of an improverishment of spirit. In consequence people as individuals have (i.e., can, should, and do have) a wide spectrum of trans-welfare goals—goals the attainment or progress toward which is definitely to be viewed as "in the interest" of a person, even though it need not be his welfare that suffers by a deficiency in this regard.

In a wholly parallel way there are legitimate goals for a society that extend well beyond the region of the welfare of its members: in the cultivation of literary, artistic, and scientific creativity and appreciation; in the forging of an attractive and comprehensively pleasant life environment; in the cultivation of enjoyable human interactions; and in preserving and enhancing the appreciation of its historical, cultural, and intellectual heritage. A society can and should look beyond the physically comfortable life comprising its welfare to the fostering of those conditions and circumstances that make life rich, full, and rewarding. The material factors at issue in welfare are only the springboard from which a society should move on to more deeply meaningful objectives.

From this standpoint it becomes obvious what answer is to be given to our question of whether the welfare-centered society is an optimal Utopia or whether it has intrinsic weaknesses and shortcomings. The position we have been developing points immediately to the second situation. The vision of the welfare-centered society does not extend far enough. The concern with welfare is all very well as far as it goes, but welfare is myopic in failing to see beyond the range of immediate human needs—perhaps even "needs" that have been substantially escalated in an affluent society—to the less mundane, but in the long run no less important desiderata that lie beyond.

We have only given some random examples of legitimate trans-welfare goals. Broadly speaking, all these have related to matters of excellence, of creative achievement, and the enhancement of the quality of human life. Now it might be objected: "Granted that these trans-welfare objectives are of value in the long run. But in the here and now, in the short run, they are luxuries. What concern has a society with the pursuit of these trans-welfare goals until after the first item of its agenda—the welfare of its members—has been properly attended to?" To this critic we reply that his reasoning is misleading and mistaken. There are priorities that cannot be translated into sequences. A physician cannot tell a man: "Postpone exercise until after your diet has been perfected." It makes no sense to advise a student to put French off until after he is perfect in Latin. A society must be prepared to cultivate the pursuit of and the taste for excellence even amidst material adversity; otherwise the taste and the capacity for its achievement will both be dead before the day of material prosperity arrives. The plant that is not nurtured through the winter cannot flourish in the springtime. The *trans*-welfare goals cannot be made over into *post*-welfare goals because such a temporally sequential ordering of priorities can render their realization very difficult or even impossible.

VI. THE POST-WELFARE STATE

In the present condition of affluence of the technologically advanced, modern societies we can already discern the making of the *post-welfare state*, able, if willing, to devote a substantial fraction of its resources and energies toward the realization of what I have characterized as trans-welfare objectives. Such a state will differ from the welfare state as it has developed in Great Britain, Sweden, and even the United States in primarily three ways as regards its basic value structure:

A. The prime focus of emphasis will be shifted away from catering to the basic human needs of the welfare complex to the forging of more pleasant operating conditions for the conduct of life under the crowded circumstances of modern times (especially in the urban centers).

B. A higher priority will be given to goals of the cultural-creative sector. It will come to be recognized in a more emphatic way than ever before that society has a commitment to and responsibility for the level of culture, higher education, and the development of the arts. Society and its instrumentalities will take an increased interest in the institutions dedicated to promoting appreciation of the arts, the preservation of antiquities, etc. There will be a renewed stress on excellence and creativity.

C. The great surge of nationwide uniformity typical of the mass orientedness of the welfare state (mass production, mass media, mass politics) will give way in the face of tendencies of fragmentation. There will be renewed emphasis on regionalisms, parochialisms, "participatory democracy," and decentralized group action of many sorts. There will be a renewed surge of diversity-in-unity and cohesiveness-in-variety. The post-welfare society will combine unity with diversification, and will be a genuine *unum e pluribus*.

These value reorientations have far-reaching implications for the political *modus operandi* of the post-welfare state. The welfare state as it has developed in the European-North American setting is based upon a comprehensive hierarchical bureaucracy and a highly centralized control structure. Unified coordination and control have been virtually inevitable because of the nature of the problem with which the welfare state has been primarily designed to cope. Three factors have been especially significant here:

A. The bulk of the problems confronted by the welfare state has been economic in nature or in origin, and a nation's economy lends itself with relative ease to centralized direction and control. (In this regard a nation's economic life stands in contrast to its socio-psychological and its cultural dimensions.)

B. Prominent among the most fundamental problems of the welfare state have been the issues of economic and political egalitarianism. The results of equality and across-the-board equity can clearly be a centralized uniformitarianism.

C. The issues with which the welfare state has been concerned have been ones that can be tackled effectively by the legislative process. They revolve about issues of control and are, thus, of such a kind as to be responsive to centralized direction.

By contrast the critical issues confronting the post-welfare state will be of a different order. The problems that confront the society it serves will, as we have submitted, in the main lie, not in the economic sector, but in that of the cultural and socio-psychological aspects of life. As such they are most effectively and naturally amenable to a decentralized treatment better adapted to accommodate regional and communal differences. In consequence much of the structure of the post-welfare state will become multicellular rather than monolithically centralized. The "table of organization" of the many sectors of the post-welfare state will look like a spider's web rather than an inverted tree. A substantial realignment of the channels in which power and authority run will be called for, involving a marked localization of control—a shift away from the pattern of control imposed downward from on high in the centralized hierarchy, toward a relocation of authority in local units with the resultant capacity for the implementation of local initiative. The individual member of the post-welfare state will have to be closer—and will feel closer—to the effectively operative sources of authority and control—so close that he can touch their levers with his own hands. This is the pattern (already to be discerned in a rudimentary way) in present towards a shift from the bureaucratic centralism of the welfare state towards the "participatory democracy" of its post-welfare successor.

The welfare state has occupied a unique historical position. The principal social goals of the era, the main issues on the agenda of the society (economic growth, economic justice, political and economic egalitarianism, the forging of adequate "social services") were such as to be efficiently and effectively handled at the level of the state. But in the more affluent and socially more complex environmnt of the post-welfare state, this circumstance no longer obtains. The "issues of the day" will in large measure be such as to lie outside the sphere of effective state action. The state as such will become increasingly less relevant to the society's problems, and the society will readjust itself to ways of achieving its goals in ways other than through the instrumentality of the state. This is not to say, of course, that the state will "wither away" in the manner familiar in the dogmas of theoretical communism. The state and its historical functions will certainly survive. Just as the traditional security functions of the state survived (and expanded vastly) with the development of the welfare state, so the established welfare function of the state will survive (and conceivably expand) in the era of the post-welfare state. The point is that the social environment of the future will see the evolution of new forms of social action—largely outside the sphere of the state, to a degree that calls for innovative structures—to cope with the "problems of the day." The public agenda of the post-welfare state—its schedule of burning issues—will be such that the instrumentalities for effective handling call for a combination of (1) a revision of decentralized redeployment of state activities together with (2) the evolution of new, increasingly influential and important non-state approaches.

A major—perhaps the main—problem (or, rather, family of problems) that faces the post-welfare state is that of untying the knot of the city, of devising the means to tame and civilize urban life. Everyone is familiar with the catalogue of problems: dirt, noise, physical ugliness, crowding, crime, friction in interpersonal contacts. And we all know the results: personal demoralization, group tensions, and the social alienation that comes about when people interact with others not as people but as parts of a system. A prime task of the post-welfare society is to devise means of securing pleasantness for urban life—to restore convenience to city living, to make the city physically attractive, and (as far as possible) to break it down into units of human scale, to facilitate civility in interpersonal dealings.

Here, then, we have one typical example of the reorientation of the focus of society's attention that will characterize the situation of the post-welfare state. In the era of the welfare state, society's attention has been directed to the basic considerations needed to make life *viable* on a mass basis in the context of a developed industrial economy. With the post-welfare state the prime task will be that of making the circumstances of life *richer and fuller* for a mass population in the context of a "post-industrial" economy oriented heavily toward the production of services rather than goods. In brief the welfare state sees its problem in terms of making life in a mass society secure; the post-welfare state faces the problem of making it pleasant.

A Measuring Unit for
the Social Value of Moral Processes

FRANZ LOESER

W ITH THE BEGINNING of capitalism the possibility and necessity arose
of directly applying the natural sciences, particularly physics, to
the productive process. This posed the problem for the scientists of
developing exact criteria and standards of measurement as well as applying mathematical and experimental methods to the natural sciences.
The revolutionary role which Galileo's definition of the standard of
measurement of motion, expressed in the famous formula $v = s/t$, played
in this respect is too well known to be further discussed here. Yet the
revolution brought about in the natural sciences by Galileo was not
only based on his ability to find a standard of measure of motion or to
apply mathematical and experimental methods in physics. Decisive
also was the fact that the basic laws of physics were known to him and
that he held a materialist philosophical position in the field of natural
philosophy. For instance, whereas the ancient Greek philosophy defined
the basic concept of physics—force—subjectively, i. e., purely as a physical property of man, Galileo's notion of force was based on the theory
of the coordinates of moving bodies. For the first time in history Galileo
conceived the concept of force as a reflection of objective natural forces,
existing independently of the human being. Galileo's genius expressed
itself in his ability to combine his materialist philosophical position
and his knowledge of the basic laws of physics with the application of
exact standards of measurement and mathematical, as well as experimental, methods. This augmentation was the basis of modern natural
science.

Today the social scientist is faced with a problem similar to that
faced by the natural scientist at the time of Galileo. Mankind, if it is
to continue to exist and to advance to higher forms of social life, must
solve the problem of eradicating war, poverty, disease, and social injustice, as well as creating a new moral human being. Whereas at the
time of Galileo social progress necessitated the development of modern
natural science, so today mankind is faced with the task of creating a
truly scientific theory of society. The reason that ethics, despite the
many significant contributions it has made in its long history, has largely
failed to supply a scientific theory and method for the creation of this

new type of moral human being can mainly be traced back to the following reasons. The objective laws of moral development were essentially unknown. This ignorance led to the attempt to explain the development of morality either subjectively—i. e., purely as an expression of human instincts, drives, or desires—or as caused by supernatural forces. This idealist philosophical position, coupled with the ignorance of the basic laws of moral development, hindered also the application of mathematical and experimental methods and the definition of exact standards of measurement in ethics. In other words it prevented the creation of a truly scientific theory of morality. The philosophical prerequisite for a scientific theory of morality and the systematic application of mathematical and experimental methods to social progress is a Marxist ethics based upon a materialist philosophical point of view and upon the knowledge and recognition of the basic laws of moral development.

The ability to introduce mathematical and experimental methods in ethics depends furthermore on the possibility of finding exact standards and criteria of measurement for moral processes—i. e., for moral actions, behavior, consciousness, relations, or qualities. One can divide the problem of measuring moral processes into two parts. First is the question of measuring the quantitative aspects of moral processes, i.e., the number of moral actions of a certain type which occur in a specific space of time. I have dealt with this question in my book *Deontik, Planung und Leitung der moralischen Entwicklung* (Berlin, 1966, chap. 5). The second part of the problem is the question of measuring the qualitative aspects of moral processes. Central to the solution of this question is the measurement of the social value of moral processes. This paper will attempt to put forward some first ideas toward the solution of this problem.

The measuring of the social value of moral processes necessitates a measuring unit. The definition of such a measuring unit would serve as the theoretical basis for the measurement of the social value of moral processes or, to put it in the words of the physicist, for the "motion" of moral development. The attainment of such a definition requires the quantitative description of the concept of social value of moral processes. For this purpose I will begin by defining the function which morality fulfills in social development. I will conceive morality as a dynamic process with a specific normative function. This normative function comprises the regulation of social development so that the moral stability of society or the social group is ensured.

The concept of stability is here used in terms applicable to the field of cybernetics. As I understand it, moral stability exists within a social group when, under changing conditions, the group realizes its moral aims and norms to the degree that it can carry out its essential social functions and perform as a social organism. Moral stability is a dynamic process which includes the adaptation of the social group to more complex environmental conditions and its ability to progress to higher levels of moral development. Under the condition of moral instability, the level of realization of the moral aims and norms of the social group does not suffice to ensure the fulfillment of its essential social functions, and the social group tends to disintegrate morally.

If the function of morality, in its most general sense, is to ensure the moral stability of the social group, then we can conclude that the social value of moral processes can be expressed in terms of their influence on the moral stability of the social group. The measuring unit which denotes the social value of moral processes must, therefore, be a standard of measurement of the influence of moral processes on moral stability or instability. For this purpose I will classify the various moral processes. Moral actions, for example, can be classified by honest and dishonest, loyal and disloyal, heroic and cowardly actions. These classes, in turn, contain specific actions of a particular kind, which I will call elements. These classes of moral processes can again be subdivided into further classes. The kind of classification which has to be used depends on the types of moral processes which have to be measured. If, for instance, it is necessary to measure various kinds of honest actions or the same kind of honest action in different situations, then we shall interpret these actions as different classes of honest actions. Such a differentiation is, however, not always necessary.

It is obvious that different classes of moral processes will have a different influence on moral stability and instability. Generally speaking, for example, impolite behavior will have less effect on moral instability than murder. The differences and similarities of the classes of moral processes in their influence on moral stability and instability express themselves in the following fact. A specific number of elements of each class of moral processes is required to ensure moral stability or to cause moral instability. For instance, a social group will require a certain number of honest actions to ensure its moral stability; and, equally, a specific number of dishonest actions will cause its moral instability. The number of elements (i.e., specific moral actions, forms of moral behavior or consciousness, moral qualities or relations) of such a class of moral processes in a particular time and situation I take as the basis for the quantification of the social value of moral processes. Thus, the social value of a class of moral processes of which ten elements are required to ensure the moral stability of the social group

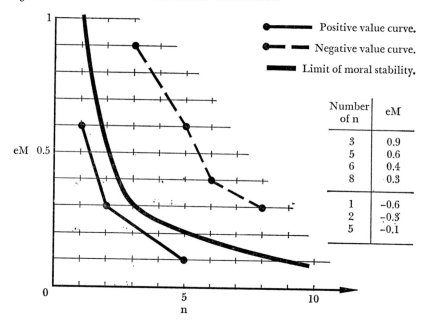

Number of n	eM
3	0.9
5	0.6
6	0.4
8	0.3
1	−0.6
2	−0.3
5	−0.1

would be $\frac{1}{10}$. The social value of a class of moral processes of which ten elements will cause the moral instability of the social group would be $-\frac{1}{10}$.

In defining a measuring unit for the social value of moral processes, one has to remember that all social values are related to a specific time and social situation. There are no social values independent of time and social conditions. This fact does not mean that certain values cannot have validity for different forms of society and historical periods. The comparatively permanent character of their validity is, however, not to be explained by their independence of time and situation, but by the similarities and common aspects in social conditions which may prevail in varying forms of society and over longer periods of history. A measuring unit of social value will, therefore, have to express the dependence of social value on time and situation. Ten dishonest actions in one day have a different influence on moral instability than ten such actions spread over one year. A certain dishonest action in one situation may have a totally different influence on moral instability in another situation.

Bearing in mind these conditions I will define the social value of moral processes in terms of an *ethometric measuring unit*, written symbolically eM. (Ethometry = theory of measurement of ethics.) I define eM as follows: *The eM unit denotes the reciprocal value of the minimal number of elements of a class of moral processes which in a specific situation and space of time will ensure the moral stability or alternately cause the moral instability of the social group.* I differentiate between a positive eM unit (+ eM), which denotes the positive social value of moral processes ensuring moral stability, and a negative eM unit (— eM), which denotes the negative social value of moral processes causing moral instability.

One + eM is equal to the social value of a class of moral processes of which one element will suffice to ensure the moral stability of the social group. Minus one eM is equal to the social value of a class of moral processes of which one element will suffice to cause the moral instability of the social group. Since 1 eM or — 1 eM is the highest social value of a moral process, the other values are expressed as fractions thereof. The greater the social value of a class of moral processes, the smaller the minimal number of elements of this class will be which ensure the moral stability or cause the moral instability of the social group. In the same manner the longer the necessary space of time is in which the minimal number of elements of a class of moral processes ensure moral stability or cause moral instability, the greater will be its social value. The reverse relations apply equally.

It is now possible to write the social value of moral processes denoted in eM units in form of a social value quotient as follows:

$$eM = \frac{t}{n}$$

The number of time units is designated by t. (A time unit may be one minute, one hour, one week, one month, one year, etc.) The minimal number of elements of a class of moral processes per t unit is designated by n which, in a specific situation, ensure the moral stability or cause the moral instability of the social group. The respective elements of the classes of moral processes must occur at least once per time unit. The following examples demonstrate the application of the social value formula:

Example 1: Twenty-five actions of a specific class which occur in 5 days ensure the moral stability of a social group. The chosen time unit is 1 day. The social value of this particular class of moral actions is then:

$$eM = \frac{5}{25} = 0,2$$

Example 2: One hundred moral (immoral) actions of a specific class which occur in 10 days cause the moral instability of a social group. The time unit is 1 day. The social value of this class of moral (immoral) actions is then:

$$eM = \frac{10}{100} = -0, 1$$

If one has to measure elements of moral processes which do not occur at least once per time unit, one has to choose a more appropriate time unit. If, for instance, a certain moral action only occurs once in 56 days, one obviously cannot choose 1 day as the time unit, but would have to use 2 months or 1 year as the time unit. Comparisons between eM values can only conveniently be made, if the time unit is the same.

It is also important to note that eM units are not additive. On the basis of the definition of eM the following relation applies:

$$-1 \leq eM \leq 1$$

The figure on page 236 shows moral actions of a particular social group which occur in a specific space of time with their respective social values. On the vertical axis the eM values are plotted and on the horizontal axis n is plotted. The positive value curve shows that within one time unit three moral actions with a value of 0,9 eM; five with a value of 0,6 eM; six with a value of 0,4 eM; and eight with a value of 0,3 eM occur. The negative value curve shows that within one time unit, one moral (immoral) action with a value of —0,6 eM; two with a value of —0,3 eM; and five with a value of —0,1 eM occur. The limit of moral stability is set by the respective eM values. If either the positive or the negative value curve cross this limit, the social group becomes morally unstable and tends to disintegrate morally. The formula eM=t/n denotes the social value of moral processes as related to time and situation. As such it is a standard of measurement for moral development or, in terms of the physicist, is a standard of measurement for the "motion" of moral development. This standard can, with appropriate adaptation, be applied equally to other aspects of ideological development.

The introduction of exact methods of measurement into ethics opens the way for the application of mathematical and experimental methods as well as the computer in this field. Thus, completely new perspectives are beginning to develop for ethics in its task to develop the scientific theory and method for the creation of the new moral man.

Old and New Types of Futurology and Their Influence on Ethics

ELFRIEDE TIELSCH

Translated by Rita D. S. Hartman

SINCE SOCRATES, either the scientist or the philosopher has been re- garded as responsible for the ethics of humanity. Socrates moved *virtue,* that is, man's ethical action or conduct, so close to *knowledge* that virtue seemed either to originate in knowledge or to be identified with it. All subsequent Socratic-Platonic philosophy—from Aristotle to Robert S. Hartman—therefore affirmed that ethical values can be de- duced from knowledge and, consequently, calculated from it by mathe- matical deduction with the help of a practical syllogism. The great hope of a Platonically schooled humanity concerning the meaning and goal of human life thus becomes theoretical understanding—and one cel- ebrates the settlement of a crisis, as, for example, the Cuban crisis, as a "victory of reason."

Before the Greek discovery—and hence overvaluation—of pure reason and its syllogistic capacity, however, man thought about the spiritual foundations of ethics very differently. The human prototype and mental function, which determined secular and religious life and action was not that of the scientist and professor in today's sense. For over seven millenia, that is, during the whole, more-or-less-conscious, first ethical epoch of civilization until today, in all corners of the earth and with all peoples and human communities, this role was performed by the prophet and his futurological revelation. It was the prophet, in the widest sense of the word, who showed man his goals, in public and private, national and supranational, big and small contexts, and in their truth or falsity. He alone made them dedicate themselves to these goals, with body and soul, with their goods and their blood, and often until death. He, the futurologist in ethics, provided the visible per- ception of what should in future be good or evil, and directed, re- sponsibly or irresponsibly, the decision for either the one or the other. He established the *agathon* as the *agathon mellon,* the "good" as the "future good."

It is true that in the constitution of the values that guide him the prophet will lean on a certain kind of knowledge which is experienced or learned, traditionally public or private and either an instilled feeling or a self-taught cognition, which in most cases is prescientific. But he pours it immediately into the form of fascinating descriptions and divinations of the future, completely sure, intellectually and instinctually, of the choice of his tools of action, with somnambulistically effective anthropological and axiological consequences. He proclaims and exploits his knowledge only in this futurological manner.

Contrary to the Socratic-Platonic notion of action as directly related to cognition, the figure of the practical-ethical prophet in his historical effectiveness—from the first Pharaohs to Buddha or Jesus to Marx or Mao—shows that only the involvement of our knowledge with the future, its futurologization, opens the way to its realization and efficiency in action. One has to produce, first, out of one's knowledge the vision and prediction of a possible future which either corresponds to or contradicts this knowledge—either promises a continuation or a change of the present. For only in the aura of the future can one possibility be preferred to another and, hence, be chosen. As such it takes on the quality of not merely a known good, advantage, or remedy, but one desired and striven for. Only by producing the conviction of choice, rather than the mere testimony of fact, does the picture of the future become so plastically attractive as to excite not only the curiosity of people but their passion to realize it. Only the value whose possession beckons in the future also causes the energy to act which, because it is intellectual, transcends short-lived instinct. For only in the focus of a goal imagined in foresight and dogmatically fixed in unshakable conviction (*Über-Zeugung*) does this energy concentrate itself completely and increase its tension further, even beyond the "natural" drive for self-preservation. Any futuristic contemplation that is big enough, by anticipating such difficulties, can assure itself beforehand against such relapse. It thus will make it possible for the energies of a person or of humanity, to be concentrated during long periods on the same task. For at the same time the other possibilities of the future will be strongly disvalued and pushed into the background. Only after a "victory of foresight" does the human being rush in the direction of his trust in the future or hold himself back with circumspection when he foresees evil consequences.

The instruction in or enlightenment of merely human understanding, and even whole centuries of enlightenment, can, therefore, convincingly represent only the circumscribed and special aim of knowledge; that is, its own wishful image of man's ever increasing future knowledge, including knowledge of man himself and his values. This understanding produces a flowering of theoretical scholarship (even in ethics), an admiration of the scientist as a theoretical ethicist, and the culture of technological-scientific and experimental practice. But this kind of en-lightenment does not suffice to initiate an advancement of man's ethical attributes and actions, either social or private, or to assure the impetus for them. For this enlightenment, prophets are needed with broader-based goals. Thus, a modern ethics will not scorn positive knowledge of values and value relations between humans; for this knowledge is, and always will be, the only reliable basis of ethical planning. On the contrary, one will have to try—the sooner the better—to gain an ever more thorough and generously elaborated survey (with the help of computers) of all known or knowable "customs" of humanity, as a whole or in part, and their precise consequences and effects in the for-mation of private and public life. But this knowledge will not be enough. In view of man's given intellectual organization, one has to secure, both today, in the year 2000, and beyond, that theoretical cogni-tions be properly converted into the corresponding forms of practical reason. Even the most modern "scientific" ethics must intend to create the human and material possibilities to foster subsequent intellectual activities and use, support, protect, and nurse them; employ them ac-cording to plan; and control them. It implies man's ability to meet the following conditions:

1. The ability to achieve a futurological conception and pre-diction involving different ethical possibilities, based upon ex-perience and knowledge.

2. The ability to choose one or more of these ethical possibilities (for instance, the principles of happiness, achievement, and edu-cation, or any combination thereof) as being the most urgent or desirable for a certain period, as well as the capacity for consul-tation about and acceptance of the responsibility for, the choice or choices involved.

3. The ability to establish an open, democratically informed public opinion in support of those possibilities recognized as ethi-cally "good" and constituting the principal results of overt action (for instance, broadening the attitudes of old religions in ethically developed countries, aiding developing countries, obliterating ra-cial prejudices, and outlawing war and violent conflict), so that, as in prescientific times of great ethical culture, powers of humanity with broad ideal and material resources can be concentrated upon specific aims.

For, if we do not succeed in activating our social and individual ethics, now available only as knowledge, the progress of ethics will for a long time and perhaps irrevocably lag behind that of technology and science.

Technology has long since left the Platonic impasse of valuing merely theoretical reason. It already cultivates in grand style the three intellectual capacities of practical reason, even though it pleads for such planning of the future in the name of the "sacred cow" of "science for its own sake" and pretends to venerate and realize it alone. A man like John Kennedy thus decided rather easily that the project of exploring the universe should have preference before all other imaginable and possible explorations on earth, or other pressing and possible actions, such as the planting and supplying of sufficient food. He therefore took the responsibility for scientific competition and ambition on a grand scale, and he mobilized unimaginable ideal and material resources for one technical-scientific goal of humanity.

Similarly generous perspectives for the ethical future of humanity have not even been worked out as possibilities or on any comprehensive scientific foundation in today's world and by today's powers. They are not even clearly present for decision-making, nor chosen and presented for democratic persuasion, let alone brought to completion with equal fervor of ideal and material resources. Rather, the future of human ethics is left, in its essential features and aspects, to prescientific types of prophecy and goal-setting. It remains, therefore, in the hands of ancient religious prophets, of half-scientific secular, individual, or social ideologies, and of science itself with its profusion of Platonic imaginings and notions, such as its fetish of theoretical reason. In this kind of ethics one succeeds at most on the intermediate level of small, administrative reformatory measures, in achieving a certain degree of consciously modern ethical planning and purposeful organization of anthropological conditions. As for the rest one either drifts in the stream of any ethical trend that happens to be strongest, or he resists this trend equally coincidentally.

A true development of prescientific ethics, as it has existed during the last 7,000 years, must go considerably beyond this state of affairs if it is to bring about results corresponding to technological advances.

Among other things—and this we can only hint at here—there is needed, as a first important step, new exact knowledge and a thorough reëvaluation of ethical futurology. One has to learn to think differently in ethics, as in all of contemporary history and civilization. The former is discovering just now (Polak) that a historically founded civilization can be mobilized only when man makes use again of his general intellectual function of anticipation. In spite of the supposed objectivity of the nineteenth century (or maybe because of it) one has forgotten, up to now, to register man's function of anticipation and planning for the future as one of the facts, or even the most effective lever, of historical action. History, too, has been under the influence of the Platonic-

Hegelian ideology of reason, which regarded man's "mere" faith in goals, and even their mere projection, as something irrelevant, if not obstructive.

This first and new historical insight into the birth of culture out of man's capacity for anticipation is not in itself sufficient to clarify the phenomenon of ethical-historical action. One has to understand that each of the prophecies which up to now have determined the course of cultural action has had to be, unique from any other. As has been the case with the oft-investigated styles of art or society, so it is with prophecy: the gifts and efforts of the ethical prophets have expressed themselves in completely different and most personal forms. Prophecy as a historical fact appears only in a very definite, specialized type of prognosis. For only one specific kind of prophecy is able to impress upon its civilization its own unique stamp. It shows up, moreover, within its own context, the character of all historical prophecy: up to now it has almost always been baroque and extravagant, even if it attempted to hide and camouflage this fact, for instance, as reason.

Besides having an eye for the significance of the general human capacity of prognosis in ethics, the future investigator and practitioner of futurology will have to be able to discern the particular "psychological" effect of any specific type of prognosis. For, aside from the purely historical interest in it, it is only this unique form of prophecy which unfolds its full effect in its own particular situation. For instance, it stimulates only specific persons or groups of persons who are attracted and appealed to only by it. It alone also shows which facets this human capacity of prophecy can, or must, assume and how to go about it; at times these are either strongly employed or completely neglected, either ecstatically intensified or left undeveloped. Only the minute investigation of the attributes of past prophecy can give an unspeculative, empirical-inductive basis to the general insight into the importance of prophecy. On it can then be built an equally unspeculative futurological instruction, close to reality and sure of efficiency. Moreover, only from the exact and differentiated observation of the early, wildly growing type of prophecy can we learn which of these kinds have most influenced the still childish individuals or groups of the past. Only thus can we gauge how to treat and circumvent the still-existing numerous adolescent symptoms of ethical life, or else can we learn how to admit that we all have barely emerged from the latest trend, the idealistic stage of puberty in ethics.

To such an idealistic scientist the connection between prophecy and ethics may appear quite dim and peculiar. He may find the following investigation of special types of prognosis quite senseless and irrelevant.

That practitioner of ethics, however, who has a practical, mature, and realistic imagination of what is still to be done in ethics in order that humanity may survive and live happily and what can be done, at the moment or in the near future, if he starts from conditions as they actually are, will understand that one must not ignore even the seemingly most unimportant marks of individual prophecy. Only in them does one recognize the full difficulty and multiplicity of the task to provide for the prophets of humanity who possess similar concrete efficiency although they are of greater sobriety and self-control. For it will not do to treat all prophecy of the future dogmatically alike as, for example, so-called scientific planning, so highly praised and propagated today.

Obviously, in a short essay such as this, we can review only a few prominent prescientific types of prognosis in early and recent ethics. We do not strive for completeness and do not even draw all the possible ethical conclusions; we shall only hint at them now and then. For both the history of futurology in general[1] and the history of futurology in its relation to ethics and technology in particular are still to be conceived and still to be thoroughly interpreted. We and all other futurologists can only make a beginning and give a certain stimulus to this task.

SPECIAL TYPES OF PRESCIENTIFIC ETHICAL PROPHECIES

Looking for special ethical types of prognosis in the most ancient history of human culture, one finds his attention drawn to the Near East before the Greek conquest, with its very peculiar, but often quite comprehensive and consciously employed effects.

1. *The Directive Civilizations of Egypt, Persia and Mycene: Ethics as Social Ought.*

The directiveness for the future of this earliest great civilization brought about secular, totalitarian empires and guaranteed both the establishment and the duration of a unified, firm administration of empire in Asia Minor, composed of very different primary tribes. It created the political, economic, practically-technical and materially-ethical[2] foundations of collective structures, maintained in adequate regions and with coercive power. In addition to those material bases—and today's historians must recognize this point—it was necessary to establish a highly developed cultural context which preceded those empires, both in time and value, and which directed the spiritual energies of the people who prepared and maintained those methods and achievements. Evidence that the specific spiritual capacities and preparations existed by which one mentally dominated, in the most efficient manner, the huge human and material resources required for that cultural context is contained in the world's oldest documents (in Egypt). It is, precisely, the "directive⁻for the future," that is to say, the imperative, or *ought*, position which was recognized very early as cause and instrument of this domination and which, consequently, was quite systematically created, developed, and employed. For these commands alone are almost sufficient to fuse the energies of all people in such heterogeneous realms in the almost antlike, synchronized and precise interaction of a body politic. Impelled by such spiritually totalitarian "fascism" the individual behaves only as a function of this highest command and commanding power, according to its good or bad will—especially if the individual is still an archaic social link of a close-knit community. He thus obeys, without any crude, direct, outwardly physical force, e.g., without the Greek-Roman form of slavery. For, instead of his body and its possibly dull reaction, the intellectual order has hit a "nerve" of his soul, which actively and cautiously stimulates him spiritually. He fulfills the ought thrust upon him, with the cooperative exertion of all his spiritual-intellectual resources, and endures to the very last ounce of his strength.

The first Pharaohs discovered, in a general manner, very coolly and soberly, that great communal acts of people who no longer lived in archaic social tribes, depended on guidance into a future which was foreseen and expressed and transmitted in writing. For without a specifically expressed and understood *ought* command—"Tomorrow we shall (or will) do so and so"—it is impossible for conscious persons to tackle social tasks, let alone master them. Admittedly, the Pharaohs specialized from the beginning on a quite definite and extremely one-sided form of direction for the future. They compressed all acts of human direction into pure commands, imperatives, and the like, for only such a spiritual initiation of human action appeared to them theoretically and practically adequate and suitable. *Prescription* alone, therefore, was to them the total spiritual prerequisite of value.[3]

Following them, all rulers in the imperial realms of Asia Minor elaborated this one-sided imperative stimulant into a comprehensive and deeply penetrating hierarchy of command and internal culture. Gradually, it became the ideal and material framework not only for the great social and political structures of the day but also for individual decision-making. Thus, it is said in an Egyptian document: ". . . and so the tasks [of government] were distributed and the positions [offices] established, which were responsible for alimentation and nourishment: [namely] through it . . . [e.g., the aforementioned command]."[4] Thus, there developed both in theory and in practice, a completely implemented chain of command, generously equipped with the most elaborate technical means (for example, the building of roads and courier services) which reached from the Pharaoh, the first and often the only originator of the highest command and total plan, down to the vizier, to the last government functionary in the village, to individual craftsmen and laborers working either alone or at gigantic construction sites.

This transmission of command was complemented intellectually by the people's cultural understanding of command, both specific and general. One of the main prerequisites for this system was the Oriental doctrine and appreciation of reading and writing, and the codification of rules and laws. For, as today in China or in Chinese-revolutionary South Yemen the Little Red Book of Mao and the skill to read it have become contributing criteria of the true believer, so there was then an appreciation for the capacity to put directions down in writing and to extract them from the paper. In this way instructions were assured to be passed on conscientiously and precisely. Thus, the prescript (and with it the script) became the common form of command prediction.

Hence, the mark of perfect education and social rank in Egypt was the scribe of commands, in the sense of drawing up and executing prescriptions, in contrast to the Greek custom, according to which one wrote down the more esteemed oral speech only for the sake of memory. The prescriber, the maker of prescriptions, accordingly became the most esteemed and sought after profession in the state by members of the officeholding nobility.[5] This purely postulative, imperative ideal, moreover, dominated not only the human realm where it originated and was first developed, but was extended to the pertinent direction of activity with objects. Even in mathematics and arithmetic the instructions were imperatives: Draw a line, calculate, measure, etc. . . . The form of command was also here the closest at hand, common and, therefore, historically the only one encountered. It yielded only gradually and very late to the Platonic form of knowledge, which contains no incentive to application and practice.

Only the historian or philosopher of intellectual prediction who does not approach history exclusively from the Platonic point of view (or prejudice) can have an eye for this Oriental culture of command. Plato, therefore, in the *Republic* (which begins to propagate the ideal of the scientific academic politician) does not see Egypt or Persia correctly. At best he accepts only the Orient's later mystical trends. Instead, it is Xenophon, who lived and made war in the Orient, who describes correctly the intellectual foundation and form of the Persian Empire of his time. As a Greek who possesses a meta-cognitive overview of human intellectual capacities and methods, he can explain them to us and describe them accurately. He calls them, and rightly so, a culture which, above all, reigns through prescience and (commanded) planning. He also coins the correct Greek technical terms for the intellectual functions which hide behind the power façade of Asiatic imperialism—terms, it is true, which in Greek do not sound imperial or imperative enough. He demands, again and again, that a sovereign—like Cyrus, the nobility, the army, or a householder, even a housewife—should above all be strong and informed in prevision ($\pi\rho o\nu o\epsilon\iota\nu$) and "preplanning" ($\pi\rho o\pi o\nu\epsilon\hat{\iota}\nu$). For only such foresight in following one's own judgment in a secular manner—even though one also uses traditionally religious methods in order to influence the will of the ignorant—was the determining factor of Persian strength.

Therefore, throughout the history of the Occident, Xenophon's books rather than Plato's remain the prototypes in the instruction of strategists, economists, and statesmen of the imperialistic school of planning, from the Roman Scipio to the mercantilists and the general staffs or the modern American business school. Even the latter goes back, unconsciously, to Xenophonic concepts when it organizes planning games, as has always been customary in general staff work. It thus deviates from the Platonic challenge of mere knowing and learning. It fosters rather the ability to *use* knowledge through training and practice in prevision of, and decision about, future possibilities. It teaches the students to evaluate and develop their disposition responsibly, pregnant as they are with consequences, even though it does so on the basis of its own Greek-democratic modification.

In the East and South, however, where the dominance of democratic forms of prognosis and planning has not occurred, the old totalitarian social-ethical form of command survives in all its purity. Thus, to the great surprise of those who dreamed too intensely the dream of the final rational maturity of man and his salvation through democracy, we find in the developing countries, in Asia and Asia Minor, and even in Europe and America, a new absolutism of imperatives, with its own imperial culture. The establishment and imposition of the social ought originates again exclusively with the president, Soviet, council, or dictator at the top, in a grandiose scheme which makes the whole population its functionary. Thus result, for longer or shorter periods, and on more or less fertile soils, other Hitlers and Stalins, Nassers, Maos, and Sékou Tourés, who arrange the same kind of "modern" world, of *ought*-ethical secular realms, and with the same totalitarian, good or bad influence on conscience and action as existed in old Egypt. The ethics of imperative and plan thus is by no means either dead or unnecessary.

It is not dead because the early phase of this culture of imperative has never yet been recognized as such, and, therefore, could never be consciously and purposely overcome. Instead, it was repressed by memory, or assailed ad hoc and overlaid with idealistic democratic slogans. The instinctive opposition against it failed through insufficient knowledge of what one was opposing and insufficiency of the intellectual means used to fight it. The primitive, courageous resistance fighter or partisan, therefore, now as ever, feels that his only recourse is political assassination, the bodily elimination of the tyrant (unless he gets stuck in the "emergency of command"). Even the well-intentioned democrat is still obliged to tinker around, like a new inventor, with a well-tailored, shrewd technique for toppling tyrants and, consequently, he remains floundering in mid-project (Dubcek). Only he who is himself authoritarian and clever can be, in fact, victorious over even the best-equipped army in the world (Ho Chi Minh). But he, after all, only gives tit for tat. He, too, employs authoritarian planning and command, the same kind of ought as his adversary. But at least he does it consciously and on the level of the intellect of his followers. For he knows that intellectual discipline has a much larger span of action than merely external discipline. So he brings about, at least, a people's revolution, obedient to such command, instead of merely a static empire of imperative establishments.

Both democratic and totalitarian authoritarians of today (and with them their friends and foes) are thus marked, with very few exceptions and quite simply and unconsciously, by the old and new imperative forms of social and personal ethics. Nowhere in the world can people withdraw, sufficiently or totally, from this kind of prophecy, not even in the West or on the European continent. In Germany, for example, the modern technician with his computer talks again the Egyptian language of command. And the instruction of our children is still demonstrably 80 per cent based on the order of obligation, of ought, which thus prepares in the child the necessary intellectual readiness for this kind of directed action. It only needs to be reawakened and polished in order to function, rejuvenated, and to flower, for better or worse. This means that nowhere in the world have we reached the comprehension, nor are we ready to reach it, of the intellectual "mechanism" of this particular *ought*-prognosis, either historically or systematically, and, hence, practically. And, therefore, we cannot master it sufficiently either materially or linguistically, nor impose it or depose it with circumspection.

For, obviously, it is not sufficient to forbid it or deprecate its horror. It has to be imposed again and again wherever other capacities or motives for action are unstable and undeveloped. But it has to be de-

posed immediately when these functions, like those of individual foresight and decision, are threatened. To depose it, however, another
system of action-guidance must be in reserve. The child must have been
trained and practiced in it, and thus must have been taught and
practiced all kinds of such systems. For others the artificial limb of
ought-ethics, useful and necessary as it is at some place under certain
conditions, and with certain persons and social organizations, will become an extreme deficiency, a crutch for persons crippled in other
initiative to action.

2. *Scientific Prophecy on the Basis of Mathematical Laws of Nature: Ethics under the Pressure of Apodictic and Causal Prediction.*

This type of prophecy is cosmic, astronomical, and mathematical,
based on the assumption of eternal, unshakable natural laws. Ethics
here stands under the pressure of fate, necessity, and causality.

In the middle of the very strong-willed, imperalistic civilization just
described, which drove people of all centuries to the great ought of
development and purification of nature and themselves, there appeared,
strangely enough in that same Orient, the very opposite kind of prophecy, of equally world-wide, later significance, namely, the Chaldean, of
culturally independent calculation of fate and causal prediction.

Its peculiarity consists in its view of the future as extrapolation of
past and present. It leans, first of all, on the observation of cosmic
nature, impersonal and, therefore, exempt from human influence.
Thus, it tries to grasp its laws by strictly mathematical deduction, and
it turns from this primary observation of nature only secondarily to the
nations and individuals in their anthropological setting. Almost instinctively, often well-nigh anxiously, it avoids combining its predictions directly with human motivation—that is, practical reason, thus
making them binding. It does not cultivate any of the "usual" prophetic attributes—neither lively persuasion, nor influencing choice, nor
grand eschatology—and keeps aloof from commands and, hence, of an
ethics of ought which prescribes something definite. It refers basically
to the proclamation of simple, sober prediction based on causality, derived from natural law, and leaves each person to draw whatever conclusion, or make whatever decision he wishes, from this one prediction
as a component of all natural possibility.

Yet, the astrologer apparently so cool and detached does, in a certain
sense and secretly, go beyond all other possibilities of influencing human action. For he sees even human talent, environment, and man's
practical reason quite rigidly enclosed in the general and supposedly
univocally recognizable and predictable law of cosmic nature. He thus

does not recommend a choice; but he does not leave a choice either, for he does not allow any differentiated possibilities to appear, or even denies their existence. He interprets his prediction of a mere possible future as a law—that is, as fate, determination, or necessity, and as truth and logically incontrovertible. His stimulating or paralyzing world-wide influence on human action is gained in silence and through his suggestion, camouflaged as science, of the all-embracing, unimpeachable, timeless natural law, recognizable for all future. This suggestion, consequently, results in a very special kind and influence of his prophecy.

The people and sovereigns of the Chaldeans, who probably for the first time developed an explicit civilization of this kind of prophecy, played, openly and politically, only a very short role in the history of the Near East. Their empire almost ends with Nebuchadnezzar, even in the memory of humanity. But as an astronomic-astrological school (for example, in Kos) and as occasional teachers and wandering sages the priests of astrology spread the knowledge of their art of prophecy over the entire antique and modern world. Together with the great natural scientists they become influential advisors of certain high leaders of humanity. Also, the greatest of the scientists, from Thales to Newton, even unite both functions in one person. They accompany emperors and popes as grey eminences and influence their decisions in the "stellar hours" of humanity. Not even today have they lost their power. The communist in India will first seek out the astrologer; he does not trust the astrologers of the Kremlin alone; and even the Western head of state questions his personal astrologer or his equally well-functioning impersonal astrological computer. They respect and esteem this kind of prediction—though secretly—just as highly as, in the Middle Ages, did Frederick the Stauffer, Wallenstein, or Luther.

Besides this role of political advice at the highest level of human leadership, the astrologer successfully reaches into the small and private circle of individuals in all lands on earth. For even they are trying, with the help of this or that astrology, to seek out the respective *kairos* for their lives and acts. To add to their knowledge of people they gratefully accept the astrological character study of the zodiac as an ethological basis; it enables them better to preview, or institute, the social contact with their fellow man. Quite secretly, therefore, there develops everywhere an astrological ethics of international dimensions.

As secretly consulted political and private advisors, the astrologers from the beginning of their history have been very differently judged, accepted, and valued. For who, especially in the technologically developed West with its pride of achievement, would recognize a "force of destiny" or conclude a reasonable compromise with it? One only reacts in extremes to this question, or suppresses the subject completely, even in today's ethics. For only in the religious realm, and there camouflaged as a punishing or loving concern of the personal godhead, does one risk to recognize the old Oriental or Greek Fate. It thus appears, legitimately, only as predestination. But already the classical imperial tyrant persecuted and disparaged the talk of Fate, or even murdered the big and little astrologers, as Hitler did. For no one should be permitted to assert that what the tyrant wants to create by his own power as a thousand-year realm is also subject to fate written in the stars. All profane and religious eschatology sees in the Chaldean-naturalistic, scientifically sober astrologer its enemy and competitor. An individual and independent stargazer, from the time of Campanella to today, can often escape political or ideological persecution only by hiding or exiling himself, or by remaining obscure.

Out of this studious and timid, voluntary or involuntary seclusion in his science the astrologer returns into the limelight only when a reflective sovereign or pope, such as Julius II, ascends to the throne and, in his hours of loneliness, needs a companion to philosophize about the lot of humanity. Astrology and astrological prediction, which pass into astronomy and from there into the whole of natural science, find their strongest ally in half-scientists—half-metaphysicians, from Democritus to Diodorus to Cicero (*De Fato*) and thence to the modern natural scientist-philosopher, such as Max Planck or Heisenberg. It is they who elaborate the one-sided reverence for conclusions from cosmic natural science, mathematics, and computer-logic, into the most perfect pseudoscientific mythos of unbreakable and fully recognizable determinism. For they constantly confuse causal prediction of the future with the causal law of the past. They grasp the relative determination of cause and effect, which is possible only by hindsight, the *causa effectus*, in only its metaphysical speculative, teleological form, that is, as absolute and efficient *prima causa*. They confuse the logic of contradiction and of finding truth in knowledge with the axiology of human decision about possibilities. They fail to separate cleanly the prediction by statistical averages for all times from the mere probability of the future. Therefore, our wholly time-bound natural science and the natural science of psychology appear to them speculatively timeless; and they believe they are able to pronounce fate and necessity, just as does astrology. Thus, one forgets in all fields—as, for example, in the astrologically named economic science of business "cycles"—that there exists the factor of human planning, which can modify the law of (past) economic upsurges and catastrophes.

Such astrological-deterministic natural scientists have, since the times of the Stoa, declared everything as fatalistic natural law, except in the final instance when, as the last and worst consequence, there appeared the notion of man's moral and educational lack of responsibility. For here begins to stir a certain, often obscure drive for freedom of choice as against the comfortably fatalistic search for excuses. Thus, one tries to deny that all ethics is ethics of fate—rather than ethics of guilt. The modern psychological and psychoanalytic doctrines, which will find ever more sophisticated reasons for so-called absolutely determined learnings, environmental differences, and childhood traumata, and thus will reach even beyond the zodiac determinations of classical astrology—though they still use similar zoological and ethological parallels and symbols—encounter, at least in practical therapy, certain intellectual capacities of man which surmount and sublimate given circumstances and native limitations. But the psychotherapist succeeds as little as the natural scientist of today to delineate more clearly the "power of man" as counterpart of the "power of fate"—or to confront these powers precisely. He is not really interested in the human intellectual possibilities of practical reason. He deals with them at most therapeutically, but neither knows nor propagates them. For in his perspective, ethics is also essentially part of the cycle of nature, and he lets it have its way.

3. The Hebrew-Christian Prophecy of Miracles and Superhuman Endeavor: Ethics as Hope against Hope.

This kind of prophecy is based on miraculous chains of unnatural events and superhuman effort and achievement. It fuses the spiritual and the sacerdotal, and relies on the hope of salvation and the faith in distant and dim aims. Yet, this unscientific Hebrew-Christian form of prophecy gives a more fitting impression of the true power of man than the pseudo-exact prognosis of natural science and astrology. For even though it pays very little attention to natural law in any of its forms, it shows the whole measure—that is, indeed, immeasurability which human ethical effort can assume in the battle with nature, so-called unrelenting fate and suffering—to the point of daring to overcome death.

Viewed historically, early Judean prophecy has some of its roots in secular Egyptian imperative ethics, even to the point of the sudden appearance of the cult of writing. Moses (who was educated in Egypt), King Solomon, and the scribes kept strictly to the ethics of the Ten Commandments in their *ought*-form and to the minutely ordered legal form of the Torah.

Besides this kind of prophecy there develops another, more specific Israelite type. For, otherwise than in the leaders in Asia Minor, the imperial secular rulers and parties of Israel did not succeed in the task of building a supranational empire. They were unable to unite the different peoples and tribes of the Jordan valley in a homogeneous, well-organized empire, as was done in the valleys of the Nile and the Euphrates. Once this failure of the kings became manifest in the interior, and the superiority of the enemies in the exterior, the tribes had to find other ways out of the hopeless imperial situation. One was the retreat to an ever-narrower national feeling of tribe and family. The other, as a substitute for the missed international imperialism on earth, was the ever intensified and sublimated hope for a future, even a heavenly, Jerusalem. Thus, there develops the prophet of this future, starting from extreme national and private suffering, and showing in his prophecy the ultimate and highest possibilities of compensation for the frustration suffered. These possibilities are not any more in the realm of normal private, social, or international strivings for happiness. The prophet emerges from a situation of unhappiness, an "emergency," or even from the wilderness, and therefore, does not preach social urbanity and harmony as do the Greeks. He mirrors rather the lack of these attributes of the golden mean. He advocates the appreciation of the unusual, the transcendent.

The future promised by the Judeo-Christian prophet, therefore, is an internal and spiritual rather than an external triumph over misery, and only after the last bitter drop of agony has been tasted—a prescription like Churchill's "blood, sweat, and tears" in World War II. Irrational, emotional, and unrealistic hope outweighs rational hope, or at least helps to carry it along. A desperate situation leaves room only for "hope against hope"–that is, for no hope that is "reasonable." One has to beat the little spark of hope out of the rock and find it in the belief in miracles. Only the faraway, vague future seems graspable and realizable. For the near future, as any one can see for himself, cannot improve anything fundamentally. Jewish prophecy thus develops a culture of long and patient waiting for success, as does Marxism today —one that interprets every setback as a stage on the road. Its faith in the future is compelled more and more to renounce empirical or logical proof. It ends finally in pure faith, faith against and beyond reason.

The prophecy of the Judeo-Christian prophets, therefore, has no connection with cosmic scientific-mathematical calculation or probability in the Chaldean sense. Instead, it is guided by a chain of unusual events of natural and human origin, precisely those which again and again have actually saved the brave and resourceful people of Israel from their predicament. Thus, one constructs with remarkable axiological-psychological skill a continuous chain of natural and anthropological miracles, from the birth of Moses to the ascension of Christ, concentrating on, and true to, the experience of salvation. In this way one trains in the believers the personal and relevant expectation of such miracles rather than "trust" in their "reason." Even today, in the whole Christian world, the expectation of, and longing for, miracles surpasses by far any other kind of prognosis. Hitler's hinting at a "miracle weapon" deterred even reasonable people in Germany from a thoughtful prognosis; and the Christian Negro in America has still to go a long road of disillusionment before he will give up the hope for a miracle and start building up his future soberly stone by stone.

Expressed without mythology, Hebrew prophecy first of all discovered the essential equality of so-called improbable with probable future. It does not make it prognosis merely in "the cage of the probable" (Kierkegaard) which logic and natural science have erected for us. Secondly, it makes the explicit anthropological experience that man will become conscious of his full power of action, beyond suffering and death, and reach his ultimate range, only when directed toward distant, supra-individual goals which by far transcend the drive for self-preservation. He who promises him the moon and the stars fires him to higher effort than he who offers him the earth. And, thirdly, it is rather the suffering person who unfolds spiritual and physical powers in the most intensive and rational manner. For he is not so scared by occasional setbacks as is the healthy one. He learns, fourthly, even when forced to a merely passive attitude, to keep his conception of the future alive as a source of strength. He thereby proclaims the future even as a martyr. Thus, in spite of its fragile support by incredible natural events and of only "those persons who have gotten the worst of it" (Nietzsche), Jewish-Israelite prophecy has set free more human potential for action and energy than scientifically exact prognosis—unless it too reaches toward the stars instead of the earth.

By exhausting the last hidden resources of human strength for its engagement with the future, this prophecy "transcends" at times the normally desirable, or even the human goals of life, in favor of exceptional states of existence or states of emergency. Its future and paradise are not of this world. They will either be transferred to the end of the present world or to its beginning, when the guilt of damnation is found in Adam's original sin. The present social and material conditions become unimportant, and earthly happiness is limited to wishful prayers and works for the future goal, without hope of immediate joy. The social ideals also grow poorer. For the exaggeration of belief is best served by asocial, isolated, and poor forms of life.

Moreover, in the Judeo-Christian prophecy there is not even permitted any personal prediction or planning of the future. Only God is "plan and counsel." The Israelite prophet thus does not conceive his prophecy by his own reason, as does the Pharaoh or the Greek or the astrological seer. He is only called to proclaim it, and he often responds to this call unwillingly. For it does not always conform with his natural gifts; it is a forced calling. Besides it is not a thankful profession. The prophet is mostly concerned with uncovering guilt and misfortune in the present and showing the future with a faint silver lining. In contrast to his great and real results, his role in the initiation of action is either disparaged or forgotten. Therefore, in medieval scholasticism, prophecy is investigated merely as a capacity and attribute of God (Anselm). And today's Christian often agrees with Dante, who simply wrings the necks of all meddlesome secular prophets and looks upon personal prediction as sacrilege. Thus, it is in the Western world, of all places—where the most distant future is most intensely worked for—that the individual, even after secularization, dares least of all to stand by his own plans and designs. Our turn toward "futurology," therefore, came about in the Western world only in another intoxication of total divestment of Christian taboos, like a sexual frenzy, or it was taken over only from the atheistic world.

Thus, Marxism, as atheistic socialism, had an especially easy time of taking the privilege of planning out of the hands of the Christian world and declaring it its own monopoly. Moreover, it can take over the field of secular planning, especially in social respects, since Christianity has sorely neglected it. But Marxian doctrine also inherited many of the Judeo-Christian characteristics of prophecy and its conceptions of society, future, and work. For it, too, trains the person for distant goals, for great hardship and blind, dogmatic belief. The Judean claim to authority and fortune of only the "unfortunate" manifests itself in the promise of paradise only to the toiling, and even they will not experience it physically. Also in Marxism what counts is the imposition of the exceptional—the emergency situation in this world—and not the intermediate realms of human existence, the so-called "bourgeois" normalcy.

Marxian prophecy is, in many instances, therefore an illegitimate child of Christianity. But its type of prognosis also sets free other previously hidden potentials of human action. It mobilizes new sectors of the populace, such as the workers. It awakens races and castes which up to now had vegetated in a dull stupor, and it stimulates peoples and cultures, which formerly had no goals, for action and striving. It thus seizes the last inactive paradises of mankind and draws them into the stream of consciously directed action, though often only in technical respects. For it neglects and rigidly controls all social-ethical directions.

The Judeo-Christian and Marxist prophecies together have initiated a sudden explosion of human energies, even though they do not dwell on what is needed here and daily, but seek the transcendent, the unusual, the restless and unsocial.

4. *Greek-Roman Prophecy and Its Modern Forms:*
Ethics as Prohairesis *and* Prosdokia (*Choice and Anticipation*)
or Enthusiasm and (Pre-)Sentiment.

Greek-Roman prophecy at first was prescientific technological or personal prediction. But it changed rapidly into either rational-scientific or conjectural irrational futurology. Amalgamating with the Judeo-Christian prophecy, it led to today's somewhat more stable forms and dimensions of our planning, based on more objective items and methods. For Greek-Roman prophecy was always sane prediction of material and social conditions, though it evolved also from certain preceding forms of archaic clairvoyance. In Greece, namely, these forms changed rapidly into scientific types of prognosis in all material and personal spheres and thus became the basis of a secular and dependable prognosis, which could count with full success. Even in Greece, however, two main forms of prophecy have to be distinguished which have become important for the Western world.

a. *Rational, Apollonian Greek Mantic and Its Seers.* The early Apollonian seers and the corresponding oracles were independent and consciously rational institutions. The great seer usually was of socially respected noble ancestry. He was recognized by the people and lived among them. He inherited his personal gift of prophecy as his other technical skills, and he exercised it as a profession. He trained pupils as did the doctor or artisan; he did not need to hide his activity or teaching, nor did he need to mystify it, but was openly proud of it. It was also his own prediction of the future for which he took responsibility and which he proclaimed clearly and openly, without necessity of interpreters or prophets. As the Greek poets said in a fully secular manner, the best seer was he who himself conjectured rightly (Euripides). Every person, one recognizes, therefore, can, may, and must imagine the future and foresee it as a possibility if he is to act.

Like the later scientists, the early rational seer made a certain metacognizant and ordering survey over his own predictions, in relation to other intellectual potentials of the person. The "seer" of the dark past who is hidden yet did exist is strictly distinguished, already in mythical time, from the "fortune teller" of the not-yet-existing, the only as-yet-thinkable future. The different *manteis* embody the Greek teaching of conjecture, which follows after them, with its separation between the supposition of the unknown past, the hidden present, and the becoming future. Even ethics distinguishes sharply between past and future, individual and social good, the latter of merely possible but predictable benefit.

The majority of Greek seers and oracles limit their activities and powers strictly to certain rules. They regard themselves only apt, for instance, for the prediction of some kind of future perspective, as against preparations for action which go beyond it. A Cassandra and an Amphiaraos, for example, experience and recognize full well that they only see the portentous future and not the *kairos*; and that, tragically, they cannot and may not avert it. For, according to legend, they will be punished if they transgress upon their specific abilities, as the "unskilled" and undisciplined seers of today frequently do. The ancient Greek seer on principle did not confound his mere ability of seeing the future with the will to bring it about—that is, in Greek, formation of purpose (*prohairesis*). He was, therefore, usually, not himself a practical reformer, a revolutionary or a leader of his people in need, as was the Israelite prophet. That occupation always remained a task for others, a special calling in itself, as that of the counselors or the speakers (rhetors) who stimulated the will to bring about the future. The ability to be clairvoyant and the profession of *mantis*, or seer, was regarded in Greece as a special "academic" career, capable of being cultivated, taught, and examined (Platon, Charmides). It was understood as the foresight of foresights and regarded equally as valuable as the abilities to learn and to know. As a particularly independent ability both the individual Greek and the state practiced and valued it. Before every undertaking, both sought, almost dutifully, the pronouncement of the seers, or oracles. Moreover, every state and statesman since the Trojan campaign employed his own seers and official advisors, as functionaries, which still Plato entrusts, in *The Laws*, with the official elaboration of the laws. The delegation to the oracle is always publicly expected, decided, and approved by the whole people. No Greek was admittedly ashamed of it, though he did not follow directly the advice of the seer. For it was not a decision by a third party about him, let alone a command. The seer was merely a mental prestate of the counselor, in a position like our scientist, only that he felt the obligation and justification, as did the early Ionian scientists, to convert his knowledge into foresight and to give counsel, and to counsel the more, the more he knew. He was, therefore, obligated and trained out of *Nous, Dianoia*, or *Doxa*, to produce *Pronoia, Prohairesis, Prosdokia*, and all the other kinds of anticipation. For, at the edge of the pragmatic-practical Orient, even his "pure" knowledge remained ethically and technically still un-platonic. It was serviceable knowledge, immediately convertible into active initiative through "expertise."

As these philosophical schools of the political-social sector developed "philosophical" advice in the market place, the councils of democracy, and the doctrine of individual lives, so the technical sector brought forth special prescient representatives and their scientific effort for progress. Prometheus stemmed himself against the "undemocratic" will of secrecy of the established Olympus. The secularized Greek manual worker worshiped neither Pharaonic *ought*-commands "from above" nor only the "work of the fist" in the later Christian-Marxist pattern. He saw the most important factor of technical invention and action in the birth of the idea of the future work, as model-idea for subsequent material elaboration, the Socratic "idea" which Plato later transformed into the static idea of Being and Knowledge. Similarly the Greek physician praised above all his art of prognosis rather than of diagnosis. The natural scientist and meterologist intended first of all to gain causal prediction from the *aition*. The builder of tunnels referred to his advance calculations as the source of his success, and the farmer and helmsman, the *kybernetes*, to their planning of tillage and "cybernetic."

Both social-technical and social-political (or ethical) preparation for action was consciously focused in Greece on the seer's public prediction and counseling. His teleological significance and efficacy were acknowledged for both the community and the individual. Thus, there developed a private and conscious theory of action. One recognized the induction of prediction on the basis of knowledge, and that of *prohairesis* on the basis of prediction. Indeed, the relativity of all popular and private customs was thus more and more elaborated and finally even overemphasized. Ethics was frequently seen as dependent on only individual peculiarities and convictions. One renounced gradually every divine, traditional, or natural call or drive for human groupings and was unable to replace it by any new social theory. The power of the individual and of his personal prediction and choice of norms was, therefore, exaggerated, and the power of pre-sentation and pre-sentiment of the common weal was restricted.

Thus, in the Stoa, man's future was seen too early and unrealistically in pure cosmopolitanism rather than, at least in part, in the *polis*. In Epicureanism, on the other hand, one found it in the unpolitical circle of closest friends. From healthy skeptical rejection of rigid traditional customs one thus fell into the opposite extreme of predicting no possible or necessary human bonds at all, either private or public, and thus exposed himself even more to conservatism and fatalism. In the hippy and yippy community of the cynics, civilization was rejected altogether and one lived, as did the early Christians, in the private renunciation of mammon, in love of one's fellow man, and outside the sober social welfare. Thus, one neglected, in an exaggeration of individual foresight and choice, the great social, democratic, national, and international tasks. In the Hellenistic age these tasks, therefore, reverted to Oriental-Roman forms of imperial direction.

Nevertheless, in the Hellenistic age there survived for many centuries the widespread and effective culture of intellectual democratic-dialectic intercourse, developed by the Greeks. Even in the Roman realm there continued to exist the Pantheon of premeditated religious and philosophical techniques of living. Thus, the ethical password in all these realms of Greek practical wisdom remained, even after the intrusion of Oriental religions, the *pro-hairesis*, the responsible choice of what is to be expected by one's own prevision of the future. It was permitted and customary in the widest circles, under Roman imperial sovereignty, to organize one's private life by rational anticipation of future possibilities (*providentia-prudentia*) as well as openly and publicly to defend one's preferences. Hence, even in late antiquity, it was only in certain realms that one had to believe or obey blindly, or submit stoically to fate or the state.

Only one of these completely private directives for life, chosen in continuation of the Greek cult of foresight and counsel through *prohairesis*, therefore, is also the profession of the scientist, who prefers satisfaction by knowledge alone, though the old Platonic school had already begun to delete foresight from knowledge and to neglect or cancel our *prohairesis* in its ethics of pure knowledge. Man's action, as we said at the beginning, according to Plato, is supposed to grow directly out of knowledge. Moreover, there is no choice among several goods since the idea of the Good is statically, indeed monotheistically presented. It is only the Platonists who lay the groundwork for Mill's saying, "A scientific observer or reasoner, merely as such, is not an adviser for practice.... Whether the ends themselves are such as ought to be pursued, and if so, in what cases and to how great a length, it is no part of his business as a cultivator of science to decide, and science alone will never qualify him for the decision."[6] No modern academic scientist has dared until recently to design new and futural ethical directions for humanity, to give expert advice, to propagate it, or to be responsible for it. Thus, he has become helpless, axiologically speaking irrelevant, and clumsy; and he again leaves the old task of the Greek-Ionian scientist—that of prognosis—to the Oriental prescientific prophets and seers, or to irrational and uncontrolled drives.

To be sure, it is the Christian teaching which has finally condemned and prohibited the autonomous profession and *prohairesis* of the Greek-rational seer as a way of life, rather than unwittingly stunting it idealistically, as the humanistic academic scientist has done. Some Hellenistic fathers of the church demanded and proclaimed rather stridently that one is not allowed any more to "induce" his future possibilities from his own knowledge of the past or "choose" them as private values (Tertullian). Instead, one receives the vision of the future and the norms for living from the hands of the Christian prophets and their teaching, and receives them in grace and faith. He who does not do so is, in the eyes of these Christian dogmatics, no "heretic," in the highly valued Greek sense, but a degraded, besmirched, and persecuted apostate, an "elector"—that is, one who demands "free choice" out of blasphemously self-assumed prescience. Thus, in the Roman-Christian empire the end of private-ethical democracy did finally arrive.

Man's own prognosis and choice of future possible goods, elaborated by the Greek seers and scientific councils, were, at the end of antiquity, being threatened by the metaphysical-astrological doctrine of fate and determinism in addition to Platonic science and Christian faith. Man in late antiquity, when confronted with this doctrine, asserted his own providence only with vague, metaphysical concepts of an undemonstrable "free" choice (instead of demonstrable "choice"). He survived only as an indeterminist, a semi-Pelagian, or heretic.

The former secularization of the consciously-rational mantic profession, with its sequence of a scientific-technological and ethical theory of action in all realms of life which was so successful in Greece, oozes away, as it were, in the sands of the less-advanced prescientific forms of Oriental religious and secular teachings of prognosis. It only surfaces timidly in the Renaissance. Under the pressure of the continued alliance between Platonic science and Christian belief it does not succeed in working itself out in the private ethical realm. For when it reappears, within the dominion of natural science and technology, especially in the Anglo-Saxon countries, the battle for the right of self-determination over one's future is fought on the collective level of democracy, the rights of the people, and social welfare measures. There one returns to a Greek dialectic system of parties, with party programs and "elections." In the individual theory of action reigns, now as then, either Platonic idealism, Christian dogmatism, or scientific determinism. They give little legitimate room to ethical foresight. It is not surprising, then, that the individual, bereft of foresight and counsel, again and again follows the prescientific types of prophets, the Christian or Marx-

ist prophets, the *ought-* and *superought-*commands of totalitarian systems, or those of scientific technology. For how can he hold his own
and establish a personal ethical prognosis if from early childhood he
is exposed to nothing but the phrases about his political possibilities
of choice and is denied, as an individual, any knowledge of his own
potentialities of foresight and choice, let alone of how to use, supervise,
or control them. Instinctively right, the youngster of today prefers to
pour his own dully felt longing for action and education into antipar-
liamentary (*ausserparlamentarische*) channels. For there he can experience at least a semblance of private initiative, which, otherwise in
the twentieth century, is stunted and suppressed.

b. *The Dionysian, Enthusiastic-irrational Seer of Antiquity: Ethics as
(Pre-)Sentiment and Enthusiasm.* What in our Occidental, Christian-
Platonic or fatalistic-deterministic school is left over from Greek rational
futurology is only its non-rational branch—that is, the inkling, the
premonition of, or enthusiasm for, the future, instilled either from
outside or by the individual's excitement. For Plato systematically
transformed the concept of a rational-technical mantic profession into
that of "personal" prediction. One deals, from Plutarch to Dodd, with
the Dionysian colleagues of the Apollonian seers and thus destroys the
interest of both scientist and layman in rational foresight.

Even in late Greece the two types are superimposed and intersect but
do not lose their original character and specific meaning. Through the
incursion of the cult of Bacchus from the north, the originally Apollonian oracle in Delphi, for instance, became again chthonic-Dionysian.
The priesthood, on the other hand, remained rational-prophetic. Pythia
is only a secondary, though important, figure beside them. As Dionysian
and irrational she speaks confusedly and stutters, or at least speaks in
unprosaic utterances. She no longer is able to master the translation of
her inner experience into clear expression, and needs for this the help
of rational prophets. Moreover, she uses or needs outside stimuli, like
the steams from the Delphic earth fissure, in order to put herself into
trance or ecstasy and to envelop in fog the seeker of good counsel himself. Thus, she surrounds herself with the symbols of darkness and of
earthly secrets and wisdom, such as the tripod, rather than those of
light. The rational seer does not need these things, and the rational
scientist of prediction long ago found the rational tripod in his own
mind—that is, he produced a conscious epistemology and science of
prediction (Democritus, Nausiphanes). The prototypes of the Dionysian
seer, therefore, are not the figures of light and reason, gods and god-

desses, such as Apollo and Athene Pronoia. They are the dark, earthly, mysterious, or ecstatic figures of logosless animals, as most women of the time were also regarded.

Yet, the Greeks secularized even this Dionysian-chthonic, thymic-mantic profession. For these dark sides of the human soul were investigated by the early physician, the poet, and the psychologist. Long before Freud they sought and found the explanation for insanity, for the formation of complexes caused by feelings of guilt, for psychic pressures and sexual aberrations; they also sought practical and relevant therapy for these ills. Unconscious cosmic prophecy by human or by bird with an animalic sensitivity for weather may have the same interest as rational-cosmic, strictly human prediction. Both are intimately connected for those who have not yet established the Platonic separation of body and soul. In ancient times both were observed as closely as today's meteorologist re-creates or rebuilds the "hearing" organ of the jellyfish to make it serviceable for his own ability of prediction. That is, one tries to release, to understand, and to utilize even irrational forms of prediction, which appear opaque only in comparison with those of the logos.

The Dionysian-thymic prediction became misunderstood and was worshiped onesidedly and alogically in Greece only when old pre-scientific or new pseudo-scientific trends and cults were added to it and gave futurological superstition a new impetus. In Empedocles we find a scientist who, at the same time, develops a rational kind of prophecy and a very un-Greek, demagogical, and fanatically enthusiastic one; and we see how he fails in this effort, which for a Greek would be a schizophrenic task. In Stoic Hellenism, with its Semitic influence, we find a whole complex of interests, mainly of "personal" mantic which, from Plutarch to Cicero (*De divinatione*), lead to entire codifications as well as a strong renaissance of pure divination. As we have seen, already Plato had consciously regenerated this Dionysian-thymic enthusiastic branch of prediction. He refused to explain the high, creative callings of politician, rhapsodian, or poet by the rational and deliberate timing-capacity of the *kairos*, in the sense of the Ionians and Thucydides. Neither did he let the lowlier technical professions of the Socratic craftsmen, tradesmen, and manufacturers take part in (predictive) reason (*phronesis* and *episteme*). Both the high as well as the low professions are defined by him either superrationally and enthusiastically or subrationally and impulsive-thymically, if not merely pragmatically. For to the degree that they cannot be identified with the "pure" knower himself they are acknowledged, both in the Platonic state and in the later humanistic state of the West, as either exaggeratedly worshiped or exaggeratedly scorned, thus always irrationally. The philosopher-statesman—that is, the ethical-political scientist—ought to develop an erotic-enthusiastic-metaphysical Idea of (all future, that is, timeless) Good, or else he has no reasonable idea at all and lowers himself, as poet, down to the third unreasoning part of the state as well as the soul, that of the merchant and the technician. All rational forms of prediction thus shift with Plato either up to the exalted figure of Diotima or down to that of the scorned, empirical scientist-technician as a mere bird watcher or gut-reader. Even the Occidental poet-prophet has, thus, only the choice between the ideas or propaganda offered by the state or irrational prophecy and divination. Only outside of Western civilization can he practice his art in his own, original manner, un-hampered by Platonic prejudice, trying to lead the people into what he regards as a better future (Mao or Solchenyzin).

In the West, therefore, we only have either highly idealistic or thymic-enthusiastic theories of action. Even in modern times there is either the romantic-metaphysical idealism of the Good (from Fichte to Schelling to Hegel) or the ethics of pure emotion, as in Hume. Although the latter has a distinct wish for sobriety, he overlooks the intellectual activity of prediction. What counts for him is instinct or feeling as source of formation of the will. Platonic reason, on the other hand, appears completely without power for action, once it has lost the ability to think ahead and, thus, to initiate action based on its own foresight of future possibilities. The most "modern" contemporary psychoan-alytical, ethological, or behavioral scientist denies any individual or social motivation by reason—and at a time when Marxist planning dominates masses of men and technocratic planning, masses of things. This situation should have drawn the attention of scholars to the fact that it is not only irrational drives that motivate people.

5. Platonic-scientific Utopia Prophecy: Alibi of Humanistic Ethics for Responsible Planning.

Utopia prophecy may be either social, technical, or literary. It is a substitute for well-thought-out, realistic, and serious planning. It, too, is an outcome of the Platonic scientist who thus has developed another form of prescientific Greek prophecy and perfected it, in modern times, to baroque heights—namely, the ancient form of Utopia. The scholar and humanist of the Occident, since the Renaissance, has succeeded in this fantastic-extravagant manner only in thinking legitimately about the future—and about the features it may or ought to have. From Morus to Ernst Bloch's *The Principle of Hope*, Utopia or science-fiction most cleverly hides the fact that it transcends the limits of pure, strictly objective science. Its author seems to be, now as before, the cool, objective scientist. Actually, however, he lets go of the reins of subjectivity and engagement and sings the "praise of foolishness" (Erasmus) instead of that of reason. He follows his inclinations impulsively, which were otherwise more repressed than overcome. The romantic literary, such as Goethe or E. T. A. Hoffmann, organizes his life with great care, dividing it, for instance, into the soberly juridical work of the day and the dreams, full of poetic fantasies, of the night. The humanist scholar gives free rein to his primitive and immature, childishly fabulous imagination of the functioning of society, quite apart from his realistic knowledge and education. An artist like Leonardo captures the borderline between the warlike, deadly technique and the musical-clock playfulness of a projected machine.

Even if a social or economic Utopia is constructed upon supposedly strictly mathematical ideals, such as the circle, or quantitatively exact equations, such as those of Campanella and Malthus, demanding exactly alike departments instead of historically grown provinces, the equality of all people in spite of their obvious differences, equal economic rings around a city, uniformly communistic living conditions, and the same ethical virtues, such imaginations are still fantastic or at least much too simple when measured by the totality and variety of human life. "*Hominem non sapiunt*" is Burke's justified objection against the democratic-Utopian constitutional drafts of Paine and Rousseau. "*Societatem non sapiunt*" one would like to object against the equally-Utopian Marxian planning of society. For, as Sorel has already observed, Marx forgot to incorporate the ethics of the complicated, everyday social relations in the wishful image of his working-class paradise. Thus, Marxism, like democracy, must try to balance upon the narrow edge of those exceptional situations on which it is based. Both produce a balance artificially, from time to time, through cultural revolutions or general elections. But the normal situation, such as the competition for money or power, reappears nevertheless again and again and denies the Utopia.

For the humanist Utopian has, at best, a very one-sided and very vague idea of the real life of the individual or society. The main part of his futurology consists, therefore, of impossible or deviant futuristic imaginations, even though some of his fragments may be illuminating and find a fertile soil. As an impractical scientist, though, he is also very reluctant to think about real consequences. He means to demonstrate only Platonic thought-experiments and not to play the role of an efficient action-oriented prophet with responsibility for his ideas. He also closes his eyes to the fact that ideas do not always remain ideas but may represent the beginning of consequences which he would not agree with. Therefore, the ethics of Nietzsche's "blond beast" could easily be seized by Hitler or the whole white race. Marx's idea of the rule of the proletariat could lead, as it did under Stalin, to the murder of other social classes. German idealism could lead to the deterioration of realism, and, thus, to docile consent to the worst ideals, if only they were ideals. Or the liberalization of sex by Freud leads to the sex wave, which would certainly not have been sanctioned by the reserved patriarchal author, though he is to blame for being one of its co-originators. This means that the futuristic imagination of the Utopian, which was meant to play its role more or less without obligation to him, in a country of Nowhere, can also bear fruit in the land of Somewhere, simply because man is capable of following Utopian aims. And since this Utopia is not thought out realistically, it may cause more havoc than good. It is, therefore, just the scientist, on whom the layman relies so much, who is leading mankind irresponsibly into quite specific labyrinths and blind alleys.

Whether the Utopian paints his future visions in glowing colors or writes them in "sober" mathematical formulae, whether he allies himself with realistic reforms or plays at them Platonically, he will always be guilty, for he errs against the common rules of practical reason for the correct planning of the future. He does not first devise the practical possibilities of the future and afterwards choose the one that seems best to him. Instead, he conducts himself like Plato who asks his listeners, before the description of the future, to release him from proving its possibility (*Republic*, 457e–458a, 472d–473a). He takes his chance, consciously and irresponsibly, whether his picture of the future can ever be realized or not. He uses his foresight not at the right time, nor concentratedly enough nor long enough. His most beautiful and far-reaching Utopia will, therefore, turn out to be shortsighted, ill-considered, and unwise.

Surely even the most extravagant, high-flying or deeply involved Utopias and their prophets have found a following, especially among those who are themselves fantastic dreamers. We may agree with Camus and see that it is too easy for man to die for mere ideals. So it is also too easy for a leader of men merely to deliver fabulous ideals and, thus, to waste time, lives, and goods while running after impossible programs. Today it is the ethical-social or technical Utopia of the scientist and humanist which is humanity's favorite. Man sacrifices himself for it with enthusiasm, while he dedicates himself only reluctantly and unwillingly to what he regards as "reasonable" ethical goals, such as those amplified by the United Nations. However, that organization lacks an effective prophet.

CONCLUSION

Looking at history as a whole, one sees that man has been stimulated and his potential for action has been developed mainly by the pre-scientific prophets. Firstly, only such prophecy promised salvation in absolute and grandiose terms and thus aroused his most eager desire for the future. Or, seen from the opposite side, it alone stirred up his guilt and fear of dire fate and thus evoked his resolve to resist with all his might. Secondly, only this prophecy "knew" that man in order to become active needed, at least unconsciously, the prefabricated piece of future which it had to offer as its spiritual base. Hence, it was superior to all reason and all drives, since it dominated, rightly, at least part of the activity which transforms knowledge into action. Thirdly, however, human prophecy fell under the slavery of other trends, such as natural science, which prevented it from growing up, except to occasional flowerings, small or great. Up to now it has been able to offer humanity only this timid blossom, which is preciously little observed, recognized, cultivated, or controlled.

The examination of a few expressions of great prescientific prophecy has necessarily led us far afield from the usual arguments and subjects of ethical discussion, such as, say, the linguistic analysis of *ought*-propositions, the minutiae of material value differentiations, special conflict situations, the metaphysical problems of liberty, or the doctrine of Good in itself. We hope, however, that this discussion has shown certain links between the great classics of ethics and the forms of their utilization, which are missing so far in the textbooks of ethics. For even though many pages in them are dedicated to the motivation of human action by drives, reason, nature, the environment, or ideals, very little mention is made of prophets and the art of prophecy by which they have guided—and will no doubt in future guide—large parts of ethical history.

NOTES

1. The material for this essay became visible only in the process of writing such a history of prediction. It had to be made fruitful for ethics, because in the majority of ethical works, both past and present, one finds no general but only specific beginnings of its treatment such as in existential philosophy.

2. Also materially-ethically, the first concept and value of justice began in Egypt, with a struggle for the corresponding social order involving all classes of society. See J. H. Breasted, *The Dawn of Conscience* (New York, 1933). The Greeks later developed their own form of virtue and gave it a scientific foundation.

3. The oldest document in the world says explicitly and without subtlety: "Thus are carried on every work and every craft, the action of the arms, the going of the legs, the movement of every member, according to this command which the heart [as the seat of the spirit!] thinks, which has come forth from the tongue, and which makes the worth of everything" (Breasted, p. 36).

4. See Breasted, p. 51, from the *Drama of Memphis*, around 4000 B.C.

5. The admonitions for the choice of professions in Egypt say throughout: "Behold, there is no profession where you are not being commanded except that of the bureaucrat; for it is he who commands. If you know how to write, this will bring you more benefit than all the [crafts or other] professions I have explained to you" (v. Bissing, *Altägyptische Lebensweisheit* [Old Egyptian Wisdom of Life], Zürich, 1955, p. 59).

6. John Stuart Mill, *A System of Logic* (New York, 1874), p. 657.

SYSTEMIC VALUE

Time and the Concept of Ought in Legal Experience

LUIGI BAGOLINI

I

THE PROBLEM OF the measurement and the passage of time at various levels of exchange in the technical and theoretical language of legal activity is considered in different ways. In the field of the so-called scientific legal theory one discusses, for instance, whether the passage of time can or cannot be considered as a legal fact. The choice of one or other of these two possibilities evidently depends also on the definition of legal fact that one proposes and accepts as useful and valid in relation to the purpose for which it has been formulated.

Speaking of the effects of the passage of time one generally refers to the efficacy of a right, to the effective existence of an obligation, to the fulfillment of an obligation, to the effect of a contract, or the fact of being in arrears in the payment of a debt,[1] etc. In some cases the passage of time is considered in relation to other circumstances, for example: the inactivity of a person as regards the actuation of a so-called legal relation. One speaks, for instance, of negative prescription whose general effect is to extinguish rights which have not been exercised. When the prescriptive period has expired the right is gone.[2]

There are also positive prescriptions that require possession, in which case by possession one means "a question of fact which may be either actual or civil, through the effective possession of tenants . . . . A title may be strengthened by prescriptive possession although the adverse right was a grant by the possessor himself or his predecessor in title."[3] "Under the term 'prescription' are included various rules of law, differing widely as to their scope and effect," but "having in common the element of the effect of lapse of time."[4]

It can be said that, in the measurement of time, the legal expert adopts standards that are related to some natural and physical phenomena on the basis of which a distinction is made between years, months, and days, etc. There are general law situations in which, for practical purposes, the unit of measurement is the day, "conceived as the indivisible interval of 24 consecutive hours following one after the other, to so-called legal midnight." Nevertheless, it is necessary in some cases to take into consideration a given instant for certain purposes, that is, to determine the precedence or, on the contrary, the posteriority of an event for the performance of a contract of insurance. These are cases where an instant may be thought of as the decisive element.[5]

What is the notion of time generally involved in the mind of the lawyer or legal expert when he acts as a registrar of time in the ordinary and practical manner to which I now refer? A contemporary lawyer rightly says from his technical point of view that the passage of time—that is, the fact that today is not yesterday and that tomorrow will no longer be today—influences legal relations and that this measurement of time is made necessary by the very need to determine, from time to time, the nature of this influence.[6]

In the legal sphere, time is reducible to a possible relationship between something which is before and something which is after, to use an expression of Maurice Merleau-Ponty.[7] Francesco Carnelutti (an Italian lawyer) says that in the sphere of law we cannot speak of pure time in contrast with the notion of place, because the concept of time approaches very closely to the concept of place and is, in a broad sense, included in it.[8] One might also agree with Henri Bergson that legal time is conceived of as objectified in space[9] or in a pseudospace.

It is, as Merleau-Ponty says, present time,[10] being present from the point of view of the jurist who registers and measures it. From the same point of view only the present is real and concrete, whereas the past and the future are unreal, in the sense that the past is no more and the future is not yet.[11]

We can thus say that, in law, time is a uniform succession of moments. In fact the jurist commonly says that we need a criterion of measurement and that, metaphorically speaking, this criterion "implies the representation of a kind of ideal thread which unwinds uniformly and without interruption."[12] Finally, the jurist's notion of time is conditioned by a practical need for measurement and does not go beyond this.

II

It seems very important to me to emphasize some basic characteristics of the measurement of time in law that I think have not as yet been sufficiently clarified. (1) The notion of time involved in legal proceedings of measurement does not coincide with what some authors who treat linguistic problems call the living and immediate experience of time.[13] (2) The legal notion of time does not coincide with the most rigorous proceedings in which physicists and mathematicians refer to time.[14] Hans Reichenbach has very well expressed the difference between a so-called scientific and an immediate, unscientific notion of time.[15]

(3) Time is generally thought of by jurists in the sense that only the present is real and concrete and that what one means by *now* or by *Jetzt* (the *now*) is time in its true reality. The only real and concrete position of the pendulum is its present position; the past positions of it no longer exist and its future positions do not exist yet. An event is real and concrete only from a point of view in relation to which it is present, neither past nor future. If we refer to the measurement of time and to time objectified in a legal sense, a past event is real only if it is thought of as present from the point of view of some spectator or observer, meaning that one cannot think of the past in itself as irreducible to the present. This reduction of time to the form of the present can be considered as a kind of subjective insight implied in the techniques of measurement. This subjective insight, however, seems to be in contrast with an objective insight and, therefore, with the objectivity of the measurement that in law, too, one attempts to achieve. Emile Benveniste has recently very clearly illustrated this so-called objectivity. This effort at objectification of time, he says, is a necessary condition of social life. What one may call social time is the time of the calendar. Calendars must satisfy certain inevitable conditions. (1) A "stative" condition means that one proceeds from an axial moment, to which a zero point corresponds. (2) A "directive" condition which may be indicated by means of the opposite terms *before* and *after* in relation to a reference axis. (3) A condition of measurement by which it is necessary to fix a repertory of units of measurement that serve to denominate the constant intervals between the recurrence of cosmic phenomena.[16]

Starting from a "stative" axis the events are located according to one or other directive orientation, previously (behind) or subsequently (ahead) in relation to this axis, and are divided in a way that one can measure their distance from the same axis—for instance, some years or months or days behind (before) or ahead (after) the axis. Each of these divisions (years, months, days) constitutes an indefinite linear series whose terms are identical and constant without inequality or gaps, so that an event can be exactly pinpointed in a temporal chain through its coincidence with a particular division.[17] Can this objective insight of time which corresponds to a general legal outlook be reconciled with that subjective insight which determines itself, as I have sought to show, through the belief that the concrete and real form of time is only present, not past nor future?

As regards time objectified in space Jean-Paul Sartre says that from a commonsense point of view (and the good lawyer must have common sense) it seems that "to be" is only present and now.[18] Consequently, there arises the following question: How may one combine the objectivity of the temporal chain with the subjectivity involved in the concept of *now*?

An exhaustive answer to this question has been given by Martin Heidegger. He has demonstrated that objectified, measurable, and localized time is the "*world* time" or the "*now* time" (*Jetzt-Zeit*), as, for instance, the time measured by the clock. When time is what we mean by our present act of calculation we say " 'now' . . . here, and so on." The process of calculation is thus constituted by a continuous series of *nows* which, from the point of view of a present *now*, are "no more" or "not yet."[19] Every time sequence is therefore conceived as a flow of *nows* constantly and simply present. "The series of 'nows' is itself conceived in a certain way as simply present. From the point of view of objectified time we say: the 'now' is in every 'now' but nevertheless vanishes in it. In every 'now' the 'now' is now, and therefore the 'now' is constantly present as itself."[20] Karl Jaspers, in his book *Kleine Schule des philosophischen Denkens*, also speaks of objectified time as present. The experience of temporality, as he says, fulfills itself in the present state.[21]

According to Heidegger, not even Hegel through his dialectical way of thinking avoided the conception of time objectified as "*now* time." The most adequate expression of Hegel's conception (using his philosophical language) of time also consists in the determination of time as the negation of a negation, or in a certain sense as the negation of a kind of punctuality. Heidegger thinks that the succession of *nows* is, in Hegel's philosophy, extremely formalized and leveled.[22]

III

Finally, the objectified and localized time is that in which the present is privileged with respect to the past and the future. It is the time involved in the operations of measurement and registration of the jurist; it is time considered as "vulgar" and non-authentic from certain points of view, for example, from the point of view of all those who contrast the so-called vulgar time, even when discussing linguistic problems[23] and even in ethnographical researches,[24] with some ordinary immediate and subjective human experience of time.

Nevertheless it is also true that without the processes of measurement and registration (and therefore without time, be it simply vulgar time), without objectified time as *now* time, social life would be impossible. The complete elimination of objectified time would involve, as has been said, chaos or madness.[25] Even in the sphere of the social sciences, of a political system (in intention, at least, considered as a science), Harold

D. Lasswell makes appeal to measurable and objectified time as both an instrument and a criterion of research.[26] This does not, however, in my opinion mean that objectified time covers the whole sphere of social phenomena. Some of the phenomena, from the point of view of objectified time, remain absurd and incomprehensible, and they are those corresponding to key-concepts or to "nuclear" concepts or to fundamental modalities in which we express the condition of the possibility of social living—for example, the concept of *ought* and, therefore, at a certain level of speech (though it may initially be approximative) the idea of *rule* and of *obligation*.

I generally use the word *ought* here to indicate what distinguishes a juridical rule from a non-normative fact, and that which distinguishes the rule from what is regulated. I take my stand from the conventional point of view according to which *ought* is a notion implied in the ideas of *duty* and *obligation*. I make use of this conventionally chosen point of view as a point of reference in the comparison of legal perspectives and doctrines different one from another.

It is necessary, moreover, to be well aware (in any case how could one critically not be so?) of the distinctions, in the various languages and in various legal contexts, in the meanings attributed and attributable to the words *ought*, *duty*, and *obligation*. We know that *duty* and *obligation* do not primarily form part of the language of law (as used in codes and statutes), "but they form part rather," as Herbert L. A. Hart says, "of the language used in referring to law and to certain types of situations created by it."[27] However, one recognizes the existence of a general and undifferentiated use of the expression "legal obligation" or "legal duty" which embraces all fields of law and which, it is necessary above all to take into account,[28] traverses all the limits of the so-called legal procedures and the so-called general theories of law. It is nonetheless true that these general theories of law must continually revise their conceptual apparatus; perhaps in their specific technical spheres the very notion of legal obligation appears too inadequate, general, and non-technical. But this does not exclude that the notion of legal obligation has a sense corresponding to an immediate need of awareness and of interpretation relative to certain aspects of the social phenomena that are not *tout court* completely reducible within the variable limits of the procedures and theories already referred to above. In a paper read at an international congress held at Vienna in September, 1968,[29] the well-known writer Georg Henrik von Wright discussed deontic logic, explicitly recognizing that the greatest difficulty concerning the applicability of deontic logic is of an "ontological" nature and corresponds to the following questions expressed literally by him:[30] "What is a norm? Namely, in what way is it possible to verify the truth or falsity of what one says when one says that there is a certain norm?"

Apart from specific problems of so-called deontic logic, to this last question there corresponds also the fundamental problem which Hans Kelsen poses relative to the distinction between normative *ought* and factual *is*. The possibility of finding this distinction is what, according to Kelsen, guarantees the boundaries between "sociological method and legal method," to use the words of a well-known essay of his.[31] The distinction between *ought* and *is* therefore constitutes the possibility of a methodology corresponding to the needs of a legal knowledge that has its conceptual autonomy with respect to the practical sciences, needs that, according to Kelsen, are adequate to a certain historically determined line of development of legal theory.

Kelsen thought he could find a distinction between normative *ought* and factual *is* that is purely formal,[32] that can, that is, be propounded independently of any (deontological, directive, valuational, ideological, etc.) content. But, in my opinion, his attempt has failed.[33]

If there is A, there is (or will be) B. For example, if a piece of metal is heated, it is (or will be) expanding. This, according to Kelsen, is the form of a relation in terms of "being," that is, a factual relation, such as the relation of cause and effect expressible also in terms of probability. On the contrary, the form of a legal norm, or in general of a norm of conduct (the form of the normative *ought* or in Kelsenian language, the form of the relation of *imputation*), is the following: "if there is A' there ought to be B'." For example, "if a man commits a theft, he ought to be imprisoned."[34] Therefore, if there is A, there is (or will be) B—a relation of causality, that can be expressed by the verbal form *is*; if there is A' there ought to be B'—a normative relation that can be expressed by the verbal form *ought*. Remaining on the formal plane of Kelsen's thought, we find ourselves respectively faced by a temporal sequence B to A and B' to A'; whether *is* or *ought* is in question. Formally, in both cases we find ourselves faced exclusively by objectified temporal sequences (that is, even in time, such as "*now* time" in the sense to which I have referred above). Consequently it is easy to discover that in Kelsen's observations the difference between *is* and *ought* is purely verbal since formally the two verbs, in the contexts in which they respectively figure, express the same thing and that is nothing more than the relation between a *first* and an *after*—A and B, and A' and B'. So that Kelsen's attempt to make a formal distinction between *is* and *ought* is vain.

Simply to say, as Kelsen also does, that the relation of causality is independent of any human act, while the relation in terms of *ought* is established by human acts[35] assuredly does not serve to give us the differential characteristic of *is* and *ought* which Kelsen would give. Since what is to be shown, within the ambit of Kelsen's statement and in accordance with his intentions, is the possibility that the idea of normative *ought* has of formally expressing the difference between the relations of different contents—that is, precisely, between relations that are prima facie dependent and relations that are prima facie independent of human acts.[36]

Substantially, a causal series, in that it is a temporal sequence of *befores* and *afters*—that is, objective temporality as *"now* time" as a succession of *"nows"*—cannot give us the concept of *ought.* Consequently, the concept of *ought* cannot even be given on the basis of the Einsteinian concept of time if, as I think, what Reichenbach used to say is true—that the "close connexion between space and time on the one hand and causality on the other, is perhaps the most prominent feature of Einstein's theory."[37] In this connection I refer also to what Hermann Weyl said: "cosmic time and causality cannot be separated from one another."[38]

The circumstance that our world appears coherently ordered in terms of a serial relation founded on a link of causality and called time is an empirical fact.[39] As objectified and measurable time the temporal order of *before* and *after* is reducible to the causal order empirically understood, where the cause is always before the effect in a relation that cannot be inverted. The consequence of this is the very fact for which Einstein admits the inversion of the temporal order of certain events in connection with the problem of "simultaneity." Precisely, "since the speed of causal transmission is limited there exist events of such a kind that neither of them can be the cause or the effect of the other. For events of this kind a time order is not defined and either of them can be called earlier or later than the other."[40] In parentheses, as Reichenbach also observes, from the causal conception of the temporal order there derives a certain indeterminacy as compared with the times of distant events, which is a consequence of the limiting character of the speed of light. From this point of view one can no longer speak of an absolute, objectified time. For the physico-objective existence of an absolute time a world would be needed in which "there were no upper limits for the speed signals."[41]

Besides, within the ambit of the physicist's observations one sees, for example, what Louis de Broglie used to say—time is no longer a form that can be thought of in itself even leaving aside its contents, nor therefore is it a "scheme" in which every phenomenon can be precisely localized independently of the dynamic processes that unfold within it.[42] This statement is certainly not, in itself, in contrast with the thesis of Reichenbach to which I have referred, and for which time within the ambit of a physicist's words (that is, I say, as objectified time)[43] is reducible to the causal processes that constitute the world in which we live.[44]

On the other hand, it is likewise true in Reichenbach's opinion that today the idea of a strict causality must be abandoned and that causal assertions must give place to pronouncements in terms of probability.

While causal laws are found to have been understood as exceptionless generalities, an *if, then, always* relation, the laws of probability are laws that admit exceptions, but these are exceptions that occur in a regular percentage of instances. The probability law is an *if, then in a certain percentage* relation. "Modern logic offers the means of dealing with such a relation, which in contradistinction to the *implication* of usual logic is called a *probability implication*. The causal structure of the physical world is replaced by a probability structure and the understanding of the physical world presupposes the elaboration of a theory of probability."[45]

Reichenbach wanted to carry to its final consequence the reduction of causality to probability, even to the extent of maintaining the probability-inductive nature of all human knowledge as empirical knowledge.[46] Consequently, by this route, from the expression of the notion of time in terms of causality one arrives at its expression in terms of probability. Kelsen, at least verbally, did not oppose the reduction of causality to probability when, for example, he referred expressly to Reichenbach's standpoint.[47] Nevertheless, Kelsen thought he was still able to continue speaking of factual *is* in terms of a causal relation. Namely, according to Kelsen, causality remains an "epistemological postulate" and a law which, as such, imposes on human consciousness the seeking of "a connexion between the phenomena observable in reality as cause and effect." That human consciousness does more or less approximately apply this law does not in any way preclude its validity as an "epistemological postulate." It is a question here of a postulate with respect to which the so-called natural laws can be considered precisely as mere laws of statistics and probability.[48] Kelsen, so to speak, substantially reconciles causality with probability without resolving the first in the second, but with the intention of fully preserving that which is for him the autonomous and irreducible meaning of the idea of causality with respect to the notion of probability.[49] There is much matter for discussion here. In any case Kelsen's point of view does not even seem —at least intentionally—in contrast with the fact, for example, of recognizing the existence of cases in which—though in a conventional manner —it becomes useful to speak of so-called causal laws (distinct from the so-called laws of probability): where certain "combinations" of laws of probability are capable, as Jacob Bronowski says, of giving very strong verisimilitudes. In any case, leaving aside for the moment the special prospect of Kelsen and the large question regarding the meaning of causality to the degree that it is distinguished from probability, let us pose the following question: is it possible in some way to express the conceptual peculiarity of normative *ought* with respect to factual *is* in specific terms of relations and of judgments of probability?

IV

Von Wright, for example, in his most recent considerations on deontic logic and the ontology of norms denies that the foundations of obligation can consist *tout court* in the strong probability of undergoing a sanction consequent on the action that violated the obligation. And this in consideration of the fact by which, for example, a clever and intelligent criminal might place himself in a position to reduce to a minimum the probability of being punished.[50]

The following formulation corresponds to a less oversimplified attempt to conceptualize an obligation in terms of probability. A certain person is obliged to perform action C in that he belongs to a class or category A of persons, a member of which would most likely incur a sanction S for failure to perform action C (A here indicates the class comprising all the persons belonging, so to speak, to the sphere of jurisdiction of a given legal order). But let us admit, says von Wright, that B indicates as regards A a subclass of persons who, while belonging to A—by virtue of their common ability or by virtue of favorable circumstances common to them—have the possibility of performing criminal actions without risk or with the minimum risk of being punished. Well, let us compare this hypothesis regarding those who are to be considered within the A order as criminals with the following hypothesis.[51]

Let us admit that is, according to the following second hypothesis, that there are persons belonging to A who may not be punished for nonperformance of C. These would be persons belonging to A, but having the privilege by which they would be permitted not to perform C. A would include in this second hypothesis two subclasses: the privileged and the non-privileged. In the ambit of this second hypothesis the smaller the privileged subclass is as compared with A; the greater is the probability that any person belonging to the A class will be punished —while there is little, or no, probability of punishment for a person belonging to the privileged subclass.[52] Moreover, according to the definition concerning the formulation of this second hypothesis, the privileged were to be subjected to the same obligation as the non-privileged, though exempt from the sanctions. Hence, we can make the analogy of their situation with respect to the situation of criminals considered in the first hypothesis.

On the basis of this analogy between the first hypothesis concerning the cunning criminals and the second hypothesis concerning the privileged, von Wright even from the standpoint of the second hypothesis excludes the possibility of one's conceptualizing obligation in terms of probability. And he excludes it, be it understood, in consideration, I repeat, of the stated analogy, and not because the existence in class *A* of a minority of persons immune from sanctions constitutes in itself a social anomaly or an injustice. He excludes it simply for the fact that such minority should be in the *A* juridical order, in the same condition in which a minority of astute criminals might find themselves. "Immunity" is not in itself unacceptable; it is unacceptable in the guise of the equalization of the situation of "immunity" with the condition of astute criminals: a reason for which the reduction *tout court* of the legal obligation to the probability of the actuation of the sanction is to be rejected.[53]

What, then, is the final general conclusion of von Wright? It is the following: the reply to the demand for which one asks whether an action is or is not obligatory may "often" ("often" the writer says and therefore "not always") usefully assume the form of a prediction concerning a probable reaction of judges. But this form does not constitute a conceptual theory of legal obligation—or of duty; it does not therefore constitute the concept of *ought*. The idea of legal obligation or duty cannot be identified with a judgment of probability regarding the actuation of a sanction.[54] That is, *ought* is not reducible to a temporal succession which assumes the form of a relation between behavior *C* and the actuation of a sanction *S*—of a relation that can be expressed, for example, in the words used by Reichenbach—if *C*, then in a certain percentage *S*.[55] At bottom, von Wright is in agreement with Kelsen on one fundamental point as regards what concerns a conviction that I cannot share. For both the temporal relation between a *before* and an *after* in terms of objectified time—that is, the relation between behavior and the application of a sanction—cannot constitute an element of "conceptual" distinction (to use the adjective by von Wright) or "formal" distinction (to use the adjective employed by Kelsen) between *ought* and *is*. With one difference: the temporal relation is verbally expressed by Kelsen in terms of causality, while by von Wright it is expressed in terms of probability. But this latter difference has little importance since, as we have seen, according to the meaning given by Kelsen to the word *causality*, there is no contrast between *causality* and *probability*.

The result of all this may then, in my opinion, be repeated and elliptically generalized by saying that certainly in terms of objectified time as causal relation—and of causality as probability—it is impossible to place and determine the concept of *ought*; there remains *is*—"law as fact."[56] Where legal experience is thought of as all exclusively reducible to objectified time, a normative knowledge—or legal, as distinct from what is called sociological knowledge—is impossible. On the other hand, I repeat, it is also indubitably true that there cannot be legal procedure of measurement and of registration of facts which do not imply objectified time as a countable succession. There evidently enters into the idea of objectified time all the "chronological" ideas used technically by legal experts such as that of "fixed time" in reference, for example, to a given due date for a bill of exchange and that of "mobile" time indicated by a number of days, months, or years from a fixed point in time, for example: "the duration of a contract for three years from the moment of its being completed, where the precise day on which the contract is determined . . . may undergo a shift according to whether the months and the years on the calendar have a greater or fewer number of days."[57] And, together with others, there evidently enters within the ambit of the prospect in terms of objectified time the ideas of "useful time," the time during which "it is possible to carry out certain legal acts, by which holidays are excluded," and of "continuous time," "which comprises holidays too" according to certain rules on which, for the purposes of our present discussion, it is useless to linger.[58] On the contrary, there cannot be included, so to speak, in the notion of objectified time—and, therefore, they cannot be "conceptualized"—those procedures and those key ideas that are employed from time to time as "connotative"[59] of the sphere of operations on which, though from a "chronological" standpoint, the technical observations of the legal expert hinge. The same circumscribing horizons of such specific spheres of operations seem to disappear the more readily the less legal *ought*, for example, appears determinable with respect to social and factual *is*. There remain the facts the "regulaciones fácticas de lo fáctico" to use an expression of Xavier Zubiri's.[60] There also remains the social reality of which it is a question of defining the meaning, insofar as it is useful to define it; and there remains the social reality perhaps as "economy," insofar as it is useful and possible to define *economy* extended to the maximum to embrace "all" the social reality (which, in parentheses, whenever it is thought of as "all," is extremely difficult and perhaps impossible to say what it may mean).

However, it is not only a question of definition of spheres of operation. It is a question of paradoxes and of incongruities in which there is manifested, so to speak, the consciousness of social living; it is a question perhaps of a crisis that goes back to the loss of the sense of *ought* in that it is irreducible to factual *is*. So that it seems to become absurd that a behavior—and, therefore, a present will—must be limited and constrained by the past will expressed by an established norm or by a normative purpose which, as such, is future with respect to the present will of the person for whom it is formulated.

V

In the objectified succession of *nows* it seems absurd that the *now* that is no longer—or the *now* that is not yet—can be binding and, therefore, prevalent as compared with the *now* that is a present moment. The obligation to maintain a promise appears especially absurd. It appears absurd that the present will of an individual, present and as such real, should be linked to—and made dependent on—a will of the same person already past and, as such, unreal or no longer real. It is the absurdity, under another aspect, pointed out by David Hume.[61] The authors of a vast literature have attempted in vain to overcome it.[62]

Last year I promised and contracted because I so willed. Now I no longer will so. Why is the past will, dead and no longer mine, to dispose of my present will? How can the past—in the objective succession of *nows*—prevail over the *present* constituting, with respect to it therefore, an *ought* and a binding element?[63] If one remains on the level of the succession of *nows* and of objectified time as "*now* time," if the *past* as past is not, if the past as past does not possess it positivity, the *ought* created by a promise appears absurd. And yet the promise is the fundamental nucleus of life and social experience. By substituting the word for the immediate performance, the promise, as Rudolf von Jhering used to say, constitutes an enormous step forward with respect to the primitive form of contract; it releases human beings from the links with the present, and as a result, men can assume as the basis of their operations their future possibilities; by directing themselves towards the *future* they can provide for their present needs.[64] From this latter standpoint the future has its positivity with respect to the present as a result of which it can *prevail* over the present. But from the point of view of objectified time as a succession of *nows*, the future is the *now* which is not yet; the future has not its positivity with respect to the present, nor can it therefore in a certain sense *prevail* over it.

In point of fact, norm, promise, responsibility, authority as justification and legitimation of power, all are absurd from the point of view of objectified time as a causal or a probable succession. Normative *ought* is not conceptualizable; one cannot explain, consequently, how a norm, in that it represents past will, can prevail over present will; one cannot explain, on the other hand, how the prospect of an end, which as such is future, can prevail over the present will and limit it. There remains the probability that the power to apply a sanction prevails or not over the power, and, therefore, makes possible the utility of avoiding it; there remains a naked struggle of power. But, on the other hand, naked power, as a pure physical or material force, lacking in any persuasive element and, therefore, devoid of all justification, whether it is given in good or bad faith, whether it is genuine or false, is perhaps merely an illusion. If even the fiercest tyrant also needs collaborators, he needs for that very reason to persuade somebody. There is generally agreement, for example, in affirming that an individual is responsible insofar as he is made responsible by norms and rules of conduct. From this point of view it follows that, if the conceptual distinction between *ought* and *is* is lost— the distinction between norms and facts and, therefore, also between norms of conduct and natural laws or *Invarianten*, in the sense in which this word is used, for example, by Max Born[65]—the notion of responsibility is also void of sense. Since, while it appears plausible to say that a man be made responsible by norms that forbid him to wound or kill, it does not in the least seem plausible to say that he be made responsible by reason of the physical laws on the basis of which *one calculates* the effect produced by the throwing of the stone with which that man struck another man.[66]

VI

In conclusion, it seems to me, as I have tried to show elsewhere, that some ideas expressing social situations which, at various levels of discussion (not only juridical but also political), reveal themselves to be fundamental, are not conceptuable and reveal themselves to be absurd to every consideration in which there is implied the notion of objectified time as "*now* time." In the light of this conclusion there are two roads open: either one accepts this conclusion to its final consequences—not only theoretical but also practical and political—or one makes appeal, whenever one thinks it possible, to the hypothesis regarding a notion of temporality which surpasses, and yet comprises within itself, objectivizable and measurable time within the ambit of a discussion in which it is possible to explain and demonstrate, from time to time, the origin and constitution of the processes of measuring and of objectivization of time. The actuation of this possibility of demonstration might function as a proof *sui generis* of the validity of the hypothesis. As for myself, I have attempted the second road, making use of Bergson, in the sense in which he has been used, for example, by Sartre and by Merleau-Ponty, while accepting the diverse criticisms leveled at Bergson by Sartre[67] and by Merleau-Ponty.[68] I have not been able to assent to the final and yet different conclusions of Sartre and Merleau-Ponty on the question of temporality. Nor, on the other hand, have I been able to accept the standpoint of Husserl, though availing myself in the field of jurisprudence of some explorations made by him.[69]

In taking this second road I have expected to be able to use on various occasions[70] some points of departure of Pantaleo Carabellese's thought which still have, in my opinion, a coherence and actuality of their own,[71] though taken for themselves and independently of their over-all conception—understood as a whole— from which they emerge.

Therefore, according to the hypothesis taken up by me, objectified time—whether it is as one finds it involved in the processes of measuring of the jurist or in those of the sociologist or whether it is as one finds it involved, at a different level, in the more advanced processes of physics —is *one* way of being (susceptible of being combined in the most diverse manners)—but it is not the *only* way of being—of conscious time.

By the word *consciousness* I do not here mean only to indicate analytical knowledge or descriptive and factual knowledge, the results of which are, in both cases, reducible to propositions that are verifiable as true or false, but every kind of prescientific, emotional, practical, directive, mythological, ideological, consciousness, etc., as well as the more or less clear and distinct consciousness that the individual has of every possibility of action offered to him by the situation and the social environment in which he lives. Broadly understood in this way, the meaning in use, so to speak, of the word *consciousness* which I have chosen comprises all that which, in its turn, is indicated by the words *knowledge, feeling,* and *will* (and by the corresponding words in the various languages). I am conscious of what I know, of what I feel and perceive, and of what I will.

To know, to feel, and to will are, from this standpoint, ways distinct one from another of my "being-conscious-of-something." There may be situations in which my knowledge (expressible in propositions of which it is possible to say in some way that they are true or false) *prevails* over my feeling or my will. In other situations my feeling may, through certain of my actions, *prevail* over my knowledge and over my will, or my will may in certain cases prevail over my knowledge and over my feeling. It will be a question, moreover, of the prevalence of the way my consciousness acts over the other two, never of the elimination of the other two. Therefore, according to the hypothesis thus considered, every conscious manifestation of human life unfolds itself through an "interpenetration" or "intension" of knowledge, sensation, and will to which the three so-called forms of time respectively correspond: past, present, future.[72]

The object of knowledge (insofar as knowledge is understood as distinct from feeling and from will) can be thought of as past with respect to the act of knowing. From this standpoint what Bertrand de Jouvenel says is, in my opinion, right: "the past is the seat of cognoscible facts"—that is, of facts which are in some way, so to speak, capable of being verified as true or false (even if speaking of *seat* may appear somewhat metaphorical). Though it is not always easy "to discover whether a fact is true or false," in effect what one is accustomed to indicate by the word *fact* is, for the most part, "as a general principle, verifiable." Impatience and irritation, which, for example, can be aroused by contradictory versions of a single fact, show the deep conviction that this *factum* is cognoscible, so that one is led to say that one of the witnesses, even if one does not know who, is lying or making a mistake.[73]

Even in terms of probability the content of *knowing* is past with respect to the act of knowing, since probability assertions always express frequencies relative to events already repeated and are derived from the frequencies observed in the past.[74]

Unlike the object of knowing which is, therefore, past with respect to the act of knowing, the objecting of feeling, on the contrary (insofar as feeling is understood as distinct from knowing and from willing), can be thought of as present with respect to the act of feeling (and of perceiving). And the object of willing (insofar as willing is understood as distinct from knowing and from feeling) can be thought of as future with respect to the act of willing.

Insofar as it is distinct from knowing and from feeling (or from perceiving), the will constitutes in fact a species of field in which, as de Jouvenel says, one is free to "place images that do not correspond" directly "to any acquired" and, as such, past "reality." For instance, "image is not pure fantasy if I have the will" and "the power to bring about subsequently a reality that corresponds to it. In that there exists the power to substantiate this image, it is something 'possible,' and insofar as there exists a will to achieve it, it is a project."[75] Independently of the basic ideas of de Jouvenel, what he says, seems to me, in relation to the hypothesis put forward here, perfectly valid and decisive. Within the ambit of the "possible" and of the "project" the will has an "intentional" character. Unlike *fact* of which one can say whether it is true or false, *intention* possesses various grades: it may be weighted, pondered, reasoned, conjectured.[76] Intention eludes the sphere of a rationality that is expressed exclusively in relations of objectified time and inductive, causal, and probability relations; intention involves the sphere of the more or less reasonable; it involves the sphere in which it is possible to speak of greater or less participation in and sympathy with the situations of others.

VII

The objection of those who would say that in actual fact what may be called the act of knowing is present and that only its content is past would not, I think, be valid against the hypothesis put forward here identifying the temporal forms (past, present, and future) with the concrete development of consciousness (knowledge, feeling, will). The objection would not be valid because one cannot think of the so-called "act of knowing" (as distinct from feeling and from willing) independently of its content. That is, to use an elliptic expression, knowing is always "knowing-something." Knowing which is not knowing-something is nothing. Consequently the "something" is the concrete determination of the act of knowing. This does not exclude, I repeat, that knowing implies the present like feeling or like perception, without which one could not think of knowing as a human activity nor of consciousness as intension or "interpenetration" of knowledge, feeling, and will and therefore, correspondingly, of past, present, and future.

From the practical point of view, from the standpoint of the action in the moment of its being effected as regards the activity of the so-called practical man, what de Jouvenel says is also true, that the *facta*, insofar as they are past, are of interest only because they "serve as the basis of presumption as to *futura* . . . . If So-and-so, for example, is preoccupied as to the departure of his plane, tell him that that particular flight has previously taken off at the scheduled time for a long series of days, and he will be reassured, since these previous *facta* will appear to him as a guarantee of the *futurum* which alone is of importance to him."[78] But even this observation—and this example—does not serve to exclude, but rather to reinforce the hypothesis and the point of view sustained here. That the *facta* are "in practice" of interest and importance in terms of *futura* means that knowledge of *facta* involves the willing of *futura*. It is a question, precisely, of a nexus of conscious involvement of knowledge, feeling, and will which is actuated and developed through social— and therefore also political and legal—"interactions" of the behavior of human beings. This definition is according to the broader meaning that I have chosen and have attributed to the word *consciousness*. Environmental and social consciousness, not understood exclusively in an intimate, inner, or static sense, etc., not consciousness as merely knowing (as distinct from feeling and willing) nor, therefore, understood as objectified in causal temporality, but consciousness in act, as a condition of possibility of all spatial and temporal objectivization. If consciousness thus understood is "interpentration" of knowledge, feeling, and will, it is not absurd (but it is explicable) what in practice appears quite evident: that *facta* are important in terms of *futura*, though being in themselves distinct and irreducible with respect to the *futura*.

VIII

This hypothesis regarding consciousness as "interpenetration" or "intension" of the temporal forms seems, moreover, to correspond to an operatively useful view in various fields. It suffices to think of certain methodological attitudes in ethnology—of some declarations of Claude Lévi-Strauss or of Gilberto Freyre.[79] In any case it is a question which can serve to open a complementary discussion at the level of which the distinction between *ought* and *is* is no longer merely verbal, unsubstantial, or illusory.

Unlike a discussion in terms of objectified time as *"now* time," wherein what is real and concrete is only present, from the point of view of conscious time what is *real* and *concrete* (to use these two adjectives at the level of a certain common and ordinary language) is also past and future: the positive binding prevalence of a past will over a present will becomes plausible. The possibility of the prevalence of common interest over self-interest becomes plausible—that is (to express ourselves in David Hume's terms), the possibility of the prevalence of a future interest over an immediate and present interest. In both cases the *ought* as a positive binding prevalence of the past or of the future over the present becomes understandable. In conclusion the distinction between normative *ought* and factual *is* becomes comprehensible in reference to a normative attitude and to a *Handlungsbezogenheit* on the basis of which, I think, it makes sense to speak of normative *ought*. In my opinion it has been Hart's merit, implicitly or explicitly, to emphasize that by reason of which, from the "external" point of view the distinction between *ought* and *is* is not, after all, tenable. It is so only from an "internal" point of view.[80] I leave aside here all specific discussion regarding the precise and most faithfully attributable meanings of the adjectives *internal* and *external* in Hart's thought and all questions regarding the utility of these two adjectives rather than others. However, the appeal to the internal point of view—leaving aside a strict interpretation of Hart's thought, which is not possible in this article—may be taken as meaning the necessity of putting oneself in the situation of the person who is under the obligation. But what situation? A purely factual situation? On the plane of a purely factual situation in which the normative obligation is also conceived as "fact," the distinction between the normative obligation and the "fact" is clearly not, in my opinion, possible. It is necessary to appeal to a situation that is not exclusively factual— that is, namely *conscious* in the sense used above. (Which does not mean falling *tout court* into a certain type of psychologism, and this precisely because of the very broad meaning I have chosen and attributed to the word *consciousness*.) It is necessary that the words *obligation* and *duty* should be used to indicate in some way consciousness of obligation and duty wherein the word *consciousness* does not have precisely the sense that is exclusively reducible to the meaning in common use of the expression "knowledge of facts." Only thus can it be completely plausible to say that the existence of a norm, insofar as it is distinct from pure "fact," implies, as Hart affirms, an attitude and, namely, in his very words, an "attitude consistent with regarding" a certain "behaviour as a model."[81] I can—it is true—be, so to speak, subjected to a norm A of which I am not aware and which I do not even know. In this case there may remain, moreover, a certain degree of probability as a result of which an action of mine—though performed without my knowing of the existence of the norm A—is followed by the actuation of a sanction. This holds in this case unless one returns to the reduction of the obligation to a mere relation of probability between a certain action and the putting into effect of a certain sanction, and one loses all specific distinction between normative *ought* and factual *is*. The fact for which the application of a sanction takes place even independently of the consciousness of the existence of a norm does not exclude the fact that the distinction between normative *ought* and factual *is* can be proposed within the ambit of such consciousness. That normative *ought* is distinguishable with respect to *is* only in consideration of the normative attitude of the person who is subject to the norm means that normative *ought* cannot be enucleated and distinguished from factual *is* independently of the *conscious* behavior of such person. We return, thus, to the hypothesis set out here, according to which in order to have really the idea of a normative *ought* distinct from factual *is*, it is necessary to have a certain prenotion of consciousness as "interpenetration" of past, present, and future for the reasons already stated.

Outside the hypothesis in whose ambit this prenotion can be outlined there remains, it seems to me, a single road, to follow to the very end, if one wishes to be coherent, and along which there is no longer *ought*, no longer *duty*, but only the power of him who commands. There is only a power to consider, from time to time, concrete and real only in the "spatially present" moment of its actuation, or to adopt the adverb used by Michel Foucault (in connection with *Traum und Existenz* by Ludwig Binswanger) in the "geographically present" moment of its actuation.[82]

IX

In order to avoid the reduction of *ought* to *power* (a reduction, as we have seen, in itself contradictory) it is necessary, I repeat, to make appeal to consciousness as "interpenetration" of knowing, feeling, and willing and, therefore correspondingly, as we have also seen, of past, present, and future. This is true because, in the configuration of such an "interpenetration," there is implied the possibility of prevalence of one temporal form over another.

This possibility of prevalence is the kernel of the question within the ambit of the hypothesis proposed here and needs to be clearly reiterated. It has no sense, I repeat, to speak of the prevalence of one temporal form over another at the level of a discussion regarding qualitative and objectified time in terms of relations of cause or probability for obvious reasons, since if the *after* in the objectified chronological chain comes after the *before*, one cannot explain how the *before* can prevail over the *after*, and vice versa. The idea of prevalence is here psychological-conscious and sets itself, on the other hand, at a level of discussion which is also different with respect to any level of speech whatsoever in which one speaks, for example, of temporal forms in terms of "quality." On this point I cannot accept the notion of conscious time as "qualitative" time proposed in a certain sense by Bergson, nor in that, though different, put forward by Carabellese. The concept of "quality" always implies an objectivization. The temporal forms at the level of consciousness are in themselves modes in the act of "having-consciousness-of-something."[83]

The "qualities" imply, on the contrary, an objectivization; they belong to the sphere of objects and things as they appear to us in their causal chain, not to the formation in the consciousness of the specifically cognoscible vision of such chain. One "quality" may, in a certain sense, superimpose itself or replace another and not, properly speaking, prevail over another.

The word *prevalence*, as it is employed by me in this context, implies rather the sense attributable, though metaphorically, to the word *tension* and also to the word *tendency*. Past, present, and future—as forms constituting my concrete environmental and social consciousness—that is my "knowing-feeling-willing-something"—are respectively the tensions or the tendencies of social and environmental development of my consciousness. And according to the diverse environmental situations in which I find myself and, therefore, according to the various modes of my "having-awareness-of-something," one (or other) of these tensions may, respectively, manifest itself, even on the plane of social relations, through a prevalence with respect to the other two—that is, it may be realized in a more intense manner as compared with the other two.

The very prospects and views of the world emerging from contemporary culture are not exempt from the dynamic of these prevalences. For example, a certain neopositivistic view of life and of the world insofar as it resolves itself in a scientistic view is conditioned by the prevalence of the past over the present and over the future, and that is by the prevalence of knowledge whether empirical or analytical, over the immediacy of feeling and willing. In fact the thought that only that has meaning which is expressible in propositions that are verifiable as true or false may imply a prevalence of knowing as compared with willing—namely, of the *factum* as compared with the *futurum*. The belief that the only time possible is empirical time, objectified in the causal chain, is a belief that arises precisely because of the prevalence of cognoscible tension over the others and therefore of the *factum* over the *futurum*.

On the other hand, the dissatisfaction that many people feel today with regard to certain absolutist attitudes implied in the neopositivistic and scientistic views of life and of the world is a dissatisfaction that has its justification in the fact that consciously the prevalence of cognoscible tension over *feeling* tension and over *willing* tension can never humanly attain the limit of cancellation and emptying of these two. In the ambit of an analysis of the very legal and social experience itself, these possibilities of prevalence—without cancellation—of one temporal form over the others have been typified by some writers. Such typifications might be more or less plausible and discussible as regards the empirico-verifiable correctness of their respective determinations. But, independently of whatever concerns their correctness from the empirical, descriptive point of view, the intentional motive of their very formulation and enunciation is, in my opinion, fully acceptable and revealing. It reveals to us that legal and social experience is conditioned in its multiform dynamism by a play of reciprocal tensional prevalences of the three temporal forms, by a play of prevalences whose results are, in some ways, important and, be it more or less provisionally and conventionally, representable and characterizable. This play of prevalences is possible insofar as one temporal form is not assumed as privileged with respect to the others in an absolute sense, insofar as, so to speak (or to use an expression of Sartre's),[84] real being is not only the "present," insofar as the environmental and social reality of human "awareness" takes form through the positivity of the three temporal forms.

From this point of view there is sense in speaking, as Husserl does, of "man of the past," of "man of the future," and of "man of the present" as three tendential types. The man of the past is dominated by the sense of a world that is finished, limited, always substantially identical with itself, from a certain extraneousness with respect to the real and present conditions in which he lives. His danger is to fall into passibility and into inactive conservatism. The man of the present is the man of action, animated by an impulse to be active and by a positivistic view of the world, in which one tends to resolve the sense of *ought* on the plane of the reality of action, of experiment, and of verification. His danger is aridity, the reduction of his view of life to that of a play of forces, the speculation of the moment, the prevalence of force over the legitimation of power. On the contrary, for the man of the future the present situations are valid in their functions as vectors directed towards the future which such situations reveal in themselves; the present is represented as projected on planes of possible subsequent achievements. The danger of the man of the future is the building of castles in Spain.

According to Husserl, as regards legal experience, the judge may tend in various circumstances to assume the role of the "man of the past." He who wields executive power has the role of "man of the present"; he who legislates, in various cases and from various points of view, is included within the ambit of the type of "man of the future."[85]

I have no intention here of discussing the details of the characterizations offered by Husserl. What I agree with fully is that the temporal forms can be respectively typified by social, political, and legal experience according to the various senses of a greater or lesser intensity of prevalence of one over another. What I do not agree with is the fact by which Husserl has privileged the "present." He says in fact: "Unter den drei Zeitdimensionen kommt der *Gegenwart* ein absolutes Primat zu."[86] The absolute primacy of the present over the past and over the future is here affirmed. This is an affirmation in which one of Husserl's fundamental convictions is expressed. But if there is an absolute primacy of the present over the past and over the future, how can it happen that the past or the future—in certain situations that Husserl has typified— should prevail and, therefore, should have, respectively in their turns, a primacy over the present? If it is true that the present has an absolute prevalence over the past and over the future, one does not understand how the past or the future can, respectively in certain situations, prevail over the present. Vice versa, if it is true, as Husserl has shown, that the past or the future can reveal themselves in certain situations as prevailing over the present, the absolute primacy of the present over the past and over the future, which Husserl also affirms, remains incomprehensible.

In point of fact, by privileging the present one does not depart from the conception of time as "*now* time," which cancels the validity of any phenomenological description regarding the prevalence of one temporal form over another on social, political, and legal levels. To avoid the difficulty that has been pointed out it is necessary, in my opinion, to pass beyond the limits of a discussion in which time is expressible exclusively in terms of "*now* time."

X

The central problem which is the object of the preceding observations concerns the possibility of a distinction between normative *ought* and factual *is*, and between *norm* and *fact* in the social, political, and legal field. Staying within the limits which I have laid down for myself, the problem is not prima facie either deontological nor ideological, even if, as I think, certain implicit so-called subjective coefficients of valuation cannot, in such subjects, be eliminated. I have directly and intentionally occupied myself with saving the dimension of *ought*, setting aside the variety of valuational contents that it may assume. It is a question of a second dimension irreducible[87] to—and yet nonetheless implied in—a view of life and of the world in terms of "*now* time," of "causality," and of "probability." It is important above all to pose the problem of the condition of concrete possibility of this second dimension in order to be able to believe in it. The problem of its contents and of its valuational determinations is included within the ambit of a second discourse concerning the choices of the contents that the "sense of duty" may and must assume. These are choices that seem today more than ever pregnant with responsibility in the profound contrasts of ideas, of aims, of interests in which the contemporary society is struggling.

NOTES

1. Among various writers I mention are Domenico Barbero, *Sistema istituzionale del diritto privato italiano*, Vol. I (Torino, 1958), p. 263; G. Branca, *Istituzioni di diritto privato* (Bologna, 1955), p. 51; M. Allara, *Le nozioni fondamentali del diritto civile*, Vol. I (Torino, 1958), p. 366.

2. See, for example, W. M. Gloag and R. C. Henderson, *Introduction to the Law of Scotland* (Edinburgh, 1939), p. 143.

3. *Ibid.*, p. 143.

4. *Ibid.*, p. 142.

5. Barbero, p. 281.

6. *Ibid.*, p. 260.

7. Merleau-Ponty, *Phénoménologie de la perception* (Paris, 1945), p. 474.

8. Carnelutti, *Teoria generale del diritto* (Rome, 1951), p. 309.

9. See, for example, H. Bergson, *Essai sur les données immédiates de la conscience* (Paris, 1948), pp. 56 ff.

10. Merleau-Ponty, p. 474. See also E. Leisi, *Die Darstellung der Zeit in der Sprache in R. W. Meyer*, ed., *Das Zeitproblem im 20. Jahrhundert* (Bern and Munich, 1964), p. 20.

11. See T. Barth, "Mensch, Natur und Zeitlichkeit," in *Atti del XII congresso internazionale di filosofia*, Venice, Sept. 12–18, 1958, Vol. II (Florence, 1960), p. 42.

12. Barbero, p. 260.

13. See, for example, E. Benveniste, "Le langage et l'expérience humaine," in Vol. *Problèmes du langage* (Paris, 1966), p. 8.

14. See F. Gonseth, "Temps et syntaxe," in *Akten des XIV. internationalen Kongresses für Philosophie*, II (Vienna, Sept. 2–9, 1968), 630. See also O. Costa de Beauregard, "Le temps et les théories physiques," *ibid.*, pp. 617–22; M. Bunge, "Physique et métaphysique du temps," *ibid.*, pp. 623–29; A. N. Prior, "The Logic of Tenses," *ibid.*, pp. 638–40; G. J. Whitrow, "Time and Mathematics," *ibid.*, pp. 641–45. As is known, Whitrow is the author of the important book *The Natural Philosophy of Time* (London, 1961).

15. H. Reichenbach, *Atom und Kosmos. Das physikalische Weltbild der Gegenwart* (Berlin, 1930), pp. 41–56.

16. Benveniste, pp. 6–7.

17. *Ibid.*, pp. 7–8.

18. Sartre, *L'être et le néant. Essai d'ontologie phénoménologique* (Paris, 1955), p. 151.

19. M. Heidegger, *Sein und Zeit* (Tübingen an der Saale, 1926), pp. 421–22.

20. *Ibid.*, pp. 422–23.

21. Jaspers, "Kleine Schule des philosophischen Denkens" [Lectures given in the first term of the study program of the Bavarian Television, fall, 1964] (Munich, 1965), p. 155.

22. Heidegger, p. 432.

23. See, for example, Benveniste, pp. 7–8.

24. See, for example, the replies of C. Lévi-Strauss to G. Charbonnier in the book of G. Charbonnier, *Entretiens avec Claude Lévi-Strauss* (Paris, 1961), pp. 29–30, 57, and on the level of a different line of research the *Nota metodologica* of G. Freyre in the book *Ordem e progresso: processo de desintegracão das sociedades patriarcal e semipatriarcal no Brasil sob o regime do trabalho livre*, Vol. I (Rio de Janeiro, 1959), pp. xxiii-xxxv.

25. Benveniste, pp. 7–8.

26. H. D. Lasswell and A. Kaplan, *Power and Society. A Framework for Political Inquiry*, (New Haven, 1950, 1957), p. xiv.

27. See H. L. A. Hart, "Il concetto di obbligo," *Rivista di filosofia* (1966), pp. 125–26.

28. *Ibid.*, pp. 127–28.

29. G. H. von Wright, "Deontic Logic and the Ontology of Norms" in *Akten des XIV, internationalen Kongresses für Philosophie*, pp. 304–11; first

An Essay in Modal Logic (Amsterdam, 1951) and *Logical Studies* (London, 1957).

30. Von Wright, "Deontic Logic and the Ontology of Norms," p. 304.

31. Kelsen, "Über Grenzen zwischen juristischer und soziologischer Methode" [Lecture presented to the Sociological Society of Vienna (Tübingen, 1911)], pp. 12–15.

32. See O. Lahtinen, *Zum Aufbau der rechtlichen Grundlagen* (Helsinki, 1951), pp. 61–65.

33. See K. Larenz, *Methodenlehre der Rechtswissenschaft* (Berlin, Göttingen, Heidelberg, 1960), pp. 68–82, especially p. 75, also with regard to the respective meanings (as used by Kelsen) of such words as *Sollen, Pflicht,* etc.

34. Kelsen, "Causality and Imputation," in *Ethics* (1950), p. 6, and in *What is Justice? Justice, Law and Politics in the Mirror of Science* (Berkeley, 1957, 1960), pp. 331–32.

35. Kelsen, "Causality and Imputation," p. 6.

36. For the criticism of another argument of Kelsen's I refer the reader to my books: *Mito, potere e dialogo. Problemi di scienza politica e di filosofia della pratica* (Bologna, 1967), pp. 95 f., and *Visioni della giustizia e senso comune* (Bologna, 1968), pp. 99–100. Such critical observations remain, in my opinion, valid even after taking account of the latest edition of Kelsen's work: "Reine Rechtslehre" (zweite, vollständig neubearbeitete und erweiterte Auflage 1960), Wien (unveränderter Nachdruck), 1967, pp. 79–95. For a criticism of Kelsen (also for the bibliography), among various writers see: L. Recaséns Siches, *Tratado general de filosofía del derecho* (Mexico, 1959), pp. 405–21.

37. Reichenbach, "The Philosophical Significance of the Theory of Relativity," in H. Feigl and M. Brodbeck, eds., *Readings in the Philosophy of Science* (New York, 1953), p. 205. This essay of Reichenbach's had already appeared in a collective volume with a list of the writings of Einstein: P. A. Schilpp, *Albert Einstein: Philosopher-Scientist* (Evanston, Ill., 1949), pp. 289–311.

38. H. Weyl, *Raum, Zeit, Materie. Vorlesungen über allgemeine Relativitätstheorie* (Darmstadt, 1923, 1961), p. 6

39. Reichenbach, *The Rise of Scientific Philosophy* (Berkeley, Los Angeles, 1954), pp. 149–50. "Space and time have their origin in the relation between events. What we observe in nature are the situations of objects in events. Physical science analyzes the fields of activity of events which determine the conditions governing the transference of objects" (A. N. Whitehead, "Einstein's Theory," in *A Philosopher Looks at Science* [New York, 1965], p. 126).

40. Reichenbach, "The Philosophical Significance of the Theory of Relativity," pp. 205–206.

41. Reichenbach, *The Rise of Scientific Philosophy*, p. 154.

42. De Broglie, *La physique nouvelle et les quanta* (Paris, 1937), pp. 6–7.

43. See V. Mathieu, *L'oggettività nella scienza e nella filosofia contemporanea* (Torino, 1960).

44. Reichenbach, *The Rise of Scientific Philosophy*, p. 155.

45. *Ibid.,* pp. 163–64.

46. Reichenbach, *Experience and Prediction. An Analysis of the Foundation of the Structure of Knowledge* (Chicago, London, 1961), for example, pp. vi–viii and the chapter "Probability and Induction," pp. 297–404; "Rationalism and Empiricism: an Inquiry into the Roots of Philosophical Error" in *Proceedings and Addresses of the American Philosophical Association,* XXI (1947–

1948), 330–46. See also A. Fischer, *Die philosophischen Grundlagen der wissenschaftlichen Erkenntnis* (Vienna, 1947), p. 85.

47. Kelsen, "Causality and Retribution," in *What is Justice?* pp. 319–20.

48. *Ibid.*, p. 323.

49. See C. F. von Weizsäcker, *Zum Weltbild der Physik* (Stuttgart, 1963), pp. 233–39.

50. Von Wright, "Deontic Logic and the Ontology of Norms," p. 306.

51. *Ibid.*, pp. 307–308.

52. *Ibid.*, p. 307.

53. *Ibid.*, pp. 307–308.

54. *Ibid.*

55. See Reichenbach, *The Rise of Scientific Philosophy*, p. 164.

56. "A unified and realistic legal science is obviously a branch of social science. No fixed boundaries in relation to psychology, sociology and economics can be recognized." K. Olivecrona, "Law as Fact" in the collective vol. *Interpretations of Modern Legal Philosophies. Essays in Honor of Roscoe Pound*, P. Sayre, ed. (New York, 1947), p. 555.

57. Barbero, pp. 261–62.

58. See A. Trabucchi, *Istituzione di diritto civile* (Padua, 1968), p. 127.

59. I refer here to the sense attributed to the word *connotation* as distinct from *denotation* by D. Easton, *The Political System. An Inquiry into the State of Political Science* (New York, 1965), p. 114.

60. Zubiri, *Sobre la esencia* (Madrid, 1963), p. 24.

61. Hume, *A Treatise of Human Nature*, book III, 2, part sec. I, ed. by L. A. Selby-Bigge (Oxford, 1946), pp. 516–17, and in this connection my book *Esperienza giuridica e politica nel pensiero di D. Hume* (Torino, 1967), pp. 54 ff.

62. See, for example, W. Schuppe, *Grundzüge der Ethik und Rechtsphilosophie* (Breslau, 1881). pp. 304 ff.; A. Reinach, *Zur Phänomenologie des Rechts: die apriorischen Grundlagen des bürgerlichen Rechts*, Munich, 1953 and in 1913 in "Jahrbuch für Philosophie und phänomenologische Forschung," pp. 11 ff., pp. 77 ff.; T. Lipps, *Die ethischen Grundfragen* (Hamburg, Leipzig, 1905), pp. 152–61, 167–70; F. Bassenge, *Das Versprechen. Ein Beitrag zur Philosophie der Sittlichkeit* (Berlin, 1930), pp. 27ff.; D. Ross, *Foundations of Ethics* (Oxford, 1939), p. 77 ff. For the criticism of these and other writers (to whom I add here H. Reiner, *Grundlagen, Grundsätze und Einzelnormen des Naturrechts* [Freiburg im Breisgau, Munich, 1964], p. 50); see also my book *Visioni della giustizia e senso comune*, p. 235 ff.

63. See G. Rensi, *Lineamenti di filosofia scettica* (Bologna, 1921), p. 166.

64. Von Jhering, *Der Zweck im Recht*, Vol. I (Leipzig, 1893), p. 265.

65. Born, *Physik und Politik* (Göttingen, 1960), pp. 16–21.

66. See A. D. Ritchie, "Can Commonsense be Trusted?" in *Essays in Philosophy and Other Pieces* (London, 1948), p. 1.

67. See Sartre, pp. 152–53.

68. See Merleau-Ponty, pp. 472–73.

69. Gerhart Husserl, *Recht und Zeit. Fünf rechtsphilosophische Essays* (Frankfurt, 1955), pp. 10–65.

70. See my books: *Diritto e scienza giuridica nella critica del concreto* (Milan, 1941); *Mito, potere e dialogo; Visioni della giustizia e senso comune.*

71. See also G. Semerari, *Storicismo e ontologismo critico* (Bari, 1960) and *Responsabilità e comunità umana* (Bari, 1960).

72. See E. E. Harris, "Some Reflections on the Nature of Consciousness," in *Atti del XII Congresso Internazionale di Filosofia*, Venice, Sept. 12–18, 1958, V (Florence, 1961), 225. See, regarding my point of view, the article of F. Baroncelli, "Luigi Bagolini: una fenomenologia del discorso politico," in *Ethica* (1968), pp. 142–153.

73. de Jouvenel, *L'art de la conjecture* (Futuribles, Monaco, 1964), pp. 13 ff.

74. Reichenbach, *The Rise of Scientific Philosophy*, p. 236.

75. De Jouvenel, pp. 13 ff.

76. *Ibid.*

77. See my book *La simpatia nella morale e nel diritto* (Torino, 1966) and S. Cotta, "Decisione, giudizio, libertà," in *Rivista internazionale di filosofia del diritto* (1968), pp. 213 ff.

78. De Jouvenel, pp. 13 ff.

79. See Charbonnier, pp. 26–27, 29, 33; Freyre, pp. xiii, xxxii, xxxiii.

80. See Hart, *The Concept of Law* (Oxford, 1961), pp. 87 ff.

81. *Ibid.*, p. 83.

82. Binswanger, *Le rêve et l'existence* (Paris, 1954), p. 88.

83. See J. Macmurray, *The Self as Agent* (New York, 1956), pp. 203–22, *Persons in Relations* (London, 1961), pp. 127–46, and also *Reason and Emotion* (London, 1955), pp. 259–78.

84. Sartre, p. 151.

85. Husserl, pp. 27–65.

86. *Ibid.*, p. 42.

87. What I say here does not preclude that for certain effects and for certain purposes the so-called reductionism may be a useful operative attitude. "Reductionism is not all bad," as says R. S. Summers speaking of "reductionist impulse" in very clear and balanced observations. "Legal Philosophy Today" in R. S. Summers, ed., *Essays in Legal Philosophy* (Oxford, 1968), pp. 10–11. See for another aspect A. Edel, *Method in Ethical Theory* (London, 1963), pp. 173–83.

Language and Human Action

ADAM SCHAFF

I FEEL MORALLY OBLIGED to revert to the problem of general semantics. Some years ago, in my *Introduction to Semantics*, I sharply criticized this school, and yet, apart from those shortcomings about which I then wrote in detail, I realize that the doctrine has certain positive aspects— if only an insistence on the social function of language which is not found elsewhere. I have primarily in mind its observations concerning the influence of language on human behavior. While the weaknesses of general semantics have been subjected to much—and unrestrained— criticism, the valuable stimuli inherent in some of its tenets have received perhaps less than their due.

The thesis with which I am concerned and which can be extrapolated from various statements of general semanticists is simple but heuristically important: human behavior is often conditioned by mental suggestion owing to the orientation of the mind—and, with it, of emotions, volition, etc.—by language. This idea is, of course, my own formulation, and it can be safely asserted that such a thesis has not been explicitly pronounced by any general semanticist. Nevertheless, I maintain that it can be deduced from their works—and I have only put it in moderate terms.

It can be claimed, naturally, that the thesis is far from original. After all, from Herder and Humboldt to the modern theory of the linguistic field in the philosophy of language, and from conventionalism to logical positivism in philosophy, it has been known that the shape of thought is connected with the shape of language—that is, that language affects thinking. And since human behavior is in one way or another associated with thinking, particularly when action is goal-directed, it is obvious that behavior is also, at least indirectly, connected with language and is somehow influenced by it. But obvious as it may seem, this notion was never stated so clearly before—and it is general semantics that has the credit for correcting this condition. *Ex post* the idea may appear banal (as often in the case of very important discoveries), but this does not change the position—particularly since, although it has great heuristic value, it, so far, has been neither fully appreciated nor turned to account in investigating concrete reality.

Anatol Rapaport, certainly one of the most outstanding exponents of general semantics, writes about it as follows:

Grammar deals only with word-to-word relations.... Logic goes further. To a logician, sentences are assertions (if this is true, then that is true).... The semanticist goes further than the logician. To him words and assertions have meaning only if they are related operationally to referents. The semanticist defines not only validity (as the logician does) but also truth. The general semanticist goes the furthest. He deals not only with words, assertions, and their referents in nature but also with their effects on human behaviour. For a general semanticist, communication is not merely words in proper order properly inflected (as for the grammarian) or assertions in proper relation to each other (as for the logician) or assertions in proper relation to referents (as for the semanticist), but all these together, with the chain of "facts to nervous system to language to nervous system to action."[1]

When speaking of general semantics we must always bear in mind that its founder, Alfred Korzybski, was above all concerned with social therapy. It is no accident that his magnum opus is entitled *Science and Sanity*. He actually believed, to the point of obsession, that all ailments are semantogenic in nature. Consequently, what one must do to cure these ailments is to operate skilfully upon the sphere of language—that is, bring home to people the semantic nature of their erroneous convictions, emotions, inhibitions, etc. Hence, his interest in semantics was primarily connected with therapeutic operations designed to preserve social sanity.

But if we ignore this obsessive aspect, what remains is surely of a rational nature—a frequent difficulty in our analyses of general semantics since it often happens that when the weak points of this doctrine have been exposed there remains much that is reasonable and provides food for thought.

This is certainly true of the three basic tenets in the field of the theory of language: the principle of non-identity (the word is not the thing it represents); the principle of non-allness ("the map is not the territory" —that is, the sign cannot claim fully to represent the object); and the principle of the hierarchy of signs (distinction between objective language and metalanguage).

These propositions are by no means original; on the contrary, all of them have been drawn from historically known sources which, incidentally, general semanticists honestly acknowledge. And it is from these principles, particularly the first two, that are derived certain rules concerning the use of language, by means of which people can avoid errors leading to semantogenic disturbances. Thus, it is necessary to index generic names, so as to avoid confusion between the individual and the general (and so as to realize that when we say *Negro* we are always referring to individuals, $Negro_1$, $Negro_2$, etc.); further, all terms and statements should be dated, so as to distinguish between the various phases of phenomena (thus, instead of saying, e. g., *Karl Marx*, we should say *Karl Marx*$_{1844}$, *Karl Marx*$_{1857}$, etc.); finally, all descriptions and evaluations should be accompanied by the phrase "et cetera," so as to make it quite clear that "the map is not the territory"—that is, description is never complete.

It is in general semantics that the phrase "the tyranny of words" was coined—a metaphor expressing the idea that language exercises a decisive influence on human behavior. Emphasis on this idea, which reached the obvious exaggeration typical of the doctrine of semantogenic pathology, is basic to the tendency to reduce social problems (such as communism, fascism, etc.) exclusively to the sphere of language as well. But let us stick to the principle that we are not interested in poking obvious fun at exaggerations and absurdities but rather in the difficult task of finding the rational kernel of ideas—even when it is buried in a heap of chaff. And there is no doubt that the metaphor about the "tyranny of words" has such a rational kernel—as have the rules about the practical use of language designed to overthrow this tyranny.

For a clearer insight into these matters we must first of all examine the implications of the thesis about the sign-character of language. We say that language is a system of signs—and we conceive the word *sign* so broadly that the opponents of this thesis must simply choose another definition as their point of departure. Because of this broad meaning we can interpret linguistic signs as having some specific characteristics by which they can be distinguished as a subclass within the general class of signs. As I wrote in another context, it is the link between the material bearer and meaning which constitutes this specific feature of linguistic signs; this makes them particularly useful in the process of abstraction and, consequently, accounts for the fact that only linguistic signs can function as names.

Let us dwell awhile on this observation and its implications. Linguistic signs, like all other signs, function in the process of communication—beyond which they cease to be signs and are simply material objects or processes. When functioning in the process of human communication they are a necessary element of thinking (what we have in mind in this context is *human* or conceptual thinking) which cannot exist without all kinds of signs. To put it more radically: the process of thinking involves all kinds of signs, but linguistic signs are a necessary element of thinking. I do not intend to argue this point in more detail here since I have already done so elsewhere. But what are the implications of this approach?

When thinking of something we always think by means of signs which represent this "something" (that is, signs which are capable of causing effects in action similar to those of sense perceptions). Now linguistic signs have particular properties in this respect, not only in view of their usefulness in the process of transmitting our thoughts to others but also —an extremely important point—in the sense of their suitability for a generalizing inspection of reality. This is what I had in mind when referring to the specific character of linguistic signs which makes them an indispensable instrument of abstraction at the level of conceptual thinking. Why this is so—and what the mechanism of this abstraction is—can best be explained by the physiology of higher nervous functions; and although its answers so far are, I think, inadequate, it is precisely from this branch of science that we can demand and expect a definite solution.

That each word generalizes is a thesis accepted by various schools of linguistics. This is why the linguistic sign is so important for the process of thinking, but this is also the source of various difficulties—including those which interest us most in this context.

The assertion that each word generalizes should be understood to mean that conceptual thinking, which is always verbal (although this is not always evident and, therefore, not always realized), takes place at a high level of abstraction and generalization. Between thinking and language, intertwined as they are in an inseparable whole, there is mutual interaction. Conceptual thinking is of a generalizing nature because it is effected by means of linguistic sign language which endows thinking with its abstract and generalizing character. But in any case this quality of linguistic sign language is conditioned by the meaning of signs which—in a certain sense of the word *meaning*—are equivalent to thought. Thus, the word establishes in its meaning what is general in things and phenomena. This is a characteristic of the names of things and properties such as *man, table, virtue, redness*, etc.; of actions—*to walk, to eat*, etc.; and finally of all kinds of particles, conjunctions, etc. like *is, or, and*, etc. Consequently, it is a feature of thinking which uses these signs as its instruments. Human thinking has also invariably the character of what is known in psychology as Galtonian photographs; these are obtained by superimposing on the same plate several photographs of objects belonging to the same class (e. g., of a human face or its parts). This means that thinking extrapolates that which is general, in the sense of being common to given things and phenomena. And since that which is general has various shapes, if only because of differences in the selection of elements shared by many things and phenomena, the generality of thinking and language also acquires various shapes. It may, for example, depend on our knowledge of the object which tends to orient our perception and condition our articulation of the world—and so our cognitive generalizations.

It is owing to this generalizing function of language and verbal thinking that what is individual in cognition is both the point of departure and the point of arrival, the result. There is no doubt that sense perception—and thus thinking—begins with individual objects. But equally incontestable, although not so evident and requiring deeper cognitive insights, is the proposition that what we extract from the surrounding reality as individual is the *result* of experience and a cognitive process which is based on a definite language. On this count Wilhelm von Humboldt was perfectly right when he insisted that we think as we speak (adding, however, that we also speak as we think). That which is individual does, it is true, exist objectively, in the onto- logical sense of this word; but epistemologically it is a product of knowl- edge, and in a certain sense of this word we can even say it is a *construct* of knowledge—meaning that what is individual and is in a sense the starting point of our knowledge is always arrived at in conceptual, verbal thinking through what is general, because we cannot think of what is individual without experiencing, in one form or another, the meaning of the proper word, without which we cannot think of anything conceptually.

We cognize what is individual not only through what is general but also by an appropriate modification of what is general. I have in mind the linguistic and intellectual operations which enable us to grasp that which is individual through the intermediary of that which is general and to transmit the contents which have been formed in this manner in the process of communication. The word *tree* generalizes, as do all other words. But we know how to use this and other general words to express something individually concrete. This ability usually is the out- come of a combination of a number of words: each of them is general, but their conjunction results in such an intersection of the various meanings that it becomes specifically individualized. Various degrees of individualization can be achieved by this process, and sometimes, when scientifically important subclasses are involved, we give them special names (e. g., "coniferous tree," or, even lower down in classification, "fir tree," "pine tree," etc.). Individuality here is always obtained by combinations of words—that is, by combinations of general meanings (e. g., "a deciduous tree of the chestnut species, the first on the right in the main avenue, near the entrance to the park"), since individual names are as a rule not used in this field.

One can, of course, imagine a language with a much smaller vocabulary of general words—indeed, one can even cite some examples of such languages being used by communities at a very low level of development (for example, certain languages of the Australian aborigines). They have names for certain fish species, but no word for *fish*; they have individual names for the trees or shrubs growing on the tribe's usual trail, but no general name for *tree* or *shrub*; they have verbs expressing such actions as "riding at a gallop" or "riding at a trot" but no word for *riding*. Such languages have the advantage of concreteness which helps them to avoid the pitfalls of languages at a higher level of generalization—but they have also one basic defect: they are inadequate for abstract reflection about reality, which is an indispensable condition of scientific knowledge. In other words, such a language may be extremely practical and suitable for certain types of action, but it is incapable of expressing —and so also inventing—a theory of relativity, which, of course, makes it inferior to languages with more developed abstracting and generalizing functions. On the other hand, a language exclusively composed of individual signs, which is theoretically possible, would undoubtedly lead to intellectual disaster since it would prevent conceptual thinking and thus paralyze action, based as it is on thinking.

A developed linguistic sign language (of, say, the Indo-European type) is free of this defect. But just because its degree of generalization is big enough to express the individual (with the exception of individual names) through the general, as a specific combination, there emerge other difficulties in the sphere of knowledge and action with which we are concerned in this context. The point is that what is general makes it difficult to cognize what is particular and individual. This is precisely what is emphasized by general semantics—although it does so in relation to analysis of human behavior, and not abstract analysis of the function of language in cognition.

Let us revert to the propositions of general semantics and to the consequent rules concerning the uses of language. They are all directed towards the same end: to avoid the misunderstanding—which affects human behavior—that the meanings contained in a word are a full reflection of reality. Our reactions to words must not be identified with reactions to reality, and we must not infer from our reactions to words that the reality to which they refer is what these reactions make us assume. No, says general semantics, the word is not the thing, the map is not the territory, and the language in which we speak of another language is not identical with it. To avoid these distressing misunderstandings (which can easily become the source of semantic disturbances) it is necessary to concretize language by means of special operations— adding signs to signs—and to study the hierarchy of generality in thinking. Particularly interesting is the rule to which I have already referred: we should always remember that behind the general word (e. g., *Negro*) there are individual names (*Negro$_1$, Negro$_2$*, etc.), which means that this word is the name of a certain class of individuals; otherwise the general name becomes a hypostasis.

It should be borne in mind that general semantics came into the limelight at the time of the rapid advances of Nazism and that its efforts were an attempt to counteract the mythologizing influence of Nazi ideology. The genetic link between this action and reaction is obvious, although I am not sure whether the founders of general semantics were fully aware of this fact.

Years ago, Adolf Hitler in *Mein Kampf* and Alfred Rosenberg in *Der Mythus des XX Jahrhunderts* propounded a cynical theory of propaganda which is, nevertheless, extremely interesting from the point of view of our subject. An idea for which we are fighting, they said, and which we want to be accepted by the masses, should be stubbornly repeated. At first people will reject and even ridicule it, but in the course of time, if we only reiterate it with sufficient persistency, they will get used to it and finally become convinced. This was not only the theory but also the practice of Hitler; and, whether we like it or not, it was successful. In any case it happens much more frequently, although only Hitler was cynical enough to formulate the principle so baldly. In fact this principle involves a serious problem in the field of the influence of language on human behavior.

Let us take a historical example. One of the basic tenets of the Nazi ideology was that the Jews were not only an inferior race but also a particularly pernicious one because they were encumbered with various vicious qualities which made them a source of all social evils. Hence, mankind's happiness depended on the physical extermination of all Jews. How was it possible to secure social approval for this doctrine? In asking this question I am not concerned with finding an explanation for the endorsement given to the savagery of this conclusion but above all for the acceptance of the ideology itself with all its irrational premises and conclusions. And there is no doubt that it was widely accepted—not only by the Germans but also by many of their opponents who conceded Nazis one service—the physical extermination of the Jews. How could this happen, what was the psychological mechanism of this acceptance in the sense of the social psychology of this process? The purely sociological explanation, with its exclusive recourse to the notion of class struggle, etc., is far from satisfactory since what we are interested in is how irrational ideas transform public opinion. These ideas are often by no means prevalent even in societies with some traditions in the field, such as Germany with its tradition of anti-Semitism. This is a purely psychological problem, but it is also connected—and this is what interests us most—with the linguistic sphere.

Let us take the bull by the horns. Linguistic signs are associated not only with concepts but also with stereotypes. While the problem is relatively clear and simple in the case of concepts (if, that is, concepts are identified with the meaning of the word), the question of stereotypes seems a little more complicated. But it is exactly the word-related stereotype which is particularly important in this context and can contribute to the solution of our problem.

Without any claim to precision we can conceive the meaning of the word and the concept (which we identify because of their cognitive contents) as a generalized reflection of reality in human cognition. These are at the same time epistemological categories, and their various names are owing to the fact they they are the result of various types of analysis. The stereotype is also a special reflection of reality, but it has such an admixture of subjective factors—emotional, evaluating, volitional—that it acquires a specific character both with regard to human knowledge and with regard to behavior.

A Dictionary of the Social Sciences, edited by Julius Gould and William L. Kolb, says:

> *Stereotype* denotes beliefs about classes of individuals, groups or objects which are "preconceived," i. e. resulting not from fresh appraisals of each phenomenon but from routinized habits of judgment and expectation. No general statement can be made about the degree or kind of distortion, exaggeration, or simplification manifested in such beliefs.
>
> The term should properly be distinguished clearly from prejudice, for it belongs to the category of beliefs. A *stereotype* cannot, however, be distinguished from other beliefs by asserting its falseness, for there are many examples in the literature which demonstrate at least a kernel of truth in what is called stereotype. Neither can it be identified as an oversimplification of attributes of the external world. Many stereotypes actually present an elaboration of such attributes. Nor does the idea of its organizing function do justice to the variety of usages in which it occurs.... There is, however, one distinguishing element implicit, if not explicit, in all usages of the term. A stereotype is a belief which is not held as a hypothesis buttressed by evidence but is rather mistaken in whole or in part for an established fact.

The term *stereotype*, introduced into the literature by W. Lippman, is understood by him as a preconceived belief about attributes of the external world. According to Lippman, a stereotype serves to organize our experience and to economize our expectations about reality—which involves the danger of premature generalizations. Much in line with this approach is the idea of L. W. Doob who, in his study of propaganda, defines stereotypes as "the knowledge which men imagine they possess." "Doob recognizes," adds the *Dictionary*, "that neither his own nor Lippman's use of the term distinguishes it clearly from concepts in general which have the function of organizing perception."

The *Dictionary*'s analysis can hardly serve as a model of clarity and precision, but it may prove useful for our further argument, if only through its attempt to explain the term *stereotype* and its relation to other categories.

A stereotype, like a concept, is a generalized reflection of reality— and this reflection is impossible without the help of linguistic signs. Where they differ is that the cognitive process which crystallizes into a concept has an objective and descriptive tendency—which, however, does not preclude an emotional or evaluating admixture; on the other hand, the process which results in stereotypes has not only a cognitive but also an evaluating tendency with all its emotional overtones. The borderline is neither clear nor fixed, depending as it does on the kind of concepts and stereotypes which often differ considerably.

The problem which interests us most in this context is primarily connected with the function of language—or, more precisely, the function of the linguistic sign in both cases. It has been pointed out that the existence of both concept and stereotype is organically connected with the word—that they cannot exist without the linguistic sign. But they are also genetically related—that is, a stereotype is born together with a concept; thus, they are genetically connected, although not identical.

There is no thinking without concepts, and this means that there is no thinking without words endowed with definite meanings. But we can think without stereotypes because a stereotype is not a mental-logical but a mental-pragmatic category—that is, it is linked to human action. Thus, stereotypes arise when, and only when, there is evaluating—which is associated with human action in situations involving not only man's cognitive functions but also his emotions, will, etc. This is exactly why we have concepts and stereotypes of an enemy or our own nation, of a hostile or own class, etc.; but, though we have a concept of "number four," we do not possess a stereotype. "A stereotyped number four" is an empty expression, but "a stereotyped German" is not.

We are not aware of the genesis of concepts—they are conveyed to us socially, together with language which is part of our social education. But similarly we are not aware of the origin of stereotypes which we also receive by way of social education. Our likes and dislikes, expressed as they are in our evaluations, are a social product and are transmitted to us, together with language, by the environment in which we are brought up. By the same token this environment tends to form our attitudes—that is, our readiness to behave in a certain way—and our behavior—that is, our reactions to certain situations. Stereotypes include, of course, an individual element which makes for their differentiation—but this is also the case with concepts. However, these individual differences are merely an ornamental appendage to something which is generally accepted and, in this sense, common.

Thus, a word is organically connected not only with the concept but also with the stereotype. In other words, it is organically connected not only with the cognitive but also with the emotional and volitional function. It is a genetic bond of which, in addition, we are not aware except in cases of especial—and penetrating—reflection. It is not easy to tell the conceptual from the stereotypical aspect of the word, and even more difficult to draw a distinct line between them. Actually it seems unlikely that this operation can be carried out in a complete and precise manner since at least some elements of the mental image are common to both aspects.[2]

The position is even more complicated when we enter the sphere of human behavior—that is, actions constituting man's more or less conscious reactions to certain environmental stimuli. Man's behavior is obviously conditioned by his knowledge about the world, which intervenes in his thinking and so in his conscious action. But it is equally evident—although we are loath to admit it either to others or to ourselves—that man's behavior is not less, but perhaps even more, forcefully conditioned by his emotional attitude to things which can dominate his will, even in the face of common sense—and so his knowledge of the world. And it is precisely the stereotype that is the bearer of this emotional attitude; in most cases it is not felt to be a stereotype, and its power is the greater the more completely it tends to blend in our consciousness with the concept. This is where the secret of that notorious "tyranny of words" lies.

The matter is, essentially, a trivial one. We are brought up in a certain environment which, by virtue of its historical experience and other reasons which can be historically traced and analyzed, tends to form certain likes and dislikes. Naturally, stereotypes are not only a matter of prejudices and phobias which affect our attitudes and actions. But undoubtedly these hates play some part, and they are particularly interesting in this context since they shed a glaring light on the problem and at the same time are a grievous aspect of human behavior. Almost at birth—and, in fact, together with language and its attendant knowledge and emotions which are transmitted to us by society, we receive "injections" of love, aversion, or even hate—and these attitudes may operate in us sometimes to the end of our lives. In any case it is difficult, extremely difficult, to get rid of their influence. Depending on time and place, there arise various, positive or negative stereotypes of some nationalities: German, Jew, Ukrainian, Pole; or those of certain occupations: worker, actor, professor, farmer, banker, policeman, etc. Any more detailed analysis of how stereotypes which are fixed in words affect our attitudes and behavior would be laboring the obvious.

This is precisely where general semantics appears with its therapeutic operations in the field of word meanings. It is true that this doctrine has not cleared the ground for its observations and suggestions—if only in the sense of what has been quoted above—but this does not change the sense of its propositions whose aim, be it remembered, is social therapy. Thus, in close association with the tenets and postulates of general semantics, we are brought back to the question of what is general and what is individual in the linguistic sign.

The word is not the thing; the map is not the territory. When we say *Negro* we must remember that this is the name of a class of individual objects and that, in fact, we have to do with individuals—*Negro*$_1$, *Negro*$_2$, etc.—while the general name is a hypostasis. People should be taught this fact by various methods, including the so-called Structural Differential, which, through its holes at different levels and mechanical training in how to insert pegs in the right holes, is supposed to pound into their heads the simple truth that there are various levels of generality and that the class of individuals is something else than the individuals that belong to it.

Will this cure caries, gastric ulcers, or other ailments, as Korzybski maintained? I do not know, but even if it does it is owing to other reasons than those the founder of general semantics had in mind. Similarly, Lourdes water or the laying-on of hands by a miracle worker does not heal because of what is officially claimed, even though it certainly does cure some people. There is no saying how therapy works in neurogenic disorders in which treatment largely depends on human faith, which mobilizes human will. Faith in the pegs of the Structural Differential may be as strong as faith in shamanic incantations—but belief in the consciousness-forming power of the tenets and postulates of general semantics belongs to another sphere and consists of another kind of action.

For, in addition to its influence on our knowledge of the theory of language, which it undoubtedly amplifies in certain respects, it also affects our stereotypes and through them the ideological sphere of our consciousness. And this is how we arrive at another aspect of the problem: the links between language and ideology, and, through their mediation, with man's social activity.

In keeping with general semantics (which in this respect follows in the footsteps of nominalism and can claim some outstanding antecedents —from Francis Bacon, with his struggle against all kinds of idols to the semantic analysis of Tadeusz Kotarbinski, which teaches us how successfully to fight hypostases) we repeat: the word *Negro* is a hypostasis whenever we do not consciously use it as the name of individual objects $Negro_1$, $Negro_2$, etc., since only these objects "exist" in the narrower sense of this word. We are not concerned here with the old controversy between nominalism, realism, and conceptualism; we are primarily interested in the influence of this usage of language on stereotypes.

Suppose that we were born into a white family in the South of the United States. Without a thorough knowledge of American history and an analysis of social relations in that part of the world, it is hardly possible to understand why the white community transmits to a child virtually from birth an aversion to Negroes. The matter is by no means unusual: we need only consider a similar attitude to the Armenians in Turkey or to Jews in many parts of the world—or even, as recent experience has shown, the mutual relations between some Negro tribes in Africa (e. g., the Hausa and the Obi in Nigeria). The fact remains that these attitudes and their resulting behavior are connected with a certain group-stereotype in which all characteristics provoking dislike, contempt, even hate, are concentrated. Now this stereotype is associated with the word; it cannot exist without the word, just as without the word no concept can be formed. When a child learns the language of a given group he at the same time assimilates its knowledge of the world, but also its ways of evaluating this world, its stereotypes. This must be so, because learning a language is not only learning the sounds of speech but also the meanings which are connected with the material bearer—the sound. It is only this unity that forms linguistic signs of which language is composed and which we learn spontaneously when growing up in a given community. These meanings constitute both concepts (with which they are identical) and stereotypes. *And*, be it emphasized, not *or*. Social transmission is not selective in this case, and whatever the pedants who insist on drawing a line between science and ideology may say, it binds them closely together, at any rate genetically, because social practice, which gives birth to language and stimulates its progress, is at the root of objective (relatively, always relatively objective!) knowledge both of the world and of world-evaluating attitudes. And this sphere—the sphere of appraisals and evaluations, which of necessity unites the cognitive with the emotional and volitional function, which gives birth to stereotypes and at the same time is based on them—is precisely the sphere of ideology.

We now have an idea—or at least a rough idea without any claim to precision—of what we mean by *stereotype*. But what do we mean by *ideology*? Before this question is answered we cannot analyze the mutual relations between stereotypes and ideology, and so account for the influence of language on the sphere of ideology.

By *ideology* I mean (as I have written elsewhere) the views held by people about the goals of social development; these are based on a definite system of values and determine their attitudes—that is, their tendencies to behavior in certain situations and their actual behavior in social matters.

This is only one of the possible ways in which this multivocal word can be used—but certainly one in keeping with our intuition of current and scientific language: we refer, for example, to bourgeois and proletarian, capitalist and socialist ideologies, etc. It is quite clear that this interpretation of the word *ideology* presupposes a close link between the cognitive and the emotional-evaluating function in the sphere of social action, at the same time inobtrusively introducing what we have described as *stereotypes*. This is hardly a directly constitutive element with regard to ideology, but indirectly ideology could not dispense with it. Socialist humanism is a well-defined ideology, but this ideology could not have been constituted without the stereotype of "complete" man with his egalitarianism, his sense of brotherhood with regard to other men, etc.—all of which are an integral part of the system of values on which this humanism is based. The position is similar in the case of the Nazi ideology of racism. In more general terms, *every* ideology has among its constituent parts certain stereotypes of human groups, occupations, behaviors, etc., which are associated with the valid system of values. Thus, ideology is not identical with stereotype and the relationship between them is not one of class and subclass, although ideology and stereotypes are closely interconnected and influence each other. For just as stereotypes affect ideology, so ideologies tend to shape social stereotypes. But this is precisely why anyone who infringes upon stereotypes penetrates into the sphere of ideology. This is probably the most important aspect of our problem.

The meaning and role of ideology in social life are so evident that I shall not dwell on them here. But the consequences are tendencies to manipulate or change ideologies when they militate against our objectives. How can ideology be governed or altered?

There are two important elements governing action. One of them is connected with knowledge—with the cognition of reality, particularly social reality. The other is linked to the world of values which controls the social ends we have accepted. While it is true that readiness to accept an ideology is closely connected with a society's knowledge of the world—which means that science deserves respect in the sphere of ideological reflection as well—ideology cannot be reduced to science, and science does not play a decisive role in the development of ideology. In any case, at a given developmental stage of human knowledge, all this depends on the accepted system of values. And how can it be changed? How to convince people that they should embrace another system of values—and, in consequence, another ideology?

A number of answers come to mind, but they can all be reduced to two types of action: a new, plausible ideology can be offered, or the old one successfully attacked. The latter possibility involves the linguistic operations as proposed by general semantics.

An ideology can be undermined only when we have undermined the systems of values on which it is based. But values and evaluations are, as a rule, not directly derived from knowledge and science, although genetically they are connected with them as well. We know that there is no logical transition, in the sense of inference, from the statements of which science is composed to evaluations and normative sentences. Thus, a system of values can be undermined only by changes in people's convictions and attitudes. Here again there can be various modes of action: some of them are constructive—a new way of thinking is imposed on people by appeals to their sense of morality; and others are destructive since they are designed to destroy the old stereotypes and attitudes. As we have said, an attack on stereotypes is an attack on ideology, simply because through stereotypes we can indirectly get at the system of values.

The persistence of stereotypes is easy to explain, above all in psychological terms; nor is there a single or infallible way of changing them. On the other hand much can be achieved by acting on their verbal substratum.

A stereotype, as has been pointed out, is not only associated with the word without which it cannot be born or exist. Another source of its influence is that the borderline between it and the concept tends to be blurred in human consciousness. As a result its subjective character finds an ally in the objectivity of knowledge embodied as it is in the concept. Hence, the conclusion that its mystification should be destroyed by proving that the objectivism of the stereotype is purely illusory—that it is something different from the concept. Difficult as it may be, the task can be accomplished precisely through the sphere of language.

When we say *Negro* we, in fact, mean a class of individuals: $Negro_1$, $Negro_2$, etc., while $Negro_1$ is a different individual from $Negro_2$. The word is not the thing; the map is not the territory. These statements now appear in a new light, since they have displayed their hidden meaning. They begin to look quite respectable in their new guise of stereotype-destroyers. For although the battle against social evil cannot be reduced exclusively to semantogenic considerations, and although influencing stereotypes through the intermediary of language is neither simple nor quick, it still seems certain that this is a mode of action which must not be overlooked or neglected in the so-called ideological struggle (and this is what, in the final analysis, is the crux of the matter). And whoever objects that this way of action is slow and ineffective should only think of the violent resistance to similar operations on the part of those against whose ideology they are directed.

Let us consider the matter of differentiating individuals when speaking of their class. Epistemologically this is an obvious platitude; yet I maintain that, in the ideological sphere, it will meet with strong resistance on the part of the representatives of every militant ideology. Rallying forces for combat calls for a unified militant attitude and hatred of the enemy, and this requirement is counteracted by recognition of exceptions and, still more, of the diversity of evaluations. Epistemologically there is little value in the statement that there are various communists, capitalists, Germans, Jews, or Negroes. But it becomes less of a truism when we reach the sphere of ideology: here evaluations must be homogeneous, and there is no room for differentiation—unless perhaps, by way of exception, for private use.

Thus, the theory of semantic disturbances contains a rational idea which must not be forgotten even in the heat of the severest criticism of this strange doctrine. This idea, with all its simplicity, is extremely important: the behavior of man, who is always a social individual, is co-created by language, and so by the culture of the society of which his language is part. And this is why human behavior can and should be influenced, and one means is through operations in the field of language.

NOTES

1. "What is Semantics?," in *Language, Meaning and Maturity*, ed. by S. I. Hayakawa (New York, 1954), p. 14.

2. It may be interesting to note that there is a certain analogy between this conception of a dual (conceptual and stereotypical) function of language and H. S. Sullivan's distinction of a *parataxis* and a *syntaxis* stage in the development of a child in which language plays such an important role.

Value of Authenticity and
Value of Revelation of the Sign

DANIEL B. CHRISTOFF

Translated by the author and Merritt H. Moore

L IKE TRUTH, authenticity is not only a value; it is also one of the characteristics of value which may be singled out for attention when it is considered from a particular point of view. Where do we encounter authenticity and truth better than in the capacity some objects have of being more or less able to represent others, of "having value for something else"?[1] Having vicarious value is peculiarly the distinctive mark of the sign, and as a consequence, semeiology must take value into consideration, whether its practitioners are aware of this fact or not. As we shall see beginning with its founder, Ferdinand de Saussure, they have been.

First of all, it may be noted that such characteristics as authenticity and "to have value for" (*valoir pour*) are fundamental to value, and their extension is unlimited. They are fundamental because the opposition implicit between vicarious value and intrinsic value (*valoir pour soi*) is different from the well-known opposition between value through something (*valoir par autre chose*)—what is called relative value —and value through itself (*valoir par soi*)—what is called absolute value —and makes it possible to relegate the latter to metaphysics. Their extension is without limit because these characteristics are peculiar to all relations and to relations only, for if "to have value for" is characteristic of the representative, of the significative, it is of the representative in relation to what is represented, of the significative in its relation to what is signified; this characteristic is germane to systems and to the elements of systems which are related to other systems and to the elements of these systems. Therefore, all logical and mathematical sets, all classifications and systems of knowledge, just as all languages, and in general all groups of signs have this character of "having value for" (*valoir pour*). For that reason it is necessary first of all to draw attention to certain characteristics: that of belonging to a system, and the distinction between that which signifies from what is signified, with neither interchange nor substitution.

Strictly speaking, vicarious value is not a characteristic of many things. To be sure, one thing may be given instead of another, one thing may be worth, i. e., equal in value to another, but only with reference to a system. Even more than being in reference to a system, it is the belonging to, the integration with an appropriate system, which makes it possible for an element of the system to be equal in value to something extraneous to the system. It is, in fact, the belonging to a system which permits differentiation, discrimination—a fundamental trait of value: in fact, difference makes possible classification, establishment, and distinction of relations with respect to the terms of the system, on the one hand, and the originality and uniqueness of value, on the other hand.

This means that we are not treating "to have value for" here as the possibility of exchange or substitution; between two or more meanings there is no equivalence other than that which may be explicitly established and maintained by a definition (thus taking the propositional definition for the clearly defined concept—setting up an equivalence between a proposition and a term); the equivalence here is not given, it is posited. There is no interchange among signs, nor between signs and things or ideas, nor between signs and their tokens or symbols. In particular we are not now considering value from the point of view of economics, any more than from the point of view of the common measure, or standard, of the "price" of each thing, or of the single quantitative valuation to which everything may be reduced; in other words, in the case of a sign, such as money, there is no representation, signification, or value.

On the one hand, the peculiar quality of that which signifies, or of that which represents—be it a flag, or even a diplomatic agent—is never to be confused with what is represented, and this difference—ordered by the appurtenance of the one to the other in its appropriate system, for example, words and ideas, language and the world—is essential in the relation of representation and signification; this is because the flag cannot be mistaken for the law, or duty, or the country that it represents, even though it truly symbolizes them. What is more, it is the very impossibility of confusion of the sort indicated above that makes it possible for a word to express the quality of the thing which is sometimes base, sometimes noble, so that its value can change from one system to another with no danger of confusion: contrary to a belief too summarily accepted, the magic formula is not to be confused with the act it is supposed to produce.

On the other hand, the sign, as such, designates without confusion, in a non-substitutionary manner (in a way in which substitution is impossible), either that the object is its "adequation" or essence, or it is the individual existence with its real properties. But the sign, a relation between the word and the idea, sometimes only *designates* an object, the absence of which is unimportant, and sometimes *indicates* the object and imputes, recalls, or suggests its *presence*. In the first case it is addressed to the understanding, and it must not be equivocal: its function is significative, designative, and will be said to be instrumental; in the second case it is addressed to the imagination: it has a significative, evocative function. It is still observed that depending upon the object, and also upon the sign, a "good sign," a good "to have value for," does not bring together to the same degree the two designative and significative functions, being on the one hand an *authentic* sign, and on the other more of an evocator, one which *reveals* or discloses. Nevertheless, it precludes neither of these functions, as we might be led to believe by our provisional and too summary distribution (some signs being applied to the understanding, others to the imagination), as if a scientific and technical symbol on the one hand and a poetic and religious on the other hand somehow differ "by the nature of things." Could such a general delineation be established, it would be because the definition of the first signs—those which designate or denote (*désignants*)—unites them into a single system, while the second—those which reveal or disclose (*révélants*)—belong to a much more complex set of systems. This double denotative and evocative function can be observed in various signs, but nowhere is it more closely joined than in the signs of language.

That is why, ignoring any other kind of signs—pictures, emblems, reproductions, or certificates—and also anything which can become a sign —fetishes, or objects crystallized by memory, from the "sociological" or "psychological" point of view—we shall examine the singular value of the language of signs. But we must state precisely that the value in question here is not simply the greater or lesser perfection of the evocative or indicative function, but rather the always singular, and so often unexplained character on which that perfection depends. Moreover, there is a great advantage in making this distinction, if one has no wish to be content with value-perfection, whether relative or absolute, and to its well-known a priori involvements, but to enter further into its analysis. But an ambition of this sort, following such great efforts and long traditions in the fields of literary and then linguistic analysis, will seem inordinate, and the difficulty in overcoming it will require nothing less than a great deal of work.

In the field of semeiology the analytical contribution outlined by Ferdinand de Saussure is a great help. The Genevan linguist used to define language as "a system of pure values that is determined by nothing beyond the momentary condition of the terms" (*Cours de linguistique générale*, 1916, p. 116). We see immediately that the notion of system permeates the notion of value. Then the linguistic sign is defined as a combination of concept and acoustical image, both sign and image being integrated into a system. The sign itself is not isolated, and it has meaning only in relation to other signs, so that the value of the sign results from the simultaneous presence of other signs. Whereas the word, the sign, may be exchanged—but not compared—with an idea whose nature is dissimilar, it can be compared—but not exchanged—with other words or signs, and, hence, this comparison holds among similar values. Now sounds and concepts are defined and differentiated in their respective systems. The combining, in signs, of the system of differences of sounds and the system of differences of ideas in which all the elements are defined differentially, negatively, give rise to the system of values. The elements of systems of that which is signified and that which signifies are defined differentially, negatively, in their respective systems, but their combination is a positive fact; among combinations that are compared there are no longer differences, but distinctions, oppositions which, in their turn, imply phonetic and conceptual differences. Here difference plays an essential role in systems, but it makes possible still more essential correlation between combinations, and, therefore, between signs: as Saussure has written, "the peculiar characteristic of the linguistic institution is precisely that of maintaining the parallelism between these two kinds of differences."

An analysis of this sort remains no more than a sketch, or outline, when compared with the changing requirements of linguistics, which is continually being improved. Nonetheless, it preserves the exceptional merit of establishing a relation at once subtle and firm between sign and value, and in that way it signalizes and discloses a characteristic which is peculiar to value. It makes it possible to establish once more that it is preferable to conceive of value "in the plural," in its irreducibility—without denying that this irreducibility is connected with (but in a different way in each language and, in all probability, in every time) differences which are themselves exact and components of systems, those of sounds and those of ideas.

However, we believe it is necessary to maintain the inclusive distinction of the indicative and the expressive functions of signs for the purpose of making evident two ways of distinguishing value, neither of which admits of a general standard. First, authenticity is the characteristic of terms which indicate something—for instance, a provision in a will, or an account which states "facts," for example, by a witness, or still more the record of an agreement, discussion, or experience. But from the point of view of denoting, or relating (values of exactness, precision, and honesty), authenticity adds something which might be called the origin, but which is clearly more than the origin, the presence of the subject, the context, or the network of relations which unites several subjects. To consider "simple" cases, some terms, for example, include a promise, a token, or an identifying mark, which are definite because they are purely conventional. Such is the case with passwords, or even the terms—or groups of letters—of coded messages which are filed as such—whether secret and peculiar to a certain human group or public like international codes. Such things are still abbreviations which take the place of words. The very uneven importance of authenticity is discovered in each example. But in all these cases authenticity plays a preponderant role; in certain cases (the password), the term selected has no other value than that.

Such values are irreducible, sometimes because terms are purely conventional and are agreed upon because as such they are discriminating in their function of authentication; at other times—in the matter of a literary work, for example—because the origin must be unique. It is clear that other comparable signs exist, not agreed upon from case to case, whose value of authenticity is beyond substantiation, such as countersigns, slogans, or the formula for an oath. Signs of this sort, whether differentiated or not, can be protected by law; and the misuse of them is sometimes punishable, while the abuse of others—of slogans, for example—remains unpunishable. It is true that, at least psychologically and sociologically, their content may be more or less rich, in direct proportion to the degree that they differ from passwords. They do not apply to only a completely determined case for a limited time.

But beyond conventional and ceremonial terms the designative function—and the significative and expressive function of language—preserve their originality, the former being protected to some extent, the latter being devoid of protection. The terms of language, except for some strictly defined circumstances, are not protected and their misuse is indefensible—ranging from perjury to mental reservation, from falsehood to metaphor. And if they are not protected it is not because they have no value, but—as the misuse itself makes evident—precisely because of their value.

It will first be observed that if signs had only a designative function, they would be limited to that function, and in that sense they could be said to be purely instrumental. According to this way of regarding them, words would have the single function of denoting or designating; and, by definition, the danger of equivocation would be excluded from such a system of signs. In such a case the value of a term would be judged on whether it denoted without equivocation; an acceptable term would be one which, being strictly defined, would denote one object, and that object only. It is obvious that such terms would be purely stipulated.

Nevertheless, it must be noted that the reference of the sign to the signified cannot be entirely isolated (even in an entirely conventional language). The term may refer only as a function of other references, and that, as Saussure observed, in the two systems of ideas and acoustical images; in a word each term, although well defined as far as it itself is concerned (and although it is possible to define and formulate new terms indefinitely), even in this case it would have value only as related to other terms; each term, then, even though defined in isolation, would be a term in a system. The relation among the terms of a system is entirely defined only in a scholarly language, or among new symbols in a system—yet even these terms in the language are developed with the aid of elements borrowed from the roots of already existing basic languages, or made up through the use of syllables, or of systems of prefixes and suffixes which usually have their proper or conventional signification already—or even of initial letters.

With respect to such particulars it may be said again that the sign is not confused with what it designates, and that it is substituted for the thing only as a result of this distinction. Moreover, we see that the sign designates the thing only when the latter is "absent" (actually or possibly); but in its designative function it does not portray the thing expressively when it is present, it does not make it appear, nor does it hold it further away in order to put it into perspective. The designative sign often makes possible the dispensing with the presence of the thing. Even in language an initial or abbreviation often permits dispensing with words, and does so specifically because the sign which is substituted for it does not completely replace the thing.

But the case just considered of purely functional designative and indicative signs is—except in the case of artificially constructed languages—theoretical and abstract. It is almost always true that signs perform the twofold indicative and significative function that we first called attention to. In being significative the sign is amenable to interpretation, and that more especially since it is important that the two functions not be confused. Consequently, it will be much more difficult to judge the value of the sign.

As long as it signifies, the function of the term is not only to designate, but to exhibit the object, to bring about the experience of the thing, making it share in what it designates. Here, more than in designation alone, it is essential that the sign remain distinct from what is signified —that it not be mistaken for it—and, despite what may have been said about it, that is true of magical signs, of words used to invoke and to conjure, as well as ordinary words. Certainly instances are to be seen of a sign assuming the sacred or profane character of the object which it designates—its beauty, its ugliness, or its vulgarity. The first consciousness of a spoken language contains an awareness of the trivial character in signs of the trivial, or it carries over to signs taboos which affect things.

An expressive sign stimulates experience; it calls for the presence of the thing that it signifies; it must, for example, render God present; it must bring whoever perceives it to the condition for receiving this presence; at least it brings this presence into consideration. Hence, we must not take the sign "in vain" or in a mistaken sense—otherwise would we not waste this power? If such interdictions are stated, it is because signs cannot very well defend themselves—this was called attention to earlier —as things do by the obstacle that they oppose; and with respect to rules of usage, those of language, often subtle, are more easily broken than those concerning the use of things and recipes or prescriptions. In this sense a "good" sign assumes a value of authenticity in relation to existence, a value that a sign which is simply indicative does not have, even if its authenticity lies in its relation to the system. A valuable sign, precisely because it precludes confusion with the signified, portrays this in such a way that equivocation—always latent in signification—may be overcome. But presence is not a simple notion; intimate, proximate, and remote or allusive presence must be distinguished. Signs may be combined to bring the described object close, to feel what is felt only by another—for example, in the theater—to make personal for the spectator the feeling of the heroes. But they may also be so combined as to give a neutral, unemotive representation, as is required in scientific reports. They may even be combined so as to express being in the actual remoteness which may be conducive to experience when it is a matter of making a distant, exotic, or historical object felt. Finally, and above all, the representation of the supernatural creates a remoteness which is not contrary to inner experience, either by weakening an existing expression or by partially evoking it—thus, Yahweh's name is not written out in full—or, on the contrary, by magnifying and exalting it. So we see that a "good" sign does not simply signify and provoke a presence; it also signifies the relation to the speaker and to the interlocutor who joins in the conversation, and, thus, to both of them with the object of experience, a relation which creates a whole experience with the object and the subject. In that signification in which signs are not wanting in presence and remoteness, they show clearly that the sign does not designate the thing, but the relation to the thing and experience, the "intention" towards the thing. And that is why, through the system of what signifies, the sign must be sufficiently stable to remain clearly distinct from the thing signified.

So we see that the sign which, by definition, must not be mistaken for what is signified, and which must somehow exclude the thing signified from itself in order to determine its place in the world, may assume very much more complex functions.

The false sign and the false arrangement of signs must at least be mentioned here. What is properly called error may certainly be omitted and, even more surely, may be deliberate deceit (which on the contrary has played its part in pseudoauthenticity). But games are played with signs which result in things other than those they signify as being experienced. These are games of sham or pretense, of ambiguity, which "show" something in order to "hide" it, which hide in order to display —these are the games of flirtation (the simplest example) but also of irony and of the communication of feelings which cannot bear direct and immediate expression. Moreover, with irony, there are pseudonyms —as found in Kierkegaard, for example—and even the masks or pretenses called for by Nietzsche, as well as every sort of revealed and revealing deceit. Signs of this sort may create a perspective, a proportion, an opening toward the ineffable; they may do so explicitly, as in Platonic comparisons of knowledge and of indirect or direct vision, by reflection or by Idea.

The same thing may also be done by a poetic image which suggests meanings that bring hyperbole into being, and often add ambiguity to hyperbole, stimulating poetic creation in the reader. In fact, the image may prompt simple or multiple significations. So the allegory—a figure of speech, narrative, or significative description—is more or less in significations which are restrained, linear, or capable of being interpreted only through a single key. The comparison "his eyes were like suns," because wholly explicit, gives the sought for signification. But the metaphor "My eyes, my eyes wide with eternal clearness"[2] expands the interpretation much more than it directs or imposes it. Above all the poetic symbol leaves the imagination free ("Delirium with crystal fingers") in such a way that the most powerful images—the most evocative, the "best" ones—are those which open the widest field to dreams and the imagination, without doing more than open it, barely directing at the outset, using economically all the ambiguity of the forms that it may let appear and which render the free signification concrete. In this case it is evident that the sign is no more than an appeal or impulse, and that the best is that which gives the impulse which is at once the most lively and the most free.

The last examples quoted are not derived from simple terms but from the play of terms which make up the significant unity of the sign. There is good reason for underscoring at one and the same time the importance of this unity and the role that each term suggesting a sign may play in it. After all, this is how it is in ordinary language: terms are arranged in it according to systems because they belong to types and are part of systems which interact. Especially since the work of Ferdinand de Saussure we know well enough that the attention of linguists is focused on these relations among the terms of a system, and what has been called in a precise sense the structure of the language—a system of acoustical images, a system of concepts whose terms are definite, but also a system made up of signs, each of which unite image and concept. We also know that in systems which are organized in this way, in which the component elements preserve similar relations among themselves—for example, in structures of kinship according to Lévi-Strauss—similar means of communication may be revealed.

But in order to stay with what is properly called language, and from the one point of view of the value of signs which is our concern, it may be added that syntactical relations also play a considerable role. They contribute to maintaining the separation of systems of things which signify and systems of things signified, and in that way assure reference to what is signified without confusion with that which signifies. So far as phonic confusion or clarity is concerned, we run across syntactical incoherence or correction even in relatively undeveloped languages. A "good" sign—one which designates explicitly and one which indicates a presence or makes it known—relates in a twofold manner to phonetic and conceptual systems set up on the basis of difference; but the syntactical order introduced, thanks to these differences again, makes possible constantly tested differential relations which contribute to the distinction between signs themselves and what is signified, and thereby they contribute to authenticity and expression.

It is sufficient to say that a sign may not be more isolated from other signs than a term from other terms or a concept from other concepts. Nevertheless, the relation of the sign to what is signified endures in its originality; it is observed and verified only in the action which relates it to the thing, to what is signified, in its intentionality. For that reason the values of authenticity and revelation and their differences—that linguistic, syntactical, and conceptual analyses help to make precise—are not understood through these analyses themselves. The latter ones particularly do not include the importance of multivocity and ambiguity to the authenticity and suggestiveness of the expression; they do not exhaust the reality of the image.

In order to approximate the value of authenticity and of revelatory expression in the sign, the twofold relation which constitutes it must be considered—relations of things to concepts on the one hand, and relations to significative systems on the other. The sign, as it bears on the thing signified, on the world, has an intentionality; and it yields only a sketch or profile of the thing in proportion to its use; however, these sketches may be organized in such a way that they seem to present the thing itself, not simply because they designate it, but even more because they express it. So they are bearers of evidence—which, incidentally, explains why people yield so complacently to transferring to the sign itself what the presence of the thing bears with it. But, on the other hand, the significant things form among themselves a system whose structure is constantly given life and repeatedly put to the test; they give us the best known structure. For that reason it is under this structure and through it that we see the world itself as a significant reality in its entirety, and we see that poets and philosophers can say that the world speaks to man and his predicament; in this relation in which the world is revealed to man, authenticity no longer signifies the explicit conformity of the sign to the thing, but the very nature of the relation, of the sign, that binds it closely to the authenticity with which it expresses not alone the world but man.

We just now recalled that, thanks to their structure, various systems of exchange may function as a signifying language, and, above all, invariably putting men who express themselves by them in relation to each other. But the world itself may be sensed as an aggregate of signs by him who lives in the world, once the designative and simply indicative or instrumental functions of the language which separate him from things have been brought into order and the signs assume for him their revelatory value and their true authenticity. Then the poet may say:

> Nature is a temple where pillars alive
> Sometimes utter confused words;
> There man walks across the forest of symbols
> Which watch him with familiar glances.[3]

NOTES

1. *Valoir pour autre chose* may be translated as *representative* or *vicarious value*. From the context it seems that the latter might be less equivocal. Therefore, the phrase *valoir pour autre chose* will be translated *vicarious value* (translators' note).

2. Baudelaire, "La beauté," from *Les Fleurs du Mal*, XVII.

3. Baudelaire, "Correspondences," from *Les Fleurs du Mal*, IV.

The Bibliography
of Robert S. Hartman

DISSERTATION

"Can Field Theory be Applied to Ethics?" Ph.D. Dissertation, North-western University, 1946.

BOOKS AND MANUALS

Author

Profit Sharing Manual. Columbus, Ohio: Council of Profit Sharing Industries, 1948.

Axiología Formal: La Ciencia de la Valoración. Mexico City: Universidad Nacional Autónoma de México, 1957.

Die Partnerschaft von Kapital und Arbeit: Theorie und Praxis eines neuen Wirtschaftssystems. Opladen-Cologne: Westdeutscher Verlag, 1958.

La Estructura del Valor: Fundamentos de la Axiología científica. Mexico City–Buenos Aires: Fondo de Cultura Económica, 1959.

La Participacion de Utilidades en Mexico. Mexico City: Asesores de Pensiones, 1963.

La Ciencia del Valor. Mexico City: Universidad Nacional Autónoma de México, 1965.

El Conocimiento del Bien: Crítica de la Razón Axiológica. Mexico City–Buenos Aires: Fondo de Cultura Económica, 1965.

El Inventario de Valores Hartman. Mexico City: El Manual Moderno, 1967.

The Structure of Value: Foundations of Scientific Axiology. Carbondale: Southern Illinois University Press, 1967, 1969.

The Hartman Value Inventory. Boston: Miller Associates, 1967; Austin: Axiometrics Incorporated, 1969. Translations in Spanish, German, Swedish, Japanese, and Hebrew.

The Hartman Value Profile. Alcoa, Tenn.: Axiometric Testing Service, 1970.

Manual de Interpretación del Inventario de Valores Hartman. Mexico City: Servicios Psicoaxiológos, 1970.

Research Manual of the Hartman Value Profile. Alcoa, Tenn.: Axiometric Testing Service, 1970.

La Situación Moral: Fundamentos de la Teleología Científica. Mexico City–Buenos Aires: Fondo de Cultura Económica, 1972.

La Estructura del Valor Intrínseco: Introducción Axiológica a la Etica y la Estética. Mexico City–Buenos Aires: Fondo de Cultura Económica, 1972.

Contributor

"Can Field Theory be Applied to Ethics?" *Summaries of Doctoral Dissertations.* Evanston: Northwestern University Press, 1946, pp. 168–72.

Introduction to *Hitler in Our Selves*, by Max Picard. Chicago: Henry Regnery, 1947, pp. 13–23.

"Cassirer's Philosophy of Symbolic Forms," *The Philosophy of Ernst Cassirer*, Library of Living Philosophers, pp. 299–333. Evanston: Northwestern University Press, 1949. German translation, pp. 187–228.

Introduction to *Profit Sharing: Democratic Capitalism in American Industry* by Kenneth M. Thompson. New York: Harper and Brothers, 1949.

"The Analytic and the Synthetic as Categories of Inquiry," edited by Albert Aevy, *Perspectives in Philosophy*, pp. 55–78. Columbus: Ohio State University Press, 1953.

"Value Propositions," *The Language of Value*, edited by Ray Lepley, pp. 197–231, 337–42, 352–74. New York: Columbia University Press, 1957.

"The Science of Value," *New Knowledge in Human Values*, edited by A. Maslow, pp. 13–37, 233–35. New York: Harper and Brothers, 1958.

"General Theory of Value," *Philosophie: Chronique des années 1949–1955*, edited by Raymond Klibansky, II, 1–39. Florence: Nuova Italia, 1958.

"The Revolution Against War," *Critique of War*, edited by Robert Ginsberg, pp. 310–43. Chicago: Henry Regnery, 1970.

"Fundamental Terms of Ethics," *Encyclopaedia of Relevant Knowledge* (New York, in preparation).

"Fundamental Terms of Value Theory," *Encyclopaedia of Relevant Knowledge* (New York, in preparation).

"Philosophy in the Americas," preface to Paul Kurtz, *American Philosophy in the Twentieth Century*, Spanish edition. Buenos Aires, Mexico: Fondode Cultura Economica, 1972.

Translator

Strindberg, August. *Der Sohn der Magd.* Zurich: Büchergilde Gutenberg, 1936. (Swedish into German.)

Hegel, G. W. F. *Reason in History: A General Introduction to the Philosophy of History.* New York: Liberal Arts Press, 1953. (German into English.)

Coing, Helmut. *El Sentido del Derecho.* Mexico City: Universidad Nacional Autónoma de México, 1959. (German into Spanish, with José Luis González.)

Aster, Ernst von. *La Filosofía del Presente.* Mexico City: Universidad Nacional Autónoma de México, 1964. (German into Spanish, with Elsa Frost.)

Stebbing, L. Susan. *Introducción Moderna a la Lógica.* Mexico City: Universidad Nacional Autónoma de México, 1965. (English into Spanish, with José Luis González.)

Kant, Immanuel. *Logic.* Indianapolis: Bobbs-Merrill, Liberal Arts Press, 1972. (German into English, with Wolfgang Schwarz.)

PAMPHLETS

Die amerikanische Produktivität und der Faktor 'Mensch'. Zurich, Switzerland: H. S. Stokar, No. 709, 1951.

Ertragsbeteiligung in U.S.A. Cologne: Deutsches Industrieinstitut, No. 24, Dec. 3, 1951.

Theoretische Grundlagen der Gewinnbeteiligung. Wirtschaftspolitische Gesellschaft von 1947, Nov. 7, 1952.

The Measurement of Value. Crotonville-Ossining, New York: The General Electric Company, Advanced Management Course, Apr. 29, 1959.

ARTICLES

"Prime Number and Cosmical Number," *Philosophy of Science*, IX, 2 (Apr., 1942), 190–96.

"Profit Sharing: A Moral Reformation," *Vital Speeches of the Day*, Aug. 15, 1947.

"The Council of Profit Sharing Industries," *America*, Oct. 11, 1947, pp. 41–43.

"Profit Sharing: Philosophy, Economics, and Technique," *Surplus Record*, Jan., Mar., 1948, pp. 32–58.

"Profit Sharing: Its Place in the Free Enterprise System," *Stores*, Apr., 1948.

"The Logic of Profit Sharing," *Social Progress* (Board of Christian Education, Presbyterian Church, Philadelphia), May, 1948.

"The Moral Situation: A Field Theory of Ethics," *Journal of Philosophy*, XLV, No. 11 (May 20, 1948), pp. 413–20.

"Is Ethics as a Science Possible?" *Tenth International Congress of Philosophy* (Amsterdam), Aug. 11–18, 1948, I, 485–87.

"Profit Sharing: Democracy's Answer," *Journal of Retail Traders' Association of New South Wales* (Sydney, N.S.W.), Feb., 1949.

"The Council of Profit Sharing Industries," *Industrial and Labor Relations Review* (Cornell University), Mar., 1949.

"Employee Capitalists," *Trusts and Estates*, Mar., 1949.

"The Epistemology of the A Priori," *Philosophy and Phenomenological Research*, IX, No. 4 (June, 1949), 731–36.

"*Vinstdelningens Plats i den Fria Företagsamheten*," *Arbetarliberalen* (Stockholm), Oct., 1949.

"The Task of Value Research," *First Report of the Committee for Cooperative Research in Values* (Wayne State University), 1950.

"Value Analysis of Justice Frankfurter's Gobitis Decision," *Second Report of the Committee for Cooperative Research in Values* (Wayne State University), 1950.

"The Teaching of Ethics," *The Teaching of Philosophy: The Proceedings and Addresses of the Conference on the Teachings of Philosophy* (Cleveland), 1950.

"Is a Science of Ethics Possible?" *Philosophy of Science*, XVII, No. 3 (July, 1950), pp. 238–46.

"*Den Goda Viljans Metod*," *Arbetarliberalen* (Stockholm), Oct., 1950.

"Profit Sharing," *Research and Technical Report 7* (Industrial Relations Center, University of Minnesota), Nov., 1950.

"The Unique Role of the Church in the World to Come," *Vital Speeches of the Day*, Dec., 1950, pp. 113–18.

"Value Analysis of Legal Decisions," *Ohio State Law Journal*, XII (1951), 23–35.

"The Secretary of Peace," *The Christian Community*, Mar., 1951, pp. 6–10.

"A Logical Definition of Value," *Journal of Philosophy*, XLVIII, No. 13 (June 21, 1951), pp. 413–20.

"Anthropology and Scientific Method," *American Anthropologist*, LIII, No. 4 (Oct.–Dec., 1951), pp. 591–93.

"*Gewinnbeteiligung in Amerika*," *Wirtschaft und Sozialpolitik*, Oct. 15, 1951.

"*Gewinnbeteiligung in der amerikanischen Wirtschaft*," *Recht und Arbeit*, Nov., 1951, pp. 401–404.

"*Grundlagen und Praxis der Ertragsbeteiligung in U.S.A.*," *Arbeitsgemeinschaft zur Förderung der Partnerschaft in der Wirtschaft*, Nov., 1951.

"*Vinstandelssystemets Principer och Praktiska Uppbygnad*," *Svensk Handel*, Nov. 31, 1951, pp. 505–508.

"*Gewinnbeteiligung der Arbeiter*," *Das ganze Deutschland*, Dec. 15, 1951.

"Research in the Logic of Value," *Graduate School Record* (Ohio State University), V, No. 4 (1952), 6–8.

"*Vinstdelning: Samarbete mellan Arbetstagare och Företagsledning i fria Företag*," *Arbetarliberalen*, Mar., 1952.

"*Die menschliche Person als Ausgangspunkt sozialer Erfindungen*," *Sozialer Fortschritt*, Aug., 1952, pp. 181–84.

"*Philosophische Grundlagen industrieller Beziehungen*," *Wirtschaftspolitische Blätter*, Nov. 1, 1952.

"*Theoretische Grundlagen der Gewinnbeteiligung*," *Mensch und Arbeit*, Nov. 15, 1952.

"The Language of Science and the Language of Value," *Eleventh International Congress of Philosophy*, 1953.

"Group Membership and Class Membership," *Philosophy and Phenomenological Research*, XIII, No. 3 (Mar., 1953), pp. 353–70.

"The Challenge of Peace," *Ohio State University Monthly*, July, 1953; also *Vital Speeches of the Day*, July 15, 1953.

"The Analytic, the Synthetic and the Good: Kant and the Paradoxes of G. E. Moore," *Kant-Studien*, XLV, No. 4 (1953–54), pp. 67–82; XLVI, No. 1 (1954–55), pp. 3–18.

"*La creación de una ética científica*," *Diánoia: Anuario de Filosofía*, I (Universidad Nacional Autónoma de México, 1955), 205–35.

"*Niveles del lenguaje valorativo*," *Diánoia: Anuario de Filosofía*, II (Universidad Nacional Autónoma de México, 1956), 254–69.

"Value, Fact and Science," *Philosophy of Science*, XXV, No. 2 (Apr., 1958), pp. 97–108.

"Value Theory as a Formal System," *Kant-Studien*, 50, No. 3 (1958–59), 287–315.

"*El conocimiento del valor: La teoría de los valores a mediados del siglo XX*," *Diánoia: Anuario de Filosofía*, IV (Universidad Nacional Autónoma de México, 1958), pp. 105–41.

"*Aspectos éticos de los Satélites*," *Cuadernos Americanos*, No. 100 (1958), pp. 183–200.

"*Crítica Axiológica de la ética de Kant*," *Revista Mexicana de Filosofía*, No. 1 (1958), pp. 75–84.

"*La diferencia lógica entre la filosofía y la ciencia*," *Diánoia: Anuario de Filosofía*, V (Universidad Nacional Autónoma de México, 1959), pp. 72–95.

"Cuatro pruebas axiológicas del valor infinito del hombre," Examen, No. 9 (Mexico City, Nov.–Dec., 1959), pp. 45–57.

"Axiología y semántica: un ensayo sobre la medición del valor," Diánoia: Anuario de Filosofía, VI (Universidad Nacional Autónoma de México, 1960), 44–77.

"El Humanismo de Samuel Ramos," Revista de Filosofía de la Universidad de la Plata, No. 9 (1960), pp. 71–78.

"Investigación sobre la lógica del valor," Gaceta del Fondo de Cultura Economica, 1960.

"Sputnik's Moral Challenge," Texas Quarterly, III, No. 3 (Autumn, 1960), pp. 9–23.

"The Logic of Description and Valuation," The Review of Metaphysics, XIV, No. 2 (1961), 191–230.

"Valor y Razón," Diánoia: Anuario de Filosofía, VII (Universidad Nacional Autónoma de México, 1961), 79–99.

"Lo analítico y lo sintético como categorías metodológicas," Humanitas: Anuario del Centro de Estudios Humanísticos (Universidad de Nuevo León, Monterrey, Mexico, 1961), pp. 99–128.

"The Logic of Value," The Review of Metaphysics, XIV, No. 3 (1961), pp. 389–432.

"Prolegomena to a Meta-Anselmian Axiomatic," The Review of Metaphysics, XIV, No. 4 (1961), pp. 637–75.

"El conocimiento del Bien en Platón," Diánoia: Anuario de Filosofía, VIII (Universidad Nacional Autónoma de México, 1962), pp. 42–62.

"Capitalismo y Comunismo," Verdad, 1962.

"The Self in Kierkegaard," Journal of Existential Psychiatry, No. 8 (Spring, 1962), pp. 409–36.

"The Good as a Non-natural Quality and the Good as a Transcendental," The Review of Metaphysics, XVI, No. 1 (Sept., 1962), pp. 149–55.

"Axiology as a Science," Philosophy of Science, XXIX, No. 4 (Oct., 1962), pp. 412–33.

"Does a Corporation Need Spiritual Objectives?" Nationwide World, Oct., 1962.

"La Simbolización del Valor," Diánoia: Anuario de Filosofía, IX (Universidad Nacional Autónoma de México, 1963), 71–101.

"Introduction to Symposium *'Valor in genere y los valores especificos'*," Thirteenth International Congress of Philosophy (Mexico City, 1963), pp. 7–29.

"Value in General and the Specific Values," Symposium, Thirteenth International Congress of Philosophy (Mexico City, 1963), pp. 99–133.

"The Logical Difference Between Philosophy and Science," *Philosophy and Phenomenological Research*, XXIII, No. 3 (1963), pp. 353–79.

"*Razón y razones del Valor: La Axiología de la Escuela de Oxford*," *Diánoia: Anuario de Filosofía*, X (Universidad Nacional Autónoma de México, 1964), 63–92.

"*La ilustración y su enfoque científico*," *Primer Coloquio Mexicano de Historia de la Ciencia*, Sociedad Mexicana de Historia de la Ciencia y de la Technología (Mexico City, 1964), pp. 7–24.

"*La nación: reliquia feudal*," *Cuadernos Americanos*, No. 3 (1964), pp. 33–61.

"Four Axiological Proofs of the Infinite Value of Man," *Kant-Studien*, LV, No. 4 (1964), pp. 428–38. Reprinted in Marvin C. Katz, *Sciences of Man and Social Ethics*. Boston: Branden Press, 1969, pp. 29–45.

"The Definition of Good: Moore's Axiomatic of the Science of Good," *Proceedings, Aristotelian Society* (1964–65), pp. 235–56.

"*Nuestra Situación existencial: Pereceremos todos juntos?*" *Cuadernos Americanos*, No. 3 (1965), pp. 63–87.

"*La ontogenia del símbolo: Prolegómenos a una filosofía de formas sintomáticas*," *Diánoia: Anuario de Filosofía*, XI (Universidad Nacional Autónoma de México, 1965), 60–78.

"*La esencia de Rusia*," *Cuadernos Americanos*, No. 5 (1965), pp. 7–40.

"*La axiomática del valor*," *Diánoia: Anuario de Filosofía*, XII (Universidad Nacional Autónoma de México, 1966), 104–31.

"The University and the World," *Vital Speeches of the Day*, May 1, 1966, pp. 442–47.

"*Die Wissenschaft vom Entscheiden*," *Wissenschaft und Weltbild* (Vienna), June, 1966, pp. 81–99.

"Formal Axiology and the Measurement of Value," *The Journal of Value Inquiry*, I, No. 1 (Spring, 1967), pp. 38–46.

"*Sentimento y Valor*," *Diánoia: Anuario de Filosofía*, XIII (Universidad Nacional Autónoma de México, 1967), 248–91.

"*La producción del valor: un marco para la Teleología Científica*," *Diánoia: Anuario de Filosofía*, XIV (Universidad Nacional Autónoma de México, 1968), pp. 182–202.

"Singular and Particular," *Critica* (Jan., 1968), pp. 15–51.

"*La naturaleza de la valoración*," *Humanitas* (Universidad de Nuevo León, Monterrey, Mexico, 1968), pp. 45–69.

"Belief and Value," *Fourteenth International Congress of Philosophy*, Vienna, 1968.

"The Measurement of Value: Set Theory as Value Theory," *Fourteenth International Congress of Philosophy*, Vienna, 1968.

"Una ciencia moral para la edad atómica," Cuadernos Americanos, No. 5 (1968), pp. 81–103.

"El método científico de análisis y síntesis," Diánoia: Anuario de Filosofía, XV (Universidad Nacional Autónoma de México, 1969), pp. 1–24; XVI (1970), pp. 42–65.

"Axiological Testing and Psychological Testing," Ninth Annual Meeting, Association for Humanistic Psychology, 1971.

"The Hartman (Axiological) Profile Test," Annual Convention, American Society of Psychoanalytic Physicians, 1971.

"El origen de la Axiometría en la República de Platón," Diánoia: Anuario de Filosofía, XVII (Universidad Nacional Autónoma de México, 1971).

"The Value Structure of Creativity," Philosophy and Phenomenological Research, 1972.

"La naturaleza del valor: Estructura de las cualidades terciarias," Episteme (Universidad Central de Venezuela, Caracas), 1972.

"Transpersonal Logic in the Gospel," Journal of Transpersonal Psychology, 1972.

"Kant's Science of Metaphysics and the Scientific Method," Kant-Studien, 1972.

"The Value Structure of Justice." In Festschrift for Paul A. Schilpp. LaSalle, Ill.: Open Court Publishing Co., 1972.

"Autorretrato," Autorretratos de Pensadores y Filósofos Latino-Americanos, São Paulo, Brazil, forthcoming.

The Contributors

LUIGI BAGOLINI, professor of legal philosophy at the University of Siena from 1942 to 1950 and at the University of Genoa from 1950 to 1965, is now full professor at Bologna University. Previously at Bologna he was the first dean of the Faculty of Political Sciences. He was visiting professor at the São Paulo State University, where he was awarded the doctorate *honoris causa* in law. His recent publications include *La dottrina della simpatia nella morale e nel Diritto*, *Esperienza giuridica e politica nel pensiero di David Hume*, and *Visioni della giustizia e senso comune*.

ROBERT S. BRUMBAUGH received his Ph.D. in 1942 from the University of Chicago. He has taught at Bowdoin College, Indiana University, and is currently professor of philosophy at Yale University. He is the author of various books and articles, including *Plato on the One*, *Plato's Mathematical Imagination*, and *The Philosophers of Greece*; co-author (with Nathaniel Lawrence) of *Philosophers on Education*; co-editor (with Rulon Wells) of *The Plato Manuscripts: A New Index*. He has been associate research fellow at the American School of Classical Studies, Athens; visiting Fulbright professor, the Hebrew University, Jerusalem; president, the Metaphysical Society of America.

CHARLOTTE BUHLER received her Ph.D. from the University of Munich. Before immigrating to the United States in 1940, she taught at the University of Vienna, was director of Child Guidance Clinics in Vienna, London, and Oslo, and was visiting professor at many European and American universities. Dr. Buhler, former chief clinical psychologist at the Minneapolis and the Los Angeles County General Hospitals, presently teaches psychiatry at the University of Southern California and is also in private practice. A former president of the American Association for Humanistic Psychology, Dr. Buhler is co-editor of the *British Journal of Genetic Psychology* and the *American Journal for Developmental Psychology*. She is the author of a number of books, some of which have been translated into several languages.

HECTOR-NERI CASTAÑEDA is now professor of philosophy at Indiana University, after teaching at Wayne State University from 1957 to 1969. He has been visiting professor at Duke University and at the University of Texas. He received his doctor's degree from the University of Minnesota in 1954. He was a British Council scholar at Oxford University in 1955–56. He has received several research awards and grants, and was a Guggenheim fellow for 1967–68. Professor Castañeda is the founding editor of *Noûs* and is a member of the editorial board of *Critica*. He is author of *La Dialéctica de la Conciencia de sí Mismo*, editor of and contributor to *Intentionality, Minds, and Perception*, co-editor and contributor to *Morality and the Language of Conduct*; and he has published more than sixty articles and reviews.

DANIEL CHRISTOFF, professor of philosophy at the University of Lausanne since 1956, was lecturer (*Privat Docent*) in philosophy at the University of Geneva from 1945 to 1956. Since 1947 he has also been the redactor for the French part of *Studia Philosophica*, the yearly publication of the Swiss Society of Philosophy. Beside numerous articles and reading-accounts, he has published *Le temps et les valeurs, Recherche de la liberté*, and, in the series "Philosophes de tous les temps," *Husserl*.

JOHN WILLIAM DAVIS received his Ph.D. from Emory University in 1959, after studying at West Virginia University and Ohio State University. He is professor and head of the Department of Philosophy at the University of Tennessee. A former officer of the Southern Society for Philosophy and Psychology and president of the Tennessee Philosophical Association, he is president of the American Society for Value Inquiry and a member of the Board of Directors of the Foundation for Creative Philosophy. He is author of articles in the fields of ethics, value theory, and American philosophy, and has contributed to four books.

ALBERT ELLIS is executive director of the Institute for Advanced Study in Rational Psychotherapy in New York City where he practices psychotherapy and marriage-and-family counseling. He has been a fellow and an officer of many professional associations, including the American Psychological Association, the American Academy of Psychotherapists, the American Association of Marriage Counselors, and the Society for the Scientific Study of Sex. He has published over 250 articles and 27 books, including *The Art and Science of Love, A Guide to Rational Living, Sex Without Guilt*, and *Reason and Emotion in Psychotherapy*.

GERHARD FREY, professor of philosophy at the University of Innsbruck in Austria since 1968, has studied philosophy, mathematics, physics, astronomy, and chemistry. He was a lecturer in the philosophy of science from 1952 to 1958 and then professor of philosophy from 1958 to 1968 at the Technical High School at Stuttgart. He has published six books and about fifty articles in different scientific journals. The most important books are *Gesetz und Entwicklung in der Natur, Sprache, Ausdruck des Bewusstseins, Die Mathematisierung unserer Welt,* and *Erkenntnis der Wirklichkeit.*

THOMAS E. HILL has taught at Macalester College, where he is now Bloedel professor of philosophy, since 1946. Having studied at Davidson College, Edinburgh, Tübingen, Harvard, and Oxford, he taught earlier at King College and Southwestern College in Tennessee. He is the author of *Contemporary Ethical Theories, Ethics in Theory and Practice,* and *Contemporary Theories of Knowledge.*

WAYNE A. R. LEYS, since 1964 professor of philosophy at Southern Illinois University, was formerly vice-president of Roosevelt University, and he has held visiting appointments at Northwestern, Michigan, Chicago, and Johns Hopkins. His publications include *Ethics for Policy Decisions, Philosophy and the Public Interest* (co-author, Charner M. Perry), and *Gandhi and America's Educational Future* (co-author, P. S. S. Rama Rao). He has been a lecturer for various U.S. governmental agencies both in this country and in South America. He has served on a number of committees of the American Philosophical Association and is currently on the Committee on International Cooperation.

FRANZ LOESER is professor for heuristic at the Humboldt University of Berlin. He studied at the University of Minnesota, Manchester University, and Humboldt University, where he received his Ph.D. and his habilitation. His most recent publications are *Deontik, Planung und Leitung der moralischen Entwicklung* and *Interrogativlogik, Zur wissenschaftlichen Lenkung des schöpferischen Denkens.*

GOTTFRIED MARTIN, currently professor of philosophy at the University of Bonn, was previously professor of philosophy at the Universities of Cologne, Jena, and Mainz. His main fields of interest are metaphysics, logic, foundations of mathematics, and physics. He is the author of ten books and numerous articles. His most important works are *Kant, Ontologie und Wissenschaftstheorie* (also in English, French, Spanish, and Japanese); *Leibniz, Logik und Metaphysik* (also in English and French); *Allgemeine Metaphysik* (also in English and French). "Socrates: On the Interpretation of His Ignorance" is taken from his 1971 work, *Platon, Logos und Mythoserscheint.*

MANFRED MORITZ has been professor of practical philosophy at the University of Lund (Sweden) since 1959. He received his Ph.D. from the University of Berlin in 1933. He became a docent at the University of Lund in 1951. His fields of research are theory of value, ethics, and philosophy of law. Among his books are *Studien zum Pflichtbegriff in Kants kritischer Ethik, Über Hohfelds System der Juridischen Grundbegriffe, Kants Einteilung der Imperative,* and *Inledning i värdeteori.* He has also written a number of articles. He is now especially interested in the theory of norms and its applications in juridical thinking.

BERTRAM MORRIS has the doctorate in philosophy from Cornell University, and is professor of philosophy at the University of Colorado. He has been visiting professor at the University of Chicago, California Institute of Technology, and the University of South Florida. His published works include *The Aesthetic Process, Philosophical Aspects of Culture, Science, Philosophy and Folklore,* with Girvetz *et al.,* and *Institutions of Intelligence.*

DAVID POLE first read history at Oxford and, subsequently, philosophy at Birkbeck College, London. Since 1955 he has been assistant lecturer and lecturer in philosophy at King's College, London. He is author of *The Later Philosophy of Wittgenstein* and *Conditions of Rational Inquiry* as well as numerous articles dealing chiefly with problems in ethics; aesthetics, especially with relation to literature and literary criticism; and the philosophy of mind.

OLIVER L. REISER received his Ph.D. from Ohio State University in 1924 and did post doctoral work at the University of Chicago. He has taught at the University of Pittsburgh since 1926. While chairman of the department he visited England to learn how British scholars "did" philosophy. On the occasion of becoming professor emeritus (1966), he was awarded an A. W. Mellon fellowship to research and write the book *This Holyest Erthe,* soon to be published in England. He has written more than one dozen books and over one hundred articles and reviews. At present he is chairman of the Committee on Cosmic Humanism.

NICHOLAS RESCHER is research professor of philosophy at the University of Pittsburgh, where he also serves as associate director of the Center for Philosophy of Science. He has written more than twenty books in the areas of epistemology, logic, the philosophy of science, value theory, and the history of philosophy. Editor of the *American Philosophical*

Quarterly, Mr. Rescher holds the Ph.D. degree from Princeton University and has been awarded an L.H.D. (*honoris causa*) by Loyola University of Chicago.

FRITZ-JOACHIM VON RINTELEN, born in 1898, became professor of philosophy, psychology, and pedagogy at the University of Bonn in 1932, and then at Munich in 1936. Excluded from teaching under National Socialism in 1941, he has been at the University of Mainz since its revival in 1946. He has been visiting professor in Argentina, in the United States, and in Japan, and is a member of the International Institute of Philosophy, Paris. His publications include *Der Wertgedanke in der Europäischen Geistesentwicklung, Philosophie der Endlichkeit-Existenzialismus, Der Rang des Geistes Goethes Weltverständnis, Beyond Existentialism, Contemporary German Philosophy,* and *Values in European Thought.*

ADAM SCHAFF is professor of philosophy at the University of Warsaw, Poland. He got his doctor's degree in philosophy at the Institute of Philosophy of the Soviet Academy of Sciences in 1944. From 1945 to 1948 he was professor at the University in Lódź, Poland; since 1948 he has been head of the Chair of Philosophy at the University of Warsaw. He was elected member of the Polish Academy of Sciences in 1951, and he received an honorary degree from the University of Michigan in 1967. He has been visiting professor at Indiana University and at the University of Vienna. He is author of sixteen books and more than two hundred articles. Among his recent books are *Introduction to Semantics, Language and Cognition, Marxism and the Human Individual,* and *History and Truth.*

PAUL ARTHUR SCHILPP is distinguished professor of philosophy, Southern Illinois University, and professor emeritus at Northwestern University. As founder and editor of the ongoing Schilpp *Library of Living Philosophers* he has already published volumes on thirteen great contemporary philosophers, including Dewey, Santayana, Whitehead, Moore, Russell, Cassirer, Einstein, Radhakrishnan, Jaspers, Broad, Carnap, Buber, and Lewis. Former president of the American Philosophical Association, he is one of two American consultants in philosophy for the *Encyclopedia Britannica* and is the author of *Kant's Pre-Critical Ethics, The Quest for Religious Realism, Human Nature and Progress,* and other books as well as numerous articles which include contributions to two dozen other books.

ELFRIEDE TIELSCH, Jur.D., Ph.D., has been professor of philosophy at the Pedagogic University of Berlin since 1964. She had to abandon her career in law during the Hitler regime, and began teaching philosophy at the Free University of Berlin after the war. She is the author of *Kierkegaard's Glaube* and *Die Platonischen Versionen der griechischen Doxalehre*. In most of her articles on theory of mind and ethics she returns to the Greek sources, but tries to find a way back from impractical Platonic logic to both the modern empirical-rational and the pre-Platonic "planning." Her latest article in ethics is "Die Zukunft der Ethik und die Ethik der Zukunft," *Ztschr f. philos. Forschung*.

PAUL WEISS is Heffer professor of philosophy at the Catholic University of America, and Sterling professor emeritus at Yale University. He taught at Harvard, Radcliffe, and Bryn Mawr before going to Yale in 1946. A Guggenheim scholar, Matchette lecturer, Rhodes lecturer, and Phi Beta Kappa lecturer, he has also served as resident scholar for the State University of New York. He was president of the American Philosophical Association, the Peirce Society, and the Metaphysical Society of America, and he has honorary degrees from Grinnell and Pace colleges. Professor Weiss founded and edited the *Review of Metaphysics* and co-edited the *Collected Papers of C. S. Peirce*. He is the author of over fifteen books and some two hundred articles. His most recent works include *Philosophy in Process* (4 vols.), *The Making of Men*, and *Sport: A Philosophic Inquiry*.

WILLIAM H. WERKMEISTER, professor of philosophy at the Florida State University since 1966, taught philosophy at the University of Nebraska from 1926 until 1953, serving as chairman of the department from 1945 until 1953. He has been a visiting professor at the University of Berlin and at Harvard, and he was director of the School of Philosophy of the University of Southern California from 1953 until 1966. He has published eleven books and numerous articles in professional journals. Among his recent books are *Man and His Values* and *A Historical Spectrum of Value Theories, Volume I: "The German-Language Group."* The Library of Congress has issued his *History of Philosophical Ideas in America* in Braille and on tape for the physically handicapped.

HENRY NELSON WIEMAN is a graduate of Park College and the San Francisco Seminary. He studied in Germany with Rudolph Eucken, Windelband, and Troeltsch before serving four years in the parish ministry in California. He left for Harvard in 1915 and took his Ph.D. in philosophy there with Ralph Barton Perry and William Hocking.

For many years he was professor at the University of Chicago. After retiring from the University of Chicago, Mr. Wieman was for ten years distinguished visiting professor at Southern Illinois University, and he now lives in retirement at Grinnell, Iowa. Among his many books are *Religious Experience and Scientific Method*, *The Wrestle of Religion with Truth*, *Man's Ultimate Commitment*, *Intellectual Foundations of Faith*, *The Source of Human Good*, and *Religious Inquiry*.

Index

Administrative Powers over Persons and Property, 92
Aesthetic judgment: as intuitive, 205, 206, 207, 214–15; and physiognomic perception, 206–207; as quasi-judgment, 211, 213; as twofold judgments, 206–208; verification of, 211–14
Aesthetic value: 191–99; and aesthetic qualities, 197; as based on intuitive judgment, 205, 214, 215; confused with extrinsic value, 193–95; and creativity, 197–98; as expressiveness, 201, 208, 209, 215; and heightened sensitivity, 210; and imaginative interplay between object and subject, 198, 207, 214; as intrinsic value, 192–94, 198; and late modern art, 198; as obstructed by the pragmatic attitude, 198; and revelatory value of signs, 320; of scientific theories, 209; and uniqueness, 192–93, 195–97
agathon, 159
Aldrich, Virgil C., 161
Allport, Gordon, 144
Analytic concept: x–xi; as abstract, 120; and extrinsic value, 192
Apology, 112, 113
Aristophanes, 112
Aristotelian logic, 52, 109
Aristotle, 91, 108, 190, 196
Ascription: of concepts, justification of, 7–12; of good, 5, 7, 22; kinds of, 8
Aufstieg im Geiste, Der, 156
Axiological fallacy: 75; descriptivistic form, 75, 80–81, 82; general form, 75, 78, 81–82; ontological form, 75, 76, 77, 78, 80; related to deriving ought from is, 83; sentential form, 75, 76, 77, 78, 82. See also Naturalistic fallacy
Axiom of value, x, 122
Axtelle, George E., 131

Bacon, Francis, 308
Becker, O., 41
Being, extensionally defined, 120–21
Bentham, J., 94
Benveniste, Emile, 273
Bergmann, Fridjof, 161
Bergson, H., 272, 283, 284, 289
"Better than," 49; in Platonic tradition, 53; R. S. Hartman's treatment, 53

Bhagavad-Gita, 162
Binary logic, 43, 45, 46; contraposition in, 45
Bloch, Ernst, 263
Bonum, 159
Born, Max, 283
Bourland, D. David, 136
Bravery, in the Laches, 108–109
Brentano, Franz, 65, 144
Broad, C. D., 86
Broglie, Louis de, 277
Bronowski, Jacob, 278
Brun, Jean, 154
Buhler, Karl, 143
Burke, Edmund, 264
Buytendijk (the author), 158

Carabellese, Pantaleo, 284–89
Carnelutti, Francesco, 272
Categorical Imperative, 177
Causality reduced to probability, 278, 280
Chesterton, Gilbert K., 152
Clouds, The, 112
Concept: analytic, see Analytic concept; and confusion of value, 76–77; defined, 3; distinguished from meaning, 158; origin, 15; three kinds of, 120; semantic, see Semantic concept; singular, see Singular concept; synthetic, see Synthetic concept
Concept of good: 3–20; analysis of, parallel approach, 23–24; analysis of, vertical approach, 23–24; analyzable, 23–36; adjective, 22; "attractively normative," 18, 19; conditions of application, 18; definable, 91; defined, 18; descriptive, 6–7; and descriptive, existential, and semantic concepts, 16–17; and desire, 13–16, 19; distinctive kind of concept, 19; distinctiveness of, 16–19; normative, 16–18; origin, 15–17, 19; and other normative concepts, 14; teaching use of, 12–14; and worthwhileness, 18
Concessional principle, 45
Consciousness: defined, 284, 286–88; and the relation between ought and is, 287–89
Constraints on experience, 64